Partner to History

Partner to History

*The U.S. Role in South Africa's
Transition to Democracy*

PRINCETON N. LYMAN

UNITED STATES INSTITUTE OF PEACE PRESS
Washington, D.C.

The views expressed in this book are those of the author alone. They do not necessarily reflect views of the United States Institute of Peace.

The opinions and characterizations in this book are those of the author and do not represent official positions of the U.S. government.

United States Institute of Peace
1200 17th Street NW
Washington, DC 20036

First published 2002

Printed in the United States of America

The paper used in this publication meets the minimum requirements of American National Standards for Information Science—Permanence of Paper for Printed Library Materials, ANSI Z39.48-1984.

Library of Congress Cataloging-in-Publication Data
Lyman, Princeton N. (Princeton Nathan)
    Partner to history : the U.S. role in South Africa's transition to democracy / Princeton N. Lyman.
       p. cm.
    Includes bibliographical references (p.) and index.
    ISBN 1-929223-36-6
    1. United States—Foreign relations—South Africa. 2. South Africa—Foreign relations—United States. 3. Democratization—South Africa. 4. South Africa—Politics and government—1989–1994. 5. South Africa—Politics and government—1994– I. Title.

E183.8.S6 L96 2002
327.73068'09'049—dc21

                                                  2002024262

To Tova, Sheri, and Lori and your beautiful children.
This story is testimony that a better world is possible.

Contents

Part III Afterword

Foreword

PARTNER TO HISTORY, I believe, is destined to become a classic account of U.S. diplomacy in action. It is honest, gripping, and enlightening. It also has much to tell us about the U.S. role in South Africa's transition from apartheid to democracy in the first half of the 1990s.

Partner to History parts company from most other studies of U.S. diplomacy —whether classics or not—in one important, and very instructive, way. Typically, such studies put the United States at the forefront of the action. Whether portrayed as orchestrating the activities of a coalition of like-minded states, launching its own mediation effort, or employing coercive measures to bring reluctant parties to the negotiating table, the United States is unquestionably and conspicuously at center stage.

There are of course good reasons why the United States is so much in the limelight: it is the world's only superpower, with interests that reach all four corners of the globe and with the ability to project unmatched diplomatic, military, and economic power. Yet the fact that the United States is often cast as a leading actor unfortunately encourages a belief that the United States can play no other role. The idea that America should act overseas purely on its own terms or not at all has its place, especially, perhaps, where large-scale military deployments in support of vital national interests are concerned. But the idea can also be damaging, both to the peace and security of the international community and to specific interests of the United States. On occasion, indeed, the art of diplomacy is to know when to let others take the lead; to offer support rather than to exercise control.

Such an occasion presented itself in the early 1990s, when the South African government and the African National Congress (ANC) struggled first to negotiate a peace deal that would end the country's apartheid system and institute majority rule, and then to keep that deal alive during the tumultuous and violent period leading up to national elections. The eventual outcome—a largely peaceful transition of power from President de Klerk and his National Party to President Mandela and an ANC-dominated Government of National Unity—was a great success. But this denouement was by no means inevitable. It is for good reason that the transition has been widely hailed as a "miracle." In the eyes of the U.S. government, which had substantial political and strategic interests in seeing South Africa become a peaceful, democratic, and multiracial society, the peace process often seemed to be teetering on the edge of collapse. As Princeton Lyman, who was U.S. ambassador to South Africa at this crucial time, describes in the following pages, on more than one occasion the U.S. government offered itself to Mandela and de Klerk as a mediator, fearful that without the direct, active, and prominent participation of the United States the process would break down. The South Africans on each occasion refused the offer, obliging the Americans to continue to play a secondary, supportive role.

It is to the great credit of the United States, and to the great benefit of South Africa itself, that the American ambassador and his staff in South Africa, and policymakers in Washington, played their supportive role with great sensitivity and skill, deploying economic incentives, political influence, diplomatic suasion, and a host of other resources to sustain and advance the peace process. "The ground rules were firmly set," writes Ambassador Lyman, "and they would guide U.S. policy throughout the next two years: the South Africans would 'own' this transition process. This did not mean that the United States and the international community in general did not have a vital role to play. What it did mean was that we had to fashion our assistance to this process to facilitate it, help it through several crises, and encourage it in a multitude of ways. . . . It was an active, intensive involvement. And it made a difference."

I will leave it to the reader to discover in the following chapters exactly what difference was made by those U.S. diplomats who, together with representatives from other states and from a host of nongovernmental organizations, worked in the wings to give the protagonists the room for maneuver and the confidence needed to steer South Africa clear of tragedy. Suffice it to say that Princeton Lyman had once considered, half seriously, entitling this volume "Best Supporting Actor."

Much of *Partner to History* was written while the author was a senior fellow at the United States Institute of Peace, an organization mandated by Congress to stimulate and disseminate first-rate research on the varied means by which international conflict can be prevented, managed, or resolved peacefully. Ambassador Lyman's book can be read as an inspiring case study of one such means: facilitation. We at the Institute work to bring to the attention of U.S. policymakers, scholars, and all interested citizens the full range of options available to the United States as it seeks to encourage international peace and stability. Facilitation as undertaken by the United States, like other activities in which U.S. diplomacy plays a supportive rather than a directly managerial or commanding role, has received less attention than it deserves. Hence the Institute is particularly pleased to publish a book that demonstrates that facilitation is a role in which the United States can excel. It serves to remind policymakers and practitioners that they have a more restrained, less frontal mode of involvement by which they can promote U.S. interests and end violent conflict.

Partner to History also offers a new perspective on the South African "miracle." The Institute has already published books that examine South Africa's transition from three very different vantage points: Susan Collin Marks's *Watching the Wind* describes the work of grassroots peace workers in the first half of the 1990s; Pierre du Toit's *State Building and Democracy in Southern Africa* asks whether democratic institutions can take root in African soil; and Dorothy Shea's *The South African Truth Commission* focuses on the politics and the performance of the body created to foster acknowledgment of the crimes committed under apartheid and to promote reconciliation within the new South Africa. *Partner to History* adds another dimension to our understanding of South Africa's narrow escape from full-fledged civil war and of the prospects for its fledgling democracy.

Ambassador Lyman's volume thus sits well alongside many other books published by the Institute. For instance, it enhances the work the Institute has supported on how new democracies deal with the legacy of human rights abuses committed by former regimes, the subject of Neil Kritz's three-volume edited study, *Transitional Justice,* to which Nelson Mandela contributed the foreword. It enlarges our knowledge of ethnic conflict and the means by which it can be managed or resolved, a topic dealt with in such varied volumes as *The Effects of Violence on Peace Processes* by John Darby, *Peoples versus States* by Ted Robert Gurr, *Federalism and Ethnic Conflict in Nigeria* by Rotimi Suberu, *Building Peace* by John Paul Lederach, and two compendious volumes edited by Chester Crocker, Fen Hampson, and Pamela Aall, *Herding Cats* and *Turbulent Peace.* And it adds to our growing series of books in which practitioners recount their efforts to contain violence and foster peace, a series that includes Mohamed Sahnoun's *Somalia: The Missed Opportunities,* John Hirsch and Robert Oakley's *Somalia and Operation Restore Hope,* Paul Hare's *Angola's Last Best Chance for Peace,* Cameron Hume's *Ending Mozambique's War,* Ahmedou Ould-Abdallah's *Burundi on the Brink, 1993–95,* and my own *Exiting Indochina.*

It is no coincidence that *Partner to History* complements so much other work that has been supported by the United States Institute of Peace. Although Ambassador Lyman's subject is specific in terms of time and place, the lessons that can be drawn from his account are numerous and pertinent to many other areas of scholarly inquiry and diplomatic endeavor. Here I have emphasized the lesson that *Partner to History* can teach us about the ability of the United States to play a variety of roles in conflict resolution: we do not always need to stand center stage in order to make a difference. But other readers will no doubt focus on other lessons. For *Partner to History*, like other classics of its kind, has a great deal of insight and experience to offer new generations of American officials, diplomats, and students of foreign policy.

Richard H. Solomon
President
United States Institute of Peace

Preface

IN THE WAKE OF NELSON MANDELA'S ELECTION as president of South Africa, one of the most dramatic events of the twentieth century, two excellent books came out that told the story. Allister Sparks's *Tomorrow Is Another Country* chronicled the slow, halting movement toward accommodation—the secret talks, the tortuous negotiations, the violence, and the resolution. Patti Waldmeir's *Anatomy of a Miracle* put a human face on this history, adding new insights and an up-front vision of the men and women who had made this history. Neither of these books, excellent as they are, gives much attention to the international role in this process. It was understandable, for most of the credit belongs to the South Africans. But it was strange in a way, for the struggle for international support and attention had marked much of the anti-apartheid effort. Moreover, for those of us present in these final years of the transition, the role played by the international community, especially the United States, was an extremely active and, without exaggerating its significance, influential one. Describing this role is the purpose of this book. Doing so adds something relevant to this history. And it adds something to the study of how diplomacy is conducted in the cause of peace and democracy.

I first visited South Africa in 1976. I was then with the U.S. Agency for International Development (USAID). USAID had no programs in South Africa at that time. I was visiting our programs in the neighboring states of Botswana, Lesotho, and Swaziland. Day after day we crisscrossed South Africa by car, passing through the border posts of the Bureau of State Security, with its intimidating emblem, BOSS, emblazoned over the gate, and had our luggage searched each time for "subversive" or "pornographic" material. I was struck as we drove through the countryside at the beauty of this country. At the same time, the sight of black farmworkers riding along the road, as they then did, in pony-drawn carts seemed like a scene from the antebellum U.S. South.

At the end of the visit, I had a day free in Johannesburg. I walked through the city, with its segregating signs for "whites" and "blacks" on park benches, water fountains, and virtually every public facility. I noted the pleasant banter between whites and blacks that hid the deeper tension. That evening I found myself at the railroad station. I wandered in and encountered an eerie silence. On the platform, hundreds of black workers, men and women, were huddled together. Hardly a word was being spoken. Workers there by day, they were not allowed to own homes in the city and were heading for the townships miles away. They were downcast, reminding me of Maya Angelou's description of cotton workers returning home from a day's labor, their early morning dreams and fantasies shattered by the reality of their toil and their position in life. But this was even worse. It was a deeply unsettling experience.

My next visit occurred in 1984. I was then deputy assistant secretary of state for African affairs and was accompanying Senator John Danforth on a trip across the continent to investigate the effects of drought. It was an exhausting trip and we had had an exceptionally emotional experience in Mozambique. South Africa was supposed to be only a transit stop for our flight home. But the embassy prevailed upon the senator to have at least one meeting with the South African government. Danforth was uneasy; he did not want to make an official visit to South Africa. Finally he agreed, but only if talk was confined to the drought. We went to meet with officials of the Ministry of Agriculture. Two of them lectured us on the many programs the government had instituted to help its farmers. Danforth, increasingly uneasy, finally said, "All the programs you are describing are for the white farmers. But it doesn't matter. As long as you confine 87 percent of your population on 13 percent of the land, you will always have an agricultural problem." One of the officials drew himself up and replied, "Senator, we have built this country on white brains and black brawn, and we will continue to do so." At that Danforth stood up and said, "This meeting is over."

As we left, I asked our deputy chief of mission, Walt Stadtler, "What was that all about?" "Well," he replied, "we always take visitors to the Foreign Ministry. They know just how to talk to foreigners, how to put a softer touch on apartheid. I thought you ought to see what the real bureaucracy is like." I had always feared that, if stationed in South Africa, an embassy officer, caught up inevitably in the privileges of living within South Africa's white society, would become slightly co-opted. Walt Stadtler taught me that was not necessarily so. Still, I did not relish an assignment there.

In 1989, however, as I was finishing my three years as ambassador to Nigeria, it was clear that changes were in the air in South Africa. I wrestled with the thought of whether this might be just the time to be there, to play a role in this unfolding drama of transformation, to help rid this beautiful country of its curse.

But I hesitated too long. When I finally made my call to Washington, I was told the department had already made the selection of my friend and colleague William Swing. I said they could not have made a better choice. And I was right.

In 1992, however, I had no hesitation. Nelson Mandela had been released from prison, negotiations were under way, there was excitement—and indeed danger—in the air. I made my move early this time. And I was gratified that Assistant Secretary Herman Cohen, Secretary James Baker, and finally President George Bush supported me for the position. My wife and I arrived in South Africa in August 1992. It would prove to be the most rewarding period of our lives.

Acknowledgments

I WAS INTRODUCED TO AFRICAN AFFAIRS BY SAMUEL ADAMS, assistant administrator for Africa in AID in the 1970s, a truly remarkable man of letters and insight. He imparted a love for and fascination with the peoples of that continent that has stayed with me ever since. I was fortunate later to work under four extraordinary assistant secretaries of state for African affairs: Richard Moose, Chester Crocker, Herman Cohen, and George Moose. Each demonstrated a deep commitment to Africa, incredible dedication, and skills that they tried their best to pass on to me. While I was ambassador to South Africa, Herman Cohen and George Moose not only provided official guidance and direct participation but also never failed to call regularly, no matter what other crisis occupied them, in order to offer help and to ask what further support we needed. James Bishop, my colleague as fellow deputy assistant secretary for five years, taught me much that I know about political-military affairs and how to address them with both intelligence and principle.

As I hope is made clear in this book, I owe tremendous gratitude and appreciation to all those Americans and South Africans, truly an exceptional assemblage, who served in the U.S. government mission in South Africa during my time there. Any success we achieved, and certainly whatever I accomplished during this period, was because of them. There is not room enough to mention them all here, but at least some can be thanked by name: my deputies, Marshall McCallie and Priscilla Clapp; political counselors Mark Bellamy and John Campbell; economic counselors Donald Steinberg and Michael Cleverly; political officers Bill Pope, Robin Hinson-Jones, Terry Pflaumer, George Southern, Lois Cescarini, and Gary Robbins; consul generals Alan McKee, Pamela Bridgewater, Bismarck Myrick, David Halsted, and David Pierce; public affairs directors John Burns and Robert LaGamma; media specialist James Callahan; cultural affairs officer Rosemary Crockett; education experts Gill Jacot-Guillarmod and Frank Sassman;

USAID director Leslie "Cap" Dean and his deputy Bill Ford; defense attaché Kim Henningsen; labor attaché Thomas Shannon; minister-counselor for commerce Millard Arnold; my secretary and indispensable source of support, Barbara Beckwith; and my driver, who took us where others may not have gone, Edison Mmusa. We were backed by a tremendous team of supporters in Washington: Ambassador April Glaspie, director of the Office of Southern Africa Affairs at State; the South Africa desk officer Dan Mozena; Leon Fuerth in the Vice President's office; Lauri Fitz-Pegado in Commerce; John Hicks and Keith Brown in AID—and many others too numerous to mention but who have my deep appreciation and respect.

Nongovernmental representatives in South Africa were equally important in making the United States relevant to and supportive of the transition to democracy. Among them were John Gerhard, the distinguished leader of the Ford Foundation office; Lois Hobson, who opened the Africare program in the country and led it into new and innovative arenas of diversity training; and Frank Ferrari, advancing on the ground the long dedication of the Africa-America Institute to a free South Africa.

I am indebted to the United States Institute of Peace for a Jennings Randolph fellowship in 1999–2000 that supported my work on this book. Joe Klaits and John Crist at the Institute were warmly encouraging and constant sources of intelligent advice. The Institute's Daniel Snodderly and Nigel Quinney provided important editorial guidance. Nigel guided the editorial process to completion with great professional skill, not to mention patience and encouragement in the face of my sometimes intemperate responses to perfectly valid requests. The prize for Institute support, however, must go to my research assistant, Sara Rogge. Truly the book could not have been completed without her. Her ability to run down even the most obscure sources, her careful reading of drafts and valued suggestions, her help in arranging and later transcribing interviews, her assistance in compiling sources and references, and her general support were absolutely indispensable.

The Department of State generously made available for my review the telegraphic records of this period, which served to refresh my memory of events, and declassified several telegrams at my request. Connie Cook in the department's Office of Programs and Services devoted countless hours to identifying and locating the relevant documents. The department's Robert H. Melone, George Taft, and others read the entire manuscript and provided valuable recommendations.

Pauline Baker, president of the Fund for Peace, made available the tapes of eight years of South Africa breakfast meetings that she chaired for the Carnegie Endowment in Washington, D.C. These were a treasure trove of evolving views of both South Africans and Americans as the South Africa drama unfolded. The

Rockefeller Foundation kindly opened its archives on foundation activity in South Africa, and the Institute of International Education similarly provided archive material that greatly enriched the discussion of nongovernmental activity in chapter 3.

Many people who were actors in this story consented to interviews for the book, which served to check my interpretations against theirs as well as to provide insights that enriched the story tremendously. They were F. W. de Klerk, David Steward, Kader Asmal, Penuell Maduna, Essop Pahad, Neil van Heerden, Franklin Thomas, Edward Perkins, Herman Cohen, Roelf Meyer, Richard Goldstone, Carl Beck, Arthur Chaskalson, John Ogilvie Thompson, Patricia de Lille, Allister Sparks, Desmond Tutu, Joe Mathews, Richard Steyn, Aubrey Hamersma, Barbara Masikela, Pierre Steyn, Constand Viljoen, Helen Suzman, Colin Eglin, Daniel Knobel, Wayne Fredericks, Donald Steinberg, and John Arbogast.

All that said, this book would not have been written without the encouragement and support of my wife, Helen. She had shared the experience. More, her daily presence in the embassy, as an instructor in information technology, made a tremendous contribution to the morale as well as the operational effectiveness of the staff. She believed in this book, kept it alive in my thoughts for the several years following our time in South Africa, and never let me waver from completing it. She read every chapter and added valuable material. She too had to put up with my intemperate reactions to computer technology that overwhelmed me and soothingly solved each and every such problem. This book is as much hers as mine.

With all this help and support, I remain responsible for whatever errors there are. I hope that, such as they are, they are offset by the value of the story.

Partner to History

1

Who Owns
This Negotiation?

IN JUNE 1992, Nelson Mandela sent word that he wanted to phone President Bush.

In South Africa, the negotiations for ending apartheid, which had seemed so promising only a month earlier, had broken down. A terrible burst of violence at a town called Boipatong had further inflamed this situation. The UN Security Council was about to meet on the situation and consider its options.

Within the Bush administration, policymakers saw an opportunity. Washington was flush with the success of the Gulf War and, more importantly in this case, the resulting ability of the United States to bring about renewed peace talks in the Middle East. The Bush advisers wondered whether here, too, American diplomacy could play a major mediating role. Why not offer the skills and high-level involvement of the U.S. secretary of state to the parties in South Africa? This indeed might be just the help Mandela wanted.

But when Mandela called, that was not his plea. Instead, what he asked of the president was strong U.S. support in the upcoming UN Security Council meeting. Mandela wanted the UN body to condemn the violence, putting primary blame on the South African government, and for the United Nations to send observers to help contain such violence in the future. It would be the first significant UN presence within South Africa. U.S. support would be critical to obtaining this outcome.

President Bush willingly offered his support. Then he ventured further, offering to Mandela the good offices of Secretary of State James A. Baker to help restore the negotiating process. Bush cited the promising steps being taken in the Middle East and suggested the same process could be useful in South Africa.

Mandela returned to the question of the UN Security Council, emphasizing how important it was. Bush reiterated his readiness to support Mandela's objectives there. And once again Bush offered the services of Secretary Baker. Mandela turned back to the issue of the United Nations. Bush tried one more time. There was a pause.

"And how is Mrs. Bush?" asked Mr. Mandela.

Bush's intentions were well motivated, indeed deeply sincere. And Mandela very much appreciated that.[1] Yet, with negotiations at a perilous stage, where the danger of further widespread violence was perhaps greater in South Africa than at any time since the mid-1980s, Mandela turned down the offer of direct U.S. involvement in the process. Months later, both he and President de Klerk would do so a second time.

The ground rules were firmly set and they would guide U.S. policy throughout the next two years: the South Africans would "own" this transition process. This did not mean that the United States and the international community in general did not have a vital role to play. What it did mean was that we had to fashion our assistance to this process to facilitate it, help it through several crises, and encourage it in a multitude of ways. But we would not be at the table. We would not be partners to the negotiations themselves, or formal guarantors.

In the end, it was this ownership by South Africa that made the final settlement as effective and durable as it has been. The agreements that were finally reached in late 1993 and early 1994 represented difficult compromises by both sides. They limited the degree of control that liberation activists felt was their birthright in a free election. They failed to give whites the protection of veto rights they had been promised by de Klerk. They left all participants and stakeholders with the feeling that much had been given up to achieve a settlement. That it was their settlement, however, and not one "imposed" or devised by outsiders, made it acceptable.

THE FACILITATING ROLE

This book is the story of how the United States played its role in this period. It was an active, intensive involvement. And it made a difference. For, as much as the parties wanted to retain control of the process, mobilizing international support was an important element in their strategy. That provided the United States with the opportunity to use its influence throughout the process, sometimes with one party to the negotiations, sometimes with another, and often with public opinion and important interest groups. This book is a case study of how this form of conflict resolution diplomacy can be done. It is also a study of managing sometimes competing priorities. Ending apartheid without civil war was the number one priority for American diplomacy. But South Africa's lingering programs for weapons of mass destruction posed a serious, complicating problem for the United States, one that continued well into Mandela's presidency.

Part II of this book tells this story from my perspective as ambassador to South Africa from August 1992 through the end of 1995. It is told therefore very much as a personal story, very much in the first person. As ambassador I had the responsibility for directing the American policy during that period and was its chief spokesman. Often too I had opportunities for personal interaction with key figures in this drama that add important details to the story. But, as I hope I make clear in those chapters, my actions and representation reflected the work of hundreds of Americans in many U.S. government agencies and in Congress, who contributed to the policies and programs and made such success as we had possible.

THE HISTORICAL SETTING

It is impossible, however, to measure the American influence only by the role of official acts of diplomacy, aid, and support in the final stages of South Africa's transition to democracy. One of the reasons South Africans were confident and able to manage the transition with such skill and statesmanship was that they had long been participants in a process of engagement with interested parties around the world. For more than a decade preceding the actual negotiations, American foundations had been providing to those opposing apartheid scholarships, financial support, and access to the finest minds in America and to its best institutions. The civil rights community made the anti-apartheid movement its own, giving it moral, political, and financial support, and exercised over time major influence on U.S. government policy. For those in South Africa's white community, both Afrikaner and English, there was also engagement, though more controversial—as Nieman fellows, in leadership exchange programs, in countless appearances before interested audiences. European countries and institutions were doing these same things.

Part I of this book thus provides important background to this story. Chapter 2 conveys, if briefly, the history of apartheid, how it came to be and the way it came to represent one of the most challenging issues on the international scene. Chapter 3 then recounts the American response, both governmental and private. It seeks to provide a sense of the commitment of those in the anti-apartheid movement who set out to challenge both apartheid and the American policy toward it. It focuses heavily, moreover, on the critical period of the 1980s, for this was the period of the greatest confrontation in American political circles over apartheid, and this period shaped the policy outcomes that I was to carry forward in the 1990s. I was more an observer of these policy debates than a major participant. As deputy assistant secretary of state for African affairs, 1981–86, I was responsible primarily for matters in East and West Africa; and I was in Nigeria from

1986 to 1989. But I was at least close enough to the events in this period that I can provide some personal observations on the intensity of that debate and the personalities of those who shaped it.

THE FUTURE OF THE RELATIONSHIP

The successful transition to democracy in South Africa was a triumph for the South African people. It also laid the groundwork for a new relationship with the United States. But, as described in chapter 11, there were some sour notes as well. South African expectations of U.S. largesse were out of touch with the realities of the 1990s, leading to bitter disappointment. Growing economic relations brought with them trade disputes. Foreign policy differences over South Africa's relations with what the United States termed "rogue" states surfaced almost immediately. In sum, the United States built foundations for a solid and cooperative relationship, but with "normalcy" came all the challenges of relationships between two countries with similar basic principles, but often very different world perspectives.

The challenge for the future is to build on those shared principles. There are many serious issues on which the United States and South Africa can partner if the will and vision are there on both sides. AIDS, conflicts in Africa, human rights, nonproliferation, and broadening substantially the benefits of and participation in globalization—all of these offer that possibility. Moreover, the transition in South Africa itself is still far from complete, especially economically. Problems of poverty, unemployment, poor educational facilities, and gross inequalities of income remain legacies of the past discriminatory system. Therein lies the challenge of the next phase of American support to the transition process.

And it will take place in a similar context. For the new South African leadership demonstrated early on, as the United States began planning for the post-apartheid system, that it would own the economic policy process, and indeed its other policies, as it owned the negotiating one. The stage is thus once again set for a facilitative, but no less critically important, program of support from the international community.

FACILITATIVE DIPLOMACY: LESSONS LEARNED

Chapter 12 puts forth the more general lessons one can learn from the South Africa story. They are lessons of conflict resolution. And they are lessons for the conduct of American diplomacy in any important, complex situation. Above all, they are lessons that we should not have to keep relearning, thus the title of that chapter. They require looking deeply into how we see ourselves as well as how we project our power and influence.

Part I
The Beginning

2

Apartheid

"Off this bus, Kaffir! Don't you see this is a white bus?" "Forgive me, mei baas. This Kaffir did not know bus for white people." Granny shoved me aside, and to my moral horror, began wiping with her dress the steps where I had trodden. This appeased the white bus driver . . . he returned to the bus and drove off.
— MARK MATHABANE, *Kaffir Boy*

R ACIAL DISCRIMINATION, WHEN INSTITUTIONALIZED, indeed made part of the national ethic, brings out the worst in all people. It attracts the most brutal into positions of authority and gives them an outlet for their brutality; it demeans the victims and forces them into servility to survive; it breeds anger, fear, and timidity on all sides, making efforts at reform tepid and violent by turns. In sum, it corrupts the entire society, oppressor and victim, liberal and conservative. So it was with apartheid.

Apartheid—meaning separateness—was the institutionalization of a policy and program of racial discrimination in South Africa. It became the policy and the national ethic of South Africa in 1948, when the National Party displaced the elder statesmen of Afrikanerdom and brought a special vigor and vengeance to racial politics that would mark the next forty years. But the National Party put into law, and carried to extraordinary extremes in both theory and practice, what was in fact a long history of racial discrimination, brutality, and deprivation that had marked South Africa from the first days of colonialism.

The first European colony in South Africa was established by the Dutch in 1652. It was not intended as a colony, but as a supply station for Dutch commercial vessels rounding the Cape of Good Hope. From the beginning there was a separation, an effort to screen off the white station from the indigenous people around it. As whites began to acquire land and to settle steadily farther inland, separation, race, and economics combined to instill a strong racial structure in both government and society. The first settlers, Dutch Protestants and later French Huguenots, brought a religious fervor to their new country. With its origins in the Protestant wars for Dutch independence and the Calvinist concept of predestination, this set of beliefs would transpose the concepts of a chosen people into a system of racial superiority. This was especially reassuring to settlers who came from a low station back home and for whom the racial divide provided evidence of, in the words of Allister Sparks, "which half of God's great divide they belonged to."[1]

From the beginning, the Dutch demeaned the indigenous people of the Cape:

> Although descended from our father Adam, [the indigenous Khoikhoi]
> yet show so little of humanity that truly they more resemble the unreason-
> able beasts than reasonable man. Miserable fold, how lamentable is your
> pitiful condition! And, Oh Christians, how blessed is ours!

The commander of the Dutch station wrote:

> [The Khoikhoi] are by no means to be trusted, being a brutal people living
> without conscience. [They are] dull, stupid, and odorous.[2]

Such concepts led in time to the almost total extinction of the local indigenes, some of whom, the San people, were literally hunted as animals and cut down. As settlers later pushed farther up-country, encountering and displacing other black tribes and needing labor, slavery, which had been introduced by the early settlers, grew to become an essential component of the socioeconomic system. Race and religion supplied the justification:

> From their earliest settlement, slavery had induced in the frontiersmen a
> belief that hard physical toil was the task of the black people. Slaves were
> black or colored, so were the indigenous inhabitants. Manual labor was their
> work, "kaffir's" work, the predestined function of a servile race, the children
> of Ham, the hewers of wood, the drawers of water. . . . What evolved was
> a [white] semiliterate peasantry with the social status of a landed gentry.[3]

It is easy, indeed was too easy for many years during the anti-apartheid movement, to look down on this history and its deep impact on Afrikaner thinking and society, and to blame the "illiterate Afrikaner" and the fundamentalist society in which he lived, as the single basis for apartheid. But the British, who took over the Cape in 1795, other white settlers, and indeed many of their descendants into modern times contributed to or openly abetted and profited from the systems of racial discrimination that marked South Africa until the 1990s. The history of British rule is particularly disappointing. At times striving for reform, particularly the outlawing of slavery, and seeming to want to restrain the worst forms of racial brutality, Britain in the end, from a combination of economic interests, the demands of its own settlers, and war weariness, walked away from the task of racial liberation.

British policy in South Africa indeed vacillated throughout much of the nineteenth century. Not only were its motives in South Africa conflicted, but changes in power in London led to steps in one direction, by one government, repudiated by the next. Liberals in London, pressed by British missionaries, urged reform of racial practices in South Africa. But Britain was trying to balance three things at once: the tension between Afrikaners and British settlers, concern over the oppression of blacks, and the British hold on the colony itself:

> Any humanitarian attempt to reconcile the interests of the black majority with the colonists was certain to compound the other two problems: to reconcile two rival colonial communities with each other, and their interests, in turn with those of the imperial power. In short, history presented South Africa with a triple formula for conflict—black against white, white against white, and white against the mother country—only a miracle could spare South Africa from an endless war.[4]

For the most part, when push came to shove, Britain sacrificed the rights of blacks to its other interests. In nine wars with the Xhosa people between 1811 and 1861, the British authorities, though often reluctant to be drawn in and goaded as much by missionaries on behalf of the blacks as by the British settlers oppressing them, gradually extended British rule all along the southern coast, eventually leaving the Xhosa bereft of their land and their cattle and with their leaders imprisoned on Robben Island.[5] Britain did outlaw slavery in 1834, but this only led the Afrikaners to go north to establish their own states beyond British control. To appease the Afrikaners and regain control, Britain acceded to extending and defending the steady northern and western takeover of black lands. In 1879, the British subdued the Zulus to alleviate pressure on the Afrikaners and then annexed the entire province of Natal to limit Afrikaner control and to secure the valuable coastal land for themselves. When diamonds and gold made the northern parts of South Africa even more valuable, Britain alternated between seducing the Afrikaners with offers of federalism and self-government and military efforts to conquer the northern states outright. In the end, this led to the Boer War of 1899–1902.

In the two years leading up to that war, the British viceroy, Lord Milner, made the same sacrifice of black rights as had his predecessors throughout the century. Milner claimed he had two great objectives in South Africa: to secure for the blacks protection against oppression and to secure the loyalty of the very men who were determined to keep the natives oppressed. It was the second, however, that took priority. Milner struck a deal with the gold and diamond interests to provoke war against the Afrikaner states, leaving natives destitute and without any protection. "You have only to sacrifice 'the nigger' absolutely," he said in 1897, "and the game is easy."[6]

The aftermath of the Boer War was no different. As Thomas Pakenham has written, "Perhaps the worst legacy of the war was the political price it extracted from [black] Africans to pay for white unity." Blacks, who had perhaps suffered proportionately more in the war than either the British or the Boers, were scarcely compensated by the British, on whose side they had fought, and many were slaughtered by the Boers without significant protest. Once victorious, moreover, the British quickly abandoned demands for black political rights as they ultimately negotiated the Union of South Africa's several states into the present configuration of the country. In the steps toward South African self-government and subsequent independence within the Commonwealth, the British acceded to restoration of the color bar for voting, even depriving the mixed-race "coloreds" in the Cape, who had long had voting rights, from direct representation in the Union Parliament. The coloreds' local voting privileges in the Cape would be revoked altogether in 1934. Only by carving out from South Africa the independent states of Lesotho, Swaziland, and Botswana did Britain salvage any legacy of protection for its former black charges.[7]

The period between the Boer War and the National Party victory in 1948 would see consistent repression of blacks, Indians, and coloreds, though with some outward signs of negotiation or moderation. It was in South Africa that Mohandas Gandhi began his struggle for equal rights against British rule, suffering the same alternating pattern of audience and prison he would later experience in India. In 1912, John Dube and Albert Luthuli formed the African National Congress (ANC) to press for black rights. For years the ANC sought to obtain these rights through peaceful protest and petition. All of this, however, yielded little fundamental change. In 1913, a law was enacted formally denying blacks rights to the land they once controlled, and they were instead pressured onto "reserves," the precursor to the later "homelands." Pass laws restricted the movement of nonwhites and job preservation protected supervisory, managerial, and almost all skilled jobs for whites. Political rights for nonwhites were virtually nonexistent. All of this, however, was under a patina of international acceptance, even honor, for South Africa. Jan Smuts, prime minister of South Africa for much of this period, personified this ability to balance domestic oppression with the garnering of international respect. He led South Africa into World War II on the side of the Allies, in spite of strong pro-Nazi sentiment within South Africa, and played a prominent role in drafting the Charter of the United Nations. Yet, when called to answer in Parliament for the ringing opening declaration of the UN Charter,

"We the Peoples of the World"—did this mean equality with the nonwhite races?—he answered, "You know well that I did not include them in those words. They are not our equal and they will never be our equal." A black South African noted bitterly that Smuts nevertheless "died having lost no honour, nor respect at the United Nations Organization."[8]

During these years, however, abetted by the depression of the 1930s, white Afrikaners too suffered both economically and spiritually. Their farms had been largely destroyed during the Boer War and jobs in the cities were scarce. They chafed under the economic domination of English-speaking whites and feared losing ground to the blacks in the competition for lower-level jobs. By the 1930s, they constituted "the world's worst poor-white problem." Perhaps 60 percent were reduced to poverty. The experience had a profound impact on their outlook on both race and politics. They felt humiliated and their sense of racial superiority was threatened, above all in the cities to which many were driven in the search for jobs. In this atmosphere, a hardened view of race relations grew. In the Broeder-bund, a secret society of Afrikaner intellectuals, a philosophy of governance based on race and intense racial pride was being developed. Its influence spread in academia and elsewhere. Leadership of people like Smuts was considered by this new generation as too soft, too collaborative with the economically dominant whites, and too soft on blacks. The result was the formation of the National Party and its stunning victory in 1948.

What distinguished the National Party from its predecessors, and its policy of apartheid from past practices of discrimination, was the thoroughness of its doctrine of racial separation. "Segregation" was the slogan of South Africa's leaders in the period before World War II; apartheid—separation—was the doctrine of the new leadership. The philosophical underpinnings were both religious and sociological and ultimately aimed at preserving white political and economic power as far into the future as possible. The policies of Smuts and his generation were ad hoc, responsive to pressures and to growing unrest among the Afrikaners on the one hand and the nonwhites on the other. Apartheid aimed at a thorough, comprehensive program of separation and repression. It aimed at not only containing nonwhite rights at the moment but assuring that nonwhites would not acquire the education, the sophistication, the means to acquire those rights in the future.

Nothing was left to chance. Apartheid was codified in minute legal definitions of race, in methods of control, in the laws against not only interracial marriage but also interracial sex. By defining race not only by color but also by tribe and subtribe, apartheid sought in its more benign guise to champion cultural autonomy and separate development. Thus ten "homelands," for tribes and subtribes, to which blacks were assigned as citizens whether they had ever lived there or not, were defended as respectful of African traditions. Even F. W. de Klerk would later defend apartheid as a mistaken but well-intentioned idea of races better getting along through separate development. But those who suffered under it, and were victims of its brutal enforcement, would never consider it so.

Apartheid purists would have separated the races entirely, but the National Party had to accommodate the mine owners' and other capitalists' needs for black labor. Laborers were thus confined to hostels; pass laws and strict controls on where different races could live were enforced; and of course black labor unions were severely restricted and strikes sometimes brutally repressed. In a policy that later provided the seeds of the system's downfall, education of nonwhites was to be narrowly conceived, designed to perpetuate servitude through lack of skills or sophistication. As one future prime minister under apartheid warned in the campaign of 1948, if blacks would "cease to be barbarians," they would ultimately obtain the vote.[9]

There is so much written on the brutalities and indignities of apartheid. Much of the humiliation came from the enforcement of its rigid racial codes. Every person was classified into one of three groups: white, colored, or African (black). The coloreds were then subdivided between Asians and persons of mixed-race origin. The Africans were subdivided into eight major tribal groups. People could apply for reclassification—if moved by their desire to join loved ones, to reunify families, or simply to move up a little higher on the scale of privilege. This was itself a humiliating process, involving probing of family histories, testing of the curliness of hair, scrutiny of facial features. Families were torn apart in the process. Hundreds were arrested each year for violating the law on interracial intercourse or marriage.

The pass laws were equally humiliating. People clamored for such passes, which allowed one to work in the cities. If caught without one, one could be jailed or deported or both. Family members, with rare exceptions, were not allowed to accompany workers, so either workers who could reside in the cities were separated from their families or members were smuggled in at the risk of arrest. Unless their job required residence within the cities, nonwhites had to leave by nightfall. All public accommodations were segregated: park benches, telephones, restaurants, water fountains. There were no hotels within major cities where nonwhites could stay. Asians—primarily Indians—unlike Africans, were allowed to travel freely, but not allowed a place to stay. An Asian lawyer, arguing a case before South Africa's highest court in Bloemfontein in the Orange Free State, had to be gone from the province by nightfall each day, as he was not permitted to stay over anywhere in the region. Outside the major cities, large townships grew up—Soweto, Alexandra, Guguletu, Kayelitsha—where blacks and coloreds lived. The townships, where business establishments were severely restricted and whose residents were forced to travel, sometimes for hours, to work and to shop each day, became the hothouses of eventual black resistance, the seething breeding grounds for resentment and ultimately violence. But whites were hardly aware of their existence. I knew many whites during my time in South Africa who had never visited a township and were amazed that we did. Out of sight, hoped the architects of apartheid, out of mind. South Africa did not allow television in the country until 1967 and then restricted international programs, so whites did not even get current news reports of the large-scale uprisings in the townships that began in the 1960s and recurred in the 1970s and 1980s.

It was in the enforcement of apartheid that its worst manifestations were seen. Naturally, this is where the brutality found its place, where the sophistication of "separate development" philosophy gave way to systematic cruelty. The roots of this fierce enforcement were in the laws enacted to preserve the regime. The Internal Security Act, the Suppression of Communism Act, the Terrorism Act, and their various refinements and amendments virtually stripped nonwhites of civil, political, and legal rights. "It is hard to think of any peaceful but effective resistance program that would not be covered" by these laws, wrote one legal scholar. Another analyst summed up the definition of crime as

> Embracing any acts designed to further or encourage the achievements of any political aim, including the bringing about of any social or economic change, by violence or forcible means or by the intervention of or in accordance with the directions or under the guidance of any foreign government or foreign national body or institution; to cause financial loss to any person or the State; to cause, encourage or further feelings of hostility between the Whites and other inhabitants of the Republic; or—most sweeping of all—to embarrass the administration of the affairs of state.[10]

As black resistance grew in the 1960s, Parliament enacted laws permitting detention for up to six months in solitary confinement of persons designated as even potential witnesses, and did so for security cases, in which the courts had no power to control the process. Preventive detention was also authorized. In the 1980s, when a state of emergency was declared, the authorities were given even more draconian power. Not surprisingly, under these circumstances prisoners were tortured and beaten, and many were killed. Only in the 1990s, with the Goldstone Commission and later the Truth and Reconciliation Commission, did the truth come out about many "unexplained" or "natural" deaths that were in fact the result of police brutality or deliberate acts of special death squads.

Famous resistance leaders such as Steve Biko, the founder of the Black Consciousness Movement, and Griffiths Mxenge and Matthew Goniwe, leaders in the Eastern Cape, were so murdered. The system bred even more brutality. Under the veneer of an ostensibly constitutional system—a parliament, a judiciary that included some distinguished members, a relatively free press, a modern university system, and many brilliant lawyers and academicians—there existed a subterranean body of veterans of the wars in Angola and Namibia, of special intelligence and police units, and sometimes of even guns for hire that were used by the regime to wipe out dissidence, intimidate potential resisters, and foment violence within the black community. I will give but two examples here of what impacted literally thousands of South Africans during this era.

One author describes the testimony of police constable William Harrington before the Truth and Reconciliation Commission:

> "I stand before you—naked and humble. I have decided to stop apologiz-ing for apartheid and to tell the truth." Constable Harrington testifies about the Seven Day War in the area around Pietermaritzburg in the early nineties, when two hundred people died, hundreds of houses were burned down and thousands of refugees left homeless. He admits he assaulted more than a thousand people during his short service of two years and eight months in the police force. This works out to more than one person every day.
>
> At night, disguised in balaclavas, his unit sowed destruction in ANC areas. They went from home to home, searched for weapons, demanded to see IFP [Inkatha Freedom Party, the rival to the ANC] membership cards. If the house was without one, it was burnt down. "I fired on any ANC house or group from my vehicle. . . . It was days of death and blood."[11]

And another report:

> Between 1963 and 1980, at least 68 people died while being held under security legislation. According to official explanations, they died from such unlikely mishaps as slipping on soap, and falling out of a window, through suicide or what human rights lawyers began to call the "induced suicide" of people who killed themselves rather than give information. Torture of detainees took many forms, from sheer physical brutality, beat-ings and whippings, to the use of electric shock treatment and sophisti-cated methods of sensory deprivation. Many detainees were kept in solitary confinement for months, with no access to family, friends, or a lawyer. They emerged disoriented and traumatised. Some had mental breakdowns: all were mentally and emotionally scarred. Sometimes these things were done to children, some as young as 11 years old.[12]

This is but a small sample of the abuses that were committed. Twenty-two thousand victims came before the Truth and Reconciliation Commission that the Mandela government established to examine the violations of human rights under apartheid, an indication of the widespread pain and suffering that occurred. Archbishop Desmond Tutu chaired the Truth and Reconciliation Commission. After listening to months of such testimony, and indeed some much worse than that described here, he wrote:

I thought of God's sorrow many times as we listened to harrowing tales of the kind of things we are capable of doing to one another. Awful things that seemed to beggar description and called into question our right to be considered fit to be regarded as human at all.[13]

THE RESISTANCE

Nonwhite resistance to this history of discrimination, extinction, and repression was constant and took many forms. In the early days of white settlement and colonial takeover, it was in the form of war. Successive black tribes struggled against white encroachment, sometimes scoring stunning victories, as the Zulus did at Isandlwhana, only to be overcome by the steady, determined white application of more modern arms and economic power.

Once tribal power was broken and traditional kingships reduced to at best silence or subservience, resistance sought to use the mechanisms of the colonial structure. Gandhi sought to appeal to the British authorities on behalf of "British Indians" denied their equal rights as subjects of the Crown.[14] The early petitions of the ANC were moderate and assimilatory. Some even offered to accept a limited franchise for those who could pass a "civilization" test. Even these tactics were rebuffed. Restrictive land laws were passed, black strikes brutally put down. By 1948, challenging the moderate approach within the ANC, there emerged a new generation, men such as Nelson Mandela, Walter Sisulu, and Oliver Tambo, who wanted the ANC to take more direct action and to develop into a true mass movement. They spearheaded the Defiance Campaign of 1952, a nationwide protest against apartheid laws. Eight thousand people were jailed; ANC membership soared to one hundred thousand. A more radical challenge came from the Pan Africanist Congress (PAC), founded in 1959. Unlike the ANC, the PAC eschewed any cooperation with whites and was dedicated to mass action. In 1960 the PAC led a mass demonstration against the pass laws, centered at the town of Sharpeville. In this instance, the police shot down sixty-nine people, many while the victims were fleeing.[15] They were shots heard around the world.

Sharpeville in many ways marked the birth of the modern resistance movement. Shortly afterward, Mandela and his colleagues persuaded the ANC to launch an armed struggle and to form Umkhonto we Sizwe (MK, Spear of the Nation) as its armed wing. In the 1970s Steve Biko founded the Black Consciousness Movement, dedicated to liberating blacks from their attitudes of subservience. The government responded to these developments with further restrictive laws and a fierce crackdown. Robert Sobukwe, founder of the PAC, was jailed in 1963 and spent much of the rest of his life in confinement. In 1963, Mandela, Sisulu, and other young leaders of the ANC were captured and sentenced to life imprisonment. Steve Biko was "banned" in 1973—a form of isolation from political and public events. In 1977 he was arrested and murdered by police.

Despite the severity of the crackdown and the apparent decapitation of the resistance leadership, resistance intensified once again at the end of the 1970s. One new source of leadership was the clergy. Just as earlier leaders had sought to play upon the ostensible principles and institutions of justice of the colonial regime, the clergy with a vengeance now turned to ostensibly Christian principles. Desmond Tutu, who would later rise to the position of archbishop of the Anglican Church and simultaneously leadership in the anti-apartheid movement, told a group of white religious personages in 1981, "You whites brought us the Bible; now we blacks are taking it seriously."[16] The South African Council of Churches would become an extremely important vehicle for the anti-apartheid movement in the coming decade. Another source of mass leadership was the unions. In a late attempt at reform, the government loosened restrictions on black unions in 1979. The move had unanticipated results:

> The designers of the new labor dispensation hoped that conferring legal status on black unions would divert them from playing a role in the political arena. In reality, the opposite happened. Strengthened by their new rights, unions were able to organize workers more effectively to become the most enduring elements in the coalition of political forces confronting the authorities. The political mobilization of workers demonstrated that, in the absence of political rights, any form of mass organization was likely to assume a political role.[17]

Finally, there came the youth. In 1976, students in Soweto, the large black township outside Johannesburg, rose up to protest the imposition of Afrikaans as the language of instruction. The language issue was but the last straw, symbolic in many ways, in the steadily dehumanizing impact of apartheid, and epitomized in the "Bantu" education foisted upon blacks. The student revolt took many by surprise. When the police fired on the students, killing two and injuring others, the situation turned into a riot. The uprising spread throughout the country, in nearly every black and colored township, and drew adult support. The government responded with brute force. Before the uprising subsided, 570 people had been killed and more than 2,000 injured.[18] But the events had shaken the foundations of the apartheid system and energized mass political activity. The first change was in the role of the youth themselves. From that time on, the youth would become a major part of the resistance movement, repudiating the apathy and fear of their elders, bearing much of the pain, at times going out of control when intimidating and even killing those they saw as insufficiently committed to the cause. As one Sowetan mother wrote, "The youth began to take command of everything. It was painful to be told that we were no longer in control of our children. Perhaps we were not."[19]

The uprising also energized other forms of resistance. Attacks by the ANC's armed wing began to increase and would multiply steadily in the next few years. Stay-aways from work and school began to be used. Trade unions began moving steadily toward straightforward political activity, culminating in a formal declaration of this role by the newly formed Congress of South African Trade Unions (COSATU) in 1985. Within the white community, a watershed was also reached:

> The Soweto uprising, which took the Afrikaner elite by surprise, demolished the remaining normative underpinning of apartheid ideology. Given the ferocity of the attack on the manifestations of white supremacy, the depth and breadth of sympathy for the rebellion within the black community, and the sustained nature of the revolt, the claim of apartheid's superiority as a moral and practical basis for social harmony simply disintegrated. The Afrikaner governing elite and its followers thus lost the ideological foundation for their self-confidence and along with it the sense that they had a correct and superior guide to ordering political and social relations.[20]

If Soweto was the beginning of the last great, and ultimately successful, resistance against apartheid, it was nevertheless to be the beginning of a long, bloody, and traumatizing process. The 1980s witnessed a steady growth of organized black and colored resistance, countered by ever fiercer acts of repression by the government. There were strikes and boycotts, followed by successive states of emergency with mass arrests and intimidation. There was a deadly cycle of killings, followed by funerals, where more violence and killings occurred and the cycle would resume. On both sides, developments were taking place that would have a profound effect on the period of negotiations that would follow. In the black population, the structures of resistance organization were being perfected. In 1983 the United Democratic Front (UDF) was formed as an alliance of anti-apartheid organizations, with support and to some extent covert direction from the ANC. In the face of the banning of all black political parties, and police crackdowns on nearly all forms of political activity, the UDF managed nevertheless to create a national movement that organized strikes and stay-aways, undermined nearly every effort of the government to co-opt or undercut the rebellion, and, through a coalition of leaders from several parties, helped raise to nearly mythic proportions the stature of the ANC and its jailed leader Nelson Mandela.

The UDF also set in motion developments that would have effects long afterward. In the mid-1980s, to demonstrate its total rejection of the government's partial reforms—a constitution in 1983 that gave limited national voting rights to Asians and coloreds and created elected black town councils—the UDF launched the "ungovernability" campaign. Township elections were boycotted. Those who took office were targeted for violence, even death. Police were killed. Residents refused to pay rents or utility bills that were the principal sources of income for the township councils. The campaign destroyed any shred of legitimacy for the reforms. But it also exacted a price on township society. It created an atmosphere of nonpayment and gave significant vent to lawlessness that would hound the government of Nelson Mandela and his successor well after apartheid had been overcome. Moreover, the ungovernability campaign in the homeland of KwaZulu pitted the UDF/ANC activists against the homeland government of Mangosuthu Buthelezi, setting in motion a period of interparty violence that would threaten the transition to democracy, and indeed the continuing unity of the country, right through the final negotiations to end the apartheid regime. Residents within the townships saw these things and agonized over the fact that the youth were sacrificing their futures as well as their lives in their boycott of the education system.[21] But the passion and demands of the struggle overwhelmed these concerns.

Within the white community, even as the government vacillated between partial, if ineffective, reforms and brutal acts of repression, the beginnings of a fundamental rethinking were taking place. In 1985, white South African businessmen and journalists traveled to Zambia for talks with the ANC, a path-breaking, even technically illegal, act. In 1987, a liberal parliamentarian led a similar white delegation to Dakar, Senegal, for a meeting with the ANC. As described in the next chapter, such meetings were being sponsored abroad, outside the spotlight. Even within the bowels of Afrikaner political and intellectual leadership, a reevaluation of the fundamental underpinnings of apartheid and of the practical future for the white race was under way. F. W. de Klerk, who would lead the government into final negotiations with the ANC, has written that, by the beginning of the 1980s, it was apparent that the "death knell" had been sounded for the overall scheme of apartheid, based on separate citizenship, homelands, and discrimination.[22] By the mid-1980s, even while supporting the suppression of rebellion, some National Party leaders began thinking of strategies for negotiation. Secret discussions were begun with Mandela in 1985 and would continue throughout the turbulent next few years.[23] It was less principle than cold, practical logic. As one key National Party operative told me later, "We knew we could hang on for another ten years, maybe longer. But it was clear that we could not hold on forever. Thus we needed to find a new strategy for survival."[24]

Part of that strategy was to crush any hope on the part of the ANC of armed or mass takeover of the government, that is, to restore a "balance of forces," so to speak, as a prelude to negotiations. On this basis, some in the government's reformist camp could look back on the government's declaration of a state of emergency in 1986, one that would last until 1990 and that resulted in the arrest of perhaps twenty thousand people and in many of the regime's worst abuses, as critical to establishing a climate for negotiation.[25] But in reality there was no unanimity within the government on the scope or pace of reform, nor on the path to negotiations. For many, it was still a battle against the forces of communism and terror. In 1986, the government scuttled a promising mediation effort toward negotiations by the Commonwealth's Eminent Persons Group. That same year, President P. W. Botha scheduled a speech that was widely heralded to mark out a bold path of reform. Instead, the president portrayed such belligerency that it was, in de Klerk's words, "the greatest communications disaster in South African history."[26] Botha would not leave the scene until 1989, and as long as he was in power he ruled through a national security structure that gave wide latitude to the security forces and the hard-liners in the party.

The regime also portrayed itself the victim of a "total onslaught," on the front lines of a broad communist-inspired attack supported by the Soviet Union and exercised through the marxist-oriented states surrounding South Africa—Angola, Mozambique, Zimbabwe—as well as through Soviet-aided revolutionary movements such as the ANC and the South West Africa People's Organization (SWAPO), which was fighting for the independence of Namibia. Under this rationale, the government not only sought to crush the rebellion within, but also made military strikes into neighboring countries, supported armed rebellions against the governments of Angola and Mozambique, and engaged in prolonged military engagement inside Angola.

With its cycle of turbulence and brutal repression, and of increasing regional instability, the 1980s brought the South African issue to the forefront of international concern. If the world's attention up to that point had been relatively detached, it could no longer be so. Dramatic television broadcasts of popular demonstrations and government reprisals, vivid journalistic accounts of heroes and victims, and the growing awareness among politicians and citizens alike of the real nature of South Africa's race-based regime and the violence by which it was maintained fired the anti-apartheid movement around the world and forced governments to react.

3

Passion, Passivity, and Pragmatism

The Complex American Response

Contradiction and ambivalence continued to be the main themes of American involvement in South Africa. The realization that this was the case dawned on me slowly.
—JOSEPH LELYVELD, *Move Your Shadow*

FOR MORE THAN A CENTURY BEFORE THE END OF APARTHEID, Americans had been involved in South Africa, its racial politics, and its political and economic developments. African American church leaders and such formidable figures as Booker T. Washington took up the cause of South African blacks' education and rights in the latter part of the nineteenth century, sometimes with the support and sometimes to the consternation of American diplomats there. America's diplomatic representatives championed the rights of these missionaries to operate within South Africa but privately urged that they not come. America's consuls worried over the reaction of South African whites who disliked the message these missionaries brought, and other white missionaries echoed their concern, as one white missionary reported to a South African government commission in 1904:

> There is a danger of great evil happening through these Blacks from America coming in and mixing with the Natives. . . . These men from America come in and make our Natives imagine they have grievances when there are no grievances.[1]

In the Boer War, Americans fought on both sides, while the U.S. government remained officially neutral. Americans in general were sympathetic with the Boers, who were seen as a brave group fighting against British colonialism, much as Americans had fought for their independence in 1776. At the same time, American bankers quietly arranged $350 million in loans to help Britain finance the war.[2] African Americans were more sympathetic with the British, believing that the latter would more likely protect blacks' rights. As noted in the last chapter, they would be disappointed.

For the next several decades, America's official focus on South Africa, to the extent it existed at all, was on South Africa's role as an ally in both world wars. Woodrow Wilson considered African issues irrelevant to the Versailles Peace Conference and rebuffed African American petitions to restore "the lands seized from Africans in South Africa."[3] Jan Smuts, as noted, was an honored figure at the conference forming the United Nations in San Francisco in 1945. As late as the 1980s, Ronald Reagan would refer to South Africa's role in the world wars in explaining his conservative approach to the cause of reform. American financial interests in South Africa meanwhile grew steadily during this period. In 1917, the Anglo-American Corporation, one of South Africa's largest mining conglomerates, received roughly half its initial capital from Wall Street. Not long after, Ford and General Motors moved into South Africa. By the 1970s, 350 American corporations were present in South Africa, with a direct investment of approximately $2 billion, and American banks accounted for between $1.3 and $2 billion in bank loans. American investment was only a fraction of that of Great Britain, but significant nevertheless.[4]

CONFRONTING APARTHEID SLOWLY

American policy toward South Africa began to take on a different caste only following the National Party's victory in 1948 and the imposition of apartheid. For the next thirty years American policy would vacillate between denunciations of apartheid and steps to pressure the regime on the one hand, and more limited actions in reflection of competing interests on the other, vacillations influenced as much by the shifting of parties in the White House as by the events on the ground.

In the 1950s, American, and for that matter international, reaction to the growing institutionalization of apartheid was largely hortatory. The UN General Assembly passed several resolutions on the matter during the decade, but they went no further than setting up a study commission and urging South Africa to respond to its pleas.[5] Following the shootings at Sharpeville in 1960, the UN Security Council took up the issue for the first time, but still more in words than by actions. Not until 1963 did the Security Council call for cessation of military sales to South Africa. The United States imposed such an embargo the following year.

But other U.S. ties, including diplomatic, military, and intelligence, continued. The Johnson administration did not impose economic sanctions on South Africa but restricted Export-Import Bank financing and adopted a policy, one that would last until the 1980s, that "neither encouraged nor discouraged" American investment.

Behind the scenes, some within the State Department were laying the groundwork for greater activism and for the advancement of human rights in U.S. foreign policy. Charles Runyon III, the State Department's assistant legal adviser for Africa in the 1960s and early 1970s, began the processes that would become a feature of U.S. action within South Africa two decades later. In a posthumous tribute to him in 1999, his work was remembered:

> Charlie did everything he could to support human rights defenders and others struggling for equality in such countries as South Africa, Namibia, and Southern Rhodesia.... He arranged for US embassies to have observers at political trials. He helped arrange for opponents of Apartheid and racism, many of them facing persecution in their home country, to receive US cultural exchange grants to visit the US.... He educated and engaged the Lawyers Committee for Civil Rights Under Law in the long and noble struggle against apartheid. Charlie helped us do the right thing.[6]

Nevertheless, American policy veered in a different direction in 1969. Richard Nixon, who as vice president in the 1950s had signaled that attention to African interests would be important to the United States, nevertheless as president shifted Africa policy more toward concern with the interests of key allies such as Portugal, then fighting to hold on to its African empire. The United States would also embark, in league with South Africa, on arming the insurgency led by Jonas Savimbi against the government of Angola when the latter had wrested independence from Portugal. Nixon continued to denounce apartheid but did not see white power being overcome in the near future and did not at all welcome violent resistance. The Nixon administration loosened the military embargo that had been placed on South Africa as well as the restrictions on Export-Import Bank financing.[7]

In 1977, the Carter administration, as part of its emphasis on human rights, adopted a different, more critical, tone toward South Africa and embarked on a dedicated diplomatic effort to bring about the independence of Namibia from South African control. Statements from the administration shifted the balance of U.S. concerns from strategic to moral:

> Our concern about southern Africa is quite unlike the basis for our interest in other parts of the world important to the United States, such as Europe, the Far East, and the Middle East. Our interest is not strategic. ... Our policy toward southern Africa is guided by our ideals of liberty and equality and by our commitment to oppose racial and social injustice. We believe that the minority Governments of Rhodesia, South Africa

and Namibia violate fundamental human rights. . . . We have based our policies on the belief that the peaceful transfer of power to the black majority is not only necessary and desirable but also possible.[8]

In 1977, Vice President Walter Mondale held a widely publicized and largely confrontational meeting with Prime Minister John Vorster. Mondale told the prime minister that the policy of apartheid "cannot be acceptable to us." While giving weight as well to the importance of changing South Africa's policies in the region—in Rhodesia and Namibia—Mondale made clear that "the basis of the problems in South Africa stem from two fundamental principles—discrimination and the absence of full political rights available to all participants." Without progress on both the regional and domestic issues, Mondale saw "increasing violence and bitterness . . . and a worsening of relations" with the United States.[9]

Carter toughened the embargo standards that had been loosened by the Nixon administration and went along with congressionally imposed restrictions —once again—on Export-Import Bank financing. The administration shied away from greater economic sanctions such as disinvestment but did support a voluntary code of conduct for American companies operating there. The Carter administration also took the initiative to break the long-standing deadlock over South Africa's continued occupation of the neighboring former German colony of Namibia despite UN resolutions calling for its independence. Andrew Young and his successor as the U.S. permanent representative at the United Nations, Donald McHenry, helped forge UN Security Council Resolution 435 that laid out the framework for achieving independence, and led a five-nation effort to negotiate South Africa's agreement. At another time, in another context, as described below, UNSC 435 would provide much of the framework for achieving that goal.

Yet by the end of the Carter administration, there was frustration that little progress had been made. Assistant Secretary of State Richard Moose would note in 1980 that, while he recognized "change" had taken place in South Africa, it would be a mistake to "interpret the difference as progress." Moreover, despite the Carter administration's emphasis on human rights and the ending of apartheid, Moose confessed that the United States had lagged behind developments within South Africa and had "lost credibility with black South Africa's increasingly diverse leadership." The administration also proved in the end unable to overcome South Africa's resistance on Namibia, nor able to contain the more virulent demands for action from within the United Nations that complicated the task. McHenry, struggling to complete the Namibia negotiations, would lament "the long litany of [UN] resolutions, immoderate in tone, which do not materially advance the chances for settlement and may affect them adversely." Moose acknowledged that while "this is sometimes difficult for Americans to accept, our ability to influence events is limited." Nevertheless, the administration pledged not to "retreat from the commitment" that Mondale had made in his meeting with Vorster, to pursue change—rapid change, Moose emphasized—in southern Africa.[10]

However, the United States would shift gears yet again in the 1980s. But this time two giant forces, destined to clash, were at work. One was the growing strength and determination of the anti-apartheid movement linking civil rights leaders, student protesters, and local government activism into a major national campaign that would eventually impact on Congress and the administration. The other was the election of Ronald Reagan and the appointment of Chester Crocker as assistant secretary of state for African affairs. The Reagan administration would introduce a policy that, while raising the ire of its critics, would change the political chessboard of southern Africa in fundamental ways. Together, these two developments would usher in the most turbulent period of foreign policy disagreement in the United States since the Vietnam War.

"WE ARE SOLDIERS IN THE ARMY": THE ANTI-APARTHEID MOVEMENT

From the beginning it had its roots in the civil rights movement. George Houser, a Methodist minister who began organizing anti-apartheid demonstrations in the 1950s, was the first executive director of the Congress of Racial Equality (CORE), one of the foremost civil rights organizations throughout the 1960s. From CORE he moved to the American Committee on Africa, an organization that would become steadily stronger in its condemnation of U.S. policy in South Africa, ultimately labeling the U.S. government "Partners in Apartheid." But the most prominent link came from Martin Luther King Jr. In 1965, when the civil rights struggle was at its most dramatic point, King denounced South Africa as a country where "medieval segregation is organized with twentieth century efficiency and drive, a sophisticated form of slavery is imposed by a minority upon a majority who are kept in grinding poverty, the dignity of human personality is defiled." King complained that American protests were so muted as to "merely disturb the sensibilities of the segregationists. The shame of our nation is that it is objectively an ally of this monstrous government in its grim war with its own black people."

King articulated the symbiotic relationship that would exist between the civil rights movement and the movement against apartheid:

> In this period when the American Negro is giving moral leadership and inspiration to his own nation, he must find the resources to aid his suffering brothers in his ancestral homeland. Nor is this a one-way street. The civil rights movement in the United States has derived immense inspiration from the successful struggles of those Africans who have attained freedom in their own nations. . . . The whole human race will benefit when it ends

the abomination that had diminished the stature of man for too long. This is the task to which we are called by the suffering in South Africa and our response should be swift and unstinting.[11]

A second constituency was also forming. That same year, the Students for a Democratic Society (SDS), which would become far better known for its antiwar activities, staged a demonstration in front of the Chase Manhattan building in Manhattan, protesting the bank's loans to South Africa. It would herald a student movement in the next decade that would add numbers and force to the cause. And finally there was the growing number of politicians who would over time make South Africa one of their major issues. The first had been Charles Diggs, the African American congressman from Michigan who since his election in 1952 had labored long and hard on the Africa Subcommittee of the House of Representatives to direct more attention to southern Africa. In 1966, Senator Robert Kennedy would make a momentous journey to South Africa. Speaking to South African students, Kennedy too made the connection between the American struggle to overcome discrimination and that in South Africa. He challenged the South African students to take up the cause in their country, saying it was up to them to create a South Africa "cleansed of hate and fear and artificial barriers." His speech caused an immense stir. Kennedy soon found himself a celebrity throughout the country, cheered by thousands when his motorcade passed, addressing as many as twenty thousand at the University of Natal in Durban. Outside the speech venue, he joined the crowd in singing "We Shall Overcome."[12] The following year, South Africa refused to give him a visa to return.

Over the next several years, a combination of civil rights organizations, religious denominations, and labor unions in the United States turned their focus on American investments in South Africa. It was the beginning of a campaign to get American companies to withdraw. One of the tactics was *divestment,* the withdrawal of deposits from banks lending money there and the selling of stock in companies that invested there. By the end of the decade, millions of dollars had been withdrawn from those banks and growing pressure was being exerted in stockholder meetings by dissident stockholders. In another symbiotic development, students protesting the Vietnam War and companies they deemed complicit in it combined their protests with those against companies and banks doing business in South Africa. Such protests occurred at Amherst, Smith College, the University of Massachusetts, Cornell, Princeton, the University of Wisconsin, and Harvard Law School. Another tactic that hit at some of South Africans' greatest passions was the sports boycott. South Africa was banned from the Olympics in 1964 and, through a campaign led by Jackie Robinson, again in 1968. The ban expanded to international matches in tennis, cricket, and boxing.

South African rugby teams provoked so much hostility in Britain that soon they were no longer invited.

The pressure on corporations and those that invested in them grew steadily in the 1970s. Spurred in large part by church organizations, the movement spread to campuses and foundations:

> The effects were slow and nearly imperceptible at first, confined to paneled boardrooms and executive suites, legal consultations and committee meetings. Eventually the leaders of hundreds of elite institutions—from pension funds like TIAA-CREF to religious denominations like the United Church of Christ, from philanthropic organizations such as the Ford Foundation to universities like Harvard—would address the morality of investing in companies operating in South Africa.[13]

Nevertheless, resistance to outright disinvestment from South Africa was strong. As a result, both corporations and some of those active in the campaign turned to at least holding American companies to standards of equality in the workplace, including desegregation of facilities and equal wages for equal work. Reverend Leon Sullivan, an African American pastor in Philadelphia who had pioneered community-based job training and other opportunity programs, was invited onto the board of General Motors in 1971. Sullivan would use his first board meeting to argue, unsuccessfully, for full disinvestment from South Africa. Subsequently, he would be persuaded to draft a code of conduct for American companies operating there and establish a system of monitoring their adherence. The principles would not only end segregation in the workplace but provide for training and other opportunities for black workers. The Sullivan principles would become a bedrock of anti-apartheid activity, but not without controversy: they were vilified by some as merely a palliative to permit continued investment, lauded by others as reordering American executives to a much higher degree of social responsibility that would have considerable impact within South Africa. Received coolly at first by most American firms, the pressure on corporations to sign was intensified with news of the 1976 Soweto riots and shootings. Two years later the murder of Steve Biko heightened tensions further and strengthened the resolve of activists in pressuring corporations and their institutional investors. So too did the election of Jimmy Carter, whose administration formally endorsed and promoted the principles. Congress would later make them or their equivalent mandatory for those companies that chose to stay in South Africa.

But for some the progress was too slow, if not infinitesimal. The year 1976, when Sullivan formulated his principles, was the era of Henry Kissinger and U.S. collaboration with South Africa in arming the opposition to the Marxist government in Angola. Kissinger's shuttle diplomacy in regard to the growing crisis in

Rhodesia, though ostensibly to bring about majority rule, was also suspect. As a result, in that same year, Diggs and Congressman Andrew Young convened a meeting of thirty leaders of African American organizations to discuss U.S. policy in the region. Out of their deliberations came a plan to create an organization designed to educate and motivate African Americans on U.S. foreign policy in Africa and the Caribbean. When the organization, called TransAfrica, was finally formed two years later, its leadership fell to an angry young man, Randall Robinson. For Robinson, even the more sympathetic policies of the Carter administration were not satisfactory. "The Carter Administration . . . had a mixed record, demonstrating resolve to Rhodesia's obdurate whites, political cowardice to Angola's beleaguered government, and for all quantifiable intents and purposes, neutrality to South Africa's white rulers." Robinson despaired of traditional lobbying:

> We could not hope to win by wiggling the conventional levers, testifying before change-deaf committees, writing futile letters to habit-glued policy-makers, or depending alone on the cogency and decency of our views. It was not nearly enough to be *right*. No group in America was listened to less in Washington than the amiable but fangless liberal church establishment. We had to find a way to set our own terms and break the long-standing control of the graybeard policy bullies.[14]

Robinson would get his chance, but not for several years. Not until the wheel of political direction had turned once again in Washington and things got visibly worse in South Africa. And not until the anti-apartheid movement coalesced against a policy that seemed to it unduly insensitive to South Africa's worst practices.

THE LIGHTNING ROD: CONSTRUCTIVE ENGAGEMENT

Chester Crocker had signaled his intentions in several articles preceding his selection as assistant secretary. He believed that South Africa could be moved not so much by a fusillade of criticism and threats of international disengagement as by an understanding of the fears of its regime and its white minority and their underlying security concerns. Through such understanding it would be possible to fashion a policy of engagement (what he termed "constructive engagement") that would move that country to accept positions in the region of critical importance to the United States and eventually to face inward to its own torridly divided society. Crocker saw the outcome as basically a win-win situation: in the end, independence for Namibia, withdrawal of Cuban troops from Angola, an end to South Africa's attacks on its neighbors, and, once left without external rationalizations, a South Africa forced to confront the need for fundamental change at home. Putting these several objectives within a single complex strategy was

Crocker's strength. That it seemed to mask a real concern over the misery in-flicted by apartheid, and a priority for ending it, was its weakness.

But the complexity of the man added to the controversy that would dog his policies for much of his tenure. Crocker had been drawn to African affairs by his association with activists, including black activists, in the 1960s. He wrote his Ph.D. dissertation on African matters when Africa was at best of marginal interest in foreign policy circles. When the anti-apartheid movement got into high gear, however, Crocker was repelled by what he saw as posturing and unrealistic de-mands. A brilliant intellectual and, as events would prove, a master strategist, he cloaked his more generous principles under a cool, clear rationality that did not run from the role that power politics and the need for hardheaded pragmatism would have to play in resolving the conundrums of southern Africa. Almost to demon-strate his disdain for what he considered unrealistic reasoning, Crocker bristled at nearly any liberal rhetoric and would often dismiss his critics as either unin-formed or disingenuous. It made him a good target for some of his harshest foes.

But behind the scenes, those who worked with him—as I did every day for five years as one of his deputies, a job I later described to him as one of the most rewarding but also most exhausting of my career—saw Crocker differently. He was surely brilliant and determined, confident almost to the point of intellectual arrogance in his fundamental analysis, an attitude that would serve him well during the dark years of the late 1980s. But he was and is also a man of principle and one open to discussion and argument. For those of us who had long labored on issues of an oft-neglected continent, Crocker's activist approach was exhila-rating. We soon learned that in our nightly round-up sessions—scheduled for 6:30 P.M. but rarely begun before 7:30 or 8:00—he wanted to know not only what was happening across Africa that day, whether in trade, economics, drought, or conflict, but what we were doing about it! He battled extreme views within the administration that would cut aid to those African countries that did not vote with the United States in the United Nations, and against trade policies that marginalized Africa in favor of other regions. Contrary to expectations, Crocker assembled a team for his southern Africa negotiations that included liberal "hold-overs" from the Carter administration along with new people with different per-spectives. They were all professionals, his one qualification, and they all grew to respect him. They functioned as a team, engaged many times for hours in his office in review, discussion, and revision as needed.

Some of us also saw remarkable kindness, such as when he extended the term of office for a political appointee from the previous administration, so that the person could qualify for a pension, and again when he saved the pension of an elderly and well-liked officer who made one foolish career-ending mistake; and we saw fairness and objectivity when he resisted congressional Republican efforts to cut off all U.S. scholarship funds for the African-American Institute, an institution that criticized Crocker's policies mercilessly and whose personnel he very much disliked. Vilified from the left, Crocker was actually engaged in equally bitter struggles with the right wing of the Reagan administration, but this fact would only be fully revealed well into his term of office and in the memoirs that followed.

For all this, Crocker came to personify the policies of the Reagan administration and to embody all that was regarded well or adversely about them. The first critical decision was to engage U.S. Cold War interests, a must for the Reagan administration, in order to justify an activist policy in southern Africa. Crocker did this by linking the withdrawal of Cuban troops from Angola to a final settlement for Namibia's independence. Crocker also saw this as the hook to obtain South African agreement on Namibia, since South Africa was holding on to Namibia in part as a staging point for its forays into Angola, where it feared communist influence the most. This linkage became the first great controversy of the policy, denounced by allies, African countries, and anti-apartheid activists as introducing an extraneous and complicating issue. A second decision, in essence a corollary of the first, was to pursue this policy through the offer of better relations with South Africa if it cooperated on this regional plan. Criticisms of its apartheid policies would not end, but they would be muted and put in diplomatic rather than public channels. Part of the inducement, finally, was to loosen—once again—some of the strictures in the arms embargo, essentially to permit more "dual use" items to be obtained by nonpolice or nonmilitary importers.

For two years, Crocker enjoyed something of a honeymoon. But South Africa, as described in the previous chapter, was engaged in the 1980s in some of the bitterest and bloodiest battles of the apartheid era. As anti-apartheid activists in South Africa, through the UDF, stepped up their struggles within South Africa, they called more and more for international solidarity, specifically for imposing harsh economic sanctions on the country. South Africa also engaged in some brutal cross-border raids during this period. To the administration's critics, constructive engagement had failed on all fronts. The negotiations on Namibia were stretching out without signs of resolution; there was no reform within South Africa, indeed the opposite; and U.S. credibility with South African blacks about which Richard Moose had worried at the end of the Carter administration had only lessened, as the United States was now perceived by blacks as in the pocket of the South African government.

A principal turning point was the South African government's proposal of a new constitution in 1983. It provided for a chamber of parliament each for the Asian and the colored populations, but none for the more than 70 percent of the population who were black. The administration, like so many before it when viewing events in South Africa, tried to see in this step, however flawed, evidence of progress that would justify continued engagement. Thus the State Department described the proposed constitution as "indicative of a larger process of change going on in South Africa." The administration seemed to move further away from the principle of "one man, one vote" by saying:

> While we fully recognize that the current proposals for reform do not address the fundamental question of national political rights for the 72 percent of South Africans who are black, a process of change is under way and we support it. The United States has no political blueprint for South Africa's unsettled political agenda.[15]

The 1983 constitution, however, was portrayed in exactly opposite terms by the anti-apartheid movements in both South Africa and the United States. In South Africa, coming along with an act to give more authority to local councils that had no legitimacy within the black community, the constitution "produced a wave of anger that swept African, Indian and 'coloured' communities [and] sparked black resistance on a scale not seen in South Africa since the mid-1970s."[16] The result was the "ungovernability" campaign, which unleashed the long series of confrontations, states of emergency, mass arrests, and other actions that revealed the full brutality of the apartheid regime in its final decade of defense. In the United States, it proved to be similarly the galvanizing point for renewed action and on a powerfully more dramatic scale. Randall Robinson, angered by the relative passivity of the administration as this new constitution made its way through the processes of Parliament, then a whites-only referendum, and finally into force in 1984, came up with a new tactic. In November 1984, he and three others, including the District of Columbia's nonvoting member of Congress, Walter Fauntroy, staged a sit-in at the South African embassy and got themselves arrested. The arrest made every major paper and news network. As in South Africa, the anti-apartheid movement was suddenly rekindled on a scale not seen for a decade.

Within weeks, prominent Americans—entertainers, senators, congressmen, labor leaders, authors—virtually lined up to be arrested. Three thousand were arrested in Washington in the next year. Across the country, thousands more were arrested in similar demonstrations. As Robinson would later exult, "Black and white. Young and old. From sea to shining sea."[17] Together with now regular television reports of the struggle within South Africa, the campaign built momentum in states and local communities, as well as in Congress, for sanctions. In a few years' time, nineteen states, sixty-eight cities, and one hundred nineteen colleges and universities had approved restrictions of various sorts. In Congress, liberals such as Edward Kennedy and members of the Black Caucus were naturally engaged. Republican leaders such as Senators Richard Lugar and Nancy Kassebaum were looking for compromises but also feeling the necessity for some action.

A group of young conservative Republicans, led by Vin Weber and Newt Gingrich, surprised many by writing to the South African ambassador to say that if immediate action was not taken to end the violence and move on apartheid, *they* would recommend both diplomatic and economic sanctions.

The handwriting was on the wall. Sanctions legislation was being drafted in both houses. To stave off legislative action, President Reagan, by executive order, instituted some sanctions, banning bank loans to the government and government-owned entities and limiting Export-Import Bank loans to American companies that adhered to the Sullivan principles. Reagan also set up an advisory council to review U.S. policy in southern Africa.[18] The compromise, if it was that, did not last long.

Criticism of the administration during this period, and in particular of the policy of constructive engagement, remained brutal. Anti-apartheid activists found the administration's policy maddeningly insensitive to the evils of apartheid and suspected the worst of the "engagement" with South Africa. Randall Robinson, in the face of the "killing, torturing, and cowing [of] dark souls by the thousands" in South Africa, railed against this "two-faced democracy. . . . This peacock that would not see itself."[19] Academics and journalists were only slightly more restrained. Joseph Lelyveld, the *New York Times* correspondent in South Africa at the time, accused Crocker and others in the administration of "trustfully or willingly blind" acceptance of assurances of change and reform from white South African officials, of not "making even a token effort to seek out black opinion."[20] Robert Rotberg, then at the Massachusetts Institute of Technology, said perhaps more kindly that constructive engagement was "less venal than naïve," carried out by "inexperienced game theorists" easily outfoxed by the South Africans.[21]

Crocker struck back with equal vitriol. He described sanctions as "the moral equivalent of a free lunch." In a chapter in his memoirs of these years, titled "Sanctions and Sanctimony," he disparaged the intentions of the critics, on both the right and the left:

> We had only limited success in keeping lines of communication open to the twin poles of "movement": conservatism and liberal and black activism. Gradually, we had learned not to fool ourselves; these power blocs had very different agendas and goals from ours. They had no incentive to work with the State Department on anything. Their role was to protest, raise funds, gain national attention, and thereby expand their political base for future battles.[22]

Crocker lamented that the "poisonous debate" over South Africa was inhibiting the strategy:

> We gradually lost the ability to tell South Africa officials with a straight face that their cooperation on Namibia, Angola, or Mozambique would make

any difference to the domestic debate over sanctions. . . . By July and August 1985 it has become obvious to Pretoria that American banks, American congressmen, American media, and (for that reason) American officials were focused mainly on the issues of violence and reform within South Africa. From a South African perspective, the test of wills over control of U.S. policy was having the effect of changing the focus of that policy.[23]

Within a year of Reagan's 1985 executive order, continued confrontations in South Africa and agitation within the United States led to new pressures within the Congress for sanctions. The administration tried to head them off this time by a presidential speech that would lay out clearly American principles and policy and thus rebuild confidence in the administration's strategy. This was the intention of Secretary of State George Shultz and Crocker, but the plan fell afoul of right-wing elements within the White House. Shultz wanted the president to add further sanctions and lay the groundwork for the United States to begin consultations with the ANC, previously outcast as a "terrorist" organization. But the others, led by CIA director William Casey and speechwriter Pat Buchanan, wanted to tilt more toward South Africa and continue a hard Cold War tone. As Shultz would write, "We lost the battle." Crocker would be even more biting in his assessment, describing some of the language the White House inserted as "vintage Afrikaner-speak . . . instantly recognized by anyone half-literate on the subject."[24]

The speech had precisely the opposite effect Shultz and Crocker had intended. It was as disastrous a public relations effort for the United States as P. W. Botha's speech had been for South Africa a year earlier. In the final version of the speech, while apartheid was firmly denounced, the violence was blamed as much on the victims of apartheid, the leaders of the resistance, as on the government. There were paeans to the progress that had been made in South Africa, while the ANC was denounced for terrorist acts and being Soviet supported. Archbishop Tutu said after the speech, "The West, for my part, can go to Hell."[25] A few months later, Congress enacted a strong set of economic sanctions and, for one of the only times in his presidency, overrode Reagan's veto.

The sanctions legislation, officially the Comprehensive Anti-Apartheid Act (CAAA), had another feature that would in the next several years become extremely significant. Along with the "negative" acts of sanctions, it greatly increased the size of the USAID program, which had previously focused almost exclusively on scholarships, and moved it in new, explicitly political, directions. Under section 202, funds were made available for assisting victims of apartheid in getting legal representation when arrested in demonstrations or other acts of resistance, in developing alternative education programs, in developing their trade unions, and in developing other ways to "resist, through non-violent means, the enforcement of apartheid policies," including such policies as restrictions on housing, forced removal from geographic areas, and "denationalization." With some hyperbole, an evaluation of the USAID program years later described it as "unprecedented in that it openly stated its purpose to be to assist in the overthrow of a friendly government."[26]

Critics of the administration were overjoyed with the passage of the CAAA, and many proclaimed it the end of "constructive engagement." Certainly the battle over sanctions and even in large part disinvestment was over. Already in 1985, American banks, led by Chase Manhattan, began refusing to roll over loans to South Africa, causing a crisis in South Africa's foreign exchange regime and forcing it to freeze many of its payments. From January 1986 to the end of 1988, more than one hundred American companies pulled out of the country, including such giants as Ford, General Motors, Dow Chemicals, Eastman Kodak, General Electric, and Goodyear.

But the policy was not totally derailed. At the very end of 1988, Crocker pulled off the settlement to which he had doggedly devoted himself for eight years. South Africa agreed to the independence of Namibia, the Cuban troops agreed to leave Angola, and South African troops pulled back behind their own borders. Along the way, South Africa's long destabilization of Mozambique was also brought to an end, permitting the resolution of the terrible civil war in that country. Against constant right-wing opposition, moreover, the United States also opened up relations with the marxist government of Mozambique and de facto relations with the government of Angola. Even his critics had to describe Crocker's diplomacy as "triumphant."[27] And, as Crocker had long believed, South Africa would now have nowhere to turn but to its own internal problems, to addressing finally and definitively the fundamental issue of apartheid.

ANOTHER, QUIETER, FORM OF ENGAGEMENT

As the anti-apartheid movement grew in force in the United States, and as the debate grew in intensity, American foundations began to focus their attention on the problem. In 1977, the Rockefeller Foundation convened a commission to investigate U.S. policy toward South Africa. The report, which came out in 1981, on the eve of the Reagan administration, had a clear warning in its title: *Time Running Out*. The report saw the window closing on the chance for reasonably nonviolent resolution of the apartheid crisis. It expressed worry over the deepening commitment to violence on the part of the youth and the lack of meaningful dialogue between the government and the majority. It recommended a stepped-up program of American attention to the problem, with tightened restrictions on exports and, while not endorsing disinvestment, recommended no further expansion of American business interests in the country. Four years later, in an update of the report, the chairman of the commission, Franklin Thomas, saw this danger as having only increased, with greater radicalization of the young and the danger of acknowledged, more moderate leaders—"many of whom paid the heavy dues of exile, banning and imprisonment"—being undermined. The report would feed the debate over constructive engagement.[28]

But it would also have another effect. Quietly, behind the scenes of the more dramatic debate going on, the foundations were forging a quite different form of engagement. American foundations had begun to be more active in South Africa in the 1970s, conducting studies and providing scholarships and small grants. But the report of the commission recommended they further increase their involvement. The Ford Foundation, under Franklin Thomas, developed the most extensive program; Rockefeller, the Rockefeller Brothers Fund, and Carnegie were also active. Together, to build leadership and dialogue, they provided scholarships and grants in education, law, human rights, journalism, the arts, and many other fields. The academic community was very receptive to such programs. American universities, particularly the Ivy League ones, anxious to deflect student pressure for disinvestment, generously offered free tuition, mentors, and other support for nearly all the scholarship and training programs the foundations could develop.[29]

Ford's strategy was to exploit the legal structure of South Africa, helping blacks use the ostensible rule of law within the country to counter the realities of discrimination. Ford began support of the Legal Resources Center (LRC), an anti-apartheid legal assistance group led by South African lawyer Arthur Chaskelson, who would go on to become the legal adviser to the ANC in the final negotiations and who today is the chief justice of South Africa's Constitutional Court. At one point, Ford was covering 80 percent of the LRC's budget, supporting not only the defense of anti-apartheid activists but the training of black lawyers. Ford, working with the Aspen Institute, also brought South African jurists to the United States to join in discussions on the internationalization of human rights. One of those judges was Richard Goldstone. As described in a later chapter, Goldstone would go on to play a vital and indeed heroic role in containing the forces of violence during the negotiating period. Goldstone wrote to Thomas that the Aspen seminar "helped open his eyes as to the role and function of domestic judges and how international norms could appropriately be applied within the constitutional constraints of South Africa." Indeed, when the South African Constitutional Court was appointed in 1995, nine of the eleven justices had attended one of the Aspen seminars.[30]

Other South Africans were similarly involved in such programs. Dingang Moseneke, a prominent member of the PAC and later of the Independent Electoral Commission overseeing the 1994 elections; Penuel Maduna, an important ANC legal adviser during the negotiations and currently minister of justice; and Albie

Sachs, now a member of the Constitutional Court, were all involved, along with Chaskelson, in a program of constitutional scholarship at Columbia Law School under Jack Greenberg.[31] When I asked Chaskelson some years later about the ANC's rejection of mediation, or even of outside expertise at the negotiating table when difficult constitutional issues were being debated, he said, "For years we had access to the best legal minds in the United States, time to shape our ideas about what kind of a constitution we wanted. When the time came, we were fully ready."[32]

The prestigious Nieman Fellows journalism program at Harvard University began including South African journalists in 1960. After a while, South Africa was given a special place in the program, assured of at least one fellowship each year. Over the next several decades many of the most prominent journalists and editors in South Africa—Afrikaans, English, and black—would be awarded Nieman fellowships, creating a strong bond among them within the country if not always producing a common outlook.[33] Of the thirty-nine South African alumni, twenty-three would become editors and eleven assistant editors. Aggrey Klaaste, editor in chief of the *Sowetan,* South Africa's most prominent black newspaper, spoke of its impact this way: "For black South African journalists who had been denied such international recognition, isolated, harassed and forced to endure the pernicious attacks on the press, this Fellowship was the first shaft of light to press freedom." Today the South African Nieman Society is one of the most active in the world.[34]

Another Ford Foundation focus was labor. Ford recognized that black labor unions not only were an important vehicle for economic advancement but clearly would play a political role. Among the labor leaders Ford brought to the United States was Cyril Ramaphosa, head of the National Union of Mineworkers, who would build his organization into the most powerful black union in the country and go on to be the chief ANC negotiator with the government for the ending of apartheid. A third area was education. Within these areas, there was an even more significant objective: bringing black and white South Africans together, in many cases bringing those in the country in touch with those in exile, which would have been impossible in South Africa, and promoting dialogue. In connection with one such seminar, a prominent vice chancellor of an Afrikaans university spent four days in intensive discussions with Thabo Mbeki, the de facto foreign minister of the exiled ANC. Afterward, the chancellor went to Franklin Thomas and told him that he had never before met with a member of the exiled community, that he was convinced that they could work together, and that he would go back to South Africa, resign his university position, and lecture on this need for dialogue. That he did.

Begun even earlier, in 1958, the United States–South Africa Leadership Development Program (USSALEP), with both corporate and foundation funding, brought black and white leaders together for a similar purpose. For conservative whites, these programs proved eye-openers. Even for liberal white politicians, they provided an opportunity to get out of the hothouse atmosphere of South Africa and "recharge our batteries, . . . to have a dose of something else, to see what is right."[35] In the 1970s, USSALEP launched a program with the American Bar Association, in connection with the Black Lawyers Association in South Africa, to train up-and-coming black lawyers and law students. South African jurists such as Richard Goldstone taught in these programs, furthering the development of judicial activism on behalf of human rights. Over the next three decades USSALEP, partnering with other American professional and educational organizations, developed programs of training and collaboration in education, law, technology, business, public administration, and other fields. USSALEP also administered the South African Nieman Fellowship program. Thousands of South Africans and Americans participated in these programs. Until 1989 all of them were funded privately.[36]

By the beginning of the 1980s broader scholarship and training programs were getting under way. The South Africa Education Program was initiated in 1979 under the Institute of International Education to provide university scholarships to disadvantaged (i.e., nonwhite) South Africans. In 1982, the USAID program began support that would provide more than $40 million over the next decade. But critical to the success of the program was the tuition waiver and other financial assistance provided from more than three hundred participating colleges and universities, spurred in part as noted above by the disinvestment debate on their campuses. Derek Bok, president of Harvard University, led the fund-raising campaign for this program with the universities and corporations. By 1989 more than thirteen hundred South Africans had received scholarships, roughly half in South Africa and half in the United States. Remarkably, under apartheid in the late 1980s 95 percent were employed on completion of the program, at a time when black unemployment ran as high as 40 percent. Participants ranked the psychological effects of the program as high as its academic benefits. A survey of graduates in 1989 found that they felt the major benefit was increased self-esteem and gaining the confidence of being able to compete with whites both academically and in the workplace.[37]

Many other exchange and training programs developed in this period. In Washington, Pauline Baker at the Carnegie Endowment for International Peace launched a series of breakfasts on South Africa that would go on for eight years, giving a platform to South African politicians, churchmen, labor leaders, academics, exiled liberation figures, and, in turn, American officials and members of Congress. It was a quiet place for debate, education, and the promotion of understanding.

A study of foundation grant making to South Africa in 1987 listed twenty-four foundations active in such programs. Although the report found the total amount dedicated to such programs "miniscule" compared to total foundation activity, the impact on individuals and on the processes of dialogue would be great.[38] The foundation programs developed in these years would also provide an important base on which the U.S. government's much larger aid program would later build.

SUCCESSES AND SCARS

In the end, Crocker's regional analysis proved largely correct. The connections, including the hated "linkage" of Cuban troop withdrawal to Namibian independence, offered the combination of incentives that, once the parties were ready, would break the deadlock of so many past years of effort. The concept of "total onslaught," to which hard-liners on South Africa's right had clung for so long and to which the country had diverted so much of its attention and resources, was no more. The southern African landscape had been fundamentally altered.

But the policy had not anticipated, nor did it encompass, the dramatic turn that events would take within South Africa during the 1980s and the visions of brutality that could not be addressed alone through quiet diplomacy. In this period, the anti-apartheid movement both within South Africa and abroad made sanctions the sine qua non of international solidarity with their struggle. Fighting that pressure, and trying amid the chaos to point to underlying "change," proved impossible for the administration and cost it dearly in public support and ultimately with the Congress.

There was also a massive failure of public diplomacy within South Africa and with liberation leaders in exile. There was already a historic divide between the ANC and the United States born of the Cold War. Many of the ANC stalwarts, and of course the Communists among them, had their ideological grounding in the Soviet Union and had imbibed an anti-imperialist attitude toward the United States. "America was the most hated country," said one of the former ANC prisoners on Robben Island. "We were unanimous in our negative attitude toward the United States," said another.[39]

These attitudes were reinforced by an American policy not well understood or articulated inside South Africa. The administration allowed the South African government to control the public explanation of constructive engagement and thereby to portray the two countries in a form of partnership. Hidden from view of most of the South African public were the rather fierce debates that were taking place behind the scenes between the two governments, not only over regional policies but about the South African governments' repression of its people. The gap in information and understanding also allowed the anti-apartheid movement in South Africa for its own purposes—in particular the campaign for sanctions—to demonize the policy even more.

Both official visitors from Washington and the embassy in South Africa failed in explaining U.S. policy, not paying nearly enough attention to the growing loss of credibility, not taking nearly enough time to reach out at senior levels to black leaders in South Africa and abroad, and not using public diplomacy within South Africa to prevent the demonization of American policy. The policy apparatus failed to make the case to anti-apartheid activists that the end of South Africa's regional destabilization, and in particular the independence of Namibia, to which the administration was devoting so much of its attention, would contribute significantly to an atmosphere within South Africa conducive to negotiations. And it did not respect enough the strong commitment of black leaders to sanctions, a step black leaders considered absolutely vital to putting pressure on the South African establishment, even with the costs to black workers.

THE IMPACT ON AMERICAN OPERATIONS

Throughout most of the 1980s, contact with the American ambassador in South Africa was almost taboo among liberation figures. Herman Nickel, ambassador to South Africa during most of the Reagan years, bore the brunt of this. Even after sanctions were enacted and change was taking place in the U.S. attitude—for example, with the opening of a dialogue with the ANC in Lusaka, Zambia, in 1987—anti-apartheid leaders continued to avoid American officials. Archbishop Tutu refused to meet with any American ambassador right through 1989. Other liberation activists made boycotting the embassy (though sometimes more in public than in private) a point of honor. Tim Bork, who set up the first on-site aid program after passage of the CAAA, and who had a distinguished record of opposition to apartheid, purposely established the USAID office away from the embassy and succeeded in building bridges to the black community. Nevertheless, black groups that received U.S. aid sometimes denied the fact in public and especially to American visitors; others kept their distance altogether.[40]

The anger generated during this period spilled over to the nongovernmental sector as well. The Rockefeller Foundation in 1984 justified stepped-up programming in South Africa, in part by the need to counter this feeling:

> The degree of hostility toward Americans among black South Africans should not be underestimated and while many are sophisticated enough to know that the Rockefeller Foundation is a non-partisan organization that does not seek to further the policies of the Reagan Administration or any other administration, some groups feel that it would be wrong to accept money from any American source.[41]

Franklin Thomas, who had chaired the Rockefeller Commission reports, *Time Running Out,* in 1981 and 1986, and had a long-standing strong relationship with the black community, nevertheless found it difficult to obtain appointments with black leaders when he took part in the outside review of U.S. policy that Reagan had ordered in 1985. Finally he arranged a meeting with two persons who knew him well:

> They sat me down and said the only reasons they were meeting with me as a member of the [Policy Review] Commission was because of my prior credibility with them, that they would not meet with other members. . . . They thought I was being exploited by the administration, that the commission would not be allowed to come up with anything that was forward-looking in the way that black South Africans would see as beneficial, and that basically I was giving cover to the administration by my participation; they were resentful of that and disappointed. That was a tough period. Every time you ventured forth to either strengthen a little bridge that was there or maybe create a bridge that didn't exist, you realized you were stepping on very, very fragile territory.[42]

To help overcome this problem, Crocker in 1985 hired Carl Beck, who had long-standing professional and family ties in the region, as the embassy's liaison to the black community. Crocker agreed Beck did not have to defend U.S. policy; Crocker asked only that he not criticize it. Beck nevertheless had to draw on his nine years of close relationships in the black community and his fluency in Tswana and Sesotho to get into the circles of those leading the resistance. He listened to scathing criticism of the United States. Many at the time believed the U.S. focus on Namibia was a ploy, a means to forever delay progress within South Africa. "Everyone [I talked to] was convinced that Namibia would only become independent when there was a black government in South Africa." Like Thomas, Beck relied on his personal credibility to cut through the hostility. On one occasion, when his taxi driver asked a young boy in one of the townships for directions, it turned out that the word had been passed in advance. The boy told the driver that "they told us not to kill him."[43]

The American ambassadors succeeding Herman Nickel did much to break down this antipathy. Edward Perkins, the first African American ambassador to South Africa, arrived in 1986, shortly after sanctions had been enacted. Perkins did much to restore a sense of dignity and credibility to the U.S. position. With his imposing physical presence, his commanding demeanor, and his outspoken views on the evils of apartheid, Perkins could not be denied. He stood out in the crowd attending the all too frequent funerals of activists slain during the state of emergency in the late 1980s. His confrontations with P. W. Botha, then president of South Africa, as well as frequent criticisms of him by government spokesmen, put paid to the idea that the United States was in league with the apartheid regime.[44] Perkins also utilized the press to get his message across to the white population, that the government of South Africa would never again have the opportunity to deal with people of the quality of Nelson Mandela, Walter Sisulu, and Thabo Mbeki. They should not miss this opportunity. When he arrived he faced racist bigotry from both sides, blacks accusing him of being a "house nigger." After he had been there awhile, he was a celebrity: "It went from this kind of racist ugly contempt . . . to the point where he was mobbed everywhere he went. On planes from Cape Town people would just want to come up and touch him and stuff like that."[45]

Bill Swing, who followed Perkins in 1989, made further inroads in this regard. With his indefatigable energy, his earnestness, his irresistible determination to make connections, Swing reached virtually every part of South African society. Swing was the U.S. ambassador when Mandela was released from prison in 1990 and met with him shortly afterward. He set in motion U.S. policy in support of the complex negotiating process that began in 1991. He made clear in his meetings with government officials that the transition could not include a veto for a white minority. The aid program was also growing significantly during this time. As the wall between liberation supporters and the American government fell away, U.S. financial support for the anti-apartheid organizations within the country became more significant and less controversial. Indeed, under President Bush the program grew from $14 million to $25 million, then $50 million, and would rise again in 1992 to $80 million, becoming the largest bilateral U.S. aid program in Africa. All of it went to nongovernmental organizations. When Swing, then American ambassador to Nigeria, returned to South Africa in March 1993 to celebrate his wedding, which I had the pleasure of hosting on the lawn of the ambassador's residence in Cape Town, Archbishop Tutu was among the guests. Ed Perkins was the best man.

These positive developments in the relationship, from the late 1980s onward, were taking place against a backdrop of dramatic changes taking place within South Africa and in U.S. policy. Nevertheless, I would find the question of credibility one of the most important challenges I faced. I will return to this question in chapter 6.

4

The Wind Shifts

*The government in power in the days of Verwoerd and Vorster
frankly didn't give a damn . . . but don't forget the impact of
the outside, it was there.*   —HELEN SUZMAN

THE 1990S WERE DIFFERENT IN SOUTH AFRICA in many ways, most of all in the developments within the country that portended a negotiated solution to its long agony. The framework for the role the United States would play in this setting was shaped by two additional developments. One was the convergence, after so much divisiveness, in U.S. attitudes and policy. The second was the role that the international community, and especially the United States, would be in a position to play as serious negotiations got under way. All of these developments were taking place in the context of, and being shaped by, the winding down of the Cold War.

THE CONVERGENCE OF U.S. POLICY

In July 1992, the State Department convened an all-day conference on South Africa at Meridian House, the stately mansion in upper northwest Washington, D.C. It is the traditional send-off for a new U.S. ambassador, to which position I had just been confirmed. It brought together government and outside specialists, including some of the most active on the anti-apartheid front. In its report on the conference, the department concluded, "Given deep differences of opinion among South African specialists over the years, particularly concerning U.S. policy toward South Africa, the degree of consensus at the conference was surprising."[1]

It probably should not have been. By the end of the decade the contentiousness of the 1980s had already begun to decline. One reason was that the debate over sanctions was over. Having been passed by Congress over President Reagan's veto in 1986, sanctions became an accepted part of U.S. policy. If the administration did not enthusiastically endorse them, it also no longer fought them. Disinvestment, not demanded in the sanctions bill, remained an issue, but a more muted one. The final serious battle in that regard came in 1988, when Congress passed an amendment to the sanctions bill eliminating corporate tax deductions for taxes paid in South Africa. The next year, Mobil Oil, perhaps the largest and certainly one of the most visible U.S. companies to remain in the country, announced it would sell its holdings to a South African firm and leave.

The second reason was the end of the Cold War. Southern Africa had been one of the fiercely contended battlefronts of that war. Throughout the region, Cold War concerns had lain heavily over U.S. policy: in Angola, where the United States had provided covert aid to Jonas Savimbi; in Mozambique, where relations became normalized only when that country began to move away from Soviet dependency; and in South Africa itself, where repugnance at apartheid was tempered by the concern over the ANC's close alliance with the South African Communist Party. Not only did the Soviet threat vanish at the end of the decade. So did much of the controversy surrounding constructive engagement, after it climaxed in 1988 with an agreement that simultaneously brought independence to Namibia and the withdrawal of Cuban troops from Angola. Southern Africa was no longer on the "front line" of a conflict regarding American global interests.

The winding down of the Cold War had a direct impact on American freedom of action with regard to South Africa. Already, in 1987, Secretary of State Shultz, seeking to repair the damage from President Reagan's 1986 speech, had met in Washington with Oliver Tambo, the president of the ANC. It was the first time such an official contact with the ANC had taken place at that level. The State Department issued a statement that same year that, rather than branding the ANC a terrorist organization, called it one with "a legitimate voice" in South African affairs.[2] In 1987, the U.S. embassy in Lusaka, Zambia, opened an official dialogue with the ANC office there. But these moves, as important as they were in relation to the ANC, were tactical, and they were still controversial at the time.[3] Moreover, in these contacts, the issue of communist influence in the ANC remained a major point of contention. In contrast, by the 1990s, with the Cold War virtually over, the ANC's alliance with the Communist Party appeared more an anachronism than a hindrance to major American engagement.

Equally significant, the end of the Cold War led to a decline in the level of interest in South Africa by conservative members of Congress. Earlier, as a counterweight to the ANC, conservatives and many others, including the AFL-CIO, had championed Chief Mangosuthu Buthelezi as the appropriate black leader to support. Buthelezi opposed sanctions, violence, and communism—all of which were anathema to conservatives—while he also adamantly and admirably opposed apartheid, the creation of independent "homelands," and other forms of white domination. He was a capitalist's dream of a liberation leader. He was (and is) also deeply religious and an impressive speaker. But in the 1990s, Buthelezi emerged, as will be detailed in later chapters, as a serious obstacle to a peaceful transition. Had a strong reservoir of American political support remained for Buthelezi in the 1990s, U.S. policy would have been far less effective and surely less adroit.

Finally, events in South Africa removed many of the areas of contention. The 1980s were characterized by harsh debates over the genuineness of reform under P. W. Botha, over gradual versus more radical reform. F. W. de Klerk replaced Botha as president in 1989 and began a process of reform that would soon change the political landscape altogether. De Klerk had come up through the National Party hierarchy and was not early foreseen as a major reformer. De Klerk describes himself as a member of a middle group within the party, neither a "radical" reformer nor one opposed to reform. But like a growing number within the party during the 1980s, de Klerk had come to realize that without major changes in the whole racial structure of the country South Africa's economy would continue to shrink, its international isolation would continue, and the danger of even greater violence would grow. De Klerk would resist calling apartheid evil, but he did believe it was a mistake and increasingly unworkable. While his predecessor had opened the door to political participation of coloreds and Indians, and indeed had fought the conservatives within the party over that issue, de Klerk went further, realizing that South Africa for all the reasons above had to develop a "constitutional relationship with Black South Africans."[4]

Moreover, as pointed out in chapter 2, de Klerk and others in the party were concerned by what might happen to the Afrikaners, and indeed all whites, if change did not come. With that in mind, de Klerk set out to establish what he described as "an orderly step-by-step process," one that he hoped would end apartheid but protect the rights and opportunities for his white constituency. It would be the guiding principle of his negotiating strategy over the next four years.

If the situation seemed ripe for reform by the end of the 1980s, few expected the drama and speed with which reform came in 1990. Allister Sparks, in a later epilogue to his brilliant book *The Mind of South Africa,* originally published in 1989, wrote that in the original edition he had foreseen that major changes would likely come under de Klerk in 1990:

> But I was wrong about one thing: President De Klerk himself. While recognizing that he was more intelligent, polished, agreeable and pragmatic than his belligerent predecessor, I did not anticipate that he would be particularly bold or enlightened. . . . I could not have been more mistaken.[5]

President F. W. de Klerk in effect moved the situation onto an entirely new plain when in February 1990 he stunned much of the world by announcing the unbanning of the ANC, the South African Communist Party, and all other liberation parties. Shortly afterward, the government released Nelson Mandela after twenty-seven years in prison. Sparks called it "one of the greatest leaps of faith in the annals of political leadership." De Klerk described the decision more modestly and pragmatically:

> I realized that we would have little chance of success in the coming negotiations if we did not grasp the initiative right at the beginning and convince the important players that we were not negotiating under pressure, but from the strength of our convictions. We had to convince them that our acceptance of a unified South Africa with universal franchise was not simply a negotiating ploy and that we were not trying to cling to elements of apartheid under a different guise. Only if we could succeed in doing so would we be able to launch an orderly step-by-step process of meaningful negotiations.[6]

As these developments unfolded, they opened the way for the Bush administration to repair some of the damage from the 1980s. Bush was loyal to Reagan and continued to view sanctions as a mistake. But he and Secretary of State James Baker had their own priorities in mind at the outset of the administration. Herman Cohen, who took over as assistant secretary of state for African affairs in 1989, was instructed by Baker that he should concentrate on two things: (1) finding ways of furthering cooperation with the Soviet Union and (2) overcoming the friction with Congress. The first of these opened the way for Cohen to pursue an active peace effort in Angola in close collaboration with the Russians. The second meant overcoming the bruising differences over sanctions. Also, Cohen received a signal from moderates within Congress: "The problem with the Reagan Administration was that the sanctions legislation was considered by the vast majority as their way of sending a signal of hatred of apartheid. And that somehow if we could send a signal back that their gesture was appreciated, not as a conflict with Reagan but a gesture against apartheid, . . . we should [look] at it in that direction."

Cohen, determined to take the bite out of the sanctions issue, found the way in a hearing before the Senate in late 1989. There was again a fight within the administration, with many in the White House wanting him to say that sanctions were useless. But Cohen, with the assistance of Under Secretary Robert Kimmit as well as Baker himself, worked out a very different response:

> We arranged that the answer would be, while sanctions had a very major economic impact on the black community, because [they] created unemployment, disinvestment, and a lot of people had to be thrown out of work, . . . they [also] had a very strong psychological effect on the white

community, indicating they, the whites, were in deep isolation and they had to rethink the whole issue of apartheid.[7]

Cohen's remarks, and similar ones he made in speeches in Washington and New York, were immediately picked up by Thabo Mbeki, who told an American audience that "he was very pleased to hear a strong statement from Hank Cohen saying sanctions worked."[8] Cohen was also able to deflect pressures for increasing sanctions, something to which Bush was adamantly opposed. Cohen had already learned from de Klerk in South Africa that dramatic announcements would be made early in 1990, including one on the release of Mandela. Not in a position to reveal that, he nevertheless won an agreement from Congress that if there was no progress over the next several months he would revisit the question of stronger sanctions with Congress in February 1990. "I knew when February came around, the demand for sanctions would no longer be valid."[9]

President Bush, whatever his feelings on sanctions, was anxious to demonstrate his true feelings about apartheid. In 1989, he invited Albertina Sisulu, wife of jailed ANC leader Walter Sisulu and herself a major figure in the anti-apartheid movement, to the White House. Carl Beck, the officer Crocker had hired as liaison with the black community in South Africa, had left South Africa by then but went back to arrange the visit. The ANC hesitated but finally agreed. Beck was ecstatic: "I just loved the thought of the look on [Foreign Minister] Pik Botha's face when Mrs. Sisulu's request for a passport must have arrived. It was one of the sweetest days of my life."[10] Bush also met with Archbishop Tutu. Bush resented the negative things Tutu had said about President Reagan, but in the end they had a "wonderful conversation." Tutu told the press afterward, "George Bush is a different president. I think I can get along well with him."[11]

Attitudes were changing in Congress as well. In January 1990 a congressional delegation led by House Africa Subcommittee chairman Howard Wolpe reported that it could still find "no evidence whatsoever of any indication of a commitment to fundamental change. No determination on the part of the government to accept a truly democratic, non-racial system."[12] But three months later, in the wake of Mandela's release, a delegation led by Congressman William Gray, a member of the Black Caucus, told a Washington audience, "The long march out of the agony of apartheid has perhaps begun." Gray's delegation was not prepared to lift sanctions but agreed unanimously that "we should not push on additional sanctions at this time." Representative Ron Dellums, who had authored the original sanctions legislation and had proposed a new, stricter, disinvestment bill, told Pik Botha that "he was so impressed with progress . . . that he would withhold pushing for this piece of legislation."[13]

The debate thereafter took a different direction. It became one of when to lift sanctions, rather than when to impose new ones. Secretary Baker, against the wishes of Mandela, who believed it was too soon for such a high-level visit, went to South Africa in 1990 and engaged in discussions over the sticky issue of the release of political prisoners, one of the conditions of the CAAA for lifting sanctions. Cohen would make this a major focus of his diplomacy in 1991–92. It was of course one of the thorniest issues in the negotiations between the South African government and the ANC, and, as described in a later chapter, it was not finally resolved until the fall of 1992.

Bush was able to signal his support more dramatically for the new processes of negotiation that were under way through two historic visits to Washington. Mandela made a triumphant tour of the United States in June 1990. He was received tumultuously at every stop. He held a three-hour meeting with President Bush and then became only the second non–head of state to address a joint session of Congress. The meeting with President Bush seemed to erase the last vestiges of unease over the path being pursued by the ANC. Mandela would say afterward that the meeting "exceeded our wildest expectations."[14] Before Congress, Mandela evoked the names of American historical figures, from Washington and Jefferson to Frederick Douglass, W. E. B. Dubois, and Martin Luther King Jr., and offered his thanks to the American people: "We are glad that you merged with our own people to make it possible for us to emerge from the darkness of the prison cell and join the contemporary process of the renewal of the world." He received a standing ovation. In the words of Robert Massie:

> In that moment, the brute cynicism of politics, the endless calculation of interests, the relentless struggle for dominance melted into a warm celebration of hope.[15]

De Klerk made a quieter but no less significant visit shortly afterward. There was no opposition to the visit, which would have been unthinkable only a year before, the only dispute being over whether de Klerk or Mandela should come first. De Klerk was taken aback at the reception he received: instead of a "cold shoulder" it was a "wonderful experience for me when I was received with full military honors at Andrews Air Force Base and when I saw our flag flying from lampposts along the street outside the White House."[16] As detailed further below, the visit would have a profound effect on de Klerk and, he believed, gave him the backing he was seeking for his own reform agenda. Events moved relatively quickly thereafter. In August 1990, the ANC formally suspended the armed struggle. In December 1991, formal negotiations for a wholly new political dispensation began under the auspices of the Convention for a Democratic South Africa (CODESA). Negotiations were now the single way forward.

As U.S. policy geared itself to this reality, it was now able to do so unburdened of the divisiveness of the past.

COURTING THE INTERNATIONAL COMMUNITY

Throughout the history of the struggle over apartheid, both the government and its opponents had seen international opinion as important if not decisive. Each had lobbied foreign governments, the United Nations, business leaders, and civic organizations on their respective positions. The start of formal negotiations in South Africa did not end those efforts. Indeed, the competition for international support would become one of the pieces on the negotiating chessboard.

International opinion could of course be a two-edged sword. There were times in the 1970s when the South African government, reacting to the stepped-up criticism of the Carter administration, explicitly rejected outside "interference" and rallied white public opinion around that theme.[17] The ANC drew heavily on outside support during its period of exile and underground activity, but the Cold War forced it to choose tangible support from one side in that war at the cost of its image with the other. Nevertheless, as the period of confrontation and, subsequently, negotiation developed in the 1980s, each actor looked for international support to buttress its position and increase its leverage.

For the South African government, the 1980s was a period of respite and re-evaluation. As controversial as constructive engagement was in the anti-apartheid movement, members of the South African government found it a source of encouragement, not only for addressing regional issues, but also for advancing the reform agenda that was brewing within the National Party and other establishment institutions. In the words of one official, "Washington was not only not shouting at Pretoria, it was also giving signs of a constructive interest in what was happening here."[18] It was important to de Klerk because reestablishing South Africa's place within the international community was an important psychological factor among the white population, and a political selling point for reform. As de Klerk has described it:

> It was . . . essential for me to be able to show my own supporters as soon as possible that the course we had adopted was producing dividends. Visible progress in eliminating the restrictions that had been imposed on South African citizens and companies would help in this regard. In particular, the removal of sanctions, a dramatic rise in our exports and our early return to international sporting competition would help to illustrate the benefits of rejoining the international community.

Furthermore, de Klerk wanted to establish, and demonstrate at home, international credibility and therefore backing for his own pace of reform:

> I wished to ensure that key international leaders would lend their support to a balanced process of negotiations in which the reasonable concerns of all South Africans would receive adequate attention. It was important to

break down the stereotypes that many people overseas had developed of white South Africans and the National Party—and to persuade them that we were no longer the problem but an indispensable part of the solution.[19]

On the eve of his assuming the leadership of the National Party in 1989, the stepping-stone to the presidency later that year, de Klerk made a trip throughout Europe. Some believe that he heard a tough message from even friendly interlocutors, such as Margaret Thatcher. The message was that the piecemeal and controversial reforms of his predecessor, P. W. Botha, would not suffice to sustain, for example, Thatcher's stance against sanctions.[20] De Klerk reports it differently, that he sought and received credibility, understanding, and a promise of support for an agenda of more thorough reform, even without indicating the details of his intentions.[21] In the spring of 1990, he again traveled to Europe to boost support for the process he had so dramatically begun in his February speech.

Following his second trip to Europe, de Klerk focused on the United States. "Despite the success of my European trip, I realized that Europe alone was not enough. It was essential that we should also make a breakthrough to the United States—the world's leading super power."[22] De Klerk considered the United States a "more difficult nut to crack" because of the comprehensive, congressionally enacted sanctions and the still hostile resistance in the anti-apartheid movement. Thus he was moved to tears at the pomp and ceremony accorded him later that year, as the first South African president to visit the United States in forty-five years. Most important, following his meetings with President Bush, the president informed Congress that the process of reform in South Africa was irreversible, a key if not sufficient condition in the sanctions legislation, and proclaimed that discussion of further application of stringent sanctions was fast becoming irrelevant. In de Klerk's view, he had achieved all his objectives with the visit.[23]

Mobilizing international support continued to be part of the government's strategy over the full four years of negotiations. In preparing for his path-breaking speech to Parliament in February 1990, de Klerk carefully orchestrated a buildup of expectations in the international community. He purposely avoided giving a date for Mandela's release, for which the world was anxiously waiting, in order to shift the attention of the gathering media to the address.[24] Throughout the next four years, de Klerk's messages to his white constituency would continue to be that a bold reform effort would reestablish normal relations between South Africa and the international community.[25] The sanctions debate would thus take on a new meaning in the 1990s, that is, whether the government or the ANC could control the pace and degree whereby sanctions would be lifted and who would get credit for their lifting.

The ANC similarly saw international support as a key element in its strategy. Of course, it had had to rely heavily on such support during its long period of being banned within South Africa. Its headquarters-in-exile and its underground activities, including military ones, depended on the good graces of the "Front Line" states, those independent African states on or near the South African border. The ANC's financial support came from sympathetic supporters in Western Europe, particularly the Scandinavian countries, and from nongovernmental supporters in the United States, along with both financial and military support from the governments of Libya, Cuba, the Soviet Union, and Eastern Europe. But the ANC's thinking went beyond that:

> The ANC understood better than most liberation movements how important international solidarity was, that you couldn't separate the two. Of course we must concentrate on internal mobilization and all of these things. But that they were interrelated, that if you intensified your struggle at home the possibilities of creating a broader base and stronger movement outside was better and vice versa, if you had a powerful solidarity movement outside it would in turn impact upon developments in South Africa. The ANC understood this very, very clearly.[26]

From the late 1970s, the ANC recognized that ultimately it would need the official support of the United States to achieve the degree of international legitimacy and clout it needed. Taking his cue from a friendly CIA contact in London, Thabo Mbeki, in charge of the ANC's international relations, began a campaign to broaden support for the ANC and its objectives beyond the civil rights and trade union activists in the United States, specifically beyond members and supporters of the Democratic Party.[27] Throughout the 1980s, the ANC worked to enlist understanding from Republican senators such as Richard Lugar and Nancy Kassebaum and representatives such as Amo Houghton, and to reach out to the American business community. This support would prove crucial in the passage of sanctions legislation in 1986 and in overriding Reagan's veto.

For those within the ANC who had lived in the United States and knew the diversity of its views and the sympathy for the anti-apartheid movement, changing the American government's official perception of the ANC as a communist, terrorist organization was critical. It was necessary not only to gain support from the United States, but to counter strong anti-American attitudes among those in the ANC whose outside links were largely with the Soviet bloc.[28] Oliver Tambo's meeting with the secretary of state in 1987 was an important step in this direction. But the ANC took even greater satisfaction from the State Department's determination that same year that the ANC was a "legitimate voice" rather than a "terrorist" organization. Mandela told President Clinton years later, "If the United States could say we were not a terrorist organization, who would any longer say we were?"[29] The end of the Cold War and the collapse of the Soviet Union in 1989 made this outreach to the United States all the more important. Shortly after his release from prison, as described above, Mandela made a triumphant visit to the United States. The adulation, high-level attention, and proffers of support were, in Mandela's words, "truly humbling." But Mandela made a point in his address to Congress to urge the United States to keep the sanctions in place.

Thus, entering the period of negotiation in 1990, each interlocutor had its eye on the degree of international support—which for both sides now meant Western support—it could garner. While international opinion would not be decisive in the resolution of the individual items under discussion, nor even in some of the major turning points in the negotiation process, it was never absent from the considerations of the parties. That gave the international community an entrée to the process and the opportunity to use its resources to influence the outcome.

THE PASSING OF THE BATON

As negotiations proceeded, moreover, diplomatic changes on the ground in South Africa were creating a more prominent role for the United States. In the early 1990s, a forceful and outspoken British ambassador, Robin Renwick, seemingly dominated the diplomatic scene in South Africa. Often dubbed a "proconsul," Renwick was highly visible and not hesitant to claim exceptional influence over the actions of all the parties. That Britain's Margaret Thatcher had been one of the strongest opponents of sanctions made this role all the more extraordinary, if not controversial.[30] But following Renwick's departure in 1992, Britain preferred to lower its profile, to shift, in the words of one Foreign Office official, to a "less prescriptive role."

The perception was thus that, from 1992, Britain's leadership on the ground gave way to that of the United States.[31] Perceptions are often deceiving. Renwick's successor, Sir Anthony Reeve, if employing a much different style, was active and intelligent and at key moments produced high-level involvement from his government. Moreover, during Renwick's tenure, my predecessor, Bill Swing, who is one of America's top diplomats, was one whose views were strongly and clearly delivered, and whose breadth of contacts and indefatigable energy gave him tremendous influence. Whatever the truth of it, however, the perception of growing U.S. influence provided us with special opportunities as well as responsibilities.

Part II
Into the Breach

5

From Mediation
to Facilitation

I WAS APPOINTED AMBASSADOR IN JUNE 1992 and confirmed in August that year. After some twenty years of work on African affairs, I considered this the pinnacle assignment. The first half of my career, until 1980, had been spent in the U.S. Agency for International Development, giving me a background that seemed appropriate for planning a postapartheid relationship with South Africa, which would emphasize economic reconstruction and development. I suspect that some people recommended me for the job with this in mind. I certainly looked forward to that part of the assignment. But the truth was that as much as I treasured my career in USAID, and my work on development, my academic background was in political science, and my continuing interest was foreign policy and diplomacy. In the subsequent twelve years in the State Department I had worked on conflict resolution and related security matters in several parts of the continent and had devoted three years of effort, as ambassador to Nigeria, to pressing for a transition from military to civilian rule there. I had also watched, and participated in to some extent, Chester Crocker's direction of the long and complex negotiations throughout southern Africa.

I suspected, based on this experience, that the transition process would in fact demand continued attention. I was not even sure that the violence that had preceded the opening of negotiations was behind us. One of the unsettling preparations my wife and I made was buying appropriate clothes for funerals. In this vein, Chester Crocker said to me as I was preparing to leave, "Remember, South Africa is a roller coaster. It is up one day and down the next." It was good advice.

Nevertheless, the mood in Washington that spring was optimistic. By May 1992, the process of negotiation had proceeded so well and so fast that it seemed like an agreement on the transition might be reached by midyear. Colleagues kidded me that "it would all be over" before I got there. That optimism was rudely shattered in June, when of a series of shocks began that would bring the process to an almost complete halt.

The first of these shocks was a breakdown in the negotiations themselves. Since Mandela's release in February 1990, talks had proceeded slowly. Throughout 1991, the ANC and the government had struggled over the nature of the transition to democratic rule. The government had argued for a two-stage process. During the first stage, an interim government, in which the de Klerk government and its allies would have a significant share of power, would develop an interim constitution and establish some "basic principles" that would bind a final constitution. The ANC agreed reluctantly in June 1991 to a two-stage process but saw the first stage as limited primarily to setting the stage for elections. For the ANC, the critical objective was a democratically elected Constituent Assembly that would write the final constitution. A multiparty forum, CODESA, was agreed on as the forum for thrashing out the principles and details of agreement on these issues. CODESA convened in December 1991 and quickly broke into five working groups.[1]

The negotiations were interrupted in February 1992 when the National Party lost a key by-election to the small but vocal Conservative Party, which had broken away from the National Party in 1982 to protest even P. W. Botha's reforms. De Klerk had in fact risen to prominence in the National Party by taking on Andries Treurnicht, the leader of the Conservative Party, in 1982. That marked what de Klerk described as the beginning of a "long uphill struggle against the Conservative Party." But de Klerk was also concerned after the by-election that the mandate he had received in 1989 was "visibly slipping away," and that his credibility had "seriously eroded." He responded by calling a whites-only referendum for March on his reform program. The referendum question was simple, but at the same time far-reaching:

> Do you support the continuation of the reform process that the state president started on 2 February 1990 and which is aimed at a new constitution through negotiations?[2]

The ANC was not happy with a whites-only referendum but went along with it. De Klerk campaigned hard and won handily, with more than 68 percent voting "yes." The whole world breathed a sigh of relief. The outcome seemed to set the stage for rapid progress. But in the aftermath of the referendum, the government toughened its negotiating position. De Klerk argues that he had made a promise to his constituency during the referendum campaign not to surrender the principle of power sharing between whites and blacks nor to submit to simple "majority rule." Others believe the government felt emboldened by the results of the referendum.

and overplayed its hand.[3] Whichever the reason, the negotiations that had seemed so promising only a few months earlier soon reached deadlock.

The nub of the disagreement came over the means by which a new constitution would be ratified in a freely elected parliament. The government proposal put forward in May 1992 would have required a 75 percent majority vote in the Constituent Assembly for approval of a new constitution. The ANC sensed a trap. Not only would the white opposition and its allies in the Parliament be able to block adoption of a majority-driven constitution, but also the likely deadlock would stretch out the time during which South Africa would be ruled by a power-sharing government under an interim constitution. The ANC made some extraordinary concessions in order to reach agreement, offering a weighted voting in the Parliament of 70 percent. At the same time, the ANC pushed for a "deadlock-breaking" mechanism whereby a draft constitution would be put to a popular vote after six months if the Parliament could not agree. Here the government sensed a trap: the ANC could deadlock the parliamentary process and quickly move to the popular vote.

As close to agreement as the parties had come on many other aspects of the transition, the differences between them on this issue were irreconcilable. On May 15, the ANC withdrew from the working group dedicated to these issues, saying further efforts were fruitless.[4] Some analysts have suggested that the breakdown was a godsend, for the ANC in particular had gotten out in front of its constituency and had perhaps come close to signing an agreement—particularly the 70 percent weighted voting concession—that would not have been supportable within its ranks. The government too, it is argued, needed a break and time to realize the limits of its political influence in the changing dynamics of South African politics.[5]

The stage was set for a battle of wills and of power. The ANC turned to what would become a frequent tactic for mobilizing and demonstrating its political power: mass action. Following the breakdown, the ANC called for a massive stayaway from work and for large-scale demonstrations. The forcefulness of these actions put the government in a bind. As Allister Sparks has written:

> by unbanning the blacks' political movements De Klerk enabled them to mobilize their mass support and literally paralyze the country. Short of reverting to old-style states of emergency and security crackdowns, which would ruin the image of moderation he had been at such pains to cultivate internationally, there was little the President could do to counter this formidable new prospect. This was the genie he had let out of the bottle.[6]

But then an uglier part of the process emerged. Violence between supporters of Buthelezi's Inkatha Freedom Party and the ANC had been building since 1990.

On June 17, 1992, just one day after the beginning of the latest mass-action campaign, a group from an Inkatha-controlled hostel in the town of Boipatong, just south of Johannesburg, went on a rampage. They massacred thirty-eight black people in their homes, including a nine-month-old baby and twenty-two women, one of whom was pregnant. The tragedy was compounded when de Klerk sought to visit the township; he was turned back by angry mobs, and in the tense situation surrounding his departure the police shot down twenty more persons.

Violence had now uprooted the negotiation process. The ANC announced it was withdrawing from the process altogether until the government met fourteen demands, including strict controls over the purveyors of violence, whether coming from within or outside the government.

AN INTERNATIONAL PRESENCE

This was the situation that led to the meeting of the UN Security Council in July 1992. The United Nations had had a long history of involvement with South Africa, but until this moment this relationship constituted one basically of confrontation with the South African government. Year after year, the United Nations had passed resolutions denouncing apartheid, had enacted sanctions—the mandatory arms embargo against South Africa in 1977 was the first such act against a member country—and in 1974 barred South Africa's government from participation in the General Assembly. The UN Special Committee against Apartheid rallied support for the liberation struggle, for further sanctions, and for aid to the liberation movements. UN funds began to flow indirectly to these movements and their supporters in the 1970s and totaled more than $75 million by the time of the election in 1994.[7]

Not surprisingly, given UN actions against apartheid, the attitude of the South African government toward the United Nations was one of hostility. Obtaining South African cooperation with the United Nations in Namibia had been no small achievement by Chester Crocker and his colleagues.[8] The UN Security Council meeting in 1992 was therefore a turning point. With the South African government's agreement, this meeting brought about a UN presence in South Africa, an observer mission that would grow to one hundred and that focused on the problems of violence. This was a major objective of Nelson Mandela, for which he sought American and other support going into that meeting.

But the meeting was also an opportunity for de Klerk. From the beginning, his strategy had been to demonstrate to his constituency that one of the benefits of his reform program would be an end to South Africa's isolation. Indeed in 1990, in the wake of de Klerk's dramatic moves earlier in the year, a UN team led by Under Secretary-General Abdullah Farah spoke of the "bold and courageous policy to which President De Klerk has committed his government"—rare praise that must have seemed like music to South African government ears after so many years of denunciation. A General Assembly resolution that same year was remarkably tame in its criticisms.[9] The stage was set for South Africa to begin a new association, and a more trusting one, with the international community. The UN presence in South Africa was the first step.

"IT IS JUST A QUESTION OF US"

The UN Security Council meeting also served as a turning point in U.S. policy. Up to that point, the idea of American mediation had been gaining momentum within the administration. Herman Cohen thinks it not coincidental that the idea took hold at the same time that the administration was suddenly doing more on Africa in general, as later exemplified in Somalia. The administration overruled bureaucratic contrary advice in many such cases, perhaps in consideration of the upcoming presidential election. But no doubt there was a genuine belief that the United States had something valuable to offer and was concerned that the negotiations should not be allowed to fail. Dennis Ross, the special coordinator for the Middle East, had accompanied Baker on his earlier trip to South Africa and was optimistic about the potential for U.S. mediation. The administration was after all still in thrall to the Gulf War and the prospect of a New World Order. South Africa could offer an important example of how that world was unfolding. Nevertheless, Cohen found it amazing, almost unseemly, that at the annual summer White House reception for the diplomatic corps, "they were racing, Baker and Bush, after the South Africans and cornering them and buttonholing them, saying you've got to have a mediator, we really want to help."[10]

Cohen, though aware that the South Africans had turned down such offers before, did not object. He noted that the American, British, and German ambassadors in South Africa, at the parties' request, were already actively engaged in helping to bridge gaps, counsel reason, and overcome differences. Cohen called it "invisible mediation." Nor did I object when the idea was put to me. It seemed to offer an important, exciting opportunity.

President Bush thus wrote to de Klerk, Mandela, and Buthelezi in the wake of the Boipatong massacre. In his letters to de Klerk and Mandela, Bush put forward the offer of an active, possibly a mediation, role for the United States. Referring to the importance of resuming the negotiation process, President Bush wrote to each of them:

> It may be that help from a third party could be useful for changing the climate and putting negotiations back on track. We are prepared to play such a role if you think it would be useful. I have asked Secretary of State Baker

... to be personally available to you if you wish to discuss this, or any other issue, further.[11]

De Klerk responded two days later. After addressing the issue of violence and reiterating his absolute commitment to the negotiating process, de Klerk replied obliquely (without referencing it directly) to Bush's proposal, but the message was clear: "It cannot be expected that South Africans should surrender responsibility for determining their own future. Neither can South Africa allow its sovereignty to be impaired. However, we value the positive role the international community can make in facilitating the negotiation process."[12] Looking back analytically on that position years later, de Klerk noted it had all along been a position of the National Party to obtain "constitutional change constitutionally":

> We did not have a situation [that necessitated] putting the process into the hands of a third party or third parties, or a conglomeration of third parties. We wanted to achieve a South African solution agreed between South Africans. . . . We would welcome support for the process and we constantly welcomed [it], we never said no, we never withheld information. . . . We realized that international pressures at times on the ANC was important on issues. But we did not in any way want to give up essential control of the process itself by us and by the institutions that resulted [from] the negotiation process.[13]

Nelson Mandela's response came in his telephone conversation with President Bush, cited in chapter 1. The ANC's rejection of mediation paralleled the South African government's. As an ANC representative told a Washington audience earlier that year, "People are talking about an external arbiter. We are sufficient to the task. It is just a question of us."[14]

But the ANC's motivation, in the eyes of the ANC, was somewhat different from that of the government. In the view of one ANC principal, de Klerk was intent on maintaining control of the process in order to preserve the legitimacy of the existing state. That legitimacy would assist in his negotiating a change in structure that was only superficial—"a black president without any power"—without a more fundamental transformation of the state itself. "The legitimacy of the state would not have been allowed to be impugned in any way, by arbitration or conciliation, or mediation . . . [the South African government would have] totally rejected that."[15]

The ANC by contrast did not accept the legitimacy of the existing state. It came at the question of possible mediation, therefore, from a different perspective, but arrived at the same conclusion:

> The debates in South Africa were about the nature of the state. . . . What kind of a state are you going to have? And of course the nature of the state debate was about the nature of the transfer [of power] to the majority.

> Our position was that we knew we were the overwhelming major-
> ity. It was a transfer of power we were talking about, and a mediator has
> no role in a transfer of power. A mediator may have a role when there is
> inability to meet together or conciliate. A mediator may put forward ideas
> for discussion, for negotiations, and stand back. But we didn't require that.
> We had already worked out our negotiating positions, we had unpaid but
> extraordinary participants in the negotiation process: people from universi-
> ties, from outside, South Africans involved in the ANC. And of course we
> had this remarkable team of Mandela, Mbeki, and Ramaphosa.[16]

If their motives were different, both sides nevertheless saw in a process controlled
by South Africans an ultimate legitimacy that would make the final accord that
much stronger. ANC negotiators take pains today to emphasize that all the elements in the final constitution—the Constitutional Court, proportional representation, the bill of rights—were "our own." When the other side pushed the idea
that a supreme court like that of the United States or India would be the final
determiner, "we said no, there's no legitimacy in that."[17] De Klerk said of the final
settlement, "Nobody could say that it has been thrust upon us from outside."[18]

The United States did not press its offer any further. Cohen took the rejection
as a positive sign: "If they're rejecting mediation it means they're determined.
Because sometimes you accept mediation as a way of avoiding an outcome." From
the summer of 1992 onward, therefore, the United States accepted the position
that the process would, indeed should, be in the hands of the parties. On several
occasions in the ensuing years, when some South Africans, including some from
within the ANC, suggested that more direct outside involvement might in fact
be necessary, the U.S. position would be to put the responsibility back on the
South Africans.

The new U.S. position was stated at the UN Security Council meeting in
July 1992. In supporting the decision to designate a special UN envoy to South
Africa—the distinguished American Cyrus Vance—U.S. ambassador to the
United Nations Edward Perkins stated that Vance's mission would not "tamper
with the complex negotiations themselves." It would not be another Namibia.

Assistant Secretary of State Herman Cohen reiterated this position in testimony before the Senate on September 23. He recalled the offer of good offices by
Secretary Baker and the response from both the government and Mandela. The
decision by the parties to continue negotiations on their own, said Cohen, "was a
good sign." At the same time Cohen clarified that the parties had welcomed foreign intervention on the violence question.[19]

This was perhaps the most significant outcome of the UN Security Council
meeting. Having given Mandela the critically important imprimatur of international focus on the violence, the Security Council—in a bow to de Klerk—did not
determine responsibility for the violence, nor did it mandate the Vance mission to

do so. But Vance's mission, which proceeded to South Africa immediately after the Security Council meeting, proved critical in putting international support behind the South African Commission, which was headed by South African justice Richard Goldstone, to investigate the causes of violence. Vance toured troubled areas with Goldstone and in his report to the secretary-general endorsed Goldstone's call for an across-the-board investigation of the security forces in South Africa.[20] The Goldstone Commission would eventually turn up evidence of shocking police and military involvement in the violence. Vance also played an important role in resolving issues impeding a return to the negotiating table, particularly that of political prisoners. On his return, Vance recommended the dispatch of fifty UN peace observers, who were augmented by some thirty more from the Commonwealth, the European Union, and the Organization of African Unity (OAU).

While both sides drew benefits from the UN decisions, the new level of involvement touched sensitive nerves about exactly what the role of outsiders would be. Foreign Minister Pik Botha hailed the Security Council meeting as a victory for the government. He pointed to the fact that the government had not been condemned, and that the Vance mission would be a "facilitating, fact-finding, goodwill mission," with no binding implications for the government. He implied that the focus would be not so much the root causes of violence as getting the ANC back to the negotiating table.[21]

Thabo Mbeki reacted immediately, saying that the government's attempt to portray the Security Council resolution as focusing on resumption of negotiations was "unfortunate and dangerous." Vance's mission, Mbeki claimed, was to see how violence could be ended, not how negotiations could be restarted. It was "self-evident," Mbeki said, that if violence were brought under control, the chances of negotiations could be improved.[22] Not all ANC officials made such sharp distinctions. One ANC leader, close to the situation in violence-torn KwaZulu and Natal, told U.S. embassy officers that the international facilitator should address "violence plus," that is, violence plus core issues blocking return to negotiations. But by and large ANC leaders preferred that the negotiating issues themselves remain between the ANC and the government.

For the United States, a commitment to a facilitative rather than a mediation role set in motion a no less active role. Indeed, if the parties asserted that the responsibility were theirs, the international community could and would hold them to that responsibility. Their degree of responsibility, and of the international community's ability to be of influence, would be severely tested in the coming months.

"CALL ANYONE YOU KNOW WHO MIGHT BE ABLE TO HELP"

As the impasse in the negotiations continued and the United Nations prepared to send in peace observers, the ANC enlarged its mass-action campaign, extending it to the so-called independent homelands that had been established by the apartheid regime. Spurred by the more radical elements within it, the ANC organized a march on Bisho, the capital of the Ciskei homeland, on September 7. This set the stage for the third crisis in 1992.

Elaborate preparations had been made by South African peace groups to facilitate a large-scale ANC demonstration that would nevertheless avoid direct confrontation with Ciskei security forces. This plan called for the marchers to gather in a stadium outside the capital city. But the leader of the march, Ronnie Kasrils, chose to seek to outflank Ciskei's security forces and break through to the town. The result was another bloody massacre. Twenty-eight marchers were killed and over two hundred were wounded. This time it was the ANC that faced harsh criticism. But elements within the ANC were calling for further marches, including one on Ulundi, the capital of Buthelezi's homeland government in KwaZulu. To most observers, this was a recipe for wholesale slaughter.

The situation cried out for finding a way out of the box of violence and confrontation.

I arrived in South Africa on August 27 and the ceremony for presenting credentials was set for September 21. Normally, prior to presenting credentials, an ambassador is a "nonperson," that is, confined to in-house work with his staff and precluded from any diplomatic or public activity. But in the wake of the tragic events at Bisho, the South African government waived that limitation, telling me I was free immediately to carry out whatever functions I felt might help.

I met on September 8 with Ambassador Anthony Reeve of the United Kingdom, in what would be the beginning of a close and cooperative partnership over the next three years. He was seeking a letter from Prime Minister Major to key leaders and I agreed immediately that we should do the same. I recommended to Washington that the president send messages that I would deliver to President de Klerk and ANC president Mandela. We asked for a twenty-four-hour turnaround from Washington, and both the White House and the department worked late into the night, producing them the very next day.

The messages were similar, but with important differences. In the message to de Klerk, which I delivered through the Foreign Affairs Ministry on September 9, the United States reiterated its long-standing policy that the South African government was responsible for the actions of the "homelands," and therefore responsible for ensuring protection for free assembly, even in those areas it regarded as "independent." Furthermore, at my insistence, this message urged the government to "establish conditions conducive to the resumption of negotiations, taking the initiative to address the legitimate concerns of the opposition." This reflected the view of many regarding the position the government had taken in CODESA 2, which had contributed to the breakdown. Specifically, the government's proposals for power sharing bordered on asking for a veto over the majority, a demand that not only was inconsistent with the principles of the transformation that was necessary, but was ultimately unacceptable to the opposition. Our concerns were not new. My predecessor, Ambassador Swing, had expressed them on several occasions to South African government officials in the months before his departure and publicized them in an op-ed in *Business Day*.

The message to Mandela carried a different emphasis. It was the ANC's proposed march on Ulundi that posed the greatest immediate threat of major violence. Some of us had the feeling that Mandela had allowed control over ANC policy to drift and be driven by radical elements. President Bush's message to Mandela recalled how closely the United States had worked with him to secure Security Council approval for UN observers to be attached to the national peace accord structures in South Africa. Going ahead with mass action that would result in greater violence would compromise the role of the United Nations even before the observers had been deployed.

I delivered the message to Mandela on September 10, at our first meeting, just before he was to address the diplomatic corps on the situation. Mandela clearly was caught between the frustration and demands of his constituency, most easily released through mass-action events, and the obvious dangers mass action posed. He responded to our message positively, recognizing immediately the damage that could be done to the UN role he had sought. In his remarks to the diplomats following our meeting, Mandela said he was looking for an "excuse" to resume the negotiations but was stymied by government stalling on issues related to the violence as well as to political prisoners. Mandela's associates that day— Chris Hani, secretary general of the South African Communist Party (SACP), and Ronnie Kasril, who had directed the fatal Bisho march—took a more belligerent position before the diplomats, arguing the right and justification for further mass action. Mandela somewhat distanced himself from those remarks but said that the rank and file would not listen if told to do nothing. "Mass action is better than what some want," he warned: "to take up arms."

We continued in the following days and weeks to hammer away on the danger of a march on Ulundi. On September 15, I met with Chris Hani in the offices of the SACP. The atmosphere was almost surreal. In the modest, almost dingy, offices, the walls were covered with traditional and by then surely anachronistic posters of marching Red crusaders, with the slogans of a bygone era. But Chris Hani was an intelligent, articulate man with a keen understanding of the situation evolving in South Africa and had perhaps the most credibility among the ANC youth. He welcomed the meeting.

There we debated the wisdom of further mass action at this time. I argued not only that it was morally questionable to put people at such risk, but that tactically it was not in the ANC's interest to marginalize the UN monitors just as they arrive and before they could be effectively deployed. This would undercut all the ANC's gains in the UN Security Council meeting. Hani argued forcefully about the importance of mass action. It was a fundamental weapon and means of mobilization for the liberation movement. Nevertheless, Hani said, the marches on homelands would be postponed. He noted that the United States and the American people commanded significant influence in South Africa. And, quite genuinely, he expressed his appreciation for U.S. help in the transformation of South Africa.

I met more formally with Mandela on September 16.[23] We discussed at length the history of the negotiation process and, in the first of what would become many such discussions, how the conflict between the ANC and Chief Buthelezi's Inkatha Freedom Party could be overcome. Mandela's prescription proved prophetic. Pressed on what he could offer to Buthelezi in return for Inkatha relinquishing its display of traditional weapons, one of Mandela's principal demands, Mandela suggested that Inkatha could participate in the cabinet if the ANC won the election. Unfortunately, much bloodshed and tragedy would pass through the country before this understanding would be reached.

I urged Mandela at this meeting to call off the planned marches, not only the one to Ulundi but another being planned on the capital of the Bophuthatswana homeland. "It would not be understood in Washington," I said, if the marches proceeded in the present atmosphere. Mandela, who had just come from an ANC meeting, said that the ANC was "listening to appeals" and would instruct the regional ANC office that was planning the Ulundi march to "reexamine" the matter.

When I arrived at the embassy on the morning of September 23, the marine guard reported to me that a call had come into the embassy the previous evening. "Someone who said he was Man-DEL-a or something like that. He wanted your home number. Of course, I refused to give it to him." Appalled, but recognizing that the guard was only doing his duty, I immediately gave instructions on who could be given my home number. Fortunately, Mandela called back that evening. He had just read Assistant Secretary Cohen's testimony before the Senate the day before, which he described as "excellent." Cohen had listed some of the same demands that Mandela had—a ban on public display of weapons, securing the hostels from which several attacks in the townships had originated—as essential for a successful resolution of the current impasse.

I spoke with Mandela by phone again on September 24. He was calling to report that agreement had been reached for a summit meeting between him and de Klerk. We were relieved, for this offered a critical step back from the abyss. I took the occasion, however, to express concern over a report I had heard that the ANC had approved in principle the march on Ulundi, but no longer with a specific date. Mandela replied immediately that this was still "under discussion."

The atmosphere in the embassy throughout this period reflected our feeling that we should find any and every way to help end this crisis. Robert Cabelly, who had been special assistant to Chester Crocker throughout the Namibia negotiations, and who had a plethora of contacts in South Africa, arrived for a visit on September 17 and plunged into the effort with us. It was important to reach everyone with the same message and to underline the importance of pulling back from the brink. One evening, after working through various matters throughout the day, Robert and I went back to my residence and went over whom we might still call. Robert was then no longer in the government and asked if I wanted to limit his contacts at all, some of whom were ties into the South African security community. "Call anyone you know who might be able to help," I replied.

Others were as active and concerned. The United Nations sent another mission, this time headed by a former under secretary-general, Virendra Dayal, in September. After learning of the U.S. and British approaches at the highest level, Dayal quickly secured messages from the secretary-general to the three key leaders in South Africa. Reports were heard that former Zambian president Kenneth Kaunda and former Tanzanian president Julius Nyerere had been engaged by the OAU to mediate between Mandela and Buthelezi. Britain's foreign minister, Douglas Hurd, warned South Africa that time was not on its side. Later he would weigh in with what would be the face-saving formula (parole) for the release of the remaining political prisoners—including some hard-core murderers whose cause had unfortunately become critical to the ANC.

As noted, on September 24 Mandela called me and several others in the international community to say that agreement had been reached for a summit meeting between him and de Klerk. The summit meeting produced the Record of Understanding that would set the tone and the parameters of the negotiations thereafter. From that point on, it was recognized that the South African government and the ANC were the principal negotiators. Their degree of agreement would determine the pace of progress. The Record of Understanding also marked perhaps the most important turning point in the process itself, namely the agreement by the two main parties that thereafter incidents of violence, while deplored and often bitter subjects of dispute between them, would not be allowed to stop the negotiations. From that point on, the advocates of peaceful transformation, not its opponents, controlled the process, as much as the latter would wreak havoc on many people's lives for nearly two more years.

The threat of the marches on the homelands did not go away so soon. We continued to hear reports of further plans, and the ANC seemed reluctant to give up the principle of being able to march. Mandela had made the point with me on September 16 that mass action had another purpose: to insist on and, if necessary, force the right to free political activity in the homelands. Otherwise, the ANC would be not only blocked from campaigning for their incorporation into a free South Africa, but kept from preventing wholesale voter fraud in the first democratic election. This would become an important theme in the later unraveling of Bophuthatswana and in the ongoing troubles in KwaZulu and Natal.

Nevertheless, in the atmosphere of late 1992, such actions seemed most inadvisable. Another problem was that there were some in the ANC who believed that mass action could prove a shortcut to power. Assistant Secretary of State Cohen spoke to this issue in his Senate testimony. Having first made clear that the South African government had the responsibility for ensuring that no such excessive and unjustified force be used as was used at Bisho, he went on: "Similarly, mass actions aimed at confrontation that add to the already unacceptable level of violence are clearly ill-advised. This is particularly the case when mass action proceeds from the false premise that easy victories can be gained on issues already the subject of serious negotiations."[24]

Not until late October had the idea of marching on these capitals become so thoroughly discredited that the threat receded. Jeremy Cronin, a principal in the Communist Party, told our embassy in October that, after Bisho, the party learned that mass action has its limits and that insurrection was simply not viable in South Africa. He nevertheless credited mass action, along with international pressure, with bringing about the Record of Understanding. The same month, Jay Naidoo, secretary general of the labor alliance COSATU, was very critical to me of the U.S. position against further mass action as enunciated by Cohen. COSATU provided much of the organizational muscle and indeed many of the participants in the mass-action campaigns. But then, having vented his criticism, he conceded that it would be "suicide" for anyone to march on Ulundi in the foreseeable future.

International pressure was an important element in the final drawing back from the brink. Obviously, the domestic pressures were as much or more compelling. But Mandela, Mbeki, and eventually others realized that, if violence between the ANC and Inkatha got out of hand, everyone would lose control of the process. Even within the SACP there was a recognition that the support of the international community was as important as any internal mobilization of forces in protecting the process of transformation that had begun in 1990. In the opinion of Essop Pahad, who attended my first meeting with Chris Hani,

> When you first came and had that interview, we were going through a difficult patch. And the question about whether or not the de Klerk government would remain consistent with its own undertakings had not been clarified fully. We didn't know whether or not right-wing elements in the military may not stage a coup d'etat. We were never sure whether we were

not going to end up in prison, having come back from exile. But we said, we're here now, we are staying. And obviously for us, one of the important elements [in that calculation] was the fact that we would have the international community, who would have reacted in an exceptionally negative way to any further shift to the right in South African politics.[25]

WHERE IS THE URGENCY?

The negotiating process had passed perhaps its worst crisis. But it was not yet on track in a credible way. Over the next several months there seemed almost a lethargy in the process. Neither side seemed eager to engage very significantly. There was a great deal of sparring with disgruntled parties such as Inkatha, extended discussions over mechanisms for returning to the table, and seemingly little hurry on anyone's part. There were reasons for this hiatus. Both sides in the negotiations now had to reevaluate their positions to see how the impasse that had developed in CODESA 2 could be overcome. The Record of Understanding had removed the obstacles to resumed negotiations, but it had not addressed any of these issues. In this "breather" period, the ANC would in fact reach one of its most significant decisions: to propose a Government of National Unity that would guarantee cabinet-level participation for minority parties. It was one of the most fundamental breakthroughs in the negotiating process and demanded exceptional effort by the ANC leadership to sell it to its constituency. The government in turn began to back away from some of its more fixed formulas for power sharing. Quiet talks between the principal negotiators—Roelf Meyer for the government and Cyril Ramaphosa for the ANC—continued; indeed they had been secretly going on all through the crises of the summer, building an atmosphere of trust between the two men.

Regardless of these reasons, and the necessity on both sides for a breather in the formal negotiations, the nation became impatient and increasingly depressed. A major reason was the economy. In the fall of 1992 it nose-dived. Sanctions, isolation, and unrest—and indeed the long-term cumulative effects of apartheid on management and labor—had led the country into decline for several years. But whereas the decline was slow and steady in the late 1980s, no more than 2 percent of GDP annually, GDP fell 6 percent in the third quarter of 1992.[26] Severe drought devastated the agricultural sector. Spending and investment reached record lows. On top of the complexities of the political transformation, the perilous state of the economy and the tremendous reconstruction that would be required of it came more clearly into view. As British foreign minister Hurd had warned in September, "The economy is suffering badly and South African society with it."[27]

Adding to the negative mood was the increasing level of violence, especially in Natal. Despite the deployment of UN observers and the courageous activities of the National Peace Accord chapters to overcome it throughout the country, violence continued to escalate throughout this period. Charges flew back and forth between the ANC, Inkatha, and the government over who was more to blame for the violence and the slow pace of negotiations. In late November, the Goldstone Commission uncovered and publicized convincing evidence of systematic programs of destabilization and violence being carried out by South African security services, involving hit squads and provocateurs. This added to the charged atmosphere.

In late October, Mandela spoke of a "fetid cloud of despair" that had enveloped the country. In November, de Klerk tried to counter the mood, rejecting perceptions of "gloom and paralysis." He compared the situation to that prior to 1990, when South Africa was isolated and there was a spiral of uprisings and a state of emergency. But the fact remained that for six months there had been no visible progress on the transition.

In late October I sent a message to Washington, warning that the lack of urgency that seemed to pervade the leadership on all sides, the spiral of violence, the deepening recession, and the growing discontent and pessimism in the country were leading the nation to a point of no return. More and more, South Africans were beginning to tell us that mediation was necessary. It was a theme we would have to address. Archbishop Desmond Tutu had called for an international peace force in the wake of the Boipatong massacre and would do so again in the next year, when violence continued unabated. As noted, some within the ANC itself had advocated that the United Nations address "violence plus." Bantu Holomisa, the military head of the Transkei "homeland" and a maverick supporter of the ANC, was arguing that only an outside, independent mediator could succeed in bringing about an agreement.

If the leadership of the two key interlocutors rejected mediation, therefore, the parties had to demonstrate more progress on their own. I proposed that we, and others in the international community, begin to press all sides to (a) fix a date for elections, that is, give themselves a deadline; (b) honestly address the core issues blocking agreement; and (c) recognize that to achieve these objectives no side could get all it wanted in a settlement. These same themes had been enunciated by Assistant Secretary Cohen during a visit to South Africa in September, and we proposed intensifying our efforts to advance them. To start, we asked for a formal State Department statement along these lines, which was subsequently issued.

I had not given any formal press interviews since my arrival, largely because of the intensive period of crisis and diplomacy of those first months. I chose to use my first such interview, published in the Johannesburg *Sunday Times* of

November 15, to emphasize the above themes. In what the *Times* called a "somber assessment," I stressed the need for urgency. How long could people be patient if the date for elections kept being put off and the likelihood of attracting new investment would take much time after that? Unless there was progress on an interim government in the coming year and elections within a year thereafter, I warned, South Africa could reach a point of no return. Looking at the dangers of a further decline into violence, I sounded a theme to which we would come back over and over in the coming year: if South Africa crossed the line into civil war, outsiders could do little to help. That was the lesson of Yugoslavia and Somalia. The responsibility lay with South Africans to control their destiny.[28]

In the next few weeks, we repeated these themes in all our contacts. In meeting with government officials, we expressed concern at what we saw as the erosion of the government's credibility. We called for decisive action in response to the disclosure of the covert campaigns against the ANC from within the government, for unequivocal support for the further work of the Goldstone Commission, and movement on the remaining political issues. Without such progress, we said, we did not see how we could question demands for greater UN and other international intervention in South Africa, including even a mediator. In return, the United States was prepared to advocate for principles in a settlement that were dear to the government's heart, viz., interim power sharing in a transitional Government of National Unity, strong constitutional and institutional guarantees against abuse of state power, some form of federalism, protection of human rights including the rights (but not the privileges) of individuals and minorities, and the principles of a free economy.

With the ANC and Inkatha, we weighed in on the agonizing negotiations, involving at this time the mediation of Kenneth Kaunda, designed to bring Mandela and Buthelezi together in the context of reaffirming the principles of the National Peace Accord. We began a long and intensive dialogue with Buthelezi and his supporters aimed at bringing them back to the negotiating table. Inkatha's vitriolic reaction to the Record of Understanding, and to the negotiating process outlined in it, had been the spark for the latest round of violence. With the ANC, as with the government, we urged progress on core points in the negotiations and welcomed the breakthrough decision by the ANC regarding a Government of National Unity.

Significant movement began to occur at the end of November. De Klerk proposed for the first time a timetable for the completion of negotiations, with elections to be held by the first half of 1994. He retired twenty-three military and police officers relating to the probe into covert actions. In December and again in January, the ANC and the government held two retreats, hammering out the essentials of what a Government of National Unity would look like. Following the first of these retreats, Mandela expressed optimism that the differences between the ANC and the government were bridgeable.[29] In a meeting in his office two days later, de Klerk told me, "We are coming out of the trough."[30] In February 1993 formal negotiations resumed.

The process now appeared firmly on track, and the key parties appeared committed to bringing it to completion. Difficult issues over power sharing still remained that would not be resolved until the very final days of negotiations. Inkatha, for a time in a strange coalition with other "homeland" leaders, would continue to challenge both the legitimacy and the mechanics of the negotiations. The plague of violence would continue right up until the elections themselves. But from February 1993 on, our policy moved to providing support for the processes and procedures the two main parties had chosen, for the general framework of agreement underlying these processes, for the timetable to which the parties had agreed, and for bringing onboard all those who were hesitant or outright opposed.

We also began serious work on the challenges of the postapartheid period. If the gloom and despair of 1992 had had any salutary value, it was to focus everyone's attention on the deep problems in South Africa's economy.

(from left to right) Helen Lyman, Princeton Lyman, F. W. de Klerk, and Marike de Klerk, September 21, 1992, after the author presented his credentials as the new U.S. ambassador to President de Klerk.

Chief Mangosuthu Buthelezi and the author, March 1994.

Photograph by Joachim Kallweit, Kurt Schlesinger Studios, Johannesburg. Reproduced by kind permission.

The author and Nelson Mandela at the signing of the USAID agreement with the Mandela government, September 21, 1994.

Jesse Jackson, leader of the U.S. election observer mission, and the author speaking to a South African journalist, April 27, 1994.

Photograph by Graeme Bridges.

6

Lending Weight to the Process

The United States and the ANC are moving closer together.
We are seeing problems from the same perspective.
—NELSON MANDELA, *August 4, 1992*

Our relationship has moved from a stern one to a warm one.
—F. W. DE KLERK, *November 30, 1993*

THERE WERE SEVERAL ESSENTIAL ELEMENTS in our lending support to the reinvigorated negotiating process. The first was establishing and maintaining credibility with the principal parties to the negotiations. Second was rallying support for the process from key elements of South African society that were skeptical or negative. Third was being proactive, using diplomacy and resources to help overcome obstacles that would continue to arise right up to the election itself. This approach was particularly important in regard to the violence that plagued the country throughout 1993. Finally, we needed to begin to lay the foundations for the postapartheid era, to set in motion the preparations that would enable a new government to begin with maximum effectiveness.

This chapter recounts our efforts along these lines with the government, the ANC, and civil society. Subsequent chapters address our efforts with the most recalcitrant parties, from the right and the left, who threatened the very transition itself.

CREDIBILITY

One of the ironies of South Africa is that the United States had problems of credibility with both of the principal negotiating parties, the government and the ANC. Critics of the policy of constructive engagement would expect that a cozy relationship had developed between the U.S. government and the South African government through the 1980s. In fact, that relationship was often stormy. Not only did the issue of apartheid constitute a constant source of disagreement and criticism, but the negotiations over the independence of Namibia and the withdrawal of Cuban troops from Angola proceeded through a series of crises, sharp exchanges, and at times the recall of the U.S. ambassador.[1] It was a classic case of parties dealing closely and in the end effectively with each other out of mutual interest rather than shared ideals.

Congressional enactment of sanctions in 1986, moreover, reinforced a view within the South African white community that American political weight was on the side of the liberation movement. The election of President Clinton, who was much closer than his predecessor to constituents of the anti-apartheid movement, added to these concerns. The government had been pleased with what it saw as growing credibility with the Bush administration, which had resisted pressure for additional sanctions, counting on assurances from de Klerk that dramatic steps were in the offing.[2] As noted in the last chapter, de Klerk had been enormously moved by his reception in Washington in 1990. In 1992, President Bush certified that the conditions in the Comprehensive Anti-Apartheid Act allowing for the lifting of some of the sanctions had been met and that the process toward ending apartheid was "irreversible." De Klerk found this action particularly heartening.[3]

But as the process in South Africa moved into the final stages of difficult negotiations, and an election loomed in South Africa, a new administration was taking office in Washington. South African government officials and their constituency wondered about the objectivity that the United States would bring to bear on the process. In the aftermath of Clinton's election, I received many a query from government, the press, and others as to whether the new administration would be an objective facilitator in the unfolding negotiations.[4]

As for the ANC, with all the progress that had been made with the liberation movement, as described in chapter 3, I had no illusion when I arrived in South Africa that credibility did not still remain fragile and in need of careful cultivation. As Archbishop Tutu put it to me in his inimitable style years later, in reflecting on all the United States did along these lines in 1992–93, "I think we began to feel that we might begin to consider you friends."[5] Moreover, credibility had to be taken to a new level if we were going to be active in facilitating the process: in providing advice, carrying messages, receiving confidences. One of the first objectives, therefore, was to establish and maintain credibility on both sides, to be sensitive to each party's suspicion of our possible motives or sympathies.

Credibility is not neutrality. It does not mean a lack of principle or a lack of readiness to take sides on an issue that is critical to the very process being supported. Credibility relates to motive and to candidness. There was no neutrality over where we should stand on the transition. The United States had to back a real transfer of power, one that gave legitimacy and effective power to the party that won the election. Anything less would not only violate principle; it would ultimately fail in winning support from the vast majority of the citizens. The United States also had to press for constitutional guarantees of human rights and protection of individual and minority rights. Again, this conformed with principle, but it also was vital to keeping peace and retaining vitality in South Africa's multiracial society and advanced economy. Finally, the United States had to be on guard constantly against developments that would throw the process into uncontrolled violence, drown the transition in blood and civil war that would change the landscape for decades thereafter.

Pursuing these positions would put us at odds at one time or another with each party. The key to credibility was in my view transparency. We needed to make our positions clear, and to operate as transparently as possible. Furthermore, the United States had to be seen clearly on the side of a transition that was basically fair and effective, even if it meant, inevitably, that all sides could not get everything they wanted. Conveying our position thus involved a careful mixture of quiet diplomacy, with careful touching of bases, and public diplomacy to dispel any doubt about where we actually stood. Public diplomacy came to play a major role. As an ANC official recalled of our public pronouncements, "We felt the U.S. was also now having to come out in the open and was participating in the process, rather than in the background privately, because [the latter] is always subject to sinister interpretations."[6]

In addition, credibility rested on giving recognition to those who were making a true effort at a peaceful transition. It was important during this period not to focus exclusively on the ANC—as the "government-in-waiting"—and to dismiss the importance and genuine contributions of de Klerk and his government. Repeatedly during this period, there was criticism of the rewards and recognition that went to de Klerk, whether in the award of the Liberty Medal in Philadelphia, discussed below, or of the Nobel Prize. These were important steps, however. At a deeper level there had to be recognition of the tremendous pressures under which de Klerk was operating, the dangers from his right wing and, potentially, from the security forces. Our policies would have been foolhardy and self-defeating had we advocated measures that would have undermined de Klerk's authority or political capacity to complete the negotiations.

Finally, symbolism becomes an important instrument in establishing credibility. There were several instances in which dramatic acts of presence or response signaled a deeper commitment to the process and the parties. Several are described below.

WITH THE ANC AND ITS ALLIES: GESTURES WITH MEANING

My first meetings with Mandela were described in the previous chapter. In those meetings, I sought to establish clearly the principles described above. More than that, I established a practice of letting him and his chief aides know of the various steps we were taking, and of seeking his advice relating to some of the more difficult parties. Thus I told him in advance of the U.S. decision, discussed in chapter 8, to have me meet with Lucas Mangope, the president of the Bophuthatswana "homeland," to try to persuade him to agree to reincorporation with South Africa. I did not want any suspicion within the ANC that the United States was abandoning our long-standing policy of nonrecognition of the homelands or had other nefarious motives. Similarly, I shared with Mandela plans to meet with other dissidents. I did not ask permission. The United States had the right and the responsibility to be in touch with as many parties as possible, to understand the situation, and to exert our influence as we could. But in the situation of South Africa, it was important to make clear what we were doing.

Mandela responded with enthusiastic support. He encouraged me to meet with Mangope, with whom he also was having discussions, and with others opposing the process, for example, Ferdie Hartzenberg, leader of the Conservative Party; Constand Viljoen, who would become the leader of the Freedom Front; and of course Chief Mangosuthu Buthelezi. I was candid, without violating confidences, in sharing with him the result of these meetings. When I told him that my meeting with Mangope had produced no progress whatsoever on the issues of reincorporation or respect for human rights, Mandela laughed and said he had had the same result.

The ANC operated in a tripartite alliance: the ANC, the SACP, and COSATU. There was of course a lot of overlapping membership between these groups. The ANC had long managed this alliance with skill and a strong emphasis on consensus, without losing overall political control. But the SACP provided the alliance with some of its sharpest strategists. Its leaders, perhaps with internal misgivings, would prove crucial in bringing about acceptance by the more radical members of the alliance of some of the key compromises, political and economic, that the ANC would make over the coming years. COSATU was critical to mobilizing the crowds on which the ANC counted in its use of mass action.

I made it a point to have some of my earliest meetings with leaders of the South African Communist Party. The SACP was influential and the Cold War issues were moot. I wanted them to know that. As described in the previous chapter, I met early on with Chris Hani, one of the most popular and intelligent leaders of the ANC-SACP alliance. He and I established an understanding on where the United States stood on mass action and we achieved some consensus on this in the wake of the Bisho tragedy. I met around the same time with Joe Slovo. He had been the bête noire of the apartheid regime for years. He not only had been general secretary of the SACP but, more disturbing to apartheid defenders, had become the leader and true creator of the ANC's armed wing. Slovo's return to South Africa, when the SACP was unbanned, was one of the hardest things for white hard-liners to accept.

At Slovo's suggestion, we met for lunch in a small nondescript restaurant in Johannesburg. Slovo was by this time convinced of the strategy of negotiations and was already looking ahead to the postapartheid era. He was and would remain to his death a committed Communist. He would in fact write a monthly column in, ironically, *Business Day,* called "Red Alert." But Slovo realized too that the Soviet system had been a disaster. As he wrote later:

> The single party state, except at rare moments in history, is a recipe for tyranny. What we've learned from the Soviet experience and from the African experience is that the concept of the party as a vanguard which has the right to rule by virtue of calling itself something and which is entrenched in the constitution as a permanent godfather of this society, is a disaster.[7]

That day we talked a little about our roots, as we were both products of Lithuanian Jewish parents. Slovo had been born in Lithuania and came to South Africa as a child. He would credit his Jewish roots for some of his social conscience, but he was never religious.[8] We then went on to talk about the process of change. Later, under Mandela's presidency, Slovo would become the new South Africa's first minister of housing. One of my most memorable meetings was in 1994, when I brought a team from Fannie Mae (the U.S. Federal National Mortgage Association) to his office to explain how South Africa might develop a secondary mortgage market to help finance low-cost housing. As the team explained this quintessentially capitalist scheme, I thought I could read Slovo's mind as he thought, "How did a lifelong leader of the Communist Party get to the position of welcoming the formation of a secondary mortgage market?" But he not only welcomed it; he implemented it. But before those days came, Slovo would become one of my most important interlocutors on the tortuous constitutional negotiations and the impact they were having on the prospects for peace.

Relations with the other leg of the tripartite alliance, COSATU, were iron- ically more difficult. The AFL-CIO, in its anti-Communist zeal, had eschewed relations with COSATU, the largest labor association in South Africa, because of the Communist influence in it. The AFL-CIO publicly supported Chief Man- gosuthu Buthelezi as the ideal black leader in South Africa and developed ties with Inkatha's trade union grouping and other small labor affiliations. Despite the end of the Cold War, the AFL-CIO's Africa relations arm, the African- American Labor Center (AALC), found it difficult to give up its anti-Communist suspicions. Individual American labor unions had established better ties with their COSATU counterparts. The American Federation of State, County, and Munic- ipal Employees was one such union, and its international secretary-treasurer, William Lucy, was a prominent anti-apartheid activist. But overcoming the his- tory of the AFL-CIO's position was difficult. Little by little, new ties were built with support from our USAID program and the diligent efforts of AALC's rep- resentative on the ground.

More relevant to our political agenda was the work of an exceptionally tal- ented labor attaché in our Johannesburg consulate, Thomas Shannon. Politically attuned, he won the confidence of labor members and their important legal ad- visers in the struggle under way in the province of Natal and the homeland of KwaZulu, between COSATU and the more radical leadership of the province's ANC chapter. Theirs was also a struggle against hit squads supporting Buthelezi's Inkatha Freedom Party (IFP). Thanks to our attaché's tireless work, and frequent travel into the area, I was put in touch with the provincial labor leaders on my visits to Natal. Their lives were in such danger that we would meet at midnight or similar late hours, after which they would slip away to their hidden and regularly changing living quarters. Our support for their efforts to forge a more peaceful and rational path in this troubled province helped them somewhat; it gave us invaluable insight into the realities of the complicated skein of ambition, rivalries, treachery, and subversion that lay beneath the terrible violence of this period.[9]

In the spring of 1993, there arose two dramatic occasions on which we pro- vided tangible evidence of the American commitment to the cause of liberation. The first came in the wake of the terrible assassination of Chris Hani in April 1993. Hani was gunned down on a Sunday morning by a white immigrant from Poland who had been egged on by right-wing extremists. It was a major blow to the ANC. Hani, as noted above, was enormously popular with the youth of the liber- ation movement. He had the charisma, and thereby the most potential, to address what was a growing problem for the ANC, control of the youth vigilantes, so valuable in the early days of mass action but now becoming not only unruly but dangerous. Hani had begun to take action to curb their access to arms and to channel them into more structured activities. His death also came at a difficult time for the negotiators. The process had been restarted, but the long delays in setting a firm election date, and the arcane nature of the debate going on at the Kempton Park center, had left the general population feeling disconnected and impatient. Hani's assassination thus threatened to set off a wave of terrible violence. Mandela was given the opportunity to speak on national television to urge calm, but he was also in danger of losing control again of his followers if he did not allow for some outpouring of anger and frustration.

The ANC scheduled two memorials for Hani. The first was in Jubilani Stadium in Soweto, the sprawling black township outside Johannesburg. The second was a funeral in Johannesburg, a more formal ceremony to which foreign dignitaries and diplomats were expected to come. On the recommendation of my political officer, Pamela Bridgewater, who was our daily liaison with the ANC, my wife and I decided to attend both. Together with my security officer, who was not at all happy with this decision, and Pamela, we drove to the stadium. Outside, we came close to driving into an armed confrontation between the police and angry youth. Just ahead of us, the police had jumped from their armored cars and taken up positions behind them with rifles pointed at the chanting youth across the road. We pulled back and moved to another entrance. Making our way into the stadium, we were immediately recognized by burly ANC security guards with SACP slogans emblazoned on their T-shirts. They almost lifted us from the ground as they took us through the crowds, down the stairs, and up onto the podium. We were the only diplomats in attendance; indeed, my wife and I were the only white people in the entire stadium.

The rally was tense. Mandela drew boos when he mentioned that de Klerk had sent condolences. His message urging calm seemed to have little resonance. In one of the few times when Mandela was eclipsed by any other leader, the head of the militant Pan Africanist Conference, Clarence Makwetu, drew cheers when he arrived and more when he delivered a fiery speech of defiance. Mandela struggled to regain control and the rally ended relatively peacefully, though reports of violence outside continued to filter into the stadium. As the rally ended, Mandela's aides told him of our presence on the podium. Though exhausted and troubled by what had transpired, he greeted me warmly. Then he noticed my wife, hanging back near the edge of the podium. He had not met her before but guessed immediately who she was and that she was both nervous and shy. He beckoned her forward and put his arms around her. It was her first meeting with Mandela. He was her hero ever afterward.

The Hani assassination tested the transition process as it had never before been tested, and it provided valuable lessons. Following the rally at Jubilani, the ANC called for mass demonstrations to release the tremendous tensions among the population. Despite widespread fears of violence, the vast majority of the demonstrations were peaceful. Only in Cape Town, where loudspeakers outside a ceremony in the cathedral failed to reach an overflow crowd, did peace marshals lose control and serious violence occur. The message was clear for all who chose to hear it. For all their anger and all their frustration, for all their fears and all their uncertainties, the people of South Africa had no desire to destroy their country. That would prove just as true of the white population as elections neared a year later. Given the opportunity, South Africans wanted to preserve their country: make it better, not burn it down.

The other message, however, was just as clear. The time for endless negotiations had passed. The process could not survive many more crises. In the wake of the tragedy, the ANC pushed hard for a firm agreement on an election date. The time frame had been set earlier, but a firm commitment to a date had been sidestepped by the government and some of the other parties. After further protracted negotiation, the principal parties agreed on June 3 that the election date would be April 27, 1994. From that time forward, one of the United States' principal positions would be that this date could not be postponed. It became the basis on which we would argue with all the recalcitrant parties who argued for more time, for more negotiations, for a more perfect set of transition documents.

The Hani tragedy and its aftermath exhausted the ANC. But within two weeks, Oliver Tambo died. Tambo had led the ANC throughout Mandela's long imprisonment and had done more than any other person in that period to win ANC worldwide recognition and respect. At first the ANC did not feel up to yet another major expression of national tribute. When the State Department indicated that the White House was putting together a major delegation for the funeral, I advised against it. The ANC, I said, did not plan a major international event. Fortunately, the White House on this occasion ignored my advice. It proved to be a singularly important decision.

Tambo's funeral took place on May 3. There were delegations from around the world, but none rivaled that from the United States. The White House put together a delegation of some of the best-known leaders of the anti-apartheid movement. It was headed by Secretary of Health and Human Services Donna Shalala. As chancellor of the University of Wisconsin, Shalala had personally helped save the life of Frank Chikane, secretary general of the South African Council of Churches (SACC), when he was poisoned by government security agents while on a visit to the United States. The delegation also included Maya Angelou, Jesse Jackson, William Lucy, Congresswoman Maxine Waters, longtime activist and head of TransAfrica Randall Robinson, New York City official William Lynch, longtime friend of Tambo Nadine Hack, and Clinton's friend and adviser Ernest Green. After first planning to seat only heads of delegations on the podium, the ANC chose to seat the entire U.S. delegation. They asked both Donna Shalala and

Jesse Jackson to speak and asked Maya Angelou to recite one of her poems. For perverse reasons, or perhaps by chance, Shalala was slotted to speak between the PLO representative (this was pre-Oslo) and the Cuban delegate. Shalala joked that this could be the end of her political career back home. But she rose to the occasion magnificently.

In a short but eloquent address, Secretary Shalala said:

> We honor this son of South Africa today for reminding us that the struggle against apartheid is to free both the oppressed and the oppressor. We honor him for his vision of a new South Africa, in which all persons, of all races, would become one people, one South Africa. We honor him for his leadership in the struggle for freedom around the world.

Turning to the issues of the day, she put the United States clearly on the side of an appropriately rapid completion of the transition process:

> Because of his leadership and other leaders of the liberation movement, the dream of all thoughtful South Africans is at hand. This is the time. This is the hour for all those engaged in the negotiating process to free South Africa once and for all from the bondage of apartheid.

Then she addressed what had been a concern of South Africans since the election of Bill Clinton, whose administration had come to power on the message of domestic concerns and a focus on the American economy:

> On behalf of President Clinton, we want to assure you that the American people are with you—not just in this moment of sorrow, but in the days ahead when South Africa sets the date for its first ever truly democratic election. We will be with you through that election and in the sometimes difficult years of reconstruction and growth that will follow.[10]

She finished by raising her arm and shouting the slogan of the liberation movement: *Amandla!* The response was enthusiastic.

Following the ceremony, the U.S. delegation traveled by bus to the burial site, with crowds recognizing and cheering such well-known figures as Jackson and Angelou. Over the thirty-six hours they were in the country, the delegates reached out to their extensive personal contacts in South Africa and to others they were meeting for the first time with a message of U.S. support.

The delegation had a tremendous impact on the ANC and the population at large. It received extensive media attention. Throughout the day, we heard people say to us they were "thrilled," "overjoyed," "elated," and "jubilant." At a reception for the foreign delegations that night, Mandela told Secretary Shalala that he was "ecstatic" about the U.S. presence. Cyril Ramaphosa, secretary general of the ANC and the lead negotiator at Kempton Park, thanked the delegations for making this "a real state funeral."

Why did this event have such impact? First of all, in the wake of decades of the United States ignoring Oliver Tambo and the ANC, the official American tribute to his memory and his contributions struck many as healing an old rift. More contemporarily, it was a signal that the division within the United States, between the executive on the one hand and the anti-apartheid movement and its congressional supporters on the other, was over. They were united in one official delegation and one policy. Third, it settled some of the uneasiness about the intentions and commitment to South Africa of the new administration. Some of Secretary Shalala's warmest applause came when she mentioned America's commitment to the economic and social development to come in South Africa. Finally, as in Ramaphosa's remark about a state funeral, it symbolized American recognition that the ANC was in fact a government-in-waiting, even if there was a long way to go before the election. As I said in my report to Washington, the delegation "was like a burst of sunshine."

Our work with the ANC was deepening in several respects. In September 1992, I invited Joe Modise, head the ANC's armed wing, the MK, to the ambassador's residence for an informal talk. It was the first time there for Modise. Discussion between the ANC and the government on the future of the security forces was just getting under way and was one of the most critical of the matters to be resolved. Modise asked for help on researching other experiences with such military integration, for example, in Zimbabwe and El Salvador. I offered to put him in touch with the U.S. defense attaché who had served in Zimbabwe. Modise accepted readily. While sanctions on military assistance to South Africa remained in effect, we had good reasons to want to assist in helping on the integration process. In the summer of 1993, getting around these sanctions by imaginative use of U.S. Information Agency (USIA) funds, we sent a joint MK/South African Defence Force team to the United States.[11] The bond that developed between them carried over to their subsequent work together. Germany and other allies sponsored similar visits.

In the spring of 1993 it came to our attention that Mandela was operating with barely minimal security. It was alarming given the tensions and violence in the country. There were complex legal problems with our offering assistance in this area. In fact, it was a classic catch-22 situation. On the one hand, U.S. assistance for VIP protection could only be offered to help protect government officials. On the other hand, if such assistance was deemed going to the South African government, it violated sanctions! I crafted a careful legal argument to get around the problem. First, I went to the minister of law and order, Hernus Kriel, and secured from him two statements: (a) the South African government was not providing Mandela, nor could it provide him, such protection, and (b) it believed such protection was valuable to the transition process. The first statement ensured that we were not assisting the government nor even (as the lawyers insisted we could not do) taking over a South African government function. The second constituted a basis for justifying such assistance under the funds to assist in the ending of apartheid provided under the sanctions legislation. Then we utilized a portion of these funds reserved for assisting the parties in preparations for the election, obtaining ANC agreement to use a portion of its share of these funds for this purpose. The training got under way in the summer of 1993 and was exceptionally well received. With similar funding machinations, we trained a second cadre of protection officers later in the year. Mandela's protection became visibly more professional.

WITH THE GOVERNMENT: WALKING ON EGGSHELLS

As important as it was to establish credibility and build capability within the ANC alliance, it was as important to maintain close contact and frank exchanges with the government. It was also important to provide visible international recognition and support to de Klerk in his steadfast determination to see the process of transformation through to the end.

De Klerk was faced at times in this period with fierce criticism from the more conservative elements within his own party and with threats of defection—indeed, at one point several National Party officials defected to the Inkatha Freedom Party.[12] There would be significant disputes over some of de Klerk's negotiating objectives and his actions in the face of violence. But even when these differences surfaced most strongly between himself and Mandela, de Klerk remained essential to the process. Mandela told me in December 1992 of his sensitivity to the pressures on de Klerk. In August 1993, after tension between the two leaders had long since surfaced, I heard Mandela answer a question at a small dinner party about his feelings toward de Klerk. "My worst nightmare," replied Mandela, "is that I wake up one day and find he is not there."

Throughout 1993, I stayed in close touch with the government's chief negotiator, Roelf Meyer. We reviewed the state of negotiations, the various steps the United States was taking to support the process, and how we might help in overcoming the resistance of Buthelezi's Inkatha Freedom Party and others. Meyer believed the U.S. support for federalism, which was announced in 1992, was designed to placate Buthelezi. Meyer himself was more skeptical of introducing federalism in South Africa and worried that the United States and other supporters of Buthelezi would use this issue as a means of prolonging the negotiations until Buthelezi was fully satisfied. Over the course of the year, however, Meyer became "relaxed" about the relationship with the United States and convinced that we fully supported keeping to the transition timetable.[13]

I met regularly also with President F. W. de Klerk. Most high-level American visitors to South Africa did as well, making a point of expressing their admiration and support for what de Klerk was doing. Particularly impressive, I thought, were the compliments paid him by such strong anti-apartheid figures as Secretary of Commerce Ron Brown and, later, the Reverend Jesse Jackson. By April 1993, de Klerk could say to visiting Assistant Secretary George Moose that he was encouraged by the Clinton administration's "pragmatic and constructive" approach toward events in South Africa. De Klerk began planning his visit to the United States to meet with the new president.

The relationship was such as to allow us to take on some of the most difficult issues in the negotiations. In December 1992, and again in May 1993, I had delicate exchanges with de Klerk on the nature of power sharing under the proposed Government of National Unity. De Klerk was searching for a formula that would ensure continued influence by what he sometimes called the "First World" element of South Africa. He had made promises along these lines to his constituency in the white referendum of 1992 and felt he could not go back on them. I reiterated that the other side also had constituency concerns, and that the negotiations on this point must not undercut the moderates within the ANC. Basically, we talked around the question of "influence" versus a "veto," with de Klerk searching already in April for a consensus approach, the structure that eventually resolved the issue.[14]

I felt it important, and perhaps helpful to moderates within the government, to voice these same concerns publicly. In a speech in April 1993, I warned those who still thought "an agreement could be reached which hobbles the authority of the majority."

> No democracy works if power is absolute. The minority must have rights and protection. Power must have checks and balances. . . . But there must also be rights of the majority. The electorate must feel that its votes count for something, that the party or parties that are in the majority have sufficient mandate and authority to lead the country in new directions, to provide for new dispensations, to make decisions and to overcome opposition after a fair debate and adherence to lawful and constitutional procedures. Any agreement short of that, in my view, will not hold.[15]

What distinguished the relations with the government side the most, however, was that the United States had other issues than the transition process. While we dealt most with the transition, issues related to nonproliferation of weapons of mass destruction were a constant subject of often difficult negotiations. These issues were not unrelated to the transition; they had a major bearing on the quest for legitimacy and respect that was so important to de Klerk as he navigated the end of white minority rule. They also bore on the image and policies of the postapartheid government and had to be discussed as well with the ANC.

De Klerk preempted one major source of concern when he announced in March 1993 that the South African government had indeed not only had a nuclear weapons capacity, but had constructed six nuclear weapons and had been at work on a seventh. De Klerk stated that the program had been dismantled and the weapons destroyed. He opened the country's nuclear facilities to thorough international inspection thereafter, meeting South Africa's full obligations under the Nuclear Nonproliferation Treaty. To meet American concerns, his government agreed to American specialists accompanying International Atomic Energy Agency (IAEA) inspectors of the nuclear facilities. For some time afterward, based on the evidence of these international inspections, I addressed lingering concerns in Washington over the remains of this capacity. Once these were satisfied, de Klerk's announcement opened the way to signing a nuclear cooperation agreement with South Africa on peaceful uses of atomic energy. The United States subsequently, though not until 1995, supported South Africa's entry to the Nuclear Suppliers Group, an international control group. These were valuable signals of assurance to de Klerk's constituency that the reform efforts, "giving away our nuclear capacity," as some put it, were paying off in terms of South Africa's reintegration into the world community.

Another proliferation concern related to South Africa's missile capacity. South Africa was hard at work on the development of a space launch vehicle. Whatever its earlier military purposes, South Africa now sought to retain this capacity and turn it to commercial use for space launches. The United States did not think this was commercially viable and believed the temptation would be great to turn it back to military use, and that the technology could even be sold to other countries. U.S. pressure on this issue drew fire from conservatives in South Africa, who accused the United States of simply wanting to deprive South Africa of a role in the space arena, not to mention weaken its potential military capabilities. But ultimately, after much negotiation and a thorough analysis by an American team of the commercial potential of space launching from South Africa, the South African government agreed to scrap this capacity. Both de Klerk and the manufacturer, Denel, emphasized that economic realities had guided the final decision.[16] But in the government's announcement there was also heavy emphasis on the significance of South Africa's taking one more step to shed its isolation from the international community:

> Although at first glance the decision to terminate the project is disappointing in that it might lead to a loss of job opportunities, there are nevertheless important benefits which could flow from it. The fact that South Africa had the capacity to produce a launch vehicle led to a suspicion that South Africa also had the capability to manufacture a missile. . . . The mere fact that South Africa was involved in the development of a launch vehicle resulted in South Africa's exclusion from important international

control bodies such as the Missile Technology Control Regime (MTCR). In light of today's announcement, I believe the most important obstacle to our membership of the MTCR has been removed. This step also has additional advantages for South Africa in terms of international cooperation in space matters.[17]

The United States agreed to contribute $500,000 toward the destruction of the relevant launch facilities and material in return for the right to inspect the results. The United States also initiated discussion of various forms of cooperation in space technology. The arrangements for the destruction and inspection proved difficult and sometimes contentious, but in the end the agreement was fully implemented in early 1994. South Africa's membership in the MTCR followed shortly thereafter.

No issue was more troublesome in this arena, however, than the case brought by the U.S. Justice Department against the South African parastatal arms companies, Armscor and Denel. Justice had evidence that these entities had not only violated sanctions against South Africa by obtaining American technology for weapons manufacturing, but also sold arms to Iraq, in violation of UN sanctions, during the Gulf War. De Klerk's government argued strongly that these transactions involved some of South Africa's leading businessmen, who had acted at the government's behest, and that in the spirit of the newly emerging relationship the case should be settled on "political grounds." The matter came up repeatedly during this period and at times seemed to be holding hostage agreement on other issues, such as the missile program. Ironically, the case became just as contentious with the Mandela government, which took up the argument on behalf of the defendants and of the "sovereign character" of the South African government. It was not settled until 1996.

Regularly during 1993, the United States briefed the ANC on these nonproliferation matters, though with sensitivity to the state of negotiations. It was important that there be continuity in these policies after the transition. Moreover, we did not want any rumors or misunderstandings about our objectives. The ANC was a staunch advocate of the nonproliferation of nuclear weapons and welcomed the developments on this score. We spent some time briefing them on the details of the missile program to win support on that as well, and to a lesser extent did so on the Armscor case. One more nonproliferation issue would arise in early 1994, with more serious political ramifications in South Africa. Arising on the very eve of the election, this issue would test our ability to balance these concerns with those of the transition. This matter is taken up in chapter 9.

In all our dealings with the government, we recognized that de Klerk's ability to retain sufficient authority and legitimacy was key to the success of the transition. This was a message that we needed to get across to Americans as well as help

convey in South Africa. Many staunch participants in the anti-apartheid movement were suspicious of the entire negotiating process, distrustful of the South
African government, and fearful of the ultimate role of the security forces. Some
confided to us that they suspected Mandela did not really understand the situation! Congress was especially important on this issue. Without congressional
understanding and support, we could not move to lift some of the restrictions on
our aid program in order to support transitional activities, such as the peace
process, or begin to make preparations for postapartheid economic development.

  We had a significant opportunity in this regard when the Aspen Institute
brought a group of Congress members to South Africa for a seminar in April 1993.
The seminar heard from all the principal parties and from numerous experts.
Cyril Ramaphosa gave a realistic but confident presentation on the negotiation
process and told the visitors that what the United States was doing—in lending
support to the process and preparing to assist in the elections—was right on the
mark. His counterpart from the government, Roelf Meyer, demonstrated that,
while significant differences remained, a bond of trust and cooperation was operating between the two men. On the last evening of the seminar I gave a reception
for the delegation. President de Klerk, to our surprise, came himself, the first time
in five years he had attended an event at the American ambassador's residence.
Watching members of the Black Caucus have their picture taken with de Klerk
gave us confidence that the integrity of the negotiating process, and the importance of balance in our relationships, had been absorbed.

  Maintaining balance in our relations between the government and the ANC
alliance, at a time when a major shift of power was imminent, was made more
difficult by their respective sensitivities. Each side professed awareness of the
needs of the other during this period, but inevitably tensions arose over status and
recognition. These difficulties were demonstrated during de Klerk and Mandela's
visit to Washington in July.

  The Liberty Foundation in Philadelphia voted to give its Liberty Medal, a
prestigious award, to both de Klerk and Mandela in a ceremony on the Fourth of
July. For de Klerk it was essential that if he traveled to Philadelphia to accept the
award he would have a meeting with President Clinton, and that there be some
distinction between his meeting, as head of state, with Clinton, and that which
would take place between Clinton and Mandela.[18] The administration at first
saw an opportunity for at least a joint appearance of the two men at the White
House, if not a joint meeting. Neither de Klerk nor Mandela wanted a joint
meeting. The White House agreed that de Klerk's meeting would come first. A
joint picture was originally agreed to by both parties, but at the last minute the
ANC canceled it, causing an awkward moment as de Klerk left and Mandela
entered the White House.

Clinton and de Klerk met for a half hour on July 2. Mandela's meeting with the president took place immediately after. Almost from that moment on, the two men publicly sparred on issues of sanctions, legitimacy, and elements of the transition. At the heart of the dispute was the competition between them for the responsibility for leading South Africa back to international acceptance. When de Klerk used the visit to meet with the heads of the World Bank and the International Monetary Fund (IMF), and talked of the need to remove sanctions and begin the process of economic reconstruction, Mandela shot back that de Klerk had no legitimate say in when sanctions would be lifted. Mandela jumped on a recent dispute over appointments to the South Africa Broadcasting Corporation to challenge de Klerk's bona fides in the transition process. Nevertheless, in their respective meetings with President Clinton, neither dwelled on these matters. At Philadelphia, each men spoke well of the other in his acceptance speech and at the luncheon afterward.

I took pains on my return to South Africa to dispel the disappointment many South Africans had over the public squabbling that had occurred. One paper had headlined the visit a "Clash of the Super-Egos." Another lamented that a great opportunity had been wasted. I suggested that Americans saw it differently, perhaps because we were more accustomed to "political exchanges taking place on nearly every occasion." Americans, I said, did not see this as detracting from the historic significance of the event. "It was precisely the contrast of the histories of these two leaders, together in their commitment to this transformation, that made the day historic. That is how it was seen and celebrated in the United States. Philadelphians and those associated with the Liberty Medal felt proud."[19]

De Klerk was not very pleased with the public squabbling, which he blamed on Mandela. It made the visit much less dramatic for him than his earlier one. He later described his meeting with Clinton in terms of the "genuine—and almost incredulous—admiration" for what had been achieved in South Africa. Almost laconically he concluded, "Clinton and Gore asked us all the appropriate questions and promised their support in our endeavors."[20] De Klerk felt he had had a warmer relationship with President Bush, and he particularly appreciated that Bush had been prepared to lift some of the sanctions without waiting for a go-ahead from the ANC. De Klerk visibly winced when I told him prior to the visit that any further action in the United States on lifting sanctions would depend on the ANC's support.

Overall, de Klerk's people felt Clinton was turning his attention almost exclusively to the coming ANC leadership.[21] De Klerk himself was perhaps more modest in his expectations. In a meeting with Assistant Secretary of State Moose in April 1993, he praised the Clinton administration's "pragmatic and constructive approach" to South Africa. Looking back on it, de Klerk credited the Liberty

Medal award, and the even more prestigious Nobel Prize later, as helpful. "That sort of recognition," he said, "was symbolically very important in establishing that there are no victors and vanquished in this process and that recognition should be given to both sides for the initiatives taken. That strengthened my hands in the final months."[22]

The United States also responded positively to de Klerk's suggestion that the international community state that it would hold any new government in South Africa to its preelection commitments, for example, to constitutionally protected principles of human rights and democratic procedure. The United States made this statement in the fall of 1993 and shortly afterward persuaded its major allies to do the same. The origins of this request and the U.S. reaction are described more fully in the next chapter, for they were linked largely to reassuring the followers of Chief Buthelezi. But in fact the U.S. statement had a positive effect on the members of de Klerk's constituency, both the more conservative and those whites "in the middle."

An editor at the time of one of South Africa's leading English-language newspapers recalled the U.S. statement: "I think it was very important because it was at the crucial stage in the negotiations. In terms of the media, I can remember fastening on to it as important."[23] More generally, the role of the United States throughout the transition period, if exaggerated in the minds of some whites, acted as a form of reassurance. The prospects of major change frightened even those whites who knew such change was both right and inevitable. One Afrikaner businessman described it this way: "Particularly in the Afrikaans community there was great fear that once political change occurred it would be chaos, everything would fall to pieces and so on. . . . The steady hand of the U.S. behind the process was seen to be very important.[24]

There were other steps the United States took to indicate America's confidence in the government's commitment to the transfer of power and that it was therefore time to begin establishing the foundations for future cooperation. In March 1993, the United States approved funding for a feasibility study for a penicillin plant in South Africa. The amount was not so significant, $450,000, but the fact that, for the first time since sanctions had been enacted, the U.S. government was actively promoting investment in South Africa attracted attention.[25] Once the ANC did give its support to lifting sanctions, in September of that year, the administration did not wait for the election or a new government in South Africa to begin establishing economic ties. In November, Secretary of Commerce Ron Brown led a major investment mission to South Africa during which the United States signed an agreement for South Africa's access to the services of the U.S. Overseas Private Investment Corporation. This occasioned de Klerk's comment cited at the beginning of this chapter.

ENRICHING THE DIALOGUE

Essential to the success of the negotiations was that the issues dividing the parties be resolved in ways that met the key principles to which we and most South Africans were committed. These included constitutionally guaranteed human rights and democratic practices, an open economic system, and the means for overcoming the legacies of apartheid. Some of the most difficult issues in the negotiations related to federalism versus centralized authority, affirmative action, amnesty for violations of human rights, power sharing, and electoral systems. On every one of these issues, the United States provided a plethora of experts, seminars, educational travel, and training.

Federalism was perhaps the most vexing issue. The ANC suspected that the government's "conversion" to this principle was a veiled attempt to preserve at the local level the vestiges of apartheid, out of reach of a new majority government. It saw in Chief Buthelezi's demand for a federal, indeed a confederal, system an attempt to divide the country and promote feudal enclaves. The United States pronounced itself in favor of a federal system for South Africa in 1992. The U.S. position gave encouragement to a wide spectrum of South African society that looked for some checks on the prospect of a one-party-dominated central system. Even though federalism had not been practiced by the National Party government, it soon became one of its rallying cries in the negotiations. But the largely white liberal Democratic Party, the lone parliamentary voice of opposition to apartheid for many years, also embraced federalism as a fundamental principle.

We argued to the ANC that without addressing the legitimate demands for federalism, it could not get past this issue with Chief Buthelezi. It was the most legitimate issue on his agenda. Until it was addressed the ANC could not expose other, deeper, sources of his resistance to the negotiations under way, nor convince other parties that the ANC had made a serious effort to reach agreement. To alleviate ANC uneasiness about a federal system, the United States and other countries—including Germany, Australia, and Denmark—sponsored visits for South Africans to examine how modern federalism operated. One member of an ANC team that visited the United States remarked on his return, "I did not realize that in the United States you have both strong federal and strong state governments." Federal action in the United States on civil rights, affirmative action, and other issues of equity demonstrated that a federal structure of government did not prevent the advancement of principles of the kind that the ANC felt integral to the postapartheid era. In the end, the ANC, thanks to an extensive international effort on this issue, found much to draw from the German system of federalism rather than the American.[26]

We were aware, however, that without clarifying our position on federalism, it could be used for purposes we would not endorse. For example, the government developed proposals for "fiscal federalism," which would have greatly restricted the roles and responsibilities of a new government. One government study recommended a major shift of resource allocation from the central to local government, which would have made it very difficult for the new government to restructure in a fundamental way the deeply ingrained legacies of apartheid that existed in every sector and at every level.[27] We made clear in our dialogue with both government and ANC representatives that this approach did not reflect our view of how the South African system should operate after the election.

Perhaps the most important breakthrough on the issue of federalism came from seminars sponsored by the Consultative Business Movement (CBM) and supported by the United States and other donors. At a "bush retreat" in February 1993, moderated by an American facilitator, political representatives and specialists went deep into the question of relative powers between central and other levels of government. The word "federalism," loaded with political emotion, was barred from being mentioned. Participants instead examined the various functions of government, the logical divisions of the country into economically and to some extent ethnically valid regions, and the division of functions and powers that responded best to the demands that would be placed on the new government.[28] The result was a consensus on regional divisions and powers that, modified gradually over the next several months, put the ANC on a path toward at least a basically federal system. In August the CBM sponsored a similar seminar on fiscal relations under such a system. There the parties fashioned compromises between, on the one hand, the national principles of equity and nondiscrimination that must guide a postapartheid South Africa in such services as education and access to health and, on the other, the desire to put such services as close as possible to the beneficiaries.[29]

Alfred and Ruth Blumrosen of Rutgers University, experts in affirmative action, made several visits to South Africa under USIA auspices. They helped reduce some of the fears of white citizens about the prospects of reversing the history of discrimination against blacks and assisted in drafting legislation that could enable South Africa to begin to redress these wrongs in a constructive fashion. Other experts shared ideas on free speech and whether to control "hate speech." Visitors from the Pentagon spoke about racial integration in the military. Utilizing our various resources, we made available to all the parties, and to the public at large, as wide an array as possible of the best expertise in America.

Nowhere was our effort more intense than in the sphere of economic policy. It was apparent to all parties by the end of 1992 that the South African economy was in dire straits and that the turnaround would involve far more than the end of apartheid and the lifting of sanctions. There were structural issues relating to the concentration of economic power—four conglomerates controlled some 80 percent of the Johannesburg stock market. Tax and other laws acted to encourage capital-intensive investment; no new net jobs had been created in South Africa for more than a decade. Foreign exchange restrictions were complex and had to be handled with care to avoid massive capital flight on the one hand while encouraging foreign investment on the other. In spite of the National Party government's rhetoric about free-market economics, the government's ownership share of the economy rivaled that in Eastern European countries. Education disparities enforced by apartheid had left the vast majority of South African workers without advanced skills and had left an education system unable to supply them.

Simple redistribution would not begin to meet the disparities in income that existed between blacks and whites. South Africa had a GDP about equal to that of Finland, but Finland had a population of five million, while South Africa had forty million. South Africa seemed rich because its wealth was so concentrated on about five million people, but spreading it out would leave the average South African little better off.

These realities were bearing down on the ANC as its leaders began to face the tasks of governing. Traditional attachment to socialism, nationalization of key industries, and redistribution economics died hard, however, especially within the labor movement. The period before the elections was thus important for opportunities to think through carefully what economic policies would make the most sense. We focused a great deal of attention on this need.

Other influences were being brought to bear. The ANC was courted by South African big business, which hastened to make the case for a market-driven economy. The collapse of the Soviet Union and the communist systems in Eastern Europe, along with the move away from state controls in other parts of Africa, were having their impact. Globalization was beginning to change attitudes among even the moderately socialist parties of Europe and Asia. Nelson Mandela tore up his previously prepared speech at his first attendance of the World Economic Forum, in Davos, Switzerland, in 1992 and voiced a more moderate tone. In his discussions with world business leaders there, as well as with European socialist ministers, he had found no prospect of foreign investment for a country ideologically attached to the socialist tenets to which the ANC had clung so long. As he recalled, "They changed my views altogether. . . . We either keep nationalization and get no investment, or we modify our own attitude and get investment."[30]

The United States focused first of all on helping the ANC develop a cadre of economic thinkers, training leaders, and funding research and conferences. Max Sisulu, one of three leading ANC economists, was supported for a year's training at the John F. Kennedy School at Harvard. Tito Mboweni, director of the ANC's Economic Department and who would later become governor of the Central Bank, was supported for several visits to the United States, including one to attend a special program on antitrust. Mboweni, who had been a longtime supporter of nationalization of key industries, became over time a champion of antitrust policies instead.[31]

Several other activities contributed to this process. In the fall of 1992, a consortium of private companies, donors including the United States, and other institutions put together a series of economic models that came to be known as the Mt. Fleur scenarios. Each was given a bird name. One model demonstrated the effect of a heavily demand-driven approach, with significant spending on social services, housing, etc., and on employment generation. This model foresaw rapid early growth, followed, however, by a sharp downturn due to deficits, inflation, and loss of investment. The ideal model, the Flamingo, contained a combination of controlled deficits, promotion of private investment, and select improvements in key social sectors. It predicted slow but steady and increasingly high sustainable levels of growth. The Mt. Fleur scenarios received a lot of publicity. The presence at the Mt. Fleur conference of key ANC economic leaders gave an early indication of the movement in ANC thinking.

The ANC did not want to rely too heavily on foreign advisers, and the United States agreed. There was considerable talent in South Africa. A cadre of well-trained economists existed at South African universities, and many of these academics had strong sympathy for, if not formal ties to, the ANC. Together with Canada, the United States helped finance the creation of the Macro-Economic Research Group (MERG), which linked by computers and conferences a network of economists across the country to advise the ANC. An American economist installed a macro-economic, computer-based model on the MERG's computers, and experts from many countries were drawn upon. MERG would produce an economic blueprint late in 1993 that tried to balance the divergent ideas within the ANC alliance, but by then ANC leaders had moved away from the more radical economic models and avoided endorsing even this study. Nevertheless, MERG and similar work going on within study groups created by the labor movement and in collaboration with the private sector were producing a wealth of analytical material and insight that would underpin the ANC's economic policies following the election.

There were other efforts, some informal. The American economic counselor Donald Steinberg, later U.S. ambassador to Angola, for two years hosted a monthly economic dinner at his home. ANC economists, government officials, and South African and American businessmen met, sometimes for the first time, to discuss economic and business issues. The dinners provided the first contact between the American Chamber of Commerce and the ANC. A prominent black

South African businessman told us he met more white South African business-people at U.S.-sponsored functions than at any other type event.

On a regular basis, Steinberg and his team also pored over each and every ANC speech on economic themes and quickly offered experts from the United States on each subject covered. "Supply outran demand," said one embassy official, "because the ANC could not readily absorb all that we and other donors were offering." But much information and expertise was shared during this period. An exchange of experts between the University of Wisconsin's Land Tenure Center and the ANC's Land and Agricultural Policy Center helped develop what would later, with additional World Bank study, become a politically workable approach to land redistribution and restitution incorporated in the constitution. Other ANC delegations investigated the taxation system in the United States as well as policies on free trade. An entire series of USIA's Worldnet programs was organized on relevant economic topics, which offered the additional benefit of bringing black and white personalities together to participate in the interactive programming.

Another particularly influential exchange came out of a USAID-funded education model. The model demonstrated clearly the enormous cost of trying to achieve all the ANC's educational goals through the government in a short period of time. Studies such as these demonstrated, as in housing and health, the economic realities that a new government would face and opened up thinking on public-private partnerships, for example, in mortgage financing and self-financed electrification programs, that would guide the new government as it set about rectifying social and economic disparities.

A major contribution to this process was a three-day conference in April 1993, jointly sponsored by the Aspen Institute and the South African Institute for a Democratic Alternative for South Africa. USAID was a major funder. A distinguished group of economists from the United States participated, including Robert Lawrence, John Williamson, Paul Krugman, Prakash Sethi, and Stephen Lewis. In addition, the sponsors brought in senior officials from Asia to share the history and policies behind the "Asian miracle." World Bank and IMF representatives were present. Nelson Mandela sent opening comments delivered by Trevor Manuel, and Mandela personally gave the closing address. More than fifty South Africans participated, representing a broad spectrum of leading thinkers from government, business, labor, the ANC, Inkatha, the Pan Africanist Congress, and the South African Communist Party.

In his report on the conference, chairman Stephen Lewis noted the widespread consensus both on the nature of South Africa's economic ills and the direction of reforms needed. These included attention to export promotion, trade liberalization, wage/exchange rate/productivity relationships, and promoting both domestic and foreign investment. Lewis acknowledged that "important differences existed," for example, over the speed by which protection of some industries should be phased out and over the role of government. But he concluded:

> Countries that have been forced into "structural adjustment programs" have often thought they could go on with the policies they had been following when in fact they could *not* do so. South Africa, through the broad consensus of disparate players present this week, knows there must be some fundamental changes in policy. That consensus was a definite highlight.[32]

The ANC was criticized in some quarters during the period leading up to the election for its seeming indecision on its economic outlook and its apparent lack of expertise. The ANC was sometimes referred to as the "African National Chaos." But critics were wrong in their prediction of the outcome of this period of introspection and absorption, viz., "the confusion itself made one thing seem sure. Whatever the [economic] policy, it would be implemented falteringly."[33] In fact, the ANC embarked on a remarkably consistent and coherent policy from the time it came to power. The period of 1990–94, of long negotiation and preparation, was particularly in the field of economic policy a valuable time for absorbing the realities of the South African economy and the lessons that experts from home and abroad could bring to the table.

As one official of both the ANC and the SACP later described it:

> As the ANC began to look more closely at the kind of economic policies it needed to pursue, you began to see that there was certainty that this was not going to be possible. For example, in terms of nationalization . . . the conditions were not conducive to such a move. Contact with the big South African conglomerates made a number of people in the ANC come to the realization that you could inherit an empty shell. . . . [I]f there was a fantastic run on capital, just after the 1994 elections, we would have been in very, very serious trouble. It would have had very serious consequences for our economy and certainly for a democratic government that was elected to do something about improving the quality of life of the people. The realization had set in inside the ANC that you are not the only actor in the economy. Then when our people got into government for the first time, the enormity of the problems we were facing [was] very, very stark.[34]

The message coming out of all these consultations on our part, in every field, was that solutions were available to each of the issues still on the table. Most of all, these interchanges conveyed the belief that in the end a fair constitutional system could protect those who feared too radical a set of changes as well as those who feared that change would somehow be made impossible by too structured a system of checks and balances.[35]

RALLYING SUPPORT FOR THE PROCESS

Beginning in late 1992, when the negotiation process appeared back on track and firmly entrenched, the embassy saw as one of our principal contributions rallying support for the process from the various sectors of South African society and providing encouragement through assurances of international support.

In a series of speeches and interviews over the next few months, I sought to send a positive message about the process itself. It was particularly important to indicate that the pessimism and concern over the lack of urgency that I had expressed toward the end of 1992 was no longer our view. In an interview with the *Star,* reported on January 20, 1993, I emphasized several themes that would be repeated in the months ahead.

> There's an optimistic air in the corridors of the US Embassy in Pretoria that wasn't there in the darker months of 1992. It seeped in the same day a tentative date for a multiracial election was announced. As Lyman sees it, the setting of a timetable for transition was important . . . because for the first time South Africans have a sense of urgency in getting the issues resolved.

I went on to stress the need to begin planning for the election and the post-apartheid period. As for the election, I pointed to the level of mistrust among the parties, which posed the biggest threat to the electoral process. This was a problem that could be addressed only by the South Africans themselves. Building the capacity to do so would become a major emphasis in our aid program.

> It's useful to bring in outside observers, but that doesn't substitute for systems of control inside the country. South Africans should not overestimate the role of foreign observers, but build on its innovative peace structures. Different political parties should have their monitors who are trained and know what to look for during an election. . . . There's a chance now to build up these systems.[36]

A principal target of my speeches throughout the first half of 1993 was the business community. Many business leaders, individually and collectively, were making significant contributions to the transition process. Both the South African and American business leadership had lent both financial and political support to the peace movement. One South African group, the Consultative Business Movement, devoted itself to facilitating the negotiations themselves, providing the administrative support for CODESA and subsequent multiparty negotiations. As described above, CBM organized an off-site set of meetings between political leaders and experts that broke the impasse in the negotiations over federalism and regional powers. It would later facilitate one last attempt to mediate the dispute with Chief Buthelezi's Inkatha Freedom Party. The CBM also urged the business community to take an active role in every aspect of the process of democratization. But in my view the corporate sector as a whole, and its principal organization, the South African Chamber of Business (SACOB), were not contributing as they could have.

In early 1993, deeply disturbed by the economic crisis, Mandela offered to call for the lifting of sanctions even at that early stage in the negotiations, if the business community would promise not only to stop further layoffs but to increase employment by 50 percent. Of course this was impractical. But the negative reaction of the business community, which heaped criticism on Mandela for the suggestion, struck me as misplaced and irresponsible. Business leaders derided the suggestion as "an offer addressed primarily to an American public with a superficial understanding of developments within South Africa."[37] In my view, the business community was dismissive of Mandela's offer, while offering no alternative vision of the future, at a time when signs of confidence in the future were badly needed. What one heard from the business community were largely negative pronouncements about the impact of continued political instability on the economy.

A second reason for targeting the business community was that I believed it was missing a tremendous opportunity. It was already apparent by the end of 1992 that great changes were taking place in the economic thinking within the ANC. Moreover, beginning in 1991 and with steadily greater participation from key stakeholders over the next two years, South Africa created a series of forums in which business, labor, community organizations, and political parties came together to shape future social and economic policies. These remarkable forums—on economic policy, housing, electricity, drought—did much to facilitate a smooth transition, perhaps as much as the political process in providing a common framework for a wide variety of stakeholders. But initially the business community's participation was disjointed and reactive. By contrast, COSATU had commissioned an impressive, if controversial, industrial strategy, developed by leading South African and foreign economists, that at least opened the door to productive debate on the future of capital, labor, and investment policies. The ANC launched the MERG. Business appeared nevertheless to be standing pat on the problems facing the economy and the society.

In speeches in November 1992 to South African and American business groups, I laid out the themes that I would repeat in various parts of the country over the next several months:

> One of the more encouraging signs in South Africa is the growing consensus among experts from all parties on the future direction of economic policy. There has been a sea change in the rhetoric and position papers of organizations like the ANC on economic policy. Instead of references to nationalization and socialist policies, there is discussion of the need for growth, the incentives required for greater private investment, and the

need for fiscal and budgetary restraint. The battles over these issues have largely been won.

What is lacking, however, is an equivalent sea change in output from the business sector. There is danger that the business community will have won the battle but will go on to lose the war.[38]

I urged the business community to begin addressing the critical social and economic issues to which it uniquely could make a contribution: employment, affirmative action, housing finance, growth with redistribution. The community, I argued, should be proactive, not reactive, in these areas. I urged it to begin examining ways to open the economy to more competition and to develop a more open trading system. Above all, I urged it to give support to the political process through its own unique capacities. The only major investments then on the horizon were two capital-intensive ones benefiting from the government's subsidies in this direction. If the political leaders were being called on to take risks—to reach compromises, to rally their constituencies to accept radical changes, to agree to share power—could the business community do less? Answering the argument of business that investments could only be made when the prospects and conditions were right, I said:

> If it is not realistic to ask for many bold new investments in labor-intensive industry, in new financial instruments that promote home ownership and small-scale entrepreneurship, in consumer products that service the black majority; if it is unrealistic to expect many investments in these areas in today's climate, surely it is not too much to expect a vision of how such investments will come once the political transition is under way.
>
> Where are the economic blueprints of the new South Africa? Where is the vision and the examples of how the vast majority of South Africans will find a place in the new economy if it is based on free-market principles? And if this vision does not come from within the business community, how can one expect the vision [of the political leaders] to incorporate the special needs of that community?[39]

The media gave these speeches extensive coverage, headlining the themes described above.[40]

Some in the business community were not happy. SACOB officials visited me to complain that I was being unfair. But other members of the business community, frustrated by some of the same problems with their leaders, quietly encouraged me to continue. Many of these same themes were in fact being advocated to their colleagues by the CBM.[41] One investment firm, Frankel Pollack Vinderine, soon afterward began an annual international seminar promoting the possibilities of the new South Africa and asked that I speak there each year, which I did. In May, the World Economic Forum scheduled an international investment forum in South Africa, picking up the same theme of what South Africans could expect in the new era.

Another benefit of these speeches was the response of Mandela and the ANC, who saw them as further evidence of U.S. support for the process under way and valuable public recognition of how far the ANC had come on economic policy. In April Thabo Mbeki expressed his concern to me about fears among elements of South African society that the moderates within the ANC would not last, and that radicals would overturn the commitments and directions the ANC was articulating. Government officials, including de Klerk, voiced the same concerns from time to time. These speeches were designed in part to dispel those fears. Mandela would also spend considerable effort throughout this period to mobilize exactly this kind of business support, for the transition and for the economic challenges ahead. By the end of 1993, through the forums mentioned above, a great deal of progress was in fact being made along these lines.

THE CONSTITUTION

In September the government and the ANC reached agreement on a transitional constitution, compromising on the final key issues of power sharing and federalism. Both parties had agreed to a binding set of principles that would be enforced by an independent Constitutional Court and not allowed to be abrogated even in the drafting of a final constitution after the election. But with Inkatha's continuing opposition and lingering uneasiness about the compromises that were made, white opinion was still unsure. Ken Owen, editor of the *Sunday Times,* had earlier criticized the international community for "rushing" the constitutional process. He expressed cynicism about the drafts that were emerging. He and others argued that it was important to get it right the first time, that is, to have a constitution that resolved critical issues such as federalism once and for all. I knew Owen was aiming at me, as I had been the most vocal on this issue.[42]

It was our opinion that the compromises reached by September created a sound basis for future democracy in South Africa. We also questioned whether further delay would not unravel the situation altogether. Since allusions were often made to the American Constitution, and some of the history was not well understood, I decided to address the issue of "getting it right" in the context of both America's history and the situation in South Africa. I chose the Johannesburg Press Club for an address that one editor later described as "diffidently" titled, "Some Thoughts on Constitution Making."

I began by pointing out that the process whereby the U.S. Constitution was drafted was challenged at the time and that the ratification battle was sometimes fierce. I noted that only thirty-nine of the fifty-five delegates in Philadelphia signed the document, and that some had walked out when their views were not adopted. The parallel to Inkatha's walkout was obvious but not mentioned. I reviewed the fierceness of the ratification battle, the demands for a new convention altogether (another Inkatha demand at that time), and the feeling of some that the rush to adoption was "temporary insanity." After all that, the Constitution, amended with a Bill of Rights, was adopted and over time was amended some twenty-six times. We had not gotten it right the first time, with the continuation of slavery and the absence of voting rights for women glaring defects. But it had been time to move forward. Federalism, which as in South Africa was one of the most controversial issues in the American process, proved to be an issue that had to be addressed over time, with powers flowing back and forth between the central government and the states. In other words, we had a living constitution.

I then turned to the possible relevance for South Africa:

> The issues under debate in South Africa—liberty versus equality, the separation of powers, cultural rights and the rights of minorities—are the fundamental issues with which a democracy must deal. But they do not yield to firm and final formulae. Rather, they are principles which must be articulated, defined, then refined and debated continuously as a democracy grows and changes.
>
> There is considerable debate in South Africa whether the process of transition is moving too fast. Some accuse us in the international community of unduly rushing the participants when so much is at stake. But when I hear people say, "We should not go forward until we get it right," I would suggest that one never gets it altogether right. Part of the process of getting it right is in operating a democratic system.

I then emphasized why it was time to move forward in South Africa:

> Moreover, how long do the people wait for the experts and leaders to get it right before they have a say? The majority of people in South Africa have been waiting for three hundred years for leaders to get it right, denied their right to participate in the political process all that time. . . . Obviously, the document put before the people should be thoroughly analyzed, debated, and reviewed by the best of the leadership and be careful to protect the rights of minorities and individuals even before being put to ratification. But . . . there is a point at which further delay can defeat the very process itself, can lead to such unrest that democracy is threatened even more by disorder and mob action than by imperfections in the initially accepted document.[43]

Initial coverage of the speech came in the Afrikaans press. A section in the speech where I emphasized that federalism was not the same as "ethnic enclaves" drew particular attention.[44] An article the same day in another paper said, "It is like putting toothpaste in a stale mouth to be confronted once again with the similarities between the local process and the American one and to hear that South Africa does not need to reinvent the wheel."[45] Two weeks later the English press gave it extensive coverage. Then in December the influential political editor of the *Star,* Shaun Johnson, made the speech the centerpiece of his editorial.

He began with this quote from the speech: "Perhaps one of the most hopeful aspects of our history is how quickly the battle lines faded once the constitution came into force. Many who had opposed it came around to supporting it." Johnson went on:

> I underlined these two sentences just more than a month ago and put them for safekeeping in my desk drawer. They were encouraging then, are encouraging now, and might point a way to South Africa's salvation beyond today's bitter words issuing from Ulundi, Mmabatho, Pretoria, and Bisho.[46]

Johnson pointed out the parallels to South Africa I had alluded to in the speech. Picking up on South African worries about the process, he wrote:

> There is a perception among large sections of our people that our negotiations process has been somehow especially fraught, inefficient, inept, vituperative and drawn out. In some circles it is even declared a failure because it has not been fully inclusive. . . . Lyman makes the following points among others about the birth of the US and its constitution. . . . Many people tend to think of that process as quick, clean, elegant and definitive. But memory deceives. In fact, the saga of production of that great document resonates loudly with our present.[47]

It was exactly the message we sought to convey.

THE PEACE PROCESS

Encouraging a sense of a brighter future was valuable. But the immediate reality of South Africa in that period was the level of political violence. In spite of the National Peace Accord among the parties, and the impressive network of peace committees and activists that emerged under it, violence continued to shake the political foundations and the confidence of the people. During 1993 over four thousand persons were killed in politically related violence. The intensity of the violence in certain areas and the threat it posed to the transition process made it a constant source of anguish. Aggravating the situation was the complexity of the violence. Some of it was clearly related to the rivalry between the ANC and the IFP. The violence between them began during the "ungovernability" campaign of the 1980s, conducted by the ANC-affiliated United Democratic Front and continued virtually unabated after the opening up of the political scene and the beginning of multiparty negotiations in the 1990s.

But convenient as it was for de Klerk and others to condemn this as "black on black" violence and put the blame primarily on the leaders of the ANC and IFP, there was growing evidence by the end of 1992 that government security units had fueled this violence through secret arms deals, training of hit squads, and infiltration by provocateurs. The debate over whether this was orchestrated from the top or the product of a largely autonomous group of military and police units continues to this day. But it was clear that this activity was adding significantly to the violence. One former member of the South African Defence Force (SADF) who later became an ANC member described it in late 1992 as a "headless monster," an "awesome list of state structures involved in clandestine and covert operations."[48] Over the next year, the investigations of the Goldstone Commission and the SADF itself would reveal a vast network of military intelligence and police units engaged as provocateurs, killers, and supporters of hit squads.[49]

It was also not always easy to distinguish between truly politically related violence and criminal violence that often hid under a political label. As postapartheid South Africa has revealed, criminal gangs flourished under the cover of apartheid and emerged subsequently as a major challenge to the new government. For example, in the Vaal Triangle, an area in the East Rand, south of Johannesburg, that was the scene of repeated instances of political attacks during 1992–93 that included the notorious Boipatong massacre, there were in the period of one year over 1,650 criminally related murders and nearly ten thousand reports of armed robbery, serious assault, and other "nonpolitical" violence.[50]

Even where the violence had a clearly political label there were other historical antagonisms, such as family feuds and local rivalries, that took on the political coloration of the moment but that had roots going back into other eras. This was particularly true in KwaZulu/Natal.[51] Nevertheless, in the 1990s, the pace and scope of violence in this region, as elsewhere, seemed to resonate with the state of political developments.

Violence threatened all aspects of the transition. Further evidence that it was inspired and provoked to stall the transition was that it spiked almost each time there was a significant breakthrough in the negotiations. For example, the number of killed in such violence jumped sevenfold after the first formal ANC-government talks in 1991, jumped up again in the period of CODESA 1 and 2, and surged again when the election date was finally agreed on in June 1993.[52] In the Katorus area of the East Rand, another center of political violence, the monthly number of killings jumped some six times following the agreement on the election date and continued at that level throughout the rest of the year.

Following the Record of Understanding in September 1992, de Klerk and Mandela held to the position that violence would not be used by either party as a reason to stop the negotiations. They had come to recognize that to do otherwise was to put the prospect for success into the hands of those most dedicated to seeing the negotiations fail. Nevertheless, the continuation of violence put pressure on both sides. Mandela came to feel that de Klerk could have done much more to bring it under control, and this led to the loss of trust he had had in de Klerk in 1990 and 1991, a loss that was never recouped throughout all the subsequent years of their working together. De Klerk also felt pressure to slow if not stop the process in the face of what some feared was the specter of future anarchy.

The violence was far too complex and demanding to expect that it could be overcome during this transition period. The government was losing power, the police were totally discredited, local governing institutions had largely collapsed, and no final resolution of the political rivalries was likely before the election. The objective could only be to contain the violence. It was one thing to have a steady, if horrifying, series of murderous attacks—in villages, on trains, at taxi stands, and in the streets; it was another if the situation deteriorated into wholesale ethnic killing or near civil war. If South Africa had crossed that line, its transition would have ended much differently, far removed from the spirit of reconciliation and measured justice that eventually occurred. Against that happening, the United States used what influence and resources it could muster.

The more uncontrolled violence was heavily concentrated in the East Rand, the black townships south of Johannesburg, and in the province of Natal—some 90 percent of political killings in the country during the latter half of 1993 occurred in these two areas. I visited a local peace operations center in the East Rand in July. It was the only time in South Africa that I put on a bulletproof vest. The violence that evening was so great that we had to abandon our planned visit to the nearby neighborhoods. Instead, we listened as the director of the center, Peter Harris—today an internationally recognized expert on conflict resolution—expressed worry over the safety of one of his colleagues, an IFP official, as she left for home. Any party official who worked with the peace center was liable to reprisal. There was also the risk that party officials who did participate there were on the outside perpetrators of the violence. As the sounds and reports of shootings came into the center, it seemed like a war zone.

Mandela's frustration exhibited itself in a meeting with a visiting U.S. official in late 1992. He wanted a stronger UN role, he said, in isolating and demobilizing all elements destabilizing the country. If the international community could not guarantee free political activity, by which the violence could be contained, "it better well pack and go home." Mandela faced problems of violence within the ANC, however. As he admitted in a speech in April, ANC cadres were engaged in some of the violence. ANC headquarters had little real control over headstrong regional leaders such as Harry Gwala in Natal. And a combination of criminal ambitions and the infiltration of government provocateurs put some of the community-based ANC self-defense units beyond the leaders' control as well.[53] Mandela also would not or could not bring about a reconciliation with Inkatha's Chief Buthelezi until within days of the 1994 election.

The United States in fact did not have a great deal of leverage in this arena. For bureaucratic reasons explained below, even our use of resources was restricted. Nevertheless, in conjunction with other members of the international community, we made significant additions to the capacity of South Africans to contain this threat.

The South Africans had established an elaborate peace structure, the National Peace Accord, in 1991. It was a unique contract between political leaders, religious organizations, nongovernmental organizations (NGOs), and communities across the country to work for peace. Shortly after I arrived, the American Chamber of Commerce announced that it would hold a dinner to raise $1 million to donate to the accord and invited me and the national chairman of the Peace Accord, John Hall, to be the principal speakers. Ambassadors are not normally allowed to lend support to fund-raising events, but I had no hesitation in this case. The event was a spectacular demonstration of the deep desire for peace and reconciliation that ran through the entire South African society. The internationally renowned Drakensberg Boys Choir gave a powerful, spirited performance, with both white and black boys singing together in Zulu. When it was over, I turned to John Hall and saw he was in tears. "This is the real South Africa," he said. In my address I spoke of the destruction that violence had left in its wake in the neighboring countries of Angola and Mozambique. "These are the signposts of violence in today's world. Let no romantic visionary lead us to believe otherwise."[54] I told the business community that they were not out of their element in sponsoring this benefit; they were at the heart of it.

At the national level of the Peace Accord, the Goldstone Commission to Investigate the Causes of Violence loomed as one of the most important instruments to combat the violence. Other donors, particularly Denmark, Great Britain, France, Portugal, and the Netherlands, were quick to lend support. They provided expert investigators, assisted in witness protection, facilitated inquiries in Europe, and gave financial support. Unfortunately, under the CAAA, the United States could not give aid to any body that also received South African government support. Because all elements of the Peace Accord, including the Goldstone Commission, received government financial support, we were prohibited from providing assistance to any of these structures. Or so it seemed.

Fortunately, funds under USIA were less encumbered than those of USAID. In the spring of 1992, Judge Goldstone decided that one of the contributions that the commission could make would be to establish the rules and procedures for mass marches and demonstrations. These were situations in which confrontations with police took place constantly, and all too often killing of demonstrators occurred. There were no ground rules for such demonstrations, as all the existing rules were of the old order, totally unsuited to the unleashed political activity of the current period.

Goldstone convened an international panel for this purpose and sought the services of American law professor Philip Heymann as chairman. Bypassing the restrictions on the USAID program, USIA paid for Heymann's participation. New York police commissioner Lee Brown was also a member of the panel and would later assist the new government in developing the concept of community policing. This panel was a major success. Although the panel was originally opposed by the government, the government came to appreciate that the rules set out by the panel, which were later incorporated into legislation, provided a common ground with the ANC and others for managing peacefully the growing level of political activity. Encouraged by this success, Goldstone in 1993 convened a second international panel to establish the procedures for limiting violence during the election period. With Heymann tapped to be Clinton's deputy attorney general, Goldstone turned to another American, Charles Ruff, to head this panel. Once again, the report established ground rules that, if not always followed, set a benchmark against which the freedom of political activity could be measured.

Under the Peace Accord, community and regionally based peace committees were also established with government funding. In these committees, community representatives, police, government officials, professional mediators, and international monitors faced each other across the table and sought ways to contain the violence and promote peace. There were some dramatic moments in this process. Not uncommonly, a community representative would find herself across the table from the very policeman who had tortured her years before. Government officials who had refused to recognize the rights of the black or colored populations found themselves thrown together with them in the search for accommodation.[55]

As violence continued to threaten the situation, I urged AID (the USAID headquarters in Washington) to reinterpret, in consultation with Congress, the rules regarding aid to the peace structures. AID consented in principle but was so concerned about going too far that it insisted on having Washington approve each project, even small grants to individual local peace committees. This was unworkable, as the bureaucratic machinery in Washington agonized so long over each proposal as to make our support useless in a fast-moving and tense situation.

Not until October did AID agree to a twenty-four-hour turnaround to every such proposal, enabling us to help at least in this small way.

More important, given these restrictions, was USAID's aggressive assistance to the numerous South African independent (thus non-government-connected) mediation and conflict-resolution organizations. These organizations in turn provided professional help to the peace committees. U.S. assistance was financial as well, through the provision of numerous trainers and experts from the United States. I estimate that USAID provided support to virtually every such body of note in the country. Millions of dollars went into this assistance. Some of the assisted South African peace organizations, such as the African Center for Constructive Resolution of Disputes, are today active throughout Africa, carrying on this mission of peace.

On the other side of the equation, it was important to disabuse South Africans as to how much they could expect the international community to come to their aid if they indeed lost control of the process. In May 1993 I recommended to Washington that we discourage South Africans from looking to an international peacekeeping force to contain the violence through the period of the elections. If South Africans fell victim to this as the only solution, they would have already failed in maintaining control of their transition. Furthermore, it was foolish to think that outsiders could root out the causes of the violence in South Africa, if South Africans had so much difficulty doing so. Moreover, I was sure that de Klerk would resist such a proposal, seeing it as diminishing the last vestiges of legitimacy and authority on which he was counting so much in the final stages of the transition. Finally, there was a growing potential for cooperation between the SADF and the ANC. Discussions were at last under way between them on future restructuring of the security forces, and this was to be encouraged, not preempted.

There were important roles for the international community short of such a force. All sides agreed that the corps of international peace observers—from the United Nations, the EC, the Commonwealth, and the OAU—had had a tremendously positive impact. The number was increased steadily during 1993 to one hundred from the United Nations and comparable numbers from the others. The EC observers, many of whom were police experts, were considered especially effective by local peace activists. But the United Nations also had made a deep impression. The United Nations' chief of mission Angela King had wisely decided not to establish a separate mechanism for the UN operation, but to attach her corps to the structures of the Peace Accord.[56] The other groups followed suit. They thus added strength and legitimacy to the indigenous effort, while still serving as valuable international witnesses at marches and demonstrations. Over fifteen months, UN observers attended some nine thousand meetings and events.

A South African minister traveling in one of the more tense areas of the Eastern Cape region told me that the presence of UN observers made his meeting with local residents one of the smoothest he had known. As we wrote to Washington in May,

> It is both undeniable and unprovable that international and domestic peace monitors have kept the level of violence lower than it would have been without their presence. Moreover, cadres of savvy activists are developing at the local level throughout the country. Together, there are over 100 international monitors, perhaps 1,000 South African monitors affiliated with the National Peace Accord, and a network of some 100 independent conflict resolution organizations working together, transferring skills, etc.[57]

King herself quickly established a reputation for scrupulous fairness and political neutrality combined with a readiness to speak out forthrightly when necessary, especially on the failure of the signatories to the Peace Accord to keep their commitments. It was a virtuoso performance and it paved the way for the government, overcoming its historic suspicion of the United Nations, to endorse a much larger UN role during the election.

It was not only the violence itself, however, that was dismaying, but also that it portended a growing confrontation between the ANC and Inkatha that could eventually lead to civil war. As long as the violence in these areas reflected these larger political forces, local peace committees there were largely helpless.[58] Equally disturbing, political leaders themselves began talking of the prospect of civil war.

A leading Inkatha official threatened that Inkatha might have to form its own private army. Retired general Constand Viljoen, who was emerging as a leader of the right wing, said that white farmers might need to be armed. Even Mandela had spoken of a possible civil war. All this talk of civil war had produced in turn new demands for international peacekeepers. Archbishop Tutu among others was calling for such, as was Bantu Holomisa, the ANC's ally in the Transkei. Holomisa told his followers that thousands of blue helmets would be needed if South Africa were to have a free election.

In July, I thought it would be timely to go public with our position. I traveled to Durban that month and scheduled a speech at the Institute for Multiparty Democracy (IMPD). The IMPD had been created by Oscar Dhlomo, a former general secretary of Inkatha who had left the party. His institute had received a generous grant from USAID to help prepare the country for elections. The speech was advertised as describing U.S. assistance to the transition process and future economic development, but I used it to deliver another message. I warned that if the country were to slip into civil war, the international community could not be counted on to salvage the situation. There was too much loose talk of violence, I said, and it was like crying fire in a crowded theater.

But there is more than loose talk. South Africans should not contemplate civil war, even in threat, as a means of settling the differences that still remain between the parties. . . . A resort to civil strife would be the worst form of folly. Some moreover seem to believe that, if it came to that, the outside world would step in to restore peace. That is a most dangerous illusion. The international community has learned all too painfully that outside intervention in civil war is hardly feasible or effective. Outsiders cannot save the country from itself.[59]

The speech drew coverage in both national and provincial papers.[60] I followed up on this matter with both the ANC and the government. Both Cyril Ramaphosa and Joe Slovo agreed that UN blue helmets were not the answer to South Africa's violence. I recalled with Ramaphosa that the government's security forces and the ANC had collaborated impressively during the funeral for Oliver Tambo and wondered whether more could be done in this direction. Two days later, on August 11, Ramaphosa proposed a joint SADF-MK force to control the most violent areas around Johannesburg.

Mandela also agreed when I raised it with him during several meetings in mid-August that an international peacekeeping force would be ineffective. Indeed, both the government and the ANC were rejecting calls for a new UN envoy, for example, Cyrus Vance. They were both still determined that violence, like the political settlement, be resolved internally. At the same time, Mandela too was moving toward support for a national peacekeeping force drawn from both the government and liberation personnel. He saw the international community's role as helping train this force and providing more monitors.

Eventually a National Peacekeeping Force (NPKF) was developed, with some advisers coming from the Commonwealth and France. It was welcomed initially in part because, as one editorial put it, "South Africa had proved not only that its people can decide their own political and constitutional future, they can bring it into effect as well without United Nations, Commonwealth, or any other external Peacekeeping Forces."[61] Unfortunately, this force proved to be more valuable politically than militarily over the next few months. Clumsily put together, lacking participation from Inkatha and therefore already compromised in the eyes of one of the parties to the violence, and hastily thrown into the worst area of violence, it proved an embarrassment when finally deployed in early 1994.[62]

Fortunately, the experience with the NPKF was not a precursor for the much more successful integration of the ANC's and the PAC's military wings into the South African National Defence Force after the election. Meanwhile, as the NPKF was being put together, cooperation between the government and the ANC did prove effective in the joint decision to replace the hated police units in the East Rand with the South African military. The latter proved to have more credibility with the black population than had been imagined. With somewhat less effectiveness, SADF units were later dispatched into Natal.

Nevertheless, the final answer to the violence lay with achieving an accommodation between the government-ANC transition process and Chief Buthelezi's Inkatha, and between the former and the white right wing's leader, Constand Viljoen. This became a principal diplomatic focus for the United States during the last eighteen months of the transition and is the subject of the next two chapters.

PLANNING FOR THE FUTURE

Beginning in March and over the next year, the United States began to plan our support for the transitional arrangements leading up to the elections and to lay the foundations for future cooperation with the new government. In the first place, the embassy and the USAID mission signaled to Washington the changes in interpretation or legislation that were needed for the United States to provide relevant assistance to the institutions being put into place by the government and the ANC. As noted, we sought to expand the assistance we could give to the Peace Accord mechanisms. But there were other cooperative institutions being put into place that left irrelevant old restrictions related to the role of the South African government. There was an increasingly effective National Economic Forum (NEF), which was hammering out agreements on economic policies between the government, the liberation parties, labor, and business. In August 1993 the NEF announced implementation of eighteen areas of agreement that had been reached among the membership. These focused specifically on job creation and retrenchments, trade and tariff policy, public-sector restructuring, and small and medium-sized enterprises. They would herald agreements later in the year on South African policy toward entrée into the World Trade Organization and agreement on the terms of an IMF emergency loan related to the drought—all of which were agreed on for action before the election of a new government. This was exactly the kind of cooperation that we had sought to encourage. As an editorial in the *Star* remarked:

> They [the agreements] show business committing itself to a new understanding of preserving jobs—not at all costs but at least with a keener sense of the privation of unemployment. They show labour influencing government in areas that had previously been well beyond its scope—such as public tendering, and even trade and tariff policy. They show government and business undertaking to commit resources and change operating procedures to expand the labour market and re-empower hard-pressed communities.[63]

There were similar forums for reaching agreement on housing and electricity. We were unable to assist these forums directly, but we could supply them opportunities to consult experts and to take investigative trips to enhance their work.

Looking ahead, we alerted Washington to the importance of institutions that would come into effect by the fall. The parties would put in place a Transitional Executive Council (TEC), which would oversee the operations of government through the election period. The TEC would in effect become a quasigovernment and many of the activities that the United States favored the most would surely receive government funds during this period. Particularly important would be the Independent Electoral Commission and the Independent Media Commission, which would be charged by the TEC with ensuring a free and fair election.

While we made some progress on these matters over the next several months, bureaucratic resistance in AID and political trepidation there about getting ahead of the perceived views of the anti-apartheid movement slowed us down. It was not until President Clinton signed the Transition to Democracy Act in November 1993, which lifted all remaining sanctions and authorized an active program of support for South Africa, that we were able to move aggressively in all these areas.

Meanwhile, we used all the flexibility we had. While military sanctions remained in place, we began to increase our contacts and discussion with the South Africa Defence Force, opening a dialogue about racial integration, peacekeeping, and further contact, after years of official distance. As noted above, we used USIA money to fund a joint SADF/MK team to visit the United States, an initiative enthusiastically endorsed by Mandela. As soon as the TEC was formed, we approached both the government and the ANC about future military relations and put before the TEC a draft agreement for military training under the U.S. International Military Education and Training (IMET) program, to begin with the new government. Opening doors to the SADF was not easy, for there was not inconsiderable resentment within the SADF over our long-standing sanctions against military cooperation. Nevertheless, a particularly skillful and patient defense attaché, Kim Henningson, gradually opened the doors to better communication and laid the groundwork for what would be a series of high-level Pentagon visits in 1994 and the signing of the IMET agreement shortly after the election.

USAID received a dispensation from Washington to work with educational institutions, even if they received government funds. This opened the door to extensive work, jointly funded with the Ford Foundation, primarily with the segregated black, colored, and Asian colleges and universities to improve their planning and academic capabilities. Support was also stepped up for scholarships for nonwhite students to attend the rapidly integrating South African "premier" universities, and for programs at these institutions to overcome poor secondary school instruction in math and science. The University of Cape Town and Witswatersrand in Johannesburg developed particularly effective programs along these lines, leading to mainstreaming of many nonwhite students by their second or third year, including in the hard sciences and medicine.

With USAID funding, over one thousand community leaders were trained in the period leading up to the election to enable them to take their places in the future elected town councils. Of the twenty-seven ministers appointed to the first Mandela administration, eleven had participated in USIA's international visitor's program. The United States even began a program for training future diplomats from the once-excluded nonwhite population.

SANCTIONS REDUX

Some of the most intense efforts in planning ahead were for a restoration of economic growth and employment. Here sanctions were a principal issue. I was particularly concerned with the long lead time between the lifting of sanctions and the implementation of foreign aid projects, as well as the generation of new foreign investment. For a new government this could be a serious problem. We estimated that it would take as much as two years between the time the World Bank began planning projects and the time the first dollar would be spent. Lifting of sanctions against investment could take longer. Most federal sanctions against trade and investment had been lifted by President Bush in 1991, but there were 179 state and local jurisdictions in the United States that had enacted sanctions against doing business with South Africa. Until these were repealed, significant American investment would not take place. In the case of Namibia, where a similar situation had existed, it had taken years after Namibia's independence before all such statutes were repealed.

Sanctions were nevertheless a particularly sensitive political issue in both the United States and South Africa. We knew that, especially for state and local jurisdictions, where strong anti-apartheid sentiment had led to their enactment, only a strong signal from the ANC would convince them that the time had come to lift the sanctions. Even some in Congress were leery of moving too soon, while negotiations were still in progress. As late as November, long after Mandela had called for the removal of sanctions, members of the Congressional Black Caucus hesitated over the necessary legislation, believing that Mandela had been "premature."[64]

Within the ANC, opinions were divided. As noted, Mandela became increasingly worried over the state of the South African economy in late 1992 and began flirting with a call for lifting sanctions shortly thereafter. But within the ANC there was strong resistance to doing so until the election had taken place, or at least had been ensured. Over the next several months, the ANC gradually refined its position to link removal to the fixing of a firm date for the election and the establishment of the TEC.

In our discussions of this issue, we did not want to appear to be reopening the 1980s debate over sanctions. Rather, accepting the importance they had to the ANC's negotiating posture, we entered into discussion about the timing of a call for their repeal and about what steps could be taken, even while sanctions were in place, to get a head start on the economic work needed afterward.

We took note that sanctions were in fact crumbling elsewhere. Sweden announced its intentions to lift trade and visa sanctions as early as March 1993 and to lift them on investments once the TEC was in place. Other countries soon followed suit. American companies were under stiffer restrictions because of the plethora of state and local legislation in the United States, but we encouraged some private efforts to bring American trade and investment delegations to South Africa and to hold investment conferences in the United States. Each of these initiatives was carefully vetted with the ANC to avoid any feeling that we were preempting the sanctions debate.

We took several other steps along this path. One was to have the ANC invite the World Bank (the International Bank for Reconstruction and Development, IBRD) to open an office in South Africa as early in 1993 as practicable. The office could begin studies necessary to developing specific project proposals in such areas as labor-intensive infrastructure development, electrification of the townships, and land reclamation. No projects would go forward before the election or, at most, without full TEC approval. Following several discussions with Mandela and his staff about this idea, I drafted a five-page "nonpaper" (i.e., a paper with no embassy markings), which I gave to Mandela in February, laying out the case. I took particular care to address the political sensitivities regarding any such World Bank activities. I proposed careful multiparty controls over the process that would ensure that no political benefit would flow from them to the current government in the run-up to the election, but that benefits could indeed flow to all the parties associated with the process.

In my discussions with the ANC and with Washington, I distinguished between a role for the World Bank and one for the IMF. There was even greater antipathy within ANC circles for the IMF than for the Bank. It did not help that IMF commentators around that time took a very negative view of South Africa and its prospects under an ANC government. This attitude came through clearly at the Aspen conference in April as well as in briefings in Washington. More substantively, I argued that South Africa did not need an IMF standby agreement. Unlike other African countries that had been driven to the IMF by debt crises and poor policies and needed a standby agreement, if for nothing else than to obtain debt relief, South Africa had a low foreign debt and a favorable balance of payments. It was not in crisis. Pushing for an IMF agreement would only further exacerbate ANC suspicion of international motives.[65]

Before giving the nonpaper to Mandela, I made a call on Archbishop Desmond Tutu to discuss this matter. Tutu had been one of the most forceful and influential South African advocates of sanctions in the 1980s. It was important that, if there was movement along the lines we were thinking of, Tutu not oppose them. Tutu himself was conflicted over the role sanctions were playing in leveraging the political process and in the growing severity of the economic situation. At a meeting with a visiting Anglican delegation in January, Tutu had said that sanctions should be lifted only if South Africa was effectively dealing with the violence and had established an interim government. But he went on: "We are deeply concerned at the inter-relatedness of things, especially because it is crucial that the economy takes off. . . . We would like to do what we can to contribute towards this."[66]

In our meeting, Tutu reiterated his linkage of sanctions with control of violence. But he agreed with the idea of going ahead with preparation of development projects. He thought it would be an incentive to the South African government, while he recognized that nothing concrete would happen until the transition was complete. The next day, February 12, Tutu issued a press statement that he would be prepared to write to President Clinton urging him to give South Africa access to World Bank and IMF resources, when "broadly acceptable transitional authority which would ensure multi-party control of the security forces" was established.

Our efforts on the World Bank, to which I personally devoted a lot of attention, ultimately came to naught. As early as May 1992 the ANC signaled its suspicion of both the IMF and the IBRD. In its "Policy Guidelines for a Democratic South Africa," the ANC stated, "Relationships with international finance institutions such as the World Bank and the International Monetary Fund will be conducted in such a way as to protect the integrity of the South African population and the economy. Above all, we must pursue policies that enhance national self-sufficiency and enable us to reduce dependence on international financial institutions."[67]

I found these views were strongly held in particular by Trevor Manuel, who would emerge as South Africa's first minister of trade and industry and later serve as minister of finance. He and I held several discussions of the matter over the months of late 1992 and early 1993. Mandela and Mbeki, with whom I raised the question, were more sympathetic. But others in the ANC sided with Manuel. Their views were shaped by deep suspicion, encouraged by other African countries, that the international financial institutions would in effect dictate South Africa's economic policies. That was anathema to the ANC leadership. As one ANC official remarked to me, "The world lenders think ANC rookies are ripe for the picking."

There was also fear of the "debt trap" into which so many other African countries had fallen. Although South Africa did not have a large foreign debt, it did have a substantial domestic one that could be increased by foreign loans to the government or loans guaranteed by it. Manuel and his colleagues proved strongly committed to reducing this debt. Finally, as Manuel explained to me, and as was echoed in the ANC document cited earlier, the ANC was already trying to dampen expectations about what could be accomplished in the new era, given the enormous dimensions of the socioeconomic legacy of apartheid. Raising expectations of considerable largesse from the World Bank would only encourage such expectations as well as foster an undesirable dependence on outside help.

In this, the ANC's economic policy echoed its stance on the political negotiations, that it was theirs to command and theirs for which to take responsibility. In the end, the World Bank was invited to open an office during 1993, and over the course of the next several years it carried out valuable studies of transportation, urban planning, land reform, and export policy that were extremely valuable to the government. But even today, the South African government has accepted only one small loan from the Bank. Similarly, in the aftermath of the election, the ANC government spurned large credits offered by Japan on the grounds that the terms were too stiff.

I was disappointed that the Bank was not allowed to play a more active role in financing badly needed programs, especially if they could have contributed to greater employment. But I also came to admire the ANC's determination to steer its own course, and to come to conclusions on policies—ones that the Bank would later heartily endorse—on the basis of its own internal decisions and conviction. In this, R. W. Johnson, an almost cynically negative commentator on the future of South Africa, was wrong, as he was on so many other matters, when he wrote in July 1993:

> Some voices within the ANC caution against a rapid debt build-up which ultimately results in the economy being placed under the administration of bureaucrats in Washington as has happened to most of the rest of Africa. But there is almost no power on earth which will prevent politicians (and certainly not ANC politicians) from taking large bags of money if their constituency is frantic for houses and jobs and the money is on offer. There will, in other words, be almost inexorably a debt-led boom, with money poured into black housing, education and welfare, into an increased public sector and, of course, into politicians' bank accounts.[68]

There were other steps that we set in motion. As early as March 1993 we circulated to the government and the ANC a draft double taxation treaty. We began discussion of a bilateral investment agreement through the Overseas Private Investment Corporation (OPIC). We signaled our interest in a civil aviation agreement and one for scientific cooperation. The OPIC agreement was signed in November. But for the others, the lead time was even longer than we anticipated. A civil aviation agreement was not signed until 1996 and the taxation treaty was not signed until 1997.[69]

The sanctions debate played itself out over most of 1993. When the negotiations over the TEC became stalled in June, George Moose urged Mandela during the latter's Philadelphia visit to call for the lifting of sanctions. But Mandela refused. Not until September 1993, before the United Nations and with the TEC agreement in hand, did Nelson Mandela dramatically call for the lifting of all remaining sanctions on South Africa. We did not want a repeat of the Namibia experience. Once Mandela made his appeal, the U.S. government, working closely with the ANC, launched an aggressive campaign to get state and local governments in the United States to comply. When some jurisdictions questioned the validity of a letter from Mandela asking them to do so, we suggested the ANC prepare a video of Mandela's asking for repeal, which it did. Within one year after Mandela's call, 164 of the 179 jurisdictions had repealed their sanctions.[70]

But there was another issue related to sanctions. U.S. federal, and some local, sanctions legislation had mandated a code of conduct, the Sullivan code, for American companies that remained in South Africa during the sanctions period. As the time for ending sanctions approached, there were calls for enacting a continuing and binding code for companies doing business in South Africa after the transition. This was a popular cause in the United States and in some quarters in South Africa, specifically within the South African Council of Churches. We argued early on with the ANC and the SACC that this would be a mistake. First of all, to make a distinction between the terms for one country and those for others would simply discriminate against that country, in this case the United States, and make attracting American investment all the more difficult. Once the transition had taken place to a postapartheid government, attracting investment would become a major priority.[71]

We brought the SACC together with the American Chamber of Commerce to think through this issue. We suggested that the SACC develop a set of guidelines, but not a set of special binding requirements. As we were urging the SACC to avoid steps that would impede investment, we also strongly urged—successfully—that the American business community pledge itself to continue the levels of social responsibility spending that it had been obligated to under the CAAA, even after this legislation was repealed. I felt strongly that sudden abandonment of these programs, as soon as the legislative requirement was gone, would send precisely the wrong signal. It would raise the specter of irresponsible capitalism and feed the demand for some special code. Whereas large American firms were not unwilling to continue such programs, the smaller firms were anxious to free themselves from what they felt was a debilitating expense, one that hurt their competitiveness. Strong support from the president of the Chamber, Johnson & Johnson's Roger Crawford, was critical in overcoming this opposition.[72]

We also argued that any code of conduct enacted by a foreign government, or aimed exclusively at one country's investors, would in fact preempt the new

South African government's role in setting the terms and conditions for investment. This would be a case of outsiders, however well-intentioned, dictating economic policy, not trusting the ANC even to set standards of fair treatment in a postapartheid era. But we warned the ANC that only ANC statements of opposition to such a code would be effective, not the pleading of U.S. business or of the U.S. government.

The ANC moved to the same position. At first, ANC opposition was confided to us, because ANC officials were loath to criticize publicly well-intentioned efforts of their anti-apartheid allies. But as the momentum in the United States for such a code gained ground, ANC opposition grew. Trevor Manuel told George Moose in September, "We the South Africans must handle this situation ourselves." The ANC not only felt strongly about the prerogatives of a new democratic government, but recognized that a plethora of laws enacted abroad would greatly complicate South Africa's plans to establish investment legislation and regulations. There was a rather sharp exchange between the ANC and the Congressional Black Caucus over this issue in November 1993, as the House was drafting the bill to end sanctions and encourage state and local governments to do the same. The caucus had been holding out for adding to the legislation a mandatory code of conduct for American investors. It backed down in the face of ANC opposition. Over time local jurisdictions in the United States also acceded to the ANC's position. Once in power, the ANC-led government enacted its own version of standards for both foreign procurement and foreign investment, which required all participating foreign companies to contribute to employment, training, affirmative action, and other social goals.[73]

SPECTERS ON THE HORIZON: NARCOTICS AND HIV/AIDS

One subject to which I gave special attention was the danger of narcotics trafficking. I had seen the insidious effects of narcotics on the government and society of Nigeria when I had been ambassador there in the 1980s. As I said in a message to Washington in July 1993, narcotics posed one of the most insidious threats to incipient democracies, corrupting their politicians and institutions and destroying their moral standing. We could see the danger to South Africa. Once sanctions began to be lifted and the country was open to the world, it would offer an extremely tempting target for the syndicates. South Africa was not yet on the map of narcotics watchers, as Nigeria was, so traffickers would move there rapidly. There was money in South Africa. There was poverty and lack of opportunity in the townships and an angry and restless youth already organizing into gangs. I warned Washington that more attention needed to be given to South Africa on this issue precisely because it was not yet, but could soon be, a major problem.

South Africa had a small and relatively impressive narcotics unit in the South African police. But the police on the whole were so incompetent and corrupt, in addition to being located outside the townships, that they could not begin to cope with the problem.

Early in 1993, I began discussions with the ANC on this danger and urged it to prepare for the problem. We included a special briefing on narcotics for the TEC's foreign affairs committee when it visited Washington in late 1993. We persuaded Washington to allow South African police to participate in the Drug Enforcement Agency's (DEA's) regional narcotics training program before sanctions were lifted. Following the election in 1994, Lee Brown, who while chief of police of New York had earlier participated in one of Judge Goldstone's panels, came out as the president's director of the Office of National Drug Control Policy to advise the new government. Brown shared copies of relevant U.S. legislation that would form the basis for similar legislation enacted by the new Parliament.

While many U.S. government agencies were desirous of setting up office in South Africa after the election, the only one I supported, and the one I lobbied hard for over three years, was DEA. Washington at first did not accord South Africa priority for drug funding, and there was competition for the siting of new DEA offices. The DEA office in South Africa was finally opened in 1996, with the FBI following shortly afterward. The State Department has since made South Africa a major recipient of its police and related training programs.

But none of this was sufficient or in time. By July 1993, South Africa had airlines coming in from all over the world, connecting it to Asia on one end and Miami, Latin America, and all major European cities on the other. South Africa was already the third largest consumer of mandrax, an Asian-manufactured barbiturate, and a large producer of marijuana. Traffickers were taking advantage of the corrupt administrations in the "homelands" to obtain false documents to enter the country. Syndicates from Nigeria, Thailand, and Columbia had moved in. Cocaine was on the street at higher prices than in New York. On the Cape "flats," the townships to which blacks and coloreds had been confined, drug-related gangs began terrorizing the local population, producing a backlash of vigilantism that became mixed with Islamic political organizations.

It was simply a bridge too far—one more problem for which the country had to prepare beyond what it could handle. Nor were the institutions at all in place for a new government to address the problem. Since the transition, the country has faced a major crime problem, in part because the entire police structure needed to be overhauled, a long-term proposition. Drugs flourished as this problem was being tackled. Fortunately, South Africa's commitment to democracy is strong and the institutions created under the constitution to protect transparency and justice are impressive. South Africa has not succumbed to the creeping levels of drug-related corruption that have plagued some other societies, but the problem adds to the misery of its people and the dangers for its future.

Another situation demanding attention was AIDS. Although the U.S. aid program in South Africa had been focused almost exclusively on ending apartheid, and was therefore more a political than a development program, aside from education we did invest in one developmental area: the growing problem of HIV/ AIDS. Following a visit by Secretary of Health and Human Services Louis Sullivan in 1991, the United States stationed in South Africa a full-time expert from the Centers for Disease Control (CDC) to oversee programs in education and training. Under the limitations of sanctions, these programs were almost exclusively with NGOs. Nevertheless, they had the advantage of developing grassroots support and increasing awareness and capability among those who would lead the new government. By 1994, USAID was spending $3.5 million annually on these programs, a paltry sum by today's estimates of the need, but then making the United States the largest donor to South Africa in this field.

The seriousness of AIDS in South Africa was recognized in the 1980s, the first case being reported in 1982, and by the early 1990s the rapid growth in the infection rate was causing alarm. Although few predicted the explosion of infection by the end of the century, marking South Africa with the highest such rate in the world, the trend was apparent. The earliest signs of an epidemic were seen in KwaZulu/Natal, because of its place on the trucking routes from East Africa and the growing traffic in its ports. From there it spread rapidly to the Transvaal— the Johannesburg area—and beyond. By 1994 the infection rate was estimated at five hundred a day. The USAID/CDC adviser predicted that if the upward trend in the infection rate continued, there would be more than five million people infected by the end of the decade. Alas, he was too close to the truth. The Joint United Nations Programme on HIV/AIDS (UNAIDS) estimates the number of people in South Africa affected in the year 2000 at 4.2 million, and the infection rate at fifteen hundred a day.[74]

We had reason to expect that the new government would tackle this issue more effectively and forthrightly than its predecessor. Under the National Party, the government's warnings on AIDS were held suspect by the black population, and the party's later election posters showing predatory black males did not help in diminishing suspicion of the government's racial motives. At the same time, a coalition of NGOs had begun working on the problem, providing education as well as care and support for victims. In 1992, a National AIDS Committee of South Africa (NACOSA), bringing together government and nongovernmental organizations, met to discuss broad approaches to the problem. Nelson Mandela opened the conference and pledged his full support. NACOSA was chaired by Dr. Nkosazana Zuma, who directed a USAID-funded HIV/AIDS NGO and would become the minister of health under the Mandela administration. NACOSA drew up a national HIV plan that was presented to the new government.

Unfortunately, the issue became embroiled in racial and political controversy within months of the beginning of the Mandela administration. There was a scandal over Dr. Zuma's financing of a musical education program, a dispute over presumed home-grown cures, a fight with the pharmaceutical companies over marketing and pricing of drugs, and sharp disputes between the government and the health professionals over whether to force AIDS victims into public disclosure. By the end of the Mandela presidency, HIV/AIDS was not on the government's front burner, as indicated by government statements, and the issue had polarized the activist community along racial and political lines. By the end of the decade, as the issue became headline news internationally, for example, when the AIDS crisis attracted UN Security Council attention, disputes continued in South Africa over the causes of AIDS and the proper response.[75]

Yet the fundamental problem in these disputes, beyond or perhaps beneath the political wrangling, is the reality of poverty and its impact on a society's capacity to address this epidemic. Wealth, as one early analyst wrote, enables a society to develop social services, coping mechanisms, and opportunities for people to have greater control over their lives, all of which have enabled wealthier societies to cope with the AIDS crisis.[76] The international community has not wanted to recognize this connection so directly, and therein lies much of the dispute with Mandela's successor, President Thabo Mbeki. We will return to this issue in chapter 11. Suffice it to say here, we did not have the handle we thought we had on this issue, and the results are grievous.

A CELEBRATION, AT LEAST A RESPITE

In November 1993, President Clinton signed the Transition to Democracy Act. This act not only lifted remaining sanctions but authorized an active U.S. program of support for the remaining transition process and the postapartheid era. President Clinton immediately dispatched Secretary of Commerce Ron Brown, accompanied by fifty business representatives, on a trade and investment mission to South Africa. Brown met with all leading political figures, with white and black businessmen, and with many others. As will be described in a later chapter, he engaged in quiet efforts on the political front. But most of all he sent a message about the future, and an enthusiastic one.

Brown announced that South Africa would be designated one of ten emerging markets that would receive top U.S. priority. He announced the formation of a joint US-SA Business Development Committee. The Ex-Im Bank was already looking into the financing of new planes for South African Airways. He reassured people worried about future ANC economic policies, saying that he was "absolutely" convinced the ANC was on the right track and would remain there after elections.[77] He promised special attention to promoting partnerships with black entrepreneurs in South Africa, yet he took pains to praise the white business establishment. "Your success represents the success of South Africa," he told members of the Johannesburg stock exchange.[78]

The mission received enormous media coverage. The highlight of the trip was the signing of the OPIC agreement with Minister of Finance Derek Keys. The ANC's Manuel grumbled a bit that the agreement had not been negotiated with the TEC, but not only did the TEC endorse it; Manuel and other TEC members attended the signing. Coming so soon after sanctions were finally and formally lifted, the agreement had as much symbolic as substantive significance.

Perhaps because the country was still gripped by violence, still uncertain over the role that dissenting parties to the agreements would play, still uncertain about the future, Brown's visit was like a shot in the arm. With his ebullient personality, his warm support for future economic relations with South Africa, and his obvious faith in the future of the country, Brown provoked an outpouring of some of the most optimistic commentary the country had witnessed all year. Exaggerating somewhat the impact of the OPIC agreement and what might follow, news reports headlined "Billions for South Africa," "Huge US Support," "Massive Boost," "Opening Up to the World," "US Firms Streaking Back into the Country."

De Klerk was extremely pleased with the visit, as it demonstrated full confidence in the irreversible direction of the transition and gave a boost to his leadership. The significance of the signing of the first postsanctions agreement with his government was not lost on him. Brown was careful to refer to him and Foreign Minister Pik Botha as "historic figures."[79] But the ANC was equally pleased. Mandela, after a breakfast meeting with Brown at the ambassador's residence in Cape Town, said, "I have come out feeling inspired by the knowledge that the democratic forces in this country have the support of the president of the United States of America."

Thabo Mbeki commented that "It's good they came so soon after the lifting of sanctions. . . . It's important to encourage the corporate world in the United States to put in money, especially to enable the black entrepreneurs. . . . The U.S. corporations seem to be the most sensitized to that issue."[80] In his meeting with Brown, Mbeki praised the mission as an important contribution to maintaining the transition's momentum. He and Brown agreed that an ANC delegation would visit Washington to investigate the full potential of the OPIC agreement and Department of Commerce programs. Months later, referring to the Brown mission, a COSATU official told a visiting American delegation, "The rest of the world watches what the United States does, and will follow your example."

If the coming months would once again put the country through a period of wrenching controversy and cliff-edge maneuvering by the various parties, this moment was at least a welcome glimpse into a better future. Brown would return on several occasions in the coming years to renew his confidence in and commitment to South Africa. He is warmly remembered in that country.

7

The Buthelezi Dilemma

It is because I feel that this dialogue needs to be strengthened that I will take the liberty, as I have done in the past with Ambassador Lyman, to speak openly and frankly as someone would do with old and trusted friends. If strong, a friendship can take and value criticism.

—MANGOSUTHU BUTHELEZI, *January 7, 1994*

MANGOSUTHU BUTHELEZI, then chief minister of the KwaZulu homeland, was critical to the success of the transition. Zulus constitute 20 percent of South Africa's population, concentrated in the province of KwaZulu/Natal. Although Buthelezi did not in fact speak for all Zulus, he had unwavering support in rural areas, exerted control over the Zulu monarchy and the structures of royal and tribal leaders under it, and presided over the homeland government of KwaZulu. He had once been close to the ANC and had formed his party, the Inkatha Freedom Party (IFP), with ANC approval. Up until the 1980s, he had been in the forefront of anti-apartheid activities. But in the 1980s, rivalry between the ANC and the IFP became fierce, as described in chapter 2. A number of missteps in the weeks following Mandela's release from prison in 1990 kept the two apart in that formative period of the transition, leading to bruised feelings on Buthelezi's part and his increased belief that he was being isolated and indeed threatened by the ANC. Mandela's enormous stature and immediate move into the leadership of the negotiating process struck deeply at Buthelezi's sense of his own place in the pantheon of South Africa's leaders. Buthelezi may not have been capable of attaining the status he so desperately wanted, but he was clearly capable of determining whether the transition would be one of a unified nation or one of a nation poised on the edge of civil war.

I first met Chief Buthelezi on October 2, 1992, in the KwaZulu capital of Ulundi. Ulundi is a small town, at that time not even serviced by commercial airlines. One drove four hours from Durban to meet in the setting in which Buthelezi preferred most to receive visitors. In such a small town, the capital complex containing offices, the parliamentary chamber, a dining room, and much more loomed especially large. Buthelezi normally met with his visitors in one of the drawing rooms and then proceeded to a formal luncheon or on occasion walked his unsuspecting visitors directly into a full meeting of the Parliament.

That first meeting was the beginning of a long, tortuous, sometimes strongly antagonistic relationship. But on this day, as indeed on our last encounter before my departure three years later, the meeting would be cordial, and he would display that exceptional courtesy that often confounds his antagonists.

Like many Americans, I was intrigued by this man. Many years earlier, when things seemed hopeless in South Africa, I had listened to Buthelezi speak to an American audience. He was a voice of reason, of seemingly impeccable logic. He administered KwaZulu within the South African system. But he had refused the ignoble "independence" accorded to other "homelands" and had refused to engage in negotiations with the government on transition possibilities until Nelson Mandela was released from prison. All in all, he held out the hope that there was a nonviolent, but no less principled, pathway to the end of apartheid. One could understand his support across a broad spectrum of Americans, from corporate boardrooms to the AFL-CIO.

Now, however, he was on the verge of a major break with the process of peaceful transition. In the weeks since Mandela and de Klerk had reached agreement in the Record of Understanding, the breach with Buthelezi had widened. Buthelezi had denounced the Record of Understanding, seeing in it his isolation from the center of the negotiating process. His officials would describe it as a "horror of horrors." He began to court an alliance with other homeland leaders and far right white parties. This was the subject of our first meeting, though it was also an initial "get acquainted" one.

In early December, Buthelezi issued a draft constitution for the province of KwaZulu/Natal. The constitution was a thinly veiled prescription for almost complete autonomy from any central government. Buthelezi stoked the fires of controversy by threatening to put the constitution to a referendum. It was a prescription for violence.

On December 8, at my request, we met again, at the Holiday Inn in Pretoria. Buthelezi was about to make a major speech to a largely white audience and I was anxious to dissuade him from creating any greater breach with the mainstream negotiating process. Assuring him that we saw him as a major player, I urged him not to take any rash actions, but to look for ways to return to the negotiating process. I warned that the referendum could be a cause for greater violence, just as the ANC's planned march on Ulundi, which we had strongly opposed, would have been. It was one of the few times Buthelezi did not begin a meeting with a prepared statement, which usually so strongly stated his position on matters that it rendered discussion afterward difficult. This evening he met us alone in his room and listened attentively. He assured me that he would not rush into any referendum. Then he went on to a packed house of white citizens and announced his determination to do just that, that is, press ahead with the referendum. The speech helped forge an alliance with some of the most reactionary forces in South Africa, setting in motion a period of turbulence, confrontation, terrible violence, and knife-edge diplomacy that would end only within days of the election itself.

Buthelezi might well have been skeptical of U.S. support for his primary objective, which was to be a principal partner in the transition process. For in truth, as early as the summer of 1992, if not earlier, the United States had recognized in practice if not publicly that the principal interlocutors in the transition were Mandela and de Klerk. For all the talk within South Africa, and often from within government circles, of a troika of leaders, Buthelezi never achieved the status implied in such talk after Mandela was released.

In his letters to Mandela, de Klerk, and Buthelezi in the wake of the Boipatong massacre, President Bush had made a distinction between them. To Mandela and de Klerk, he stressed that they should work together to find the compromises necessary to restore the negotiating process. He urged Buthelezi to do his best to stop the violence and, "as a key figure," to use CODESA—a forum of twenty-six parties—to work through the formation of an interim government. In September, Bush wrote only to Mandela and de Klerk, in recognition that the solution to the impasse rested with them.[1]

Buthelezi was key, however. Without his participation in the electoral process, the specter of civil war hovered over the country. At the American embassy, the "Buthelezi dilemma," as we came to call it, would be one of our major preoccupations. It was a dilemma because as key a figure as Buthelezi was, his demands were almost untenable. As noted, Buthelezi sought national recognition and power, on an equal basis with Mandela and de Klerk. As that ambition faded, he fought all the more fiercely to hold on to control of his base in KwaZulu/Natal. His demands, and even more the demands of those advising him, were tantamount to giving KwaZulu/Natal virtual confederation status within South Africa. Moreover, as the struggle between the ANC and the IFP intensified, Buthelezi moved more and more to fanning the flames of ethnic violence, and more toward traditional rulers and feudal means of political control than open, democratic ones. His KwaZulu police were seen as defending his regime more than providing protection for all the province's citizens and, more disturbing, they were accused of active participation in and collaboration with the violence itself.

The dilemma was how to engage him without either accepting the premise of his more extreme demands or ignoring the encouragement to violence that issued from his increasingly strident speeches. It was a dilemma our allies shared. If Buthelezi had long been viewed favorably by elements within the United States, he had even stronger sources of support, financial and political, in the United Kingdom and Germany. The governments of these nations had to take steadily firmer positions with Buthelezi over the coming months. It was not easy for them, though in the end they were as firm, if not as public, as we were.

The embassy laid out this dilemma to Washington in February 1993. We pointed out that, in addition to the issues described above, the politics were tricky. Precisely as Buthelezi moved to the right, he became all the more attractive to white conservatives as the preferred black partner. This put pressure on de Klerk from within his own party. Indeed, in 1990–91, de Klerk himself had hinted at a coalition made up of his party, Inkatha, and the colored votes as winning in the coming election. De Klerk in effect forfeited this possibility with his recognition of the ANC's primary negotiating role in the Record of Understanding, and later in his rejection of Buthelezi's more extreme demands. But he was dogged by conservatives within his government for doing so, and the prospect of an alliance with Inkatha never quite disappeared from the National Party's calculations. The question we posed in early 1993 was how much could we expect de Klerk to rein in Buthelezi, either by blandishments or, more difficult, by financial and political pressure.

The ANC was not blameless either. Much of the bitterness between the two parties began in the early 1980s, when the ANC/UDF's "ungovernability" campaign targeted Buthelezi's regime in KwaZulu along with apartheid rule elsewhere. Violence, drawing on deep historical rivalries, became fierce then and did not relent later, when Mandela was released and the transition process began. The ANC's Natal chapter, moreover, was led by one of the most radical and violence-prone members of the organization, Harry Gwala. As Mandela would later acknowledge, most notably in a speech in April 1993, the ANC was a part of the problem. Much later, well after the transition of 1994, it would come out that the ANC, like Inkatha, had in fact been infiltrated by government provocateurs; Gwala's chief lieutenant would be exposed as one of them.[2] During the period of 1993–94, however, the evidence pointed more to Inkatha's having been so subverted, thus making the path of peace between the ANC and Inkatha all the more difficult.

How were we to maneuver through this thicket? Our strategy was to work along several fronts. On one front, we were to do all we could to help close the gap between Inkatha and the ANC on the substance of the principal constitutional issue dividing them: federalism. The ANC had begun with a distinct distrust of federalism, seeing in it a "plot" to protect apartheid at the state and local levels. A strong central government, in their view, was essential to undertaking the fundamental transformation needed in the country. Inkatha, on the other hand, struck a sympathetic nerve with far more than conservatives when arguing for strong regional powers. The liberal Democratic Party had long argued for federalism, and de Klerk had seized on it as a means of assuring his constituents that it would constrain the power of a majoritarian government. The United States had indicated as early as September 1992 that we saw a federal structure as the most appropriate for South Africa.

We would thus urge the ANC to revisit this issue. Our emphasis, as noted in the preceding chapter, would be twofold: (1) federalism did not mean a weak central government, nor one incapable of rooting out apartheid, and (2) only by responding reasonably on this issue could the ANC carry the high ground against the more extreme "confederal" demands of Inkatha. As the ANC began to move on this issue, we struggled, as message carriers between them, to get Inkatha to recognize this movement on the part of the ANC as legitimate and as an opening to meet their basic demands.

On a second front, in seeking to overcome the violence between the ANC and Inkatha, we sought in a dozen different ways to encourage dialogue at both the most senior levels and between the principal negotiators of the two parties. Both Mandela and Buthelezi are proud men. Neither forgets a slight. Beyond that, each was wary of a meeting that would produce more shine than substance and damage them as a result. Bringing about such meetings thus proved a Herculean task, not just for us but for the many in South Africa and outside who worked toward the same objective. When such meetings did take place, they often did offer but fleeting promises of peace or reconciliation. One such meeting took place in June 1993, on the urging of Archbishop Desmond Tutu and Methodist bishop Stanley Mogobe, only to be followed by a spate of violence in both KwaZulu/Natal and the outskirts of Johannesburg. Nevertheless, opening lines of communication between them remained a major objective of ourselves and others.

Third, we felt it necessary to explore quietly with the parties what exactly Buthelezi's bottom lines were, and how they could be accommodated. Our German and British colleagues were less willing to go here, but we felt that some sort of power sharing with Inkatha, in KwaZulu if not at the national level, would eventually be the price to pay. This would be particularly hard for ANC activists in Natal to swallow, engaged as they were in literal war and convinced that they had potential majority support in the province. The trick was how to achieve such power sharing without compromising the principles of democratic choice and national unity. We felt we had to explore as well the difficult issue of policing in this province and the guarantees of free political activity in the run-up to the election, areas of great sensitivity.

Fourth, we would reach out to the business community, especially in Natal, to determine if there was any real support for what was the most dangerous scenario on the horizon but one being bruited: secession by KwaZulu and Natal. We would argue strongly against that and encourage the business community to work for resolution of the conflict and a return of Inkatha to the negotiations. This line of action would culminate in a speech I would give in Durban in March 1994 that both Mandela and some of Buthelezi's supporters would mark as signaling a turning point in the long process of bringing Inkatha back into the fold.

In sum, we determined that we could not cut ourselves off from Buthelezi. Indeed, none of our South African interlocutors wanted us to do so. Nor could we assume that the South African government on its own could rein him in, as the ANC sometimes argued. Rather we would keep open our lines to Buthelezi and repair them each time they became frayed. And we would step up our efforts to bridge the gaps between the ANC and Inkatha wherever possible.

DIFFICULT EXCHANGES

The dialogue with Buthelezi was made more difficult by the distraction of issues not really central to the power struggle under way. One issue that dominated debate in late 1992 and early 1993 was the right of Inkatha marchers to carry "cultural weapons." These spears, hatchets, and so on were defended by Buthelezi as symbols of Zulu culture and denounced by Mandela as provocations to violence. Banishing them had been one of Mandela's principal demands in the Record of Understanding with de Klerk. I suggested to Buthelezi at one point that his emphasis on this issue, when so much violence was going on, was not helping his image. Because of my advice or that of others, the issue dropped from Buthelezi's speeches shortly afterward. Another issue was how the Zulu king Goodwill Zwelethini would be represented in any resumed negotiations. Buthelezi insisted that the king have representation in addition to Inkatha, signifying that there was both a political and a monarchical tradition to be accommodated. This thorny issue, which took much of everyone's time for months, was finally resolved, only to have Buthelezi—who was by then having some differences with the king—drop the matter. The king never participated.

These were distractions. The key issues were federalism, security, and power sharing. In February 1993, Buthelezi and I held what I described at the time as "a tightly focused and at times difficult meeting." The first issue we discussed was the state of the negotiating process. Buthelezi refused to accept any of the results of the Record of Understanding and therefore was unwilling to agree to participate in resumed multiparty negotiations. He especially rejected the agreement hammered out between the government and the ANC that a permanent constitution would be drafted by an elected Constituent Assembly. To Buthelezi, having the rights of regions determined by such a body would result in "another demoralizing dictatorship." His distrust of the ANC was deep on this score. What he wanted was a constitution drafted before the elections, with Inkatha having a major say. He questioned further Mandela's willingness to include Inkatha in a Government of National Unity and insisted that the ANC's armed wing be disarmed before any election.

I sought to bridge the gap between his position and that of the others on the constitution by suggesting that agreement could be reached in advance of the election on a set of principles that would be binding on the assembly. This idea was already gaining currency between the government and the ANC. In this context, I said, the ANC was also moving in its position on federalism. But Buthelezi distrusted the ANC to abide by any such agreement. I then suggested, in the context of a proposed but still contentiously debated meeting between himself and Mandela, that perhaps an agreement was needed between them on the future of KwaZulu/Natal. He sat back and said, "Yes, definitely."

But on security we found ourselves on more sensitive ground. Buthelezi angrily rejected the idea that his police might be investigated by the Goldstone Commission, despite charges of KwaZulu police misdeeds. He would only countenance investigation of individual incidents. I went further, suggesting that in order to avoid charges of bias or misconduct during the election, there might be some form of joint political control over all security forces in the country. Buthelezi glowered at me for a full minute, saying nothing. I moved on to less important issues.

The difficult tone of the meeting, so unlike at earlier ones, was affected by Buthelezi's growing resentment of foreign pressure. British junior minister Lynda Chalker had visited him the previous day, obviously pressing him on similar matters. There were reports that foreign investors had been urging him to reach agreement on the transition. He complained to me that "Western diplomats" were advising other parties to bypass and marginalize him. I denied that this was our position; to the contrary, we were steadfast in our belief that Inkatha must be party to a final agreement.

Buthelezi's mood was not improved by the announcement a few weeks later that de Klerk and Mandela were to be awarded the Liberty Medal on July 4 by the Freedom Foundation in Philadelphia. Each would be received by President Clinton beforehand and Clinton would attend the ceremony. The award put pressure on the government and the ANC to reach agreement by then on several major sticking points in the ongoing negotiations, specifically, the arrangements for a transitional executive, the timetable for elections, and the principles that would bind the Constituent Assembly.

Tensions were running high in South Africa at the time. Only a few months earlier, Chris Hani, one of the ANC's most popular leaders, had been assassinated. Controlling and channeling the popular outcry proved extremely demanding for Mandela. That had nevertheless pushed the parties to agreement, at last, on a firm date for elections. Then, on June 25, a group of right-wing whites invaded the World Trade Center, where the negotiations were taking place. They smashed through the glass doors, beat up several delegates, trashed the building, and tore up papers on the desks. It was shocking, but in a way it represented the last gasp of the extreme right. De Klerk responded by pressing ahead on the arrangements for the transition; indeed, negotiations resumed the very next day, sending a message that no longer would violence disrupt the negotiating process.

Buthelezi was feeling more isolated and his rhetoric was becoming more strident. Hints of secession and warnings of civil war were becoming more frequent. Talk of civil war was entering the discourse of the media and other leaders.

Assistant Secretary of State George Moose arrived at this time to see how progress could be facilitated in advance of the Philadelphia celebration. In a round of meetings with leaders, he pressed them to improve communication, to make greater progress, and to step back from the use of violence. Moose and I met with Buthelezi in Durban. Buthelezi was flanked by his principal negotiators, who had been in on-and-off talks with the ANC and the government. The meeting went past midnight. Moose and I challenged the advisers on their insistence that no progress had been made on the issue of federalism. They finally agreed that it had, but complained about Inkatha being basically sidelined if not demeaned in the process. Moose nevertheless secured Buthelezi's agreement that time was of the essence and that bilateral talks with the ANC should resume immediately.

But Moose found Mandela himself in a feisty mood the next day, speaking of possible civil war. He took a hard line on the role of an elected Constituent Assembly, saying that it would have the right to overturn any prior agreements on principles. He was not keen on Moose's appeal for him to consider, on his forthcoming trip, calling for a lifting of sanctions in order to speed up economic recovery. All in all, he appeared intransigent and belligerent. Moose left South Africa discouraged.

But mood swings did not necessarily reflect policy. In the next few days, in a flurry of meetings designed to "close loops and bridge gaps," I discussed the situation with key negotiators in the government, the ANC, and Inkatha. The ANC's Cyril Ramaphosa and Joe Slovo, while skeptical, agreed to reach out once more to their Inkatha counterparts. I reminded Inkatha's Joe Matthews of the commitment made to George Moose in Durban, and he agreed to undertake further talks. Nevertheless, persons close to the talks did not believe that Buthelezi would come to any sort of agreement on the eve of the Philadelphia ceremony and make it any more celebratory of his rivals. Indeed, on June 29, Inkatha complicated the entire process by introducing a whole new set of demands, going back to the earliest issues on the nature of the transition process. As I prepared to board the plane for Washington and Philadelphia, I hammered at Buthelezi's constitution adviser, Mario Oriani-Ambrosini, the author of this latest set of Inkatha proposals. My wife pulled me aside to say I was shouting. I too was becoming exasperated.

In July, in the speech I gave in Durban on the rising tide of violence (see chapter 6), I also chose to address the state of the negotiations and the degree to which the parties, specifically the ANC, had moved on the question of federalism. It was a direct public refutation of Inkatha's claims. Inkatha had continued to boycott the multiparty forum, arguing that it was stacked against Inkatha and that no real progress was available there on this issue. It insisted on a whole new negotiating structure. Pointing to the fact that the United States had taken a specific position in favor of federalism for South Africa, I said:

> It is timely for us to say that we see in the present negotiating process the basis for achieving that objective. In the positions that have been developed by the various parties over the past several months . . . the basis for satisfactory agreement on this issue is available. It can be achieved within the present negotiating process and procedures. . . . Thus it would be a costly error to jettison that process now, or even threaten to do so.[3]

During my visits to Durban, in July and again in August, I met with leading businessmen to see whether there was indeed support for secession, or even for the confrontational tactics of Buthelezi. I found virtually no support for secession. There was considerable sympathy for Buthelezi, whom they admired and had worked with, and whose battle with the ANC made his fears justifiable in their eyes. Nevertheless, they did not relish a continuing standoff. I encouraged them to work for compromise.

Even before the speech in Durban, I was aware from his advisers that Buthelezi was angry over the lack of political support from the United States. His more extreme advisers did not help matters, of course. At one point one of them threatened to mobilize right-wing pressure in the United States to put the "spotlight" on the U.S. government's "exclusive support" of the ANC. The same adviser sounded us out on an independent KwaZulu state.[4] Statements like these, as with the Inkatha paper produced on the eve of Mandela's and de Klerk's trip to Philadelphia, contributed to the suspicion that Buthelezi was aiming at secession, or for a deal quite outside the current political framework.

Knowing of Buthelezi's unhappiness with my speech, I set out our positions at length in a personal letter to him shortly afterward. I began by rehearsing the discussion between Buthelezi and Assistant Secretary Moose in June. In particular, I reminded him that we believed the situation in the country would only worsen if the election were delayed past the spring of 1994. I reported that Assistant Secretary Moose had followed up on his meetings with Buthelezi in June by conveying to the ANC and other negotiators Inkatha's concerns over regional powers. I too was following up on those issues. Nevertheless, I wrote, there had been considerable progress on these issues. I was explicit on where we believed the debate over federalism had gone. "No one of any stature in the present negotiations is any longer proposing a unitary state, or is denying the right of regions to have specific and significant powers." In this situation, I argued, public statements that other parties were still trying to stifle or destroy regional government were not only misleading but also dangerous. "What concerns me and my government," I emphasized, "is the growing belligerence in these public statements."[5]

I pointed out also that Inkatha's absence from the multiparty negotiating forum was putting us in a quandary. We were pressing the parties to recognize and respond to the issues of federalism, which were at the top of Inkatha's concerns. But by being absent from the negotiations, Inkatha gave credence to the charge that its real goal was to delay, even prevent, an election.

I then turned to the sensitive issues of ethnic identity and ethnic fears. Alluding to accusations that the Zulu people were under dire threat, I said, "I know of no threat in the present negotiations to the Zulus as a people, nor to the king, nor to the regional powers of a KwaZulu/Natal region under a new constitution. For Zulu leaders to sound alarms of that kind, therefore, strikes us as unnecessarily dangerous." The threat to Zulus, I argued, came from those who had recently murdered Inkatha supporters in the East Rand and who were "doing their utmost to provoke you and other belligerent leaders into statements that arouse ethnic rivalry. They are the enemies of everything you have stood for over the past thirty years of your leadership as one of South Africa's greatest liberation figures."[6]

I closed by assuring him that I was urging others to avoid equally unfair and misleading charges against him: "I am urging all to shape their public statements to be supportive of reconciliation and a peaceful process of negotiation."[7]

Buthelezi responded within a few days. He referred to a "dangerous" U.S. misunderstanding of the negotiation process and suggested observers focus more on what he saw as "the systematic extermination of the Zulu people which goes on almost daily." He maintained his opposition to the two-stage process of constitution making and denied that the proposed binding principles were sufficient protection against the ambitions of an elected assembly.[8] Two days later he went public with his criticisms of the U.S. position.

Shortly afterward, Buthelezi undertook a visit to several European countries. He got no better support, however. The degree of negative reactions Buthelezi was receiving was such that de Klerk suggested that the international community show some greater warmth to him, lest Buthelezi feel isolated.

SEEKING FORMS OF REASSURANCE

In fact, we continued to work on ways to reassure Inkatha and Buthelezi personally. Whatever frustration we felt at Inkatha's seeming obduracy, we recognized that the fears among Buthelezi's people were real in their minds. I remember vividly an exchange with one of Buthelezi's more moderate officials. I had asked, with the constitutional guarantees being put into place, what the remaining concerns were? He turned to me, with a look I will never forget, and said, "When the election is over, they will kill every one of us."

I thus inveighed with the ANC to avoid rhetoric that worsened the situation, in particular personal attacks on Buthelezi. We urged more explicit, public ANC commitments to regional powers and to other agreements reached in the negotiations. The ANC had its own internal problem with the two-stage transition process that was developing. Conceding first a list of principles that would bind a future elected assembly, and then conceding the preparation of a fully fleshed-out interim constitution to guide the country after the election, the ANC felt it had compromised the principle of South Africa's final constitution being written by a democratically elected assembly. It worried about losing its constituency on these matters. Thus it kept referring to the sweeping powers of that assembly once the election had taken place. Nevertheless, following my Durban visit, I urged Joe Slovo to find another phrase for "total revision" of the constitution when referring to the powers of the assembly. I was gratified when, that afternoon, he proposed to the negotiating body dropping the phrase altogether.

Another tack was on the international front. Early in the year, the government's foreign minister had suggested that the United States and other members of the G-7 "guarantee" the new constitution. During his meeting with Secretary of State Warren Christopher in July, President de Klerk elaborated on the idea, suggesting that the G-7 hold any new government to the principles to which its members had earlier agreed. Assistant Secretary Moose picked up on this idea and advanced it over the next several months. He broached it with Buthelezi in his meeting in June and pursued it over several months with the ANC. In September the United States made a public statement regarding its guarantee, which was elaborated by Moose in congressional testimony. The United States, he said, "expects the new South African Government to abide by preelection constitutional promises and the United States will support the government in that context."[9]

The United States urged the European Community and the other members of the G-7 to make similar statements, which they later did.[10]

The agreements to which these statements referred were in particular those on the constitutional principles that were to be binding on an elected body that would write the final constitution, including not only principles of human rights and due process, but also the principle of regional powers being devolved to the provinces. Moose also urged Mandela and the ANC to make a public pledge to honor all such agreements. The ANC resisted at first. Mandela argued that any ANC statement to this effect would not assuage those who did not trust the ANC in the first place. Thabo Mbeki thought such a statement would create problems with the ANC grass roots and complicate talks then under way with right-wing representatives.

But in November, at a ceremony honoring the late Chris Hani, Mandela took the floor and made the statement in dramatic fashion. Mandela noted that there had been approaches from members of the international community asking all parties to adhere to preelection commitments. He went on: "The ANC regards these appeals as very important and its track record shows consistent adherence to agreements made in the course of negotiations. The stability of the nation would be undermined if current undertakings were not honored."[11] It was an important pronouncement. It acknowledged the uncertainty that hovered over the transition, and also acknowledged the need to provide constant reassurances to the not inconsiderable number of South Africans who were uneasy about an ANC-led government.

Discussions among the parties continued into the fall. Although Inkatha boycotted the formal multiparty negotiations, it held an important meeting with de Klerk in September. They agreed on "negotiating principles" that each would pursue: entrenched regional powers in a new constitution, an independent Constitutional Court, a constitutional state, and the right of regions to write their own constitutions. Both took issue with ANC proposals for how any deadlock in an elected assembly could be broken in approving the final constitution. Differences with the ANC aside, this kind of agreement on the basis for negotiation was a hopeful sign. The difficulty with Inkatha, however, was the disconnectedness between these seeming breakthroughs and the later interpretations by some of Buthelezi's hard-line advisers.

Shortly after the Buthelezi–de Klerk agreements, several Inkatha officials met with the State Department in Washington. The more moderate Dr. Ben Ngubane (now minister of science and technology) said that, based on these agreements, Inkatha could foresee returning to the multiparty forum. It would have to protect the Zulu monarchy, the Zulu nation, and the KwaZulu administration. However, a more hard-line adviser, Walter Felgate, denounced the interim constitution, now largely negotiated in the forum, as "fatally flawed," which did not suggest a promising basis for return. This statement harked back to what another adviser, Oriani-Ambrosini, had said to us a few months earlier, that Inkatha's intention was to start the entire process de novo. Oriani-Ambrosini was even more frank on this occasion. He said if the present transition process continued, Buthelezi would be "defeated." If it failed, he added, the ANC would be defeated. As long as these latter positions dominated Inkatha policy, there was little basis for negotiation. Indeed, in late August, Thabo Mbeki, who had always looked for lines of communication with Inkatha, was coming to the conclusion that there was no constitutional concession the ANC could make that would satisfy Buthelezi. In Mbeki's view, Buthelezi was operating from fear.

We had no choice but to make clear to the advisers that we would have little sympathy with any party that did not participate in the electoral process. The State Department made the point again to Ngubane in October.

In September, at a farewell dinner for our consul general, Bismarck Myrick, and again in October, Buthelezi reiterated his public attack on the U.S. position. Concerned that the lines of communication between the United States and Buthelezi might be becoming strained to the point of rupture, a mutual friend, Sal Marzullo, called me to suggest a quiet, very informal, three-way meeting. Marzullo had been the Mobil Oil representative in South Africa and, for many years afterward, Mobil's spokesman on South Africa in New York and Washington. He had worked to counter the pressures for disinvestment that swelled in the 1980s; he worked strenuously to make the Sullivan principles and other aspects of corporate good citizenship models of responsible behavior. When Mobil decided to withdraw, Marzullo retired. Concerned with more than business, however, Marzullo was also a dedicated supporter of communication and dialogue, being an active and important member of USSALEP, one of the few mechanisms for dialogue between Americans and South Africans from various quarters during the apartheid years.

Marzullo was a close friend of Buthelezi. He knew the Buthelezi of moderation, of deep religious conviction, of democratic and capitalist ideals. He was sure that there was a pathway for fruitful cooperation and political participation by Buthelezi in the new dispensation. He also mourned the growing strain between Buthelezi and the United States. I had known Marzullo since the 1980s and liked him very much. I agreed immediately to the meeting.

The three of us met for two hours on October 6 in a small sitting room at Ulundi. The meeting was relaxed and friendly. We began with talk of our grandchildren and of the charms of San Francisco, and I even joked a little about Buthelezi's recent criticism of the United States. Besides meeting in September with de Klerk, Buthelezi had recently received Thabo Mbeki and Jacob Zuma to discuss ways in which he and Mandela could work together to lower the level of violence. Nevertheless, Buthelezi remained suspicious of suggestions that any real progress had been made in any of the bilateral discussions. He brooded about signs of betrayal by the National Party. He smarted over what he saw as the ANC trying to appropriate Zulu cultural events by sponsoring such events, to which it invited the king. He even expressed suspicion about reports of efforts under way to define further the rights and roles of the Zulu king, even though Buthelezi's own advisers were conducting these. At the same time, he denied any knowledge of, and promised to repudiate, a flyer circulating in the United States that denounced the "left-leaning" State Department in his name.

Buthelezi did not avoid reading a formal statement. More in sorrow than in anger, he expressed his "astonishment" at the lack of U.S. support for "principles dear to the U.S." that he was defending, for example, federalism, checks and balances, a bill of rights, and guarantees of constitutional processes. Instead, he charged, we were pressuring him to accept whatever documents came out of the multiparty forum. He was also upset by President Clinton's statement welcoming the formation of the Transitional Executive Council.

I replied that the United States was not pressuring him to accept whatever came out of the multiparty forum. Rather we believed it was important for Inkatha to be at this forum in order to improve the outcome. I reiterated our conclusion that the ANC had moved considerably on the issue of federalism, for which Buthelezi could take much credit. We too, I said, had urged the ANC in this direction, pointing out that on this issue Buthelezi reflected the views of many South Africans and that, in any case, without movement on this issue, agreement was impossible. As for the TEC, the United States saw in its formation a formal step by the South African government to bring apartheid to an end. This was what the president spoke to and how it was seen in the media. All that being said, I went on, we felt that the process had to move forward to an election soon. Without it, violence would increase and a further breakdown of society would occur.

Finally I pointed to Moose's testimony on holding the parties to their pre-election commitments. Buthelezi asked me what this meant. I said I presumed it meant that a new government could not count on U.S. support for drawing on IMF or IBRD resources, nor our encouragement of private investment, if it proceeded to trample on human rights or otherwise break its constitutional commitments. Buthelezi appreciated this very much, though with his customary reserve about whether anyone could hold the ANC to its promises.

The meeting also allowed me to pick up on the sensitive issue of how to create a neutral security force. On this occasion I focused on proposals to create a new security force from the various parties in South Africa. I noted Buthelezi's position that he could not accept the ANC's military arm, the MK, "which is killing my people at night," reappearing in the daytime as part of the new security force. I wondered, however, if one could distinguish the integration of regular armed forces for defense purposes from a police force. Could he contemplate individuals who had formerly been MK members being recruited for a police force, along with former KwaZulu policemen and Inkatha members? Buthelezi said he had not thought about such a distinction and would think further about it.

We parted amicably. But the very next day, Buthelezi announced the formation of the "Freedom Alliance," an association with the homeland leaders of Ciskei and Bophuthatswana, the white Conservative Party, and the Afrikaner Volksfront, a newly emerging party of Afrikaners under retired general Constand Viljoen. He stated that Inkatha would engage in no more bilateral discussions with other parties and would now participate in discussions only in league with its new partners. It was a step backward. And it put Buthelezi in strange company. When the Freedom Alliance briefed the diplomatic corps a few days later, presumably on behalf of South Africa's "many minorities," Buthelezi was the only black African on the dais. At a later briefing, when Buthelezi was absent, there were none.[12]

THE SPECIAL ENVOY

George Moose was already preparing another idea. In August, he had broached the idea of the United States naming a special envoy to reach out to Buthelezi and to facilitate reconciliation with Mandela and with the transition process in general. He suggested his idea to Buthelezi in September but received no reaction. Mandela, when Moose raised the idea, told Moose he would think about it, raise it with his advisers, and get back to me with his views.

The White House and the State Department agreed that the ideal person would be Franklin Thomas. I heartily agreed. Thomas was president of the Ford Foundation and had been involved in South Africa for many years. He was known most in this regard for leading in 1981 the Commission on U.S. Policy toward South Africa, which issued the report *South Africa: Time Running Out.* He was well-known and respected by both Buthelezi and Mandela.

Thomas was asked by Washington in October and agreed to undertake the assignment but was pleased with my suggestion that we first sound out both Mandela and de Klerk. Others had made efforts at mediation, sometimes haplessly. A South African religious group that had approached me earlier in the summer claimed to have lined up a meeting between Mandela and Buthelezi with former secretary of state James Baker as mediator. I was asked to help ensure Baker's participation. I checked with the two parties and discovered that there was not only no agreement by the two leaders to meet, but not even an agreement for a meeting of their senior advisers. I cautioned Baker, who was prepared to be helpful if he could be, that the arrangements were not in place and in large part he was being invited on false premises. He wisely declined the invitation.

For reasons explained below, we put off the discussion of the envoy with de Klerk and Mandela until late October. Meanwhile, the White House began to back away from the idea of an envoy of the president, thinking more of a "second-track," private mission. In my view, this limited our options. I believed that having an envoy repeat the same arguments again to Buthelezi that we had been making these past several months would have little impact. Buthelezi now regularly complained of "foreign pressures" and seemed not to be moved by them.

Another option would be to take a much harder line, which would indicate that, if he did not move toward compromise, we would disassociate ourselves from him publicly and otherwise. Under these circumstances, we would support further steps to isolate him internationally and perhaps encourage steps that were then being threatened by the government, for example, taking away his budget, withdrawing his control over the KwaZulu police. This was risky, however. It could drive Buthelezi further into a corner, convince him he had no other option but armed resistance. We could also share responsibility if a government crackdown or Buthelezi's own actions led to even more violence.

Alternatively, an envoy could explore in more depth Buthelezi's real bottom line. This would mean getting beyond general debates about issues such as federalism and capitalism, and to the hard issues of power sharing. The danger here would be to enmesh ourselves in extremely sensitive power relationships among the main parties and players. We might find ourselves urging compromises that would later be rejected by the rank and file of the ANC.

But we would lose these options, I argued, if the envoy were on a "second-track" mission. Only an authoritative messenger from the White House could convey the harder-line option or even, at this late stage in the negotiations, undertake the more intrusive role of power sharing.

Thomas, however, saw it differently. Given his long association with South Africa, including his long personal relationship with Buthelezi and his more recent but close relationship with Mandela, he believed he could be most useful in coming as a friend, not wearing the mantle of an official emissary. He would thus be able to talk more candidly and deeply with his interlocutors. He even declined to carry a letter from the president, believing such communications were best conveyed through the ambassador. He saw his mission thus as helping overcome deep differences in perceptions between the two leaders, not as mediating over power sharing or other critical issues in the negotiations. He also sensed some division between the White House and the State Department about how to approach Buthelezi, which reinforced his preference for acting privately.[13]

It was not fruitful to broach the idea of the envoy with de Klerk until early November. Both de Klerk and Mandela were traveling in September, including to the United States. There was then a flurry of meetings between the various parties in September and October designed to overcome the impasse. The government was meeting with the new Freedom Alliance, and Mandela was reaching out to General Viljoen.

When I did raise the subject, de Klerk was at first skeptical of what an envoy could accomplish. The government and the ANC were now close to agreement on outstanding constitutional issues, and a parliamentary vote on an interim constitution was scheduled for midmonth. De Klerk's latest meeting with the Freedom Alliance had not gone well, but he had invited them to a bush retreat the following week and was hopeful some progress could be made there. If not, he contemplated presenting the looming government-ANC agreement to a referendum. If a referendum was not presented, then the agreement could be presented to the parties as the best and most reasonable compromise on these issues, and the recalcitrant parties would be told the government was prepared to go ahead without them, if necessary.

After some thought, de Klerk concluded that the envoy might be helpful in one of two ways. If there were agreement on some basic issues with the Freedom Alliance, perhaps the envoy could help persuade Mandela to agree to a "leaders meeting," one of the Freedom Alliance's pet demands, as a way of helping the alliance out of the corner it had painted its way into. If there were no agreement, then the envoy might usefully convey to opposing parties, including Buthelezi, that the offer on the table by the government and the ANC was a fair and reasonable one. The envoy could make clear that the international community would not support parties in their opposition to it being put into place.

De Klerk added that he felt that every step by the international community to concretize the normalization of relations with South Africa helped to lock in the transition process. I told him that the United States was nearing completion of legislation that would set U.S.–South African relations on a positive footing, and that Secretary of Commerce Ron Brown would be visiting South Africa shortly to give new impetus to economic and commercial ties.

I raised the proposal with Mandela a few days later. With his customary graciousness, Mandela made clear that he was deeply appreciative of President Clinton's focus on South Africa and of the impetus behind the proposal. He appreciated as well our consulting with him on it and made a point of saying that we were under no obligation to agree with his response. Nevertheless, Mandela took an even dimmer view than de Klerk did of the proposed mission. He saw nothing an envoy could say that had not been said by others. There had been appeals by the UN secretary-general, who had met with Buthelezi in Mozambique, by Chancellor Kohl of Germany, by Prime Minister Major of the United Kingdom, and by several African leaders, including Robert Mugabe and Sam Nujoma, to say nothing of Western ambassadors in South Africa. Mandela thought Buthelezi was getting more attention by staying outside the negotiating process than he would if he were part of it. An envoy would feed this impression. Rather, Mandela suggested, President Clinton should send a message that if Buthelezi would join the multiparty negotiations, he would be received by the White House, but not otherwise. The envoy could be sent as a follow-up if Buthelezi agreed.

Mandela was also strongly opposed to the idea of a "leaders meeting." He felt the impetus behind this was to discredit the ongoing negotiation process. Within the ANC, moreover, there was lingering opposition to elevating Buthelezi to a position as member of a troika settling South Africa's future.

Like de Klerk, Mandela was anticipating the end of the long period of constitutional negotiations. Like de Klerk as well, he contemplated testing the strength of opponents such as Buthelezi. In this he made a distinction between Buthelezi and Viljoen. Mandela was very much focused on his talks with Viljoen—indeed he would be seeing him following our meeting. He anticipated Viljoen splitting from the Freedom Alliance, further isolating the remaining recalcitrant parties.

We did not have to act right away on these cautious soundings, for Buthelezi was himself traveling in November to the United States, where there was an opportunity to convey a high-level message. Thomas, meanwhile, decided to put off his mission until January so as to take advantage of a ceremony inaugurating the new Ford Foundation office in Johannesburg.

I urged that Buthelezi be invited to Washington during his visit in November, not at the presidential level, which was not appropriate under the circumstances, but perhaps at the vice presidential level. It seemed worth making such an effort. Washington demurred, however, and Buthelezi's people made clear that he would not accept an invitation from any level lower than the White House. In the end, the secretary of state sent him a letter while he was in New York. The letter set out some of the main points of our position on the federalism debate in stark but still encouraging tones. Washington wanted to make clear that the U.S. position on federalism did not envision establishing ethnically pure enclaves or undemocratic autonomous units. But the secretary reiterated the U.S. position that had been stated publicly a few weeks earlier that we would hold a new South African government to its preelection commitments, including shared power and the protection of minorities. Buthelezi could expect strong support from the American people and government if he would take the political risk and pursue his cause within the proposed constitutional arrangement.

At the end of November, Secretary of Commerce Ron Brown made his highly publicized visit to South Africa. Brown met with Buthelezi in Durban. Buthelezi declined Brown's invitation to meet one-on-one, suspecting that it was only a way of putting more pressure on him. Brown's meeting was cordial but made little headway on the issues dividing Inkatha from the other key negotiating partners. Brown nonetheless later urged Mandela to meet with Buthelezi, lending U.S. support to an initiative being undertaken by Archbishop Desmond Tutu and Methodist leader Stanley Mogope.

Inkatha was to some extent feeling the pressure. Buthelezi adviser Oriani-Ambrosini called the State Department in November to deny accusations that Inkatha was not negotiating seriously. Buthelezi would later make the point to a visiting congressional delegation that, while having withdrawn from the multiparty forum, Inkatha had continued to negotiate with other parties "as hard as we ever did before."[14]

But events continued to move forward, leaving Inkatha isolated. The ANC and the government reached final agreement on the interim constitution in early November, including on the long-outstanding issue of voting on a permanent constitution. After one last unsuccessful effort to reach accommodation with the members of the Freedom Alliance, de Klerk moved forward without them. He submitted the interim constitution to the Parliament and, with its approval, the transition process was formally under way. The Transitional Executive Council, a multiparty structure that would oversee the administration of the country through the elections, came into being. Shortly afterward, the Parliament restored South African citizenship to the formerly "independent" homelands of Ciskei, Bophuthatswana, and Transkei. Preparations for the elections in April 1994 gained momentum.

Buthelezi reacted strongly to these developments. In a memorandum prepared for his meeting with Archbishop Desmond Tutu on December 15, which he provided me shortly afterward, Buthelezi stated:

> Once the South African Constitutional Bill becomes law, everything I am, and everything I am associated with, and all my political leadership will be directed to opposing the constitution itself. . . . I reject the principal functions of the TEC. I reject it in part and in whole. I will have nothing to do with it. I will not lift one single finger to co-operate with it. In fact, I will defy it every time it looks in my direction. For me, the TEC is drawn up as an instrument for the annihilation of KwaZulu and the IFP—most certainly for the annihilation of KwaZulu.[15]

As for international pressure, Buthelezi was blunt:

> I am utterly sick and tired of being told how wrong I am by a world out there that is accepting a settlement, just any settlement, so long as it is a

settlement, and being told to accept it at whatever cost. I am utterly sick and tired of being told that I have no democratic right to oppose a constitution in which I fail to get fundamental amendments which would have led to an all party solution.[16]

The stage was thus set for denouement in 1994. Little by little, the pillars of the Freedom Alliance would fall in the coming months—Bophuthatswana would collapse into violence and be taken over by the TEC in March; within days, two other homelands, Venda and Ciskei, would go the same way; the Volksfront then registered for the election, breaking with the more conservative Afrikaner parties. But reconciliation with Buthelezi, upon whose cooperation a peaceful transition still depended, would come only within days of the April 24 election, and then only after one major effort at international mediation.

8

Looking Left and Right

For all South Africa's leaders now face a decision: whether to plunge this country into further turmoil and violence, which no leader will later be able to control, or bravely to defy the fomenters of violence and lead the country in another direction. The latter is the more difficult challenge, but it is the only noble one open to the country, the only real role for a leader.
—PRINCETON N. LYMAN, *September 1, 1993*

WHILE MUCH ATTENTION WAS NECESSARILY FOCUSED ON BUTHELEZI and the Inkatha Freedom Party, other elements resisting the transition demanded attention. From the radical left of the anti-apartheid movement, the Pan Africanist Congress (PAC) stood out as a party that rejected the mode of negotiations, the leadership of the ANC in those negotiations, and, most critically, the suspension of the armed struggle. The PAC's armed wing, the Azanian People's Liberation Army (APLA), would visit violence upon innocent people in this period in a way that shook the confidence of the population and divided the anti-apartheid movement. From the right, an even more complex situation emerged. A combination of right-wing elements in the "homelands," recalcitrant Afrikaners, particularly in the rural areas, and disgruntled elements within the security forces posed a threat, even of a coup, that proved hard to measure as the process came ever closer to the moment of truth: the election of April 1994. Addressing these threats was crucial to the success of the transition.

THE PAN AFRICANIST CONGRESS

The PAC was formed in 1959. It drew its inspiration from a collection of efforts within the liberation movement that distinguished themselves from the racial inclusiveness of the ANC. Most prominent in this movement in the early period was the Azanian People's Organization (AZAPO). Inspired by the Black Consciousness Movement articulated by Steve Biko, adherents of AZAPO and related organizations rejected any prominent role for whites in the liberation struggle and were critical as well of the prominent role of Indians within the ANC. Also, though not unambiguously, they saw the struggle in terms of class as well as race and were more firmly committed than the ANC to a socialist South Africa. AZAPO, the PAC, and other adherents split off from the ANC-inspired United Democratic Front's "ungovernability" campaign in the 1980s. One of the defining moments of their differences with the UDF was in the debate in 1985 over whether to receive Senator Edward Kennedy, who was in a way making a reprise of his brother Robert's dramatic visit of 1966. For AZAPO, Kennedy was simply a representative of the capitalist class, whereas the UDF gave him a cautious welcome. Deeper issues drove the rivalry, of course, particularly competition for adherents among the youth and labor. Eventually, rivalry between them led to violence.[1]

By the 1990s, however, AZAPO was no longer a force to be reckoned with. Although appealing to intellectuals, and with adherents in the press and a number of important civic organizations, it had lost the support from some of Biko's strongest adherents, who questioned the intellectual depth of its leaders with regard to the meaning and message of Black Consciousness. AZAPO seemed unsure of itself as elections loomed, unable to decide whether or how to participate, unable to launch a truly popular following or political base. At the same time, the PAC had established itself both outside and within South Africa. It had established a smaller but significant rival labor federation to that allied with the ANC and a vocal youth following. African states such as Nigeria, Zambia, Tanzania, and Zimbabwe were sympathetic with the PAC's militancy and had urged the ANC and PAC to join forces. The Organization of African Unity (OAU) recognized both the ANC and the PAC as legitimate representatives of the South African people. When de Klerk unbanned it along with other anti-apartheid groups in 1990, the PAC faced decisions on how it would participate in the transition process. Its initial decision was not to do so, or at least not to do so on the terms agreed to by the ANC.

In October 1992 the PAC walked out of the alliance of anti-apartheid groups, the Patriotic Front, which the ANC had formed to proceed with the negotiations. The PAC objected to the negotiations taking place within South Africa, to the participation of the chairs (South African judges), and generally to compromises of form and style that recognized the South African government as a legitimate partner. For the next fifteen months the PAC would move in and out of the process but also undertake its own separate negotiations with the government regarding the conditions for suspending its armed struggle. These conditions were basically an agreement on the joint control of security forces and a "mutual cease-fire" of the two parties.

The extent of PAC support among the black population was questionable, but the PAC was in a position to act as spoiler. One of its ideological allies, for example, was the leader of the Transkei, Bantu Holomisa. Holomisa was an ANC supporter; indeed, he would go on to be one of its most popular members after the election. (Holomisa was expelled from the ANC, however, in 1996, after accusing the ANC, and Mandela personally, of taking secret funds from entrepreneur and hotel-gambling magnate Sol Kerzner.)[2] But in the period leading up to the election, Holomisa shared the PAC's skepticism about the negotiating process, as he constantly urged the inclusion of an outside "neutral" chair and argued the need for an international peacekeeping force to ensure a free election. On the former point, if not the latter, he was much closer to the PAC's position than that of the ANC. More important, it was widely believed that Holomisa gave sanctuary within the Transkei to APLA guerillas. APLA was suspected in vicious attacks that took place on a golf course in the Eastern Cape in November 1992 and attacks on white patrons in a restaurant in Queenstown in December, in a pub in Cape Town, and, most horribly, in July 1993, at St. James Church in Cape Town. In the latter incident, five gunmen burst in on an all-white service, began shooting round after round of bullets, and then hurled several hand grenades before leaving. Twelve people were killed, including the wife of the minister, and fifty-six were injured, some maimed for life. An attack on a church was seen as particularly unsettling:

> Never before had white South Africans suffered so grievously from the violence that had long racked the black townships. A few blacks sneered at the white cries of outrage because of this, but for the most part the shock was universal. Archbishop Tutu denounced the massacre as "a devilish deed—low and despicable," and the ANC said it would launch its own search for the killers.[3]

Among the youth, however, the PAC found resonance for its more militant stance, especially when the transition process experienced crisis. As described in chapter 6, one of the few times when Mandela lost the crowd, in a disconcerting moment for those of us watching, was during the Jubilani Stadium rally in April 1993 following the assassination of Chris Hani. Mandela was booed when he reported de Klerk's message of sympathy and there were murmurs of dissent when he called for calm. At that very moment, Clarence Makwetu, president of the

PAC, arrived on the podium. There was a roar of approval as he was introduced and again as he issued a much harsher message than Mandela's.

In the long run, both the PAC and Makwetu would prove to have little underlying support among the electorate. And the militancy that their message aroused in the youth would prove, in a tragic incident, their undoing in the final stages of the election. But in the months leading up to the election, the PAC was a threat to a peaceful transition.

The dilemma for the PAC, however, was that the longer it stayed out of the process, the more difficult it became to organize itself for the elections and win support from moderate groups within the black population. It was this dilemma on which the United States played as it sought to bring pressure on the PAC to end its violence and rejoin the transition process.

As will be described in more detail in the next chapter, the United States put in place an elaborate program for election support. One element of this was a joint project with the National Democratic Institute (NDI), the International Republican Institute, and the Joint Center for Political Studies. This project provided professional advice to each of the South African parties that would for the first time be participating in an election. Assistance covered polling, platform development, constituency mobilization, and campaigning, among other things. It was a hands-on, highly practical course in electoral politics taught by political professionals from the United States and other countries. In one case, President Clinton's principal pollster was employed by NDI on the project. The training was invaluable and the PAC recognized from the beginning that this was something it desperately needed.

The United States also was instituting programs to train future diplomats, administrators, and other professionals who would be needed from the majority population in the new South Africa. However, in December 1992, in the wake of the attacks attributed to APLA and the PAC's assumption of an intransigent position on the transition process, the United States made the decision to exclude the PAC from any of these programs. This became the leitmotif of numerous discussions I would have with PAC officials over the next thirteen months. Each time they approached me about participation in one of these programs, I reemphasized our position that we could not support any party that did not renounce violence and suspend its armed struggle. Our official position was stated by George Moose in June 1993:

> No element of the administration's support for democracy in Africa is more basic than our support for the negotiating process in South Africa. The important ingredients of that policy are that we must continue to applaud those acts of positive compromise. . . . [W]e must also continue to criticize those who fail to join in that process. . . . And we must continue to

speak out against those who perpetrate violence regardless of their political views or grievances, those who would undermine the effort to conclude a peaceful negotiated change.[4]

In December 1992, one of the PAC's most distinguished members, Dingang Moseneke, resigned as vice president of the PAC. Moseneke saw the handwriting on the wall, namely, that the future lay with the transition process, not with armed revolution.[5] Nevertheless, Moseneke urged us not to write off the PAC, but if possible to involve its members in our programs. Our position on PAC participation remained firm, but I carried on a continuing dialogue with the PAC leadership, in particular with Foreign Secretary Gora Ebrahim, General Secretary Benny Alexander, and probably the PAC's most intellectually capable representative, Patricia de Lille. It became apparent that the PAC was itself torn and in disarray. Moderates within the party earnestly wanted to end the armed struggle, recognizing that this was a precondition to participating fully in the negotiating process, but they were thwarted by the more militant members, who insisted that "we must keep one foot in the bush."[6] Another important weakness was the lack of strong political control by the PAC over its armed wing. This lack of control was laid bare when the PAC tried to distance itself from APLA's reputed attacks in the Eastern Cape, claiming that it did not dictate to APLA.

Mandela recognized this weakness in the PAC, contrasting it unfavorably with the strict political supremacy within the ANC. In an interview with the *Sowetan* in December 1992, while careful to show respect for the PAC's liberation credentials, Mandela noted:

> The PAC is a liberation movement—it is entitled to have a liberation army. . . . It's entitled to conduct operations when the time is appropriate.
>
> But I am highly critical of the fact that there does not appear to be political control over APLA. The statement that has been made by Deputy President Johnson Mlambo [to this effect] has created a great concern in me. Any liberation army, if it's going to be a disciplined and well-organized army, must be under strict political control—as Umkhonto we Sizwe [the armed wing of the ANC] is. . . . We will not allow them to conduct operations without the express consent of the ANC. It is distressing, alarming, that APLA is under no control of the PAC.[7]

We had another worry, however. The militancy of the PAC aroused threats of South African government military action against suspected APLA sites in Zimbabwe and the Transkei. Understandable as this reaction might seem, such raids would resurrect the image of a South Africa lashing out at its neighbors and create a dilemma for the ANC, which had little use for the PAC or APLA's tactics, but which would be honor-bound to denounce these attacks on a fellow liberation movement.[8] It did not help the government's case, moreover, that, as dastardly as

these APLA attacks were, there was enough suspicion of "third force" provoca-
teur activity in South Africa that some questioned where these attacks were really
coming from. APLA at the time denied responsibility for the attack on St. James.
Only years later, in hearings before the Truth and Reconciliation Commission,
did APLA admit to it.[9]

Thus we directed our efforts to dissuading the government from any cross-
border attack on Zimbabwe, seeking instead for the neighboring states to distance
themselves from APLA. In late 1992 and again in 1993, the United States urged
these states to withdraw support for any further armed actions within South
Africa. In late 1993, Tanzania and then Zimbabwe made such statements. The
UN secretary-general, Boutros Boutros-Ghali, appealed to the PAC in October
to abandon the armed struggle and join in the elections. Increasingly, the PAC
was being isolated.

We also appealed to Holomisa to defuse the crisis over his possible harboring of APLA guerillas in the Transkei. Holomisa was the one homeland leader
with whom the United States was in regular official contact, since he had announced that the Transkei would reincorporate into South Africa as part of a
negotiated settlement. He and I exchanged views often. He had taken over the
Transkei by coup from a leader beholden to the South African government and
almost immediately had set himself up in opposition to the apartheid regime. A
clever political operator and a well-trained military leader, Holomisa was extremely popular with the grass roots of the ANC for his populist views, his belligerent denunciations of the South African government, and his readiness to
confront the government on almost any occasion. While he was a member of the
ANC, his views on the transition and the peace process, as noted, were closer to
those of the PAC, and such militancy added to his popularity, especially among
the rank and file. Holomisa was personable and had an appealing sense of humor.
When meeting visiting American dignitaries, he would introduce himself with a
deprecating smile as "the military dictator of Transkei." Holomisa seemed pleased
at being able to play it both ways, as a popular member of the ANC with a bright
future in a new government and as a populist with alternate support from the
constituents of the PAC and the radical left.

But in March, following a string of attacks on whites in areas neighboring the
Transkei, the situation became very tense. To defuse the situation, de Klerk requested Justice Goldstone to investigate the incidents, including the charge that the
Transkei was harboring APLA forces. Holomisa rejected the charge and refused
to cooperate with the Goldstone Commission. The commission, he said, was a
creature of the South African government and therefore had neither credibility
nor authority in the Transkei. Holomisa would countenance only an investigation
by the Transkei's chief justice. When it appeared the South African government

might undertake military action, Holomisa threatened that he would use such a step to bring the entire negotiating process to a halt.

After conferring with Justice Goldstone, I called Mandela and urged him to persuade Holomisa to find a way to cooperate with the Goldstone Commission and avoid what could be a major destabilizing situation. Mandela, who thought of Holomisa as a promising but impetuous young man, arranged a meeting between de Klerk and Holomisa. That, however, produced only more bitter exchanges. On April 7, Goldstone asked me once again to help in working out a compromise. Goldstone had a high opinion of the Transkei's chief justice and was prepared to work with him. I phoned Holomisa that day. Holomisa was in a belligerent mood. He said he did not care about international opinion, that he did not trust Goldstone, and that he would endorse only a purely Transkei investigation.

Carefully but firmly, I reminded Holomisa that neither the U.S. government nor virtually anyone else in the world recognized Transkei's independence. While the embassy had counseled the South African government not to take military action, we had consistently held the South African government responsible for whatever transpired in the homelands and could not argue with the government on security grounds if no other alternative than military intervention was available. I went on to caution Holomisa that anything that upset the negotiations only played into the hands of the opponents of democratic transition. I therefore urged him to work out something with Goldstone, who alone, I said, could give credibility to any investigation of the truth about APLA operations in the Transkei. Holomisa finally said he would instruct his chief justice to work out something with Goldstone. The OAU's special representative in South Africa, Ambassador Joseph Legwalla, weighed in with Holomisa along the same lines, as did the ANC. By the end of the week, after an exchange of faxes between Holomisa and myself, and further intervention by Mandela, a compromise was struck. Goldstone left for the United States on April 9, satisfied that a solution had been found.

But on April 12, following the assassination of Chris Hani, Holomisa announced that the whole investigation would be canceled. According to information passed to me by the Foreign Ministry, Holomisa sent a bitterly worded message to de Klerk blaming him for, in the words of the ministry official, "virtually every problem in South Africa including the assassination of Hani." I sent an urgent message to Holomisa asking him to reinstate the investigation, but to no avail. The turmoil within South Africa in the aftermath of the Hani assassination diverted attention from the Transkei, and the immediate crisis faded. But the problem of the PAC and its inability or unwillingness to give up its militant stance continued, producing another tragic event.

In August the Congress of South Africa Students (COSAS), affiliated with the ANC, and the Pan Africanist Students Organization (PASO), affiliated with the PAC, launched "Operation Barcelona," a militant strike against the school system of the Western Cape. Every day, youthful marchers roamed the streets of townships in the Western Cape, with the more militant among them repeating the ominous trademark slogan of the PAC: "one settler, one bullet." "Settler" originally referred to Afrikaners who had first settled the land and pushed aside and killed the indigenous population, but in current parlance it referred to any white person. On August 25, a young American Fulbright scholar, Amy Biehl, was driving one of her South African colleagues home to the township of Guguletu. Amy drove unwittingly into one of the demonstrations. Seeing her blond hair and white face, the demonstrators shouted "Settler!" and attacked. She was hit by a rock as she fled her car and then stabbed. She died against the fence of a gas station to which she had been fleeing.

I had met Amy Biehl at a reception for Fulbright scholars just a few months earlier. Like everyone who met her, I was taken by her sunny disposition, her unpretentious commitment to freedom in South Africa, her promise, and her spirit. She had just been accepted to graduate school and was scheduled to leave South Africa on August 27. I was in Pretoria when the news came of her death. I was completely depressed. I had been hosting a reception for visiting stars from the National Basketball Association, there to start a basketball program for township youth, when the news came. I left the reception to make a phone call. The very worst responsibility of an embassy is informing an American family that one of their loved ones has died overseas, far from them. I always felt, however, that this was my responsibility. I called Amy's parents that night. I will never forget the words of her mother. After the initial, terrible shock of what I had to tell her, Mrs. Biehl said, "I hope she did some good. She so loved the people there."[10]

Amy Biehl's death epitomized the senselessness of much of the violence. Amy had spent nine months working on women's issues for the Community Law Clinic of the University of the Western Cape. She had been dedicated to the liberation of South Africa's majority and to the advancement of black women, who had borne so much under apartheid. She was held in esteem by such ANC notables as Dullah Omar, who would become Mandela's minister of justice, and Kader Asmal, who was a leading constitutional lawyer in the negotiations and who would also join Mandela's cabinet. Amy Biehl's death provoked enormous mourning in the Western Cape and further outrage at the violence accompanying the transition. It was front-page news throughout the country, and the memorials for her in the coming year would be attended by personages and township folk alike.[11] Only a day after her death, COSAS suspended Operation Barcelona, admitting that it was out of control.

Some again questioned all the attention to the death of a white person, when so many blacks had died in this struggle. In the embassy's press release on Amy's death, we dealt with the special character of Amy and that issue as well:

> [Amy's] death was senseless, as she only innocently drove into where the people attacked her. Indeed, it is more than senseless, for she was a tireless worker on behalf of democracy and equality in South Africa.
>
> Amy Biehl's murder is another of the brutal and terrible crimes against innocent people by those who perpetrate violence in South Africa. Only a few days ago, a three year old child was killed. Other women, children and elderly have been killed. It must stop if this society is to build a decent and safe future for all its citizens. This is what Amy devoted her time here to, and what millions of South Africans work toward every day.[12]

The impact on the reputation of the PAC bore out this conclusion. Despite PAC disclaimers and attempts to shift the blame to the ANC, several PASO members were eventually tried and convicted of the murder. Moderates within the PAC nevertheless sought to distance themselves from the act. In a letter, Gora Ebrahim asked me to convey the PAC's condolences to the family. But in my view this was not enough. In my reply to Ebrahim I wrote:

> I appreciate your saying that it is not the official policy of the PAC and its component structures, including PASO, to engage in attacks on innocent civilians. Yet, I must tell you that, in my opinion, this is not enough. At one level, PAC and PASO say they do not condone such violence. But their words at other levels say something else. Today [September 1, 1993], Transkei Regional PAC Vice Chairman Gilber Seneke is quoted as saying to high school students in Umtata that it was their duty to adopt such slogans as "Kill the Boer, kill the farmer." . . . The PASO youths arrested for the killing of Amy Biehl demonstrated at the courthouse with the slogan, "One settler, one bullet," the very slogan used by the wielders of the knives when they killed her. It was very clear what this slogan meant to them.

Ebrahim had tried to explain the anger and frustration of the youth as an underlying cause of the violence. To this I replied:

> It is not enough, Gora, to say that one understands the anger and frustration of the youth. Political leaders are not anthropologists, they are leaders. It is their job not to feed and foment that anger, not to play with it, but to channel it in other directions. Leaders must understand the meaning of their words and slogans on their followers, not pretend that they do not have that meaning. The meaning of these slogans with the youth has been made crystal clear. Leaders can no longer duck from it. Talk of the armed struggle carries exactly this connotation.

Ebrahim had pointed out, correctly, that the much greater violence that was occurring between the ANC and Inkatha did not involve PAC at all. But the difference was that the ANC and, in principle, the IFP officially deplored the violence and had committed themselves to the National Peace Accord. Only the extreme parties continued officially to encourage a policy of violence. I warned Ebrahim that the PAC could not escape from their association with this incident:

> It is true that until recently, the PAC was not involved in the senseless carnage in the townships. But that is no longer true. PAC is involved, directly and indirectly, when the perpetrators take encouragement from PAC and PASO statements and slogans. There is a price for everything. The price for talking loosely about violence is to reap the whirlwind of violence.

I concluded by referring to the repeated appeals from the PAC for participation in our electoral programs:

> Recently, we had another meeting with PAC officials to discuss assistance to the PAC's election campaign. Once again, we had to make clear that we cannot provide such assistance when the PAC's slogans call for armed struggle. Where in the world do parties campaign in elections without even calling a cease-fire? How can the US help the PAC fashion its message of "Kill the Boer, kill the farmer?" You and I have discussed this issue before. I wait for the day when we can establish a cooperative relationship with the PAC, but first the PAC must come to terms with its position on violence.[13]

The PAC did not recognize fully for some time the impact on its reputation and the cost of its inability, or unwillingness, to modify its militant slogans. Several times I complained to the PAC and asked it to rein in youth who were demonstrating in front of the trial of Amy Biehl's murderers and clearly trying to intimidate witnesses. The PAC finally took steps to curb them. In December, PAC general secretary Benny Alexander was visibly upset when I told him that the PAC had been excluded from meetings with Secretary of Commerce Ron Brown because of the Amy Biehl murder and the intimidation of witnesses by PASO-affiliated youth outside the trial chambers. Once again Alexander pleaded for participation in our electoral programs.

Increasingly isolated internationally and domestically, the PAC undertook negotiations directly with the South African government in October and November. This followed the long-threatened military raid by South Africa on a suspected APLA hideout in the Transkei. The raid was a total disaster, killing several unarmed youth and failing to uncover the suspected arms cache.[14] There was an outcry, including from the ANC, but by this time, the transition process had long passed the point at which Holomisa could stop it. In November, the PAC reached a tentative agreement with the government on a "mutual" but, on the part of the PAC, still conditioned cease-fire and plans for joint control of their respective security forces. On November 9, the PAC announced it would participate in the elections.

In January 1994, the PAC went a step further, announcing a suspension of the armed struggle, but again somewhat conditioned. Washington still refused to let PAC members participate in our programs, even as individuals not identified as party members. Finally, on January 16, 1994, Makwetu declared a "unilateral" suspension of the armed struggle, changing previously stated "preconditions" to "concerns" to be negotiated. The threat from the left was over.

Within days, we incorporated the PAC into our programs. Not a moment too soon. Our exclusion of the PAC had been objectionable to South African entities, such as Oscar Dhlomo's IMPD, that were partners in carrying out our electoral programs. Since the PAC was participating in the elections, the IMPD felt barring PAC members from the programs threatened the nonpartisan status of the institutions. Only a few days before the final PAC announcement, the director of the Joint Center for Political Studies informed the State Department it was "through" in South Africa if the ban could not be lifted.

The PAC never achieved its aims. Its clinging to the armed struggle and its consequent failure to understand the changes that South Africa was undergoing put it outside the mainstream. Throughout 1993 and early 1994, PAC officials bravely described a solid and growing base of support. But on one occasion they surreptitiously asked the embassy to help them pay their election registration fee, which of course we refused to do. In the election, the PAC polled only 1.2 percent of the vote. In a postelection assessment, PAC political secretary Jaki Serote told an embassy officer that the PAC had made three mistakes. One was that the slogan of "one settler, one bullet" had obscured everything else the party leaders tried to say. A second was the weak leadership of Makwetu. Third was not joining the TEC until the very eve of the election.[15] Serote spoke appreciatively of the U.S. electoral trainers to whom the PAC had late received access, adding ruefully, "thanks to whom we knew where our preparations had gone wrong."

Patricia de Lille, currently one of the PACs' few members of Parliament, echoed those sentiments:

> One of the other mistakes made was that we did not realize that in elections, the success of your participation, depends largely, or about 90 percent, on organization, coordination, management. So we were very weak on that. We still had to catch up on that. And we had missed the opportunity to work with those [American] NGOs to give us the capacity that could at least put us in a position to compete with the other older parties. So I think we lost, because [though] we did start working with organizations like NDI, that was only a couple months before the election.[16]

De Lille in particular, campaigning in the Western Cape, felt the repercussions of the Amy Biehl murder, even eight months after it happened. Asked how much it impacted the image of the party, she replied, "A lot. I was the premier candidate here and I know on just about every occasion, you could not get off any platform without addressing that issue. It really became a big stumbling block."[17]

And so it should have.

THE WHITE RIGHT

One of the things that made assessing the depth of right-wing opposition to the transition difficult was that the threat was often advanced, in stark and alarming terms, in order to push back against American or other foreign pressure on the government to make further concessions in the negotiations. The government was often of two minds on this. To demonstrate that it was in control and indeed confident of its negotiating ability, it conveyed reassurance that the security forces were loyal, that the government had taken their concerns into account, and that the transition could be well managed without any outside intervention. But the government also at various times warned darkly of unhappiness among the *Volk*, the National Party's and de Klerk's base constituency, and of potential discipline problems within the security force structure. Persons outside government variously shared these worries, either in hopes they were true or to warn us of the dangers.

For example, there was Hernus Kriel, minister of internal security, who had oversight of the police and with whom I made it a point to meet regularly. Kriel was known as one of the conservative hard-liners within the cabinet. He was sly and genial and held his cards close to his vest. Our conversations often took on a philosophical tone, to mask the issues we were really addressing.[18] Kriel, without amplification, would assure me in these meetings that the police would in the end stay loyal to the process and enforce the transitional arrangements. Yet he took the occasion in June 1993 to tell me that the right wing was in a position to start a civil war. APLA attacks and the provocative remarks of some of the ANC's radicals had hardened right-wing views. Almost casually, Kriel described a recent attack on the negotiating forum by white right-wing extremists, who broke in the doors and temporarily occupied the site, as "just the right's form of mass action."

The foreign minister, Pik Botha, would similarly from time to time raise the specter of right-wing resistance. He talked for more than an hour on this with Donna Shalala during her visit in connection with Oliver Tambo's funeral in May 1993. He became even more emotional in his meeting with Secretary of Commerce Ron Brown in November. Putting on his "gorilla suit," as one colleague of mine described these performances by Botha, he painted an ominous picture of the 600,000 whites in the country who had received military training and who could be mobilized in the cause of rebellion. The potential for trouble was great, he thundered.

De Klerk's attitude toward the military mirrored the conflicting assessments we were sometimes given. In his autobiography, he states, "I had personally never shared the concerns—often expressed by foreign visitors—regarding the loyalty of the security forces. I was always able to reassure them that the SADF and the police were professional organizations that would continue to accept the authority of constitutionally mandated governments."[19] Yet de Klerk admits that his relationship with these forces was a delicate one indeed. In a rather telling analysis, he writes:

> In my relationship with the security forces, I sometimes felt like a man who had been given two fully grown watchdogs—say, a Rottweiler and a bull terrier. Their previous owner [P. W. Botha] had doted on them. He had given them the tastiest morsels from his table and had allowed them to run free and chase cats all over the neighborhood. I had put a stop to all that. As a result, they did not particularly like me—although they had an ingrained sense of obedience. When I took them for walks in the neighborhood, I put them on leashes and stopped them from chasing cats. I could determine the general direction in which they would move, but they would walk at their own pace, sometimes wanting to go back, sometimes straining to chase a passing cat, sometimes happily walking in my direction. I could guide them, but I knew if I pulled too hard, I might choke them—or they might slip their collars and cause pandemonium in the neighborhood.[20]

HOW REAL WAS THE THREAT?

In the embassy, we were constantly reassessing this threat. Embassy personnel stayed in touch with all the parties, including even the most extreme, such as the Afrikaner Weerstandsbeweging (AWB), to gauge their mood and their degree of support. I also drew on the observations of astute visitors, some of whom had especially valuable entrée to retired military officers and intelligence experts. Though our contacts with the SADF had been seriously curtailed under sanctions, I worked to build these back in the months leading to the election so as to establish both communication and a vision of the future under a democratic regime. We exchanged views and assessments with our key allies as well, particularly with the German and British ambassadors, with whom I had a monthly breakfast to share views and assessments.

To thwart the threat, we sent signals to the security forces of the dire consequences for South Africa if the transition was indeed cut short by military action. But as the threat derived over time from the action of various leaders outside the government, we focused great attention on them, seeking to help bring them into the process. In the end, it was noble leadership emerging on the right that made the difference.

Assessing the threat required doing away with stereotypes. Just as the threat from Inkatha was magnified by romantic visions of a warrior Zulu nation asserting itself as of old, the threat from the Afrikaner population was often exaggerated by visions of the stout resistance that nearly defeated the British in the Boer War. Stories of Afrikaners leaving their farms, carrying their rifles, and banding together for long guerilla campaigns were recycled as people warned of the depth of resistance that could be encountered. Some of this resistance was indeed manifest, for example in the sometimes comic antics of the far right AWB, whose leader, Eugene Terreblanche, issued the most intransigent statements and rode up to the party's rallies on a white horse. Rural Afrikaners were perhaps the most threatened by change. Managing large farms and dependent on sizable government subsidies and largely docile farm labor, they were potential victims of future land reform, the organization of farm labor, and, most of all, a deteriorating security situation in which elder farm families in particular were already being victimized. A series of killings of farmers in this period heightened tension in the countryside.

But the Afrikaner population in the 1990s was not the same as that of 1948, when the National Party came to power on the same sentiments and fears and instituted the formal policies that came to be known as apartheid. In what Nelson Mandela once called the most successful affirmative action program of all time, the more than four decades of National Party rule, with its racial quotas and other forms of favoritism, had moved Afrikaners from rural poverty into government, the universities, business, media, and the arts. As the embassy noted in one of our assessments of the threat, the white right and the Afrikaner people were not coterminous:

> Unlike 1948 when the National Party came to power, most Afrikaners are not rural but urban or suburban. They are part of the modern economy with taxes, mortgages, and school fees to pay. There are now only 60,000 white farmers in South Africa [out of a white population of 5 million], from whom the militant right draws much of its support, along with some miners. There is little evidence among the larger Afrikaner community of support—or even toleration—for organized violence.[21]

The situation among the security forces was more complex. The South African army had a rather small nucleus of full-time personnel. For extensive operations, it relied on calling up men from a much larger part-time set of reserves organized as the Citizen Force, the Commando Force, and national servicemen. The Commando Force in particular was likened to a local militia, and it was about this group along with the Citizen Force that concern about loyalty was greatest. Would they respond if called on to put down an insurgency of their fellow white residents? Would they fire on any white insurgent group? On this, opinions varied. But the critical factor was who would organize and lead such an uprising. Scattered resistance was worrisome, but it could not threaten the transition. The real threat would be if there was leadership on the right sufficient in stature to mobilize these groupings and overcome the historically fractured right-wing politics among them, and to do so with the skill to make such an uprising politically significant.

One such possibility came from within the highest level of the security forces themselves. Justice Goldstone had uncovered frightening plots of murder, provocation, kidnappings, and arms smuggling within both the military intelligence community and the police designed to undercut support for the ANC and to exhaust the black population in internecine warfare.[22] In late 1992, General Pierre Steyn verified these activities within the military after an investigation ordered by de Klerk.

De Klerk reacted to these reports by firing or suspending twenty-three senior military officers, including two generals and four brigadiers. Nevertheless, de Klerk himself admits that he dared not carry out too sweeping a restructuring of the armed forces lest he "cripple the force's morale." His reasoning was partly based on the need to keep the SADF intact through the difficult final months of the transition. But he confesses also that he did not know then how deep or high up the rot went, nor could he pursue the matter.

> Under normal circumstances, the obvious course would be to carry out a thorough purge of all those involved in wrongdoing and in the line of command which had allowed such wrongdoing to occur. I seriously considered the option of dismissing General Liebenberg [chief of the SADF] and a few other generals in the top structure of command. However, these were not normal circumstances.[23]

However, by the following July Liebenberg was retired and General Georg Meiring was appointed to succeed him. Minister of Defence Kobie Coetsee told me Meiring's assignment was to cut the ties between the SADF and the right wing.

Nevertheless, worries over the potential alliance between recalcitrant right-wing elements and capable military leadership persisted. In a private communication to me from a colleague with extensive contacts within these circles, the situation was described in his typically colorful terms:

> Yes, this place will probably muddle through without the Big Bang, but don't count on it. . . . There are hundreds of lunatics out there who already are trying to tear the place apart and are planning every conceivable form of *serious* mischief. . . . If they can pick up some serious SADF/exSADF leaders to organize their efforts they will be immeasurably more dangerous. They are working hard at that.[24]

In July 1993 I had received another private communication, based on discussion with knowledgeable sources, that put the threat in similarly nuanced terms, that is, "yes, but":

> There is a "third force" and it encompasses not only former high-level officials of the military and security establishment . . . but also rogue elements who still serve within the state. Moreover, the intelligence services must know who the key players in the "third force" are because they stem (in both past and present) from the intelligence and security apparatus. A particular problem is military intelligence, which de Klerk does not control.
>
> The objective of these "third force" operations is to strengthen the hand of the conservatives in the negotiating process. Thus, once a settlement is reached and a transitional government is in place, the third force will begin to melt away, no longer having a strategic goal on which to focus. Moreover, at that point, when the government and the ANC military forces are merged, the third force will be fighting against greater and greater force, increasingly against the state itself. . . . Intelligence files or support will have to be shared, and that will be the point of no return. For this reason the third force can only go so far, and will eventually begin to lose its force and rationale. To some extent, it is bluffing in its implicit threat of ongoing civil war.[25]

REACHING OUT TO THE MILITARY

The military, like any other institution, was not monolithic. Analyzing its intrinsic culture was always a matter of generalizations that had to be refined in practice. Within the military hierarchy, some officers had begun to question the direction of South African policies as early as the 1980s, and to voice their opinions openly after 1992.[26] The tradition of loyally following orders, moreover, cut both ways. In the 1980s, the military carried out the orders of its political leaders; in the 1990s it bowed to the changes under way:

> For many years, especially during the 1980s, the ministers of defense and cabinet members, the most influential cabinet members, considered the military as the most effective tool to sustain or implement their political objectives. And I think the culture in the defense force has always been, "so what do you want, we'll do it." But then, towards the second half of the 1980s, and especially in the early 1990s, there were attempts to question whether what we were doing is really lawful or legal. And it was quashed.
>
> So when P. W. [Botha] was replaced by F. W. [de Klerk], they were surprised that this man had new and fresh ideas, more capable of visualizing what the future would hold if we persisted with the present policies and so on and the courage to say, "Look, I think we're wrong. We've got to make changes." And the inherent discipline and loyalty compelled those

who even thought [otherwise] to say "fine, we'll do it." Even a guy like
Georg Meiring fell in line, because he was taught and trained that way.
He might not have enjoyed doing it, and he would have mumbled in his
soup, but he did it and everybody did the same.[27]

Moreover, there was recognition among the military's more thoughtful officers
that change was coming and that as an institution, and as individuals, they had to
begin preparing for it. Pierre Steyn, who would later help restructure the SADF
in fundamental ways, recalls:

> There was a growing tendency among seniors and even middle and ju-
> nior ranks to start voicing their opinion. Prior to 1992, nobody dared do
> that really. Towards the end of 1992 and 1993, people realized that polit-
> ical change in South Africa was inevitable and that it would affect every-
> one and every organization and it would affect you as an individual and
> your family and especially the Department of Defense. . . . The ordinary
> airman or soldier didn't really think about it, but as a senior officer I real-
> ized that what lay ahead was going to change our way of doing things
> fundamentally.[28]

Both de Klerk and Mandela reached the same conclusion about the senior
military: they needed to be co-opted to the transition. In 1992, the MK and the
SADF began meeting secretly to scope out the future structure of defense forces
after the election. Professional camaraderie developed rather early and soon the
two found common ground.[29] By November 1993, sources told the embassy, they
had come to an agreement. The SADF was satisfied that the basic structure of the
defense forces would be preserved, indeed with existing SADF cadres remaining
for a time in the upper ranks. The MK cadres would be integrated, with those
retired out given full military pensions.

Mandela and de Klerk also moved to reassure SADF officers that they had
little to fear from a new government. Mandela told me he began such meetings in
1993 and stepped them up in 1994. Mandela believed the right wing's hold over
the commandos was greatest in the Transvaal and Orange Free State but was
reassured from his contacts that the SADF had the will and resources to contain
the threat. For Mandela, however, the issue of amnesty for past crimes was tricky
because of his anger over government-provoked violence and the existence of a
third force within the security forces. Nevertheless, Mandela, in a key meeting in
early 1994, reportedly provided assurances to senior SADF officers that an amnesty
program would be put into effect that would basically preserve their freedom.[30]

De Klerk was accused of going even further. In the first flare-up between
de Klerk and Mandela after the election, de Klerk was accused of having engineered, in the final days of his administration, a mass application for amnesty of
some thirty-five hundred policemen.[31] Whatever the truth of this matter, it was

clear that concern over amnesty was on the minds of key officials within the government and the ANC in the months leading up to the elections. I had the clear impression from my frequent meetings with Minister of Defense, and concurrently Minister of Justice, Kobie Coetsee, that this was a key factor in ensuring the loyalty of the top military officers in the final stages of the transition.

From the embassy, we undertook several initiatives directed at the military. In 1993, USIA began a series of Worldnet programs, visits, and exchanges on civilian control of the military, affirmative action, and other aspects of civil-military relations in a democracy. We encouraged the work of Jakkie Cilliers and his Institute of Defence Policy (IDP). Cilliers is a South African war hero, decorated for his service in Angola, and highly respected within the SADF. Cilliers came out of his service convinced that the SADF needed to be fundamentally restructured to meet the demands of a new era. He believed it needed to shed the image and outlook that dominated the "total onslaught" period if the government was to establish a system of civilian control over military budgets and operations, a system that was basically absent in South Africa, and prepare for integration with the military wings of the liberation movement.

Working with former members of the ANC's MK, Cilliers created the only in-depth defense analysis institute in the country at the time and produced a series of reports and analyses on these issues. We directed American experts to IDP for seminars and exchanges with the institute staff and helped publicize its work. Retired lieutenant general Pierre Steyn, who would after the election become the first civilian defense secretary, did much of his preparatory work for this position at IDP.[32] He and Cilliers would in fact write up the concept and "engineer" the establishment of a civilian-directed Department of Defence under the Mandela administration, and Steyn would subsequently draw on the U.S. Department of Defense for assistance and advice, to which the doors had been opened during this period.[33]

But at the same time there were some ominous sounds coming from the security forces, and we felt it equally important to send a strong message back. In January 1994, as part of our steadily increasing contact with the SADF, we arranged for a briefing for a visiting congressional staff delegation by the SADF's military intelligence unit. The briefers openly raised the specter of significant divisions within the military should there be a violent confrontation between the government and the right wing. While acknowledging that they were positing a worst-case scenario, they described a potential sixteen-thousand-man right-wing guerilla army that could plunge South Africa into chaos. If this happens, the briefers said, the SADF would split.[34]

We knew that assessments by the National Intelligence Service (NIS, South Africa's equivalent of the American CIA) were less pessimistic. NIS assessments went directly to the president, while those of the military intelligence were trans-mitted through the SADF chief of staff. We wondered if the message we were receiving from the military was more than an assessment. There were other com-ments being made to us and to other embassies by military and intelligence per-sonnel to the effect that the transition should not be rushed, that there would be dangers if it was, that maybe the security situation would demand special measures. We also heard reports that the right-wing elements within the military were sow-ing rumors of crisis, trying to force the government to establish a state of emer-gency, and that some senior officers were sympathetic.

It seemed to us that some of the comments we were getting might well be feelers as to the American reaction if the security forces felt it necessary to estab-lish a state of emergency, even to delay the transition. We decided to send a clear message back. Through various channels, we made clear that we felt it critical that the transition timetable, now firmly fixed with elections on April 27, be maintained. We said that in our analysis there would be a greater security threat, from the majority, if the transition was derailed. Further, we said unambiguously that should there be a military coup or other security force intervention to delay or stop the transition, South Africa would become more isolated than ever before.

We had occasion to make this point more emphatically during the visit by Assistant Secretary of Defense Chas Freeman in February 1994. I had encouraged Freeman to make time in his schedule for a visit to South Africa. Freeman had extensive responsibilities across all the Middle East as well as Africa, but as a for-mer deputy assistant secretary of state for Africa, he appreciated the significance of South Africa. For the visit, Freeman made a special effort to assemble a formi-dable array of senior American military officers, including Rear Admiral Robert M. Nutwell from CINCEUR (Commander in Chief Europe) and Brigadier General James C. Riley of the Joint Chiefs of Staff. It was the highest-ranking military visit to South Africa in more than thirty years. In his meetings and brief-ings, Freeman encountered some of the same dire predictions as heard by the congressional staff, for example, reports that the country was bordering on anarchy. Freeman replied with two messages. One held out the vision of the kind of mil-itary cooperation that could come with a democratic South Africa, including military training, high-level exchanges, and specialized attention to such tasks as peacekeeping. Freeman said he would soon recommend rescinding the so-called Duncan guidelines, which restricted military-to-military contacts between the United States and South Africa throughout the 1980s and 1990s.

The second message related to the security situation. In a well-attended speech at Cilliers's IDP on February 11, Freeman took note of the level of violence that still marred the transition process. He reiterated that there was no disposi-tion within the international community to provide international peacekeepers to South Africa; the South Africans had the resources and capacity to control the situation. He then again described the opportunities that existed for cooperation after the election. In contrast to this vision, he went on to say that if there were any steps taken to thwart or overturn the election, South Africa would instead be thrust back into the isolation of the past.[35] Freeman made the same point in his press contacts.

I addressed these issues again in March 1994 in the face of persistent rumors of discontent within the security forces. In Johannesburg on March 23, just thirty-five days before the election, in a speech titled "Flying through the Storm," I made our most explicit public statement about the role we expected from the SADF:

> There is one institution that carries an especially great responsibility in this period. That is the security establishment. The loyalty and the patriotism of the security forces are vital to the success of this transition. It is a heavy responsibility to bear. Charges of third force activity within the security establishment make it even more difficult. . . .
>
> But there is a golden opportunity here as well. A modern democracy depends upon a loyal security establishment, one which takes its direction from civilian leadership and which defends the constitution of the state. The security establishment of South Africa, suffering as it has from charges, investigations, and the prospects of restructuring, has the opportunity to demonstrate its professionalism and its place in the new order.

I took the occasion to praise the work of the SADF in the East Rand, where it had brought down dramatically the level of violence, and to praise other, less-heralded, security force efforts to promote peace and stability. The key was that this attitude prevail.

> There is enormous professionalism in the SADF. I have seen it on many occasions.
>
> Nothing would damage that professionalism more than to waver for even a moment in defending the transition to democracy. In the face of internal crisis, there is no choice but, and I use the phrase intentionally, to soldier on in the cause of constitutional rule and democracy.
>
> The same is demanded of the security establishment by the level of violence it is called upon to contain. There can be no shortcuts, no reversion to martial law or other forms of military rule. That would plunge South Africa instantly back into the position of being a pariah state.[36]

The position of the international community on this issue reinforced the message Mandela was sending. In a meeting he held with retired generals who were leading a right-wing movement, Mandela talked of the consequences of civil war:

> If you want to go to war, I must be honest and admit that we cannot stand up to you on the battlefield. We don't have the resources. It will be a long

and bitter struggle, many people will die and the country may be reduced to ashes. But you must remember two things. You cannot win because of our numbers: you cannot kill us all. And you cannot win because of the international community. They will rally to our support and they will stand with us.[37]

COURTING A TROUBLED GENERAL

In several meetings he and I held during 1993, and in his meetings in Washington in July of that year, Mandela indicated his concern over the right-wing threat (for example, this subject came up in three of my meetings with Mandela during August 12–17), but he also indicated confidence that he could address this threat. Indeed, his confidence in this regard grew in the latter part of the year. Sometimes, I thought this was just a way of his getting me to back off from pressuring him, one more time, to reach out to Buthelezi. In these meetings, Mandela would say that Buthelezi was de Klerk's problem. But, in truth, Mandela had gauged correctly, as we did, that the emerging leader of the white right wing, retired general Constand Viljoen, was a man with whom one could deal on matters of principle and honor and the peace of the nation. We had made an assessment along these lines within the embassy, if still tentatively, in May, when Viljoen first emerged on the scene. In a press conference on May 11, Viljoen had said, "I have always been a responsible person and I see no reason to change now. I'm not here to lead a rebellion, train a white army, or do irresponsible things." Mandela met with him for the first time in August 1993. In the words of ANC aides, "General Viljoen won the old man's heart."[38] Viljoen would prove in the end the key to defusing the remaining threat of civil war from the right. But for many months he vacillated between peace and war.

If there was an epiphany for Viljoen, it came with the fall of Bophuthatswana in March 1994. As described in an earlier chapter, the right had congealed in 1992 in a strange alliance of two homeland leaders (Bophuthatswana's Lucas Mangope and Ciskei's Oupa Cqozo), the Conservative Party, some other, minor, white conservative parties, and Buthelezi. The association was variously known as the Freedom Alliance (FA) and the Concerned South African Group (COSAG). Buthelezi was out of place in this constellation and, as described in the preceding chapter, deserved individual attention. In late 1992, the question arose as to whether some of these "independent" homeland leaders could be brought around to accepting reincorporation into South Africa—as Transkei and Venda had done —and thus to break away from this alliance. There was another concern, however. Even if the question of reincorporation was left to the electorate, as some were considering at that time, confrontation with these homelands over the conditions for election was looming as an increasingly serious threat to the peace.

The ANC was dead set on obtaining the right to campaign freely in the homeland areas in any election. Otherwise, it foresaw a significant bloc of potential ANC votes taken away through either campaign fraud or intimidation. But in homelands other than the Transkei and Venda, such freedom was being denied. Rumblings of "mass action" against these homelands were thus repeatedly heard. The leader of Ciskei was feckless and not worth approaching on this matter. The most important such leader, therefore, the one with a significant resource base and some claim to legitimacy, was Lucas Mangope, leader of Bophuthatswana. Bophuthatswana was the largest of the homelands, contained some lucrative mining properties, and was known internationally for the lavish resort at Sun City, to which Bophuthatswana had doggedly invited celebrities to enhance its legitimacy. As described in chapter 6, I sought permission from Washington to meet with Mangope, a move that Mandela, who was also meeting with him, encouraged.

On December 15, the date of our appointment, a fleet of cars drove up to our residence in Pretoria. Immediately a group of some fifteen security personnel fanned out across the property. Once the security men were satisfied and had taken their positions around the house, Lucas Mangope, accompanied by one of his ministers, came in for coffee. I told my wife that I had never felt so secure in my own house.

It was the first meeting for Mangope with an American ambassador, and he was immensely pleased. He is a large man and handsome in an imposing way and on this occasion was impeccably dressed. Though I had made clear in setting up the meeting, and did so again as soon as it started, that the meeting did not indicate any change in the American policy of not recognizing the independence of the homelands, Mangope was eager to be able to make his case for the first time. Mangope argued that independence had not been imposed on Bophuthatswana by South Africa, but "seized" by the Tswana people, who had been forcibly incorporated into South Africa by the British. How could they have refused this historic opportunity? Mangope saw no reason to reincorporate into South Africa, even if it was democratic. It was apparent that Mangope was no democrat. He ran a one-party state that was propped up in part by subsidies from South Africa and enjoyed a cozy, if rather questionable, relationship with white figures who seemed able to move between ministerial positions in one homeland after another as they worked to slow the transition process.[39]

Mangope's suspicions of the ANC ran deep. He recounted efforts on the ANC's part to undermine him and to destabilize the homeland. The accompanying minister described the ANC as a "seven-headed monster." Thus Bophuthatswana would refuse the principal demand of the ANC to permit free political activity in Bophuthatswana. Mangope expressed equal suspicion of the multiparty negotiating process under way, arguing that none of the safeguards being discussed would prevent an ANC takeover after the election. On other issues I raised, such as allowing access to Bophuthatswana by UN peace observers and the International Committee of the Red Cross, Mangope indicated he might relent —but in fact he never did.

There was no give in Mangope's position. As I reported to Washington, we did not expect to sway the essentially nondemocratic Mangope from his positions, and we did not do so. We had hoped to open the door to some compromises that would avoid confrontation, but if Mangope would not modify his stance on any such possibilities, we said, we feared there would be a serious confrontation eventually. Over the next fifteen months Bophuthatswana continued, in its alliance with its conservative partners, to go in and out of the multiparty negotiations and to engage within that alliance in "bush retreats" and other negotiations with the government and with the ANC. In February 1994 Mandela announced further concessions to this alliance in regard to constitutionally guaranteed regional powers. But it was not enough to overcome their resistance. However, Mangope seriously miscalculated.

Probably instigated by the ANC, which promoted rumors that employees of the homelands risked losing their pensions if the homelands did not reincorporate, civil servants in Bophuthatswana began a major strike in March 1994. The situation quickly deteriorated. Mangope then turned to his white partners in the FA, asking for armed defenders. It was a disaster. His own troops rebelled at the sight of the white Afrikaners from the outlandish AWB rolling into Bophuthatswana, some of them shooting blacks indiscriminately. The troops turned on the "invaders." The AWB, always boasting of its white superiority, was humiliated: in front of photojournalists, Mangope's troops coldly executed three AWB members as they lay helpless on the ground. In short order, the TEC determined that the SADF should occupy Bophuthatswana and an interim administration should be established under South African control. Bop's "independence" was over.[40] Ciskei collapsed shortly afterward in almost exactly the same manner.

The Bophuthatswana saga was important for many reasons. It broke apart the alliance of white conservatives with black homeland leaders and exposed the falseness of the alliance's pretension that it represented a broad collection of minorities, especially black but also white, who were resistant to simple majority rule and especially an ANC majority. It also gave indication in the final weeks before the election that the SADF would not fall apart in the face of white-aided insurgency and would indeed be prepared to carry out orders to extinguish it. This was not cut and dried. General Meiring was initially prepared to have the SADF stand aside and allow Viljoen to organize a white militia to shore up Mangope. But when confronted by ANC members of the TEC and ordered by de Klerk to help the government take over the homeland instead, Meiring—if perhaps "mumbling in his soup"—bowed to authority and took appropriate action.[41] This left honorable conservatives such as Viljoen with some hard truths to absorb.

Constand Viljoen had been chief of staff of the SADF during the 1980s. He had been a hero of the South African operations in Angola and was deeply respected within the armed forces. He had retired in 1985 and returned to his farm, where he expected to live out the remaining days of his life. But fate decreed otherwise. Viljoen was deeply committed to the survival of the Afrikaner people —its language, its culture, its freedom. He did not begrudge the black South Africans their freedom, but he wanted the Afrikaners to have their own land, their own place—a *Volkstaat*. He gravitated to the protests of white farmers and shared their fears of ANC domination. Viljoen was strongly anticommunist and he saw in the ANC-SACP alliance the evils against which he had long defended his country. At a rally of angry and armed farmers on May 7, 1993, Viljoen was called on to speak. He described what he saw as the weak position from which Afrikaner interests were being pursued in the negotiations, a situation in which the government would "crumble and shiver" in the face of ANC-orchestrated mass action. "I said you don't negotiate with communists like this," he later recalled, "when you aren't in a position of strength. You have to get your own piece of cake, you can't give in all the time."[42] His vigorous speech was followed by shouts of "lead us, lead us." Thus he was catapulted into the political arena. Shortly afterward, the right-wing parties came together in the Afrikaner Volksfront (AVF), with Viljoen at its head.[43]

That is one version, at least, and it has some truth to it. But there is probably more, for Viljoen was flanked in his assumption of leadership by several other retired generals.[44]

It was not likely happenstance. Rather, these men saw in the fractured and politically inept leadership of the right wing a formula for at best fruitless protest, at worst a bloodbath in which no one would win.[45] Viljoen and his retired military allies provided a more formidable and at the same time more respected front with which to protect Afrikaner interests. In a meeting with Secretary of Commerce Ron Brown in December 1993, Viljoen said the generals had been "called to give guidance to our people." The Afrikaners were politically divided, and only the generals had strategic vision. Without the generals, Viljoen explained, the various factions would be left in the hands of hard-line politicians who were unwilling to compromise at all. "Ironically," said Viljoen, "the generals were preventing war."[46] They proved indeed sophisticated and intelligent as they weaved their way through the labyrinth of crises, confrontations, and negotiations that would follow. So opportune was their appearance on the scene in the spring of 1993 that rumors arose that the new front had been secretly created by the government to put pressure on the ANC and bring more pragmatism to the right wing, a rumor for which, however, there is no evidence.[47]

Throughout the next several months, Viljoen would vacillate between demon-strating the leadership needed for a military-based resistance and warning his fol-lowers of the difficulties and costs, indeed almost the futility, of such resistance:

> You see, the Afrikaner always thinks back to the Boer War and they said to me that the Boers in 1899 were in a worse position than we were, [so] why are you not prepared to fight? So, I said, the conditions are completely different and there are so many other reasons why it would be foolish to fight. But they kept on pushing me.[48]

Viljoen wanted to keep open the military option, but as only one option, while pursuing a negotiating alternative. He remained tempted by the military option, especially if it could be done without a major split within the SADF, with all the violence that would bring with it:

> Quite frankly, I realized that the choice to go to war would have created a very awkward situation in South Africa. Because I would have had to fight my own SADF, and even if I could alienate the commandos from the defense force, I still would not have helicopters and tanks. . . . But at that stage you also play a game of adding weight to your arguments [with] the mere fact that we were in a position to wage war. I think we could field about sixty thousand people very quickly, all lightly armed.

Viljoen also held the idea that it might be possible to create and defend a *Volk-staat* without civil war.

> My idea was not to start a new Anglo-Boer War with people joining in. My idea was to demarcate, like the UDI [Unilateral Declaration of Inde-pendence in Rhodesia/Zimbabwe], a certain area, say the Eastern Transvaal, and say to the negotiating persons, "Look here, you either demarcate this into a *Volkstaat* for the Afrikaner, or if you attack us we will resist. We're not going to attack you." This was the general idea I had.[49]

This combination of military skill and political ambivalence made Viljoen and his generals both potentially dangerous and yet also the best hope for overcoming the threat of right-wing violence. Ironically, in looking back on this period, de Klerk told me he doubted that the United States had had much influence on Viljoen. To which I replied, "It's interesting that you say that, because I spent a lot of time with Constand Viljoen."[50]

The embassy's dialogue with Viljoen began in October 1993 and intensified over the next seven months, down to the final dramatic decisions made just days before the election. At our first meeting, Viljoen said the situation was balanced on a knife's edge. He urged us to weigh in on delaying the installation of the TEC, though not the election date. He spoke of his ties to the SADF irregulars —the Citizen Force and the commandos—and predicted that the SADF would never fire on Afrikaners. Yet he was ready and authorized by the AVF to open

negotiations with the ANC (his earlier meetings had been secret). I told him that
the TEC was essential to the progress of the transition and, not incidentally, its
formation was an ANC condition for the lifting of economic sanctions. We could
not agree to advocating delay. I encouraged him to pursue an understanding with
the ANC. From then on, Viljoen and I agreed to stay in close touch.

Increasingly over the next several months, Viljoen called or visited me to
express either his hopes or his frustrations over his negotiations with the government and the ANC and to ask for our intervention. For our part, we appealed to
Viljoen's patriotism, his love of country, and his sense of honor in order to encourage him to eschew thoughts of violent resistance and to find his way into the
election process. Recognizing that between Viljoen's dream of a *Volkstaat* and the
ANC's determination to end race-based structures in South Africa once and for
all there was no real common ground, we urged, as did the ANC, that Viljoen
search for other ways than a *Volkstaat* to achieve the preservation of his people's
heritage and culture.

The idea of a *Volkstaat* was inherently impractical. First of all, there was no
natural, identifiable region of the country in which Afrikaners were a majority.
Second, if one was carved out artificially, it was questionable that it could be sustained economically unless it was given some of South Africa's premier economic
assets, which was not likely to be acceptable to the black majority.[51]

More fundamentally, preserving Afrikaner domination in any one region,
especially if Afrikaners were to become a minority there over time, was not possible without some form of race-based voting system. Indeed, given the nature of
the South African economy and the mobility of its labor, no such region would
be guaranteed to remain demographically static. Efforts to define this problem
away through "resident" versus "nonresident" voting rights, euphemisms describing a race-based system, only raised the specter of a separate nation, not a region
within a federal South Africa. Advocates of a *Volkstaat* also had to address the
question of what rights Afrikaners would have in other parts of South Africa if
they preserved special rights in that one region. Likely, not all Afrikaners would
move to a homeland when they had jobs, homes, and other roots in other parts of
the country.

But Viljoen and his supporters had to reach these conclusions themselves.
Thus in our conversations my staff and I would raise these practical questions,
press Viljoen and his staff for answers, and suggest the problems that resulted.
One of Viljoen's greatest difficulties was that he could never get his people to agree
on just where the *Volkstaat* should be.[52] For a long time, therefore, Viljoen was
unable to produce a map of the proposed *Volkstaat*. When he did, and it included
the capital, Pretoria, the impracticality of it all was evident. The ANC, led by
Thabo Mbeki and Jacob Zuma, was pursuing a similar dialogue. Their purpose,

like ours, was not to ask Viljoen to abandon his fundamental objective, that is, to protect the lives, the culture, and the identity of the Afrikaners; for Viljoen to do so would mean the loss of his constituency. The objective was to see if it was possible to define the future in different ways.[53]

Our objective was also to encourage him in his talks with the ANC. Viljoen was impressed with Mandela, but uneasy over the ANC as a whole. As he said to me one day, "I think I can trust Mandela. But can I trust all those Communists around him?" Viljoen also fell victim to splits within the ANC. Mbeki and Zuma, always the consummate negotiators, engaged Viljoen in almost endless discussions and proposals. They toyed with the concept of self-determination, how to accept it in principle without creating a new apartheid. By late December, they had negotiated with Viljoen's AVF an "interim strategic agreement," which would have pledged both parties on the one hand to "the introduction of non-racial democracy" and on the other to seeking ways to address expeditiously the commitment of many Afrikaners to "the ideal of self-determination in a Volkstaat." A committee would be set up to work on the problem further. Another intriguing idea was being developed. The ANC, it said, wanted evidence that there really was sentiment for a *Volkstaat*. If the AVF would stand in the elections, its vote could be seen as a referendum on the idea.

But as these discussions were proceeding in Johannesburg, Cyril Ramaphosa and Roelf Meyer were in protracted negotiations with the Freedom Alliance as a whole on constitutional matters. And on these Ramaphosa and Meyer were taking a hard line, with little concern for the impact on Viljoen's position. Moreover, in these latter negotiations, Viljoen was becoming hostage to the agenda of his FA partners, which did not always serve his interests.

On December 7, Viljoen asked to see me urgently. He was concerned over the ANC's insistence, coming from Cape Town, that the Freedom Alliance commit itself to the elections as a condition of any agreement. I called Mbeki to understand the ANC position and then phoned Viljoen to explain that the ANC would accept a commitment from the AVF to participate, "if agreements were reached between them" on other matters. But the ANC was dealing with the FA parties separately and not always consistently. Thus on December 13 Viljoen called me to report he was once again pessimistic. Again the ANC had demanded the FA commit itself to the election date before any agreements could be reached. For its part, the Freedom Alliance had issued its "bottom-line" demands in Cape Town. These demands were in my view totally unrealistic. Among other things, the FA demanded that the structures and assets of the existing homelands be preserved through the elections. It was a transparent attempt to deprive the parties of free political activity in the homelands during the campaign and leave them with no assurances of reincorporation afterward.

I advised Viljoen that he urge his FA partners to issue a statement committing themselves to the April 27 election date. Ramaphosa and Meyer were growing increasingly convinced, I told him, that the true aim of the Freedom Alliance parties was to use negotiations to postpone the elections and the transition process. (This suspicion would arise again in the final stages of negotiations with Buthelezi the following April.) Viljoen accepted the inevitability of the April election but was unable to persuade his partners to acknowledge the same.

At the last minute, Viljoen pulled back from signing the agreement he had negotiated with the ANC. Loyal to his conservative allies, he balked at what he saw as intransigence in the ANC's and the government's negotiations with the FA. He also did not perceive the kind of support from Mandela he needed. But most of all, Viljoen was under attack from his conservative white allies for even talking with the ANC. He thus had prepared a belligerent statement to announce his refusal to sign the agreement but was persuaded at the last minute by the ANC to soften it. His statement thus held out the prospect for further negotiation and eventual agreement. His press officer was distraught at this reversal. He told one of our embassy officers that an agreement with the ANC would "be our Munich. . . . I will never be able to sell what he is doing today to our people. Our people are going nuts. In public I will say that everything is wonderful, but it is not. This is a disaster for us." Mandela did not help matters when, on January 9, he stated publicly that there would never be a *Volkstaat*. Although discussion proceeded behind the scenes, the AVF formally broke off negotiations with the ANC a couple days later.

Meanwhile, Viljoen and I continued our dialogue. On January 25, we had a long discussion of ways in which an agreement could be reached with the ANC short of recognition of a *Volkstaat*. The ANC, Viljoen reported, was trying to separate self-determination from a geographic concept and tie it to one of general policy and perhaps cultural protection. It had raised the idea of a *Volksraad,* that is, an Afrikaner advisory council, which would work with the new government along these lines. I repeated candidly that I thought a formal *Volkstaat* was impractical and that no solution could be founded on race-based voting. But hearing the ANC proposals, I thought there was potential for creativity and flexibility on both sides of the issue. Viljoen agreed that there was a need to define self-determination more clearly and also recognized that the election provided him with his strongest leverage with the ANC. He was attracted to the proposal to use it as a referendum on the *Volkstaat*. However, he still thought that the threat of violence was a form of leverage. I said that the ANC needed no lesson in appreciating the danger of violence and that the focus should be on the negotiating track.

Viljoen's growing attraction to contesting the elections, however, suffered a setback just a few days later. At a rally of Viljoen's AVF on January 29, Viljoen was roundly booed, so much so that he had to leave the stage, when he suggested that the party might want to participate in the elections. For Viljoen it was a humiliating experience, even though he recognized that in part the incident had been staged by his rivals in the Conservative Party. Nevertheless, Viljoen took up a harder line. "I cannot leave my people in the lurch," he told me two weeks later. "Now is the time for resistance."

It was in this atmosphere that Assistant Secretary of Defense Freeman and his team of senior American military officers met with Viljoen at the embassy on February 11. Drawing on all the military professionalism they shared with Viljoen, Admiral Nutwell and General Riley began with an exchange, military to military, on strategic theory and experiences. They then appealed to Viljoen on behalf of his duty as a soldier to respect the authority of his government, to remember the oath of office he had taken as chief of staff, and to abjure going to war against the government he had served so bravely. I added that if the right turned to violence, there was no way for the United States to help as we were trying to help now. Viljoen was clearly troubled. He was shaken by the events of January 29. He said his followers cold not stomach participating in the elections. But still he held out the hope for negotiations. Responding to the senior American military men, he made clear he did not relish confronting the state security machinery he had so long served. In a speech he had given a few days earlier, he had described the terrible damage to the economy and the terrible divisions within the security forces that an uprising would produce.

Viljoen continued to contemplate participation in the elections but hoped he could do so in the context of others within the FA, particularly Buthelezi and Mangope, agreeing to do so as well. Facing a deadline for registering his party by March 5, Viljoen, without asking for authority from the Executive Committee, did so at the last moment, in the name of the Freedom Front. I called him on March 8, praised him for this patriotic step, and urged him to take the next one, that is, to submit a list of candidates as required by law, for which a deadline loomed just one week later. Again I offered any help we might give.

I shared the results of these discussions with Mandela. He believed Viljoen was being held back from an agreement with the ANC because of pressures from the Conservative Party. Mandela recommended I see Ferdinand Hartzenberg, the leader of the Conservative Party (CP) and chairman of the Executive Committee of the AVF. I was not optimistic. Hartzenberg had succeeded the late Andries Treurnicht in 1993 as leader of the party. Treurnicht had walked out of the National Party in 1982 in opposition to even the limited reforms of then president P. W. Botha and created the CP. Hartzenberg, perhaps to demonstrate his right to leadership, had from the moment of assuming the mantle taken such a hard-line stance on the transition that, as noted, Viljoen and his generals emerged to bring more mature leadership to the white right cause. Hartzenberg had done everything he could to hem Viljoen in within the AVF. He had refused to go along with earlier agreements from the multiparty negotiations, even when other conservative parties had done so, and had been critical of Viljoen's discussions with the ANC.[54] Nevertheless, I was fully willing to try. We met on March 9 for a long discussion.

I began by arguing for the AVF to contest the election. It was an opportunity to demonstrate the party's support. Hartzenberg immediately disagreed. If the CP agreed to participate in the election, "No one would listen to us or negotiate with us any more." Moreover, he insisted that the election would usher in a communist state. It was better to sit out this "interim period" and proceed directly to "freedom." I recalled for Hartzenberg the statements by the United States and other countries that they would hold any new government to its preelection commitment. This should provide some assurance. Hartzenberg, with what I have to admit was a biting insight into great power politics, replied: "If the government acts in ways that are unacceptable, we know you will object. We also know that you will not interfere. We who live here will have to experience the oppression long before you become involved."

The argument then became circular. Hartzenberg argued that each of the ethnic groups wanted its own kingdom or state. I countered that if all the Zulus really wanted their own separate kingdom, there would be peace in KwaZulu/Natal, rather than the violence there of Zulu against Zulu. Moreover, if he was right, if all the Zulus would vote for Buthelezi, the Tswanas for Mangope, the Afrikaners for the AVF, the Freedom Alliance should sweep 60 percent of the vote. Participating in the election was therefore in the FA's interest. Hartzenberg countered that the election would not be free and fair and, in any case, the Afrikaners would refuse to vote. I said that in reality the vast majority of South Africans wanted to vote in an election and they could not be denied that right much longer. I could not resist adding, "Isn't it funny that the FA, which says it speaks for the people, is opposed to elections? And it is the FA that wants all the agreements to be made before the people can speak for themselves."

If there was no common ground on elections, I urged Hartzenberg, speak out against right-wing violence. He would only say he would not advocate it. But he added that he would encourage "peaceful takeover of towns." "We are only claiming what is ours," he said. "That does not cause violence." There was no give in these discussions. Hartzenberg was determined on a course of resistance—to negotiations, to elections, to the reality of a fundamental change in South Africa's politics. If Viljoen was to move his followers on a different course, he would have to emerge from the constraints of his right-wing allies. The realization of this came for him in the Bophuthatswana debacle just three days after my meeting with Hartzenberg.

When Mangope called for help from his FA partners, Viljoen saw an opportunity to demonstrate the strength of his following while pursuing his hope of avoiding a confrontation with the security forces. He got Meiring's agreement to allow a force of some three thousand volunteer farmer-soldiers and other white militia to go to Mangope's aid. Viljoen promised that the volunteers would not carry arms through South Africa, but only receive arms from the Bophuthatswana Defense Force after crossing the border.[55] Viljoen gave instructions to his people that Terreblanche's AWB followers, who leaped at the opportunity to participate in the action, were not to cross into Bophuthatswana until the main force was assembled. Mangope had told Viljoen that AWB participation would be unacceptable, and Viljoen sought at least to control it. But the AWB broke ranks, raced into the homeland, and, as noted earlier, so disgusted the Bophuthatswana Defense Force that it mutinied against Mangope and struck back at the AWB. Before Viljoen's main force could get there, it was virtually all over. A last-minute attempt by Viljoen to work out another compromise with Meiring collapsed in the face of the TEC's and de Klerk's determination to remove Mangope from power.[56]

It was not the first time Viljoen had been embarrassed by his partners on the right. In June 1993, Viljoen was part of a protest rally in front of the World Trade Center, where the multiparty negotiations were taking place. Suddenly, AWB members at the protest drove their vehicles across the barriers and crashed through the front door of the building. As delegates scattered for cover, the invaders took seats at the table, threw aside or destroyed documents, and even urinated on the premises. It was a shocking event, but it did nothing but discredit the right wing. The multiparty forum resumed the very next day and the leaders of the raid were arrested.

Viljoen now came back from Bophuthatswana not only convinced of the foolishness of this type of opposition, but also in further disdain of his partners and suspicious even that the AWB had been infiltrated by government provocateurs who pressed the AWB forward in order to create the very chaos that resulted. Coming back in a small aircraft, Viljoen made up his mind to participate in the elections. Landing in Pretoria, he went directly to meet with other leaders of the AVF. He later said,

> I had made up my mind. The military option cannot be successful, we have to go for the other option. Fortunately, I had developed the other option [registering the party]. But [the other leaders] refused it and that is when the split took place and eventually I went to Kempton Park [to file

the list], minutes before closing time, because I was trying to convince Hartzenberg that they should go along with us.[57]

But like so much in South Africa, it was not over until it was over. Viljoen's supporters kept telling him that the ANC would eventually cheat him. Viljoen therefore felt that he must have a written agreement with the ANC before the election, establishing the basis for pursuing the proposals for a *Volkstaat*. The agreement he negotiated recognized Afrikaner desires for self-determination and promised that, following the election, a Volkstaat Council would be established to analyze the possibilities. The agreement was ready by April 12, but the ANC kept postponing the signing ceremony. Viljoen grew suspicious. "This gave me the impression that the ANC was playing us for a fool and that they were trying to push me to the 27th and then put me into a very difficult position, hoping that I would then accept the fact."[58]

Viljoen recalled what happened next between us:

> You remember, between you and me, we had a gentleman's agreement. . . .
> We met quite often, and you said "before you do anything, promise me you will first come to me." And I said yes I will do so, and you remember we used that eventually. . . . I came to you and said, "I'm going to let the dogs loose," and you said, "Give me a half an hour."[59]

The call that Viljoen referred to came to me on April 16. Postponement of the signing had resurfaced in Viljoen all the deep suspicions about the ANC, indeed about the whole transition process as far as protecting the basic interests of his people was concerned. What Viljoen now meant by letting the dogs loose was that he would disrupt the elections. The military establishment of a *Volkstaat* was no longer possible, he knew, but "a disruption of the election would have been very easy."[60] I immediately called Thabo Mbeki's office, reaching his chief aide, Yusuf Saloojee. I explained the situation, that Viljoen felt he was being betrayed, that all the work that had gone into negotiating an agreement with Viljoen, in breaking down right-wing resistance, was at risk. I knew the ANC was not trying to fool Viljoen, but not focusing on the signing ceremony had created that impression. In a few minutes, Saloojee called back. The signing ceremony was set for April 23.

I called Viljoen with the news. He made another request. Would I sign the agreement as a guarantor? I replied that neither I nor any foreign representative had been signatory to any of the other transition agreements, so I did not see how the United States could sign this one. However, if the parties agreed, I would be pleased to be present as a witness. On Saturday, in the old, imposing Union Building, which houses the South African government, the signing ceremony took place. Although other ambassadors were invited, I was the only one to attend.

Klaus Freiherr von der Ropp, a German correspondent and author who followed South African events closely and was intimate with the right wing and
sympathetic with its concerns, sent me copies of articles he wrote about these
events. On one he penned, "Without you, SA in my opinion would never have
got the chance it did get on April 23, 1994."

It was of course an exaggeration. Many other forces were at work. Most of
the credit goes to those statesmen—Mandela, Mbeki, Zuma, and Viljoen—who
found something in common between them and who pursued it to a positive
conclusion.

The United States, however, did play its role. In a retrospective analysis the
embassy sent to Washington in 1995, we said, "At the very least, these exchanges
[with Viljoen] contributed to Viljoen's decision to enter the elections and helped
establish a relationship of candor and trust between Freedom Front leaders and
this Embassy."[61] Viljoen commented on the particular character of the American
approach:

> I recall one meeting with [a European country]. That was a terrible meet-
> ing, they were trying to intimidate me. I must say that the U.S., you the
> ambassador and the people that came from the Pentagon, you were very
> professional . . . [and] didn't try to point a finger at me and say, "Don't
> move or else we'll kill you!" And I think that helped a lot, because in a sit-
> uation like this, a form of mutual trust is of great importance. And I was
> always very happy, eventually, very satisfied with the approach of the
> Americans in this regard.[62]

Viljoen's party went on to capture just over 2 percent of the vote in the election and win nine seats in the Parliament, and Viljoen would become an important
and constructive member of Parliament. But his dream of a *Volkstaat* faded as the
practicalities bore down on it. The Volkstaat Council was appointed, as the ANC
had promised, immediately after the election. It was diligent and submitted a long
report to the government, but all the difficulties in the proposition remained.
Viljoen succeeded in getting a clause on self-determination in the final constitution, which was adopted in 1997, but by then he knew that the dream was fading.
By 1995, he was already talking of soft boundaries, of a cultural and educational
"home," rather than a political one.[63] Even the cultural sanctuaries were fading,
however. Bastions of Afrikaner intellectualism and language, such as Stellenbosch
University and the University of Pretoria, were welcoming masses of students
from the majority population, and English was rapidly becoming the standard
language of instruction.

In 1999, Viljoen's party suffered a major decline in votes, from 424,000 to
270,000. Many of his constituents had decided to throw in their lot with the
more liberal Democratic Party, which emerged as the principal opposition party.

With his characteristic candor, Viljoen recognized that his constituency was moving from the hope for a separate home to wanting to be part of the political mainstream:

> The Afrikaner people have decided to accept their minority position as de facto but they are not prepared to accept that they have no political role to play. And they oppose the idea that I have had for developing self-determination as the main line. They say no, we want to be fully part of the mainline politics of South Africa and we do not wish to have a political party just tending to the rights of the Afrikaners themselves.[64]

Viljoen, the man who said he was not a politician, indeed that he hated politics, once more contemplated going home to his farm. In 2000 he made the decision to do so. His dream of a *Volkstaat* was all but dead. But he had played his role on the magnificent plain of South Africa's transition. And, in my view, he played it heroically.

9

Denouement

And then I cried out to God, why me? Why must it be me that has to take the hard and rocky road to democracy, and security, and prosperity?
—MANGOSUTHU BUTHELEZI, *March 11, 1994*

THE FINAL MONTHS LEADING UP TO THE ELECTION IN SOUTH AFRICA were a mixture of excited anticipation and deep anxiety. The election was now firmly set for April 26–28 and campaigning was well under way. The reality of a major transformation, one of enormous consequence for every citizen, was sinking into the country's consciousness. Yet the resistance of significant parties on the right and the left, the ongoing violence, and the threat that perhaps the election would usher in a period of civil war weighed on the public. In a speech in March of that year, I referred to the entire process as "flying through the storm." The period was marked by intense negotiations, crises, fears, and ultimately triumph.

For the United States, there were three priorities. One was support for the elections. We poured $40 million and enormous energy into this objective. Second was our effort to help bring the remaining recalcitrant parties into the election. The previous chapter describes the outcome of these efforts with the homelands, the right wing, and the PAC. This chapter describes the dramatic climax with regard to Chief Buthelezi's Inkatha Freedom Party, a drama that went down to the last moment and involved leading personalities from around the world. In the midst of these events, we had to address the explosive issue of South Africa's programs in chemical and biological weapons and manage it urgently but without upsetting the delicate political transition under way.

THE ELECTION

As soon as the election date was finalized, which did not happen until July 2, 1993, less than a year before the elections, the United States and other international actors began to focus on how to assist a country in which 80 percent of the electorate had never voted outside of church or similar elections. Parties representing them had never participated in an election campaign. American election programs focused on four objectives: mitigation of violence that could upset, even derail, the elections; voter education; assisting new parties in preparing for the campaign; and monitoring of the election by both South Africans and international observers. In several of these activities, our impartiality and credibility were again tested.

Mitigation of Violence

As described in the preceding chapter, mitigation of violence had been a major objective throughout the negotiating period. But in the months leading up to the election, USAID stepped up its funding of South African conflict resolution organizations, community-based groups, and experts to the tune of $8.2 million. The Independent Mediation Service of South Africa was a major trainer and mediation service that received USAID support. Along with organizations with such national reach, USAID funded small but influential local groups and specialized ones close to targets of violence, such as the Convention of the Democratic Taxi Association. Nearly thirty South African organizations were targeted for violence mitigation efforts in 1993–94. Moreover, mitigation of violence and voter education went hand in hand. In one USAID-funded project, the Martin Luther King Jr. Center of Atlanta teamed with the King-Luthuli Center of South Africa to train hundreds of young South Africans in both nonviolence and voter education skills, and those young people reached thousands more as they went into their communities to carry the message.

Voter Education

Efforts to educate voters were considered extremely important. However, the Independent Electoral Commission (IEC), which had been created by the TEC in December 1993 to organize and administer the elections, was initially reluctant to accept outside assistance. Justice Johann Kriegler, the chairman of the commission, insisted that these had to be South African elections, not internationally administered ones. Another commission member, Zack Yacub, a brilliant blind lawyer, was even more suspicious of Western offers of assistance. The United States could not have been in more agreement that the elections must be South African run, but we also recognized that the IEC had an enormous task on its hands and only four months to accomplish it. As one writer describes the situation,

In four months the IEC had to recruit 250,000 people; train them in elections procedures; organize voter education programs for millions of people, many of them illiterate; ensure that millions obtained identity documents; monitor election meetings; mediate elections disputes; assist free electioneering; handle thousands of inquiries; and deal with complaints and contraventions of electoral law from all quarters. Polling stations had to be identified without reliable demographic data or electoral rolls.[1]

Most of these tasks could be administered only by an official agency such as the IEC. But there were many organizations able to contribute to voter education. And this was the area, besides basic procedural instruction, where the IEC probably had the least time and capability. On January 24, 1994, I along with several of our USAID and USIA staff met for two hours with the IEC. In the meeting, we worked out the means for assisting the IEC directly with various experts and equipment, among other things; but more important, we worked out an understanding on our funding programs of voter education outside the IEC, run by groups such as universities, NGOs, and churches. We promised to keep the IEC fully informed of these programs and to make sure that these groups did not violate IEC guidelines. USIA would also provide expertise to the South African Broadcasting Corporation (SABC) to help it in voter education programs through both radio and television.

But by late 1993 USAID funds were almost totally exhausted. The embassy therefore made an appeal to AID in Washington for additional funds, even though the South Africa program was already AID's largest in sub-Saharan Africa. Our appeal was abetted by Mandela having made a similar plea to President Clinton during his visit to the White House in July 1993. At the same time, we appealed to other donors to increase their funding in this area. The European Union was heavily engaged. Japan was initially less so but, responding to pleas both in South Africa, by me to Japan's ambassador, and in Tokyo, by our embassy there, added several million dollars to its efforts. In January 1994 the AID administrator, Brian Atwood, arrived in South Africa to announce an additional $10 million from the United States for voter education. These additional funds would prove crucial in the final months before the election because of rapidly changing circumstances.

One of these was in the nature of the ballot. The ANC had held fast to the position that there should be a single ballot for both national and provincial elections. Both the government and Inkatha had argued strongly for two ballots, believing that this would give them some greater chance for vote splitting at the provincial level. The ANC was convinced that a double ballot would add to the confusion for first-time voters. In his meeting with Mandela in January 1994, Atwood pledged that the United States would use its $10 million in an intensified education effort on the double ballot if the ANC would relent on this point.

The ANC finally gave in as part of a package of concessions aimed at appeasing the still recalcitrant parties on the right, but only two months before the election. By that time, voter education efforts across the country had used a single sample ballot in their training sessions and all their advertisements. The IEC, overwhelmed by other matters, planned no new special campaign on this issue, so USAID launched a tremendous campaign through its grantees, printing up thousands of new sample ballots for both the national and provincial elections and retraining as many people and organizations as possible.

Voter education played a significant role in proving wrong some of the dire predictions about the election. Most experts predicted a large number of spoiled ballots in the election. Some worried that the threat of violence would keep large numbers from the polls.[2] Neither prediction proved valid. There were problems in the election, described in the next chapter, but turnout was huge, close to 86 percent, and, most remarkably, only some 1 percent of the ballots were spoiled.[3]

A survey of voters undertaken by SABC between April 7 and 18 indicated the impact of voter education efforts. The survey found that 97 percent of respondents reported receiving some form of voter education. Of potential black voters, the most vulnerable group given illiteracy rates and the number in rural areas, 60 percent said they knew how to vote; the number was higher outside KwaZulu/Natal, where agreement had yet to be reached on Inkatha's participation and where education efforts were therefore negligible. While radio was the medium that reached the most people with voter education (82 percent of the electorate), only 44 percent of those who relied on radio said they felt they knew how to vote. But more than eight out of ten potential voters who said their most important source was either voter education organizations, political party visits, newspapers, or television said they knew how to vote. These were sources that received most of American as well as other donor attention. The survey also found that those who received some form of voter education were far more likely to vote and by a large margin were less afraid to vote.[4]

Voter education programs were not without partisan controversy. An awkward moment for the United States arose during President Mandela's meeting with President Clinton in July 1993, when Mandela made an unabashed appeal for a U.S. government financial contribution to the ANC to help it in its election campaign. When President Clinton demurred, saying that the U.S. government could not put money into a foreign political party, only nonpartisan voter education efforts, Mandela scoffed, saying, "You would be surprised at how many governments say that but are in fact willing to do so." As noted, the United States agreed to provide $10 million in additional nonpartisan voter education funds. When in early 1994 I discussed with Mandela the use we were making of the additional $10 million in voter education funds, he suggested we look at some of the organizations known to be working closely with the ANC. I promised to look into them, but in the end we chose not to utilize any of these organizations.

There was a gratifying moment in all of this rather awkward set of exchanges with Mandela, someone whom we obviously admired tremendously but could not support in electoral terms. In an appearance before the International Press Institute in Cape Town on February 14, Mandela was asked about the U.S. role in the South African elections. Mandela mentioned the additional $10 million and acknowledged, if with some regret, that the United States could not fund political parties but concluded, "I have confidence that Ambassador Lyman will, in consultation with all parties, spend these funds in the most effective and fair way." That we tried to do.

Assistance to Political Parties

Probably the most controversial form of American assistance in the election, but also perhaps among the most valuable, was our assistance to political parties. No black-led party had ever been allowed to participate in an election in South Africa. This potentially put them at a considerable disadvantage, since de Klerk's National Party and the liberal Democratic Party had long experience in this area. Earlier, Congress had authorized $10 million specifically to assist the ANC and Inkatha, as well as some nonpartisan groups, to prepare for elections.

Once the formal electoral process was agreed on, additional U.S. assistance was provided to thirteen parties, though the most significant assistance was for the ANC and Inkatha. As noted in the preceding chapter, the PAC benefited only late, after finally renouncing its armed struggle. Assistance covered voter education, party and civic organization training, legal and administrative guidance, and election studies and observation.

Here again it was important to avoid perceptions or the reality of partisanship. The vehicles through which the United States provided this assistance were the National Democratic Institute (NDI), the overseas assistance arm of the Democratic Party; the International Republican Institute (IRI), the equivalent wing of the Republican Party; and the Joint Center for Economic and Political Studies. In this case, I particularly wanted to avoid the perception, based on historical linkages, that in the election the Democratic Party in the United States was supportive of the ANC and the Republican Party was supportive of Inkatha. So I asked that the organizations do what they had never done before, that is, work jointly in every case. This meant that teams assisting the ANC were made up of members from both NDI and IRI and that those assisting Inkatha were also. This not only worked extremely well, but was an education for the advisers as well.

One issue that arose was whether the United States should, under this project, assist Inkatha at all. As noted earlier, Chief Buthelezi had refused to recognize the interim constitution, under which the elections were to be administered, and had not agreed to participate in the elections. Technically, we could have excluded Inkatha from this project, as we did AZAPO, which had opted not to participate in the elections. But our whole policy in this area was to draw Inkatha into the electoral process. Being poorly prepared would only add to the reluctance of the party to engage. We were also receiving messages from high-ranking Inkatha officials that, despite Buthelezi's strong denunciations of the elections, preparations were under way within the party to participate and that assistance would be well utilized. We thus included Inkatha and were not sorry. U.S. support for Inkatha as a party, both earlier and in this period, made an enormous difference in Inkatha's ability subsequently to participate in the election process with confidence and capability. In the opinion of one of its chief electoral strategists,

> This injection of US funds . . . was very crucial and no one else had come in, you know, on such a large scale. . . .[It] virtually was important for establishing a political party as distinct from a broad movement which would be associated with conflicts and so on, but here you had a political party, with an office, with telephones, with staff, . . . with transport all over the country . . . and it was clearly provided by the U.S.[5]

Election Observers

Election observers were deemed indispensable to the success of the elections, but coordinating the many indigenous and foreign bodies involved posed a tremendous problem. In November 1993 I hosted a meeting of the EU and UN representatives to discuss more rapid and coordinated action in support of the elections. The TEC was slow in requesting additional UN involvement and the IEC was still not in operation. We believed that the United Nations should be asked to provide a high-level representative in South Africa for the election period, to increase the UN observer mission and to help in coordinating international assistance. Denmark's ambassador, Peter Bruckner, had been urging action along the same lines, as well as in voter education programs, and provided a great deal of impetus within the European Union on these matters. USAID was charged with coordinating donor efforts in these areas. Two weeks later, the dean of the diplomatic corps went over the same ground with the entire diplomatic community.

In December the TEC, urged by the international community, adopted a resolution requesting that the United Nations, the European Union, the OAU, and individual governments provide observers and that the United Nations coordinate all international observers in cooperation with the IEC. In January the UN Security Council approved the expansion of the UN mission. Secretary-General Boutros Boutros-Ghali appointed Lakhdar Brahimi to head the mission. It could not have been a better choice. Ambassador Brahimi, with Angela King as his deputy, brought tremendous skill and perseverance to assisting the government through the election process. Coordination with the United States and other donors could not have been closer.

But the IEC and the United Nations were limited to coordinating official international observers and were allowed to provide only indirectly—through establishing rules and procedures—for the flood of independent ones. In the embassy, we anticipated an enormous outpouring of interest from American NGOs, church groups, labor unions, and other organizations in providing election observers. This was, after all, the culmination of the decades-long fight against apartheid. We therefore turned to the American NGO, the Lawyers' Committee for Civil Rights under Law. Under a USAID grant, the Lawyers' Committee played an indispensable role in facilitating and coordinating the American presence. It assisted observers in receiving accreditation with the IEC, a requirement for all observer groups and individuals; arranged or assisted in accommodations and transportation; determined in conjunction with the IEC where each group would be deployed; provided briefings, maps, and tool kits; and collated and passed on to the IEC the daily reports of the observers once they were in the field. In sum, through the Lawyers' Committee's work, the American observers fit into the national network of electoral monitoring.

One of the key requirements was to keep South African observers in the forefront of the process. The United States along with other donors funded training and deployment of thousands of South African observers. South African NGOs, church groups, the political parties, and many civic organizations undertook to field observers. The Lawyers' Committee saw to it that, whenever possible, American observers were teamed with South African organizations.

THE CHALLENGES OF NONPARTISANSHIP

In its briefing book for American observers, the Lawyers' Committee wrote:

> Many of you began your involvement with South Africa in the anti-apartheid movement in the United States. In many ways, participating in the election is the culmination of the dream which many have harboured, the institution of a democratic and non-racial political system in South Africa. To be effective observers, however, we must all set aside whatever biases we hold for or against any party or movement. Foreign observers must be especially careful not to allow their actions to undermine the delicate political process. . . . Observers must be non-partisan in their words and behavior.

The committee was hitting on what was a difficult and often challenging task for private individuals as well as officials from America during this period. There had been so much identification with the liberation movement, with the agony of Mandela's imprisonment and the exhilaration at his release and the prospect of ending apartheid, that it was hard for people to resist the pressures to endorse the ANC or other liberation parties in the election. And the ANC was ready to take advantage of those sympathies.

One example was the experience of the Artists for a Free South Africa. This was a group of prominent Hollywood figures that had for years worked on behalf of the anti-apartheid movement. Once the elections were firmly agreed on, however, it threw itself into promoting voter participation and education on a non-partisan basis. On a visit to South Africa for this purpose in January 1994, a group that included Danny Glover, Angela Basset, and other wonderful and dedicated film stars was invited to what they had been told was a voter education seminar in the Cape flats. It turned out to be an ANC rally. Blindsided into appearing at a party event, several of the members demonstrated their displeasure by refusing to attend a dinner given for them that evening by ANC provincial leader and longtime anti-apartheid figure Alan Boesak.

But the most painful experience for me was a decision with regard to Secretary of Commerce Ron Brown. As noted, Brown made a historic and deeply appreciated visit to South Africa in November 1993. As part of that visit, Brown prepared a major address, directed especially at the youth. Brown was conscious of the significance of such an address in that, nearly thirty years before, Robert Kennedy had come to South Africa and given an electrifying speech to black youth. Brown wanted to recount his own history and that of African Americans generally and their relevance to the transition at last under way in South Africa. It was an uplifting speech.

The ANC offered to provide a large venue for Brown's address, promising to bus in perhaps thousands of attendees. We thought that this could only be a party rally, with Brown seen as implicitly endorsing the ANC in the election. I vetoed the offer. Instead, the speech was scheduled at the University of Cape Town, which we believed would be a more neutral venue. But it was vacation time, few students were on campus, and the crowd was disappointingly small—a handful of faculty, administrators, and students. They were immune to the power of the address.

It was a decision on my part that I regret to this day. The speech deserved a much larger audience. It deserved taking the risk of partisanship.

I quote only a part of it here. The full text is in the appendix. But reading it does not give the full flavor of Brown's emotional delivery that day. Ron Brown said:

> Today I stand before you representing the President and the people of the United States because I, too, believe in my dream and because my ancestors believed in theirs. They came from Africa. Some two hundred years ago

they were led in chains onto slave ships bound for the Caribbean and for the American South. For generations they labored in the fields, dehumanized, disrespected, reduced to the status of a machine, but they survived. And then when declared free they labored again under the chains of racism and the chains of poverty, but again they survived. They began the fight, the movement, the struggle that we carry on today. And their son now stands here in this chamber as Secretary of Commerce of the United States of America. A man whose ancestors were brought to America by the international slave trade, now helps shape the international trade policy of the United States.

So when we think of our nation and how far we have to go, let us remember how far we have come. If we have learned anything in the past few years, it is that nothing is forever, that every thing is possible, that people can rise above difficult circumstances and recreate themselves, recreate their people and recreate their nation.

ONE MORE THING . . .

In early 1994, information became available to both the British and American intelligence services that South Africa's chemical and biological warfare programs had been much more extensive than previously known. More disturbing, and contrary to instructions by de Klerk upon assuming the presidency, they had not been dismantled.

South Africa's programs in chemical and biological warfare had a long and nasty history. Though highly classified and secret at the time, the programs and the controversy surrounding them are today detailed in work by Chandre Gould and Peter Folb for the Centre for Conflict Resolution in Cape Town; in the proceedings of South Africa's Truth and Reconciliation Commission; in the trial of the program's mastermind, Dr. Wouter Basson, beginning in 1999; and in a study by the U.S. Air Force Institute in 2001.[6] Ostensibly developed as a precaution against use of such weapons by neighboring African countries or by anti-apartheid forces against the South African regime, the projects in fact moved into the testing of agents against liberation leaders, possibly against ANC camps in neighboring countries, and against anti-apartheid activists as far away as Europe. Following five years of investigation, Basson was charged in 1999 with sixty-seven counts of murder and attempted murder, including charges in the deaths of some two hundred detainees in the former Southwest Africa (now Namibia), as well as fraud and drug charges.

The issue, when it came to our attention in early 1994, was of paramount importance. First of all, it was important to know what aspects of the program had been continued after de Klerk issued his instructions and if they were still under way. Second, there was concern over whether the personnel and scientific information relevant to such programs were in danger of being acquired by other states, in particular Libya. There was evidence that some of the scientists formerly involved in the program were in fact being solicited by Libya for work there. Third was the integrity of the chemical and biological weapons conventions. South Africa was in the process of preparing its "confidence building measure" (CBM) submission under the Biological Weapons Convention, and the report underplayed the depth and extent of South Africa's past programs. We could not let that submission pass without challenge; it went to the heart of the integrity of that convention. Finally, if reports of actual use of such material against opponents of the apartheid regime were true, they documented one of the first known uses of such agents and had to be investigated.

None of this could wait until a new government was elected. It was imperative that the situation be investigated and that processes of securing the data, identifying the key personnel, and ensuring that the issue would not become lost in the transition were accomplished by de Klerk, who alone at this moment retained the levers of power and authority over the military and intelligence services. But asking de Klerk to take this on in the midst of the crises of transition posed its own problems.

De Klerk's efficacy in these final months of political transition was absolutely essential to ensure that the security forces stayed loyal to the process, that the final negotiations for the transition were consummated, and that the elections would take place in an atmosphere free and secure. Broaching the issue within the government could create further strains between de Klerk and the security forces. De Klerk was already balancing actions against perpetrators of the "third force" activity exposed by Justice Goldstone, for example, de Klerk's cashiering of twenty-three military and police generals at the end of 1992, with measures to appease security forces' concerns over their fate after the election through efforts to secure some form of blanket amnesty. Partial leaks of explosive information such as these allegations could roil the political situation and possibly weaken de Klerk fatally. Our concern about how we handled this information was made more acute, moreover, because we were working with terrible allegations that were still unproven. Indeed, Basson proved to be a combination of Dr. Strangelove and Walter Mitty, boasting of truly terrible things one day, denying them the next.

We also had to consider when and how to share this information with Mandela and the ANC. Allegations made later by Basson and Surgeon General Daniel Knobel that the United States and Britain "did not want the program to fall into the hands of the ANC Government" were simply misleading and misinformed.[7] This was a matter that would unquestionably carry over into the new government; getting it under control, which we were sure Mandela would want to do, would fall to the ANC government later. As noted in an earlier chapter, moreover, we had made it a point to share a good deal of information on our policy and programs with Mandela during the transition period in order to alleviate suspicions about the U.S. role and build lines of consistency between the outgoing and incoming administrations in areas such as nonproliferation. But now, the parties were engaged in a hard-fought election campaign. Could we share this information in a way that did not seem to be affecting the election, for example, by undercutting and embarrassing de Klerk? And if that happened, could we still obtain de Klerk's cooperation on this matter in the waning days of his presidency?

Throughout the period of January to April, the United States wrestled with these and related issues. At the embassy, given the sensitivity of the issue, I confined knowledge of it and responsibility for working on it to only one other senior member of my staff, much later to two. In Washington, however, the issues were debated between the NSC, the CIA, the Arms Control and Disarmament Agency, and the State Department. There was also need to coordinate with the United Kingdom, with whom we shared both knowledge and responsibility. Washington had several concerns that went beyond the political situation in South Africa. One was whether to press the South African government to admit, in its submission to the Biological Weapons Convention (BWC), that it had engaged in an "offensive" program. South African officials were adamantly opposed to making such an admission, arguing that any such offensive uses were done without proper authorization and against official policy. This was an issue that required extensive technical as well as political analysis, much of which would have to wait until Mandela took office. Another contentious issue was how we should handle the allegations of usage.

Washington was divided on many of these questions and delayed providing us with clear guidance. To break the logjam, I proposed that we focus first and foremost with de Klerk on securing the relevant data and bringing any continuing rogue practices under control. Determining the exact nature of South Africa's submission to the BWC should be the product of detailed technical exchanges with all the relevant South African specialists, including those who had worked on these programs. We would aim to get de Klerk's agreement to begin these exchanges as soon as possible. On the question of usage, perhaps the most contentious issue, I reminded Washington that the allegations of use of these agents would be part of the much larger question for South Africa of how to handle the many human rights abuses of the apartheid regime. The outlines of a Truth and Reconciliation Commission were already being debated, and these allegations should properly be handled in that context. We should urge the South Africans to address these charges in that context, but not try to address them separately ourselves, especially with our still limited information. To avoid any possible implication of our participating in a cover-up, it was agreed that we would put de Klerk's government, and later Mandela's, on notice that we were bringing these charges to their attention and urging that they be properly investigated and handled. Furthermore, we agreed that in any public disclosure of the charges we would go on record as having so alerted the government. When the issue did in fact break into the news, in a story in the London *Sunday Times* of February 26, 1995, American sources were quoted extensively on the allegations of usage. Our press guidance also made clear that we had made these known to the government.[8] Finally, we recommended that de Klerk be the first to brief Mandela, before the election if possible but for certain before the inauguration, rather than our going to Mandela first. The British concurred on all these points and Washington subsequently agreed.

Tom Mangold and Jeff Goldberg, in their book *Plague Wars*, are wrong in writing that the British and American ambassadors met with de Klerk on this matter in late 1993. It was not until April 11, 1994, in the midst, as described below, of immense political jockeying and Buthelezi's continuing resistance to the elections, that we were able to secure the meeting. To prepare for this meeting, we had asked the South African officials with whom we had been discussing the matter to brief senior South African government officials and then de Klerk, which was one of the reasons for the long delay.

The meeting was vintage de Klerk. Cool, clear, professional, he neither admitted nor denied any of the information we brought to him, but he also reasserted that much of what we said, if true, went counter to his instructions. He had been shocked by the briefing from his staff. He particularly appreciated that in our presentation British ambassador Anthony Reeve and I noted that he had instructed the government to end this program as far back as 1990.[9] He probed us for more detailed information he could use to investigate the matter further. We said this could come out of the technical exchanges we were proposing. In terms of the immediate politics, de Klerk had no problem with briefing Mandela and was grateful that we gave him the opportunity to develop his response and to bring Mandela onboard before our doing so. He noted that Mandela had been angry over the way the nuclear program had been canceled, not because of the decision, with which Mandela heartily concurred, but because he had not been brought into it by de Klerk.

De Klerk asked for an opportunity to study this information further, and specifically for our proposals for technical meetings and handling of the data, and he asked that we meet again.[10] Shortly afterward, de Klerk ordered his people to work toward a full disclosure of the program in the submission to the BWC. This opened the door within days to the beginning of all-important technical meetings between South African, American, and British experts, meetings that would continue for another year, well after the formation of the new government.

The second meeting with de Klerk took place on April 22, only four days before the election. This time, de Klerk was more defensive. He now argued, contrary to his earlier stance on such programs, that a defensive program in both chemical and biological weapons was completely justifiable for South Africa, as it was for other nations, and that the program data that resulted were a "national asset." Thus he could not agree to destroying them. After some discussion, he said that in any case this was not a decision he should make, but was one for the new government. I suspected that he was less interested in salvaging the program than in taking advantage of what he saw as an opportunity to earn the confidence of Mandela about the type of relationship the two would have in the Government of National Unity. Unlike with the nuclear program decision, he would be bringing this one to Mandela as a colleague. De Klerk was also establishing with us his own importance in the Government of National Unity. Responding to our concern over proliferation if these data were maintained, de Klerk said he was absolutely committed to nonproliferation and would be our "insurance policy in a new government."

De Klerk agreed to steps to further secure the data in the interim before the new government came into being. He also instructed that the technical exchanges among experts continue. De Klerk renewed his commitment to briefing Mandela on the program, but not in the waning days of the election campaign, lest it explode into the political arena. Instead, de Klerk promised, he would do it before the inauguration, set for May 10.

We waited impatiently in the final days before the change in government for de Klerk to meet his obligation to brief Mandela. As the time grew short, and de Klerk and Mandela were both preoccupied with so many matters, we worried that our credibility would be damaged with Mandela if we said nothing. We also wanted him to hear our concerns before turning this issue over to his new team. There was much to-ing and fro-ing over this between Washington, London, and us in South Africa in these final days before the inauguration, and over who would broach the issue with the ANC. Finally, on May 4, only five days before Mandela's formal election as president by the Parliament, and though Washington was still divided on the matter, the British, with my consent, alerted Thabo Mbeki that there was a proliferation matter of great concern that we would need to address very soon with the new government. De Klerk was aware of it, Mbeki was told, and we had urged de Klerk to brief Mandela. We recommended Mandela seek a full briefing as soon as possible and meet with us soon thereafter. Two days later, de Klerk provided Mandela only a ten-minute briefing on the issue as part of the overall transition process.[11]

Mandela would not receive a full briefing from within the government for several months. Nevertheless, the groundwork had been laid for what would be another full year of discussion, this time with the Mandela government, of this most sensitive issue. Eventually, it would become a major public issue in the deliberations of the Truth and Reconciliation Commission and in the sensational trial of Wouter Basson.

BUTHELEZI: THE ENDGAME

The anticipation and excitement over the forthcoming election could not help but be dimmed by the continuing holdout of Chief Buthelezi. Although it was possible to foresee holding elections without his party's participation, and while preparations proceeded far down that path in the final months, most saw in that alternative the prospect of bloody confrontations and possibly wholesale civil war. Confrontations were in fact increasing in these months. Inkatha brought the reality of this situation into the heart of the white business district with a march of some forty thousand followers in Johannesburg on January 18. Shots were fired, at least two persons were killed, and eleven were wounded. For the white community, the violence was no longer far away.[12]

Early in January, Congressman Harry Johnston, chairman of the House Foreign Affairs Subcommittee on Africa and one of the most determined and energetic advocates on Africa policy, had led one of a series of congressional delegations to South Africa. The delegation flew to Ulundi on January 7 to meet with Buthelezi. Buthelezi's appeal for American support indicated how far out of touch he had become with the mood in America. As he stressed that his party never advocated the establishment of any federal system based on ethnic subdivisions, his appeal to communal rights almost sounded like nostalgia for the homeland system under the apartheid regime:

> You . . . need to realize that each of the peoples of this country, such as the Zulus, the Afrikaners, the Tswana, the Sotho, the Xhosa, and so on and so forth, have until now been provided with an area of virtual self-determination. Simply put, the Zulus, who are 95 percent of the population of the region of KwaZulu/Natal for instance, have until now had their own way of life deciding as they best see fit about matters such as communal land, inheritance, family law.

His second appeal sought to rekindle Cold War concerns:

> The American people should not make the mistake of believing that communism is dead merely because of the fall of the Soviet empire. It might no longer be a threat to the essential interests of the United States of America, but communism is of terrifying relevance to the people of this country, [as] 75 percent of the members of the National Executive Committee, which is the controlling body of the ANC, hold membership of the South African Communist Party. . . . It is possible that international communism will reorganize themselves [sic] to become the ideology of the developing countries.[13]

But the delegation was more concerned with what it saw as an unholy alliance Buthelezi had established with the right-wing parties and homeland leaders. Taking his visitors by surprise, Buthelezi ushered them without warning into a plenary meeting of the KwaZulu Parliament and asked them to address the crowd of stalwart Inkatha supporters. Johnston was not deterred. He shocked the audience by likening Inkatha's membership in this alliance to a partnership between the NAACP and the Ku Klux Klan. The reaction was almost riotous, and Buthelezi's chief adviser, Walter Felgate, responded with barely controlled fury. The delegation left South Africa deeply worried.

Later in January, Franklin Thomas, the special envoy selected by the White House, arrived in South Africa. Thomas had few cards to play; for example, he was unable to get a commitment from the White House to give Buthelezi a meeting with President Clinton if Buthelezi decided to enter the election. Nevertheless, Thomas enjoyed great respect and entrée with both Buthelezi and Mandela and met privately with each of them. Buthelezi reiterated to Thomas his objections to the whole process by which the interim constitution had been developed and his determination to have regional powers firmly entrenched in a final constitution before entering the election. Buthelezi did suggest that he have a one-on-one meeting with Mandela to discuss their differences. Thomas urged Mandela to take up this offer and in particular to make a direct call to Buthelezi himself. Intermediaries could not address Buthelezi's underlying concerns and sensitivity to status. Mandela only agreed to discuss the possibility of a meeting with his advisers, unsure what it might achieve.

In mid-February, Mandela announced further concessions he and de Klerk had agreed on with regard to the issues raised by Buthelezi and his allies. These included giving further powers to the provinces in finances, constitution writing, and structuring of provincial governments; a new binding constitutional principle precluding the writers of the final constitution from "substantially reducing" the powers of the provinces inscribed in the interim constitution; and another principle respecting self-determination, with specific references to consideration of an Afrikaner *Volkstaat*, postponement of the date for registering for the elections, and acceptance of a double ballot. Mandela moved quickly to make calls to President Clinton and other world leaders to emphasize the forward nature of these commitments and to urge international pressure on the members of the Freedom Alliance to accept them. However, these same concessions had in fact been rejected by the alliance in December and Buthelezi remained obdurate.[14]

A few days later, with Mandela under great pressure to meet with Buthelezi, I reiterated Thomas's recommendation to him of making a personal call to the head of Inkatha. Mandela agreed to a meeting, but only if he were assured of a positive response from the Inkatha leader. With Thabo Mbeki's concurrence, I asked Franklin Thomas to obtain that assurance. Once this was done, Mandela made the call. Bishop Mogoba of the Methodist Church, along with others, had been working assiduously on such a meeting and he made the final arrangements. USAID provided some funding to assist Mogoba in this effort. The meeting took place on March 1 in Durban. Like so many others, it both helped and hurt the process.

As so often with Buthelezi, his defiant public stand contrasted with his personal demeanor. In a statement issued at the start of the meeting, Buthelezi was not only defiant but threatening. He denounced the concessions Mandela and de Klerk had made two weeks earlier. He demanded that the elections be postponed and international mediation of issues between them be undertaken. He called the interim constitution a "prescription for disaster" and warned:

> We will exercise our democratic right to oppose a constitution we reject and to oppose the election under it. We will also exercise the democratic right to resist the jurisdiction that the TEC assumes it has over us. The ANC of all organizations must know that when the power of resistance politics has the potency that it will have in South Africa, resistance is more accurately an arbiter of what the people want than the polls will ever be.[15]

The tone of the meeting, however, was different. "'Buthelezi is very strange, he is like a child in front of Mandela. And he was just overwhelmed,'" said one participant."[16] Whatever the possible exaggeration of that observation, Buthelezi has always treated Mandela with great respect, even deference, in person. The talks made progress and set the stage for later final agreement. Mandela agreed to examine the idea of international mediation on constitutional issues and Buthelezi in turn agreed "provisionally" to register Inkatha for the election. These understandings were reflected, if vaguely, in a conciliatory joint statement.

But the positive atmosphere did not last long. Shaken by events in Bophuthatswana and by efforts of Mandela to woo the Zulu king away from him, Buthelezi sharpened his attacks and made more explicit his demand that the election be postponed as a condition of any agreement. After having met his promise to register his party for the election, he allowed the March 11 deadline for entering the list of candidates go by. On March 17, Buthelezi poured out his wrath on a visiting government minister, Andre Fourie, expressing his special sense of betrayal by de Klerk's government:

> I must speak of the betrayal of the people of KwaZulu by your Government and the National Party. I must speak of the betrayal of democracy and the betrayal of the trust that we so foolishly placed in the expected response of the Government to our sincere and greatest endeavors to remedy that which the Government and the ANC/SACP alliance were doing together. . . . I am making no threats. I do not even think I am making a

prediction. I am just talking about the very fundamental dimensions of politics among people such as ourselves, who have been betrayed, been manipulated, been subjected to violent onslaught and finally been subjected to the might of the State being deployed against them. I am talking about that which will emerge out of the present cauldron being prepared for KwaZulu/Natal.[17]

Buthelezi was scarcely less scathing in his reply to British pressure. Both British prime minister John Major and President Clinton had written to Buthelezi, as well as to Nelson Mandela, on the eve of their meeting to urge them to reach an agreement and proceed to the election. In his reply to Major, Buthelezi wrote, "My first appeal to you, Mr. Prime Minister, is to realize the extent to which we perceive your stand, and the stand of your Government, as reflecting views and positions which are totally incompatible with the norms, values, and democratic practices that underpin decency in British politics."[18] Buthelezi's reply to Clinton was milder in tone but concluded, "I make an earnest appeal to you to understand that your attitude, and the attitude of your Administration to the ANC, casts you in a divisive role."[19] In both letters, Buthelezi referred to international mediation and linked it to the question of the election.

Marking his bottom line in the reply to Minister Fourie, cited above, Buthelezi declared: "If international mediation could take place swiftly, if amendments could be made and dates for registration of the Electoral Act and dates for the Polls could be reconsidered, we would participate in the elections."[20] It was these twin demands—for international mediation and postponement of the election— that would in a strange and contradictory way constitute the elements of the denouement of this long and protracted process.

Before events could play out, however, the nation witnessed further violence. On March 28, Inkatha staged another mass march in Johannesburg. This time, a major confrontation took place in front of ANC headquarters. Patti Waldmeir sums up that tragic day:

> On the morning of March 28, 1994—exactly a month before the planned elections—Inkatha said it would stage a demonstration in Johannesburg. The day that ensued was to prove the bloodiest the white city had ever seen: thousands of Inkatha supporters marched through the modern business center, their spears, shields, and clubs in stark contrast to the glass-fronted skyscrapers of this American-style city. They were gunned down by snipers, in the large square in front of the public library, and outside ANC headquarters at Shell House. ANC security officers killed eight demonstrators, claiming Inkatha had tried to storm the building; eyewitnesses disputed this. After a day of appalling carnage, of the kind that had previously been confined to distant townships, fifty-three people lay dead, most of them from Inkatha. South Africa was shocked, not least by the fact

that Mandela personally prevented police from searching Shell House after the massacre. Prospects for a peaceful election had never seemed worse.[21]

It happened that on that very day two high-powered American delegations had arrived in South Africa. The first, led by Madeleine Albright, permanent representative to the United Nations, was housed at the Carlton Hotel, only a few blocks from Shell House, where Albright was scheduled to meet with Thabo Mbeki on March 28. At one point the ANC wanted to go ahead with the meeting in spite of the crisis, but, talking by cell phone with an American political officer trapped on the first floor of Shell House, we decided this was impossible. Mbeki himself agreed and called Albright instead. Albright almost surrealistically carried out her meeting by phone with Mbeki, as shots could be heard from the street below.

That same day, another congressional delegation arrived, this one led by John Lewis. Crouching down in the bus carrying them through the city, they witnessed firsthand the terrible tensions that marked this final month before elections. Two days later, I accompanied them to Durban to meet with Buthelezi. It was there that I would make one of the most important and, evidently, influential speeches of my time in South Africa. Because it was deemed to be of such significance, I will examine it here at some length.

The venue was the annual dinner of the Durban Chamber of Commerce. It was a black-tie affair and brought together the most powerful and influential of the business elite, who were almost entirely white, of KwaZulu/Natal province. Chief Buthelezi and I were both on the dais. Congresswoman Pat Schroeder, who was a member of the congressional delegation, found the atmosphere "haunting"—an "unholy alliance" of local makers and shakers with Buthelezi, "the only black person in the room."[22] But I had spoken with many of the business leaders of Natal over the preceding months and knew that while they were sympathetic with Buthelezi and were close to him, they desperately wanted a solution to the crisis, not civil war. Indeed, this was the desire of business leaders throughout the country. Only ten days earlier, I had been invited to a private dinner (as a "friend" of the host) for Buthelezi to bring him together with some of the major business figures in the country. They offered him substantial contributions if he would enter the race. Buthelezi was testy and belligerent in his response, a performance one businessman viewed as "depressing." But the sentiment of big business was clear.

I had been invited to give the principal address at the Durban dinner. I was determined to make a strong appeal for peace, for Inkatha's participation in the election, and, most critically at this moment, for keeping to the election dates of April 26–28. I was convinced, as were the major figures in both the ANC and the government, that delay of the election would jeopardize the long patience of the majority and open the door to possibly endless further negotiations. It could upset the entire transition. The tragic events in Johannesburg two days earlier only underlined the need for moving to a new dispensation. They showed the need to cease testing the ability of Mandela to keep a leash on the passions building up between the ANC and Inkatha and, equally important, to cease testing the capacity of the South African government to continue governing effectively.

I was aware that the American position on these matters was unpalatable to Buthelezi. On March 21, Buthelezi had written to Clinton that "the attitude of your Administration to the ANC and your rejection to what we in our IFP are doing, casts you in a divisive role." But I was convinced that the pressure of events, and the opinions of the vast majority of South Africans, called for moving forward.

I began my speech by again recounting the travails of American constitutional development. I repeated the theme that even without unanimity on a constitution, even without a perfect one, there comes a time, if the basic principles of democracy have been preserved, when it is essential to move forward. Moving to the contemporary situation in South Africa, I made an urgent plea for eschewing further delays.

> The structures and institutions of the apartheid era have lost their legitimacy and their authority. The single most important task of the present government is to bring a new dispensation into being, a new legitimacy and new government. All around us, ahead of the careful and neat timetable of the transition documents, the older structures are tottering and collapsing. New programs that are desperately needed . . . cannot go forward because the legitimacy and authority are not there. Trade negotiations are stalled, investment held in abeyance, security is becoming more tenuous.

Then I moved to a subject closer to the dark realities of the recent violence. This was the existence of a "third force" and the implications for Inkatha of its covert relations with security elements within the government, which had been revealed by the Goldstone Commission:

> There is another chilling factor in South Africa and we must now face it frankly. That is the existence of a group, however small, that is dedicated to the destruction of this process. It sees its opportunity in the exploitation of fears, of legitimate ethnic pride and demands, of political rivalries. By exploiting them, it seeks to wreak havoc and thus prevent culmination of this transition to democracy. We have not faced anything like this in our history. It is a terrifying force. It can only be beaten by an absolute commitment from each and every party to renounce the use of violence for settling disputes and to pledge to root out the perpetrators. But that is not enough, because this force is still hard to identify. So there is only one other way, to do the one thing that this force is trying so hard to prevent:

complete the transition to democratic rule. Whatever the issues that remain, do not delay further. Find ways to resolve issues in other ways; but it is time, it is essential to move on.

I then emphasized the needs of the majority at this moment in history:

> There is another reason [for not postponing the election] as well. That is the impatience of the majority of South Africans to exercise their democratic vote. I realize that voting itself, if not within a system sufficiently democratic, can be an insignificant act. But that is not how most South Africans see the choice being offered them today. I have seen hundreds of elderly people sitting for hours in the hot sun waiting to practice voting. I have seen people who have walked for miles to attend a voter education seminar. Across this country hundreds of thousands of people have attended voter education workshops, been trained as educators and monitors, and in other ways have expressed themselves eager to exercise this right. They have been waiting a long time. It is positively dangerous to ask them to wait longer and unfair as well.

I appealed to the business community in particular to rise to the occasion of this crisis. I urged them to be vocal, no longer to act just behind the scenes, in their support of the agreed-on transition process. I suggested they take initiatives to demonstrate that the opportunities exist for resolving the outstanding constitutional issues through negotiation and use of the provisions of the interim constitution. The choices for addressing this crisis, between going forward and risking more violence, were stark. I continued:

> Here then in Natal, we are in the eye of the storm. And you, as leaders of the business community, must participate in that difficult choice. I can only urge you to help find a way out that neither impedes the electoral process nor ignores the fears of those opposed to it. Above all, the descent into violent confrontation must be firmly and publicly opposed. If the community does not stand up strongly against that option, the field will be left to those for whom violence is a means to a destructive end.
>
> All of us have a role in this effort. We are not all involved in the negotiations. And some will feel they are not responsible for what happens. But I was recently reminded of the words of a prominent theologian, Abraham Herschel, who addressed the issue of past sins and present demands for rectification. He said, "We are not all guilty, but we are all responsible."[23]

As Schroeder recounts, the congressional delegation "clapped frantically" at the end of the speech, but they were soon joined by the audience as a whole, which to my surprise rose to its feet in applause. As I walked back to my seat, the applause still continuing, I leaned over to Buthelezi and said that I hoped he was not offended by my remarks. In his inimitable manner, he responded, "Why? Were you talking about me?"

But in fact Buthelezi was furious. The next day he met with the congressional delegation, which urged him to accept the current constitutional dispensations and join in the elections. Buthelezi replied that he could absolve them of their misperceptions because of the "philosophical pollution" and briefings they must have received from the American ambassador. He reiterated his opposition to the interim constitution and his deep distrust of an ANC-led government. Countering arguments that his stance threatened the peace of the nation, he argued that there was indeed a crisis, but only by resolving it with further changes in the constitution could the country avoid civil war. Congressman John Lewis did not back down. "South Africa is not an island," he told Buthelezi. "We're all in this thing together. . . . We [will] not stand by and see a modern-day holocaust in South Africa."[24]

The speech and the reaction to it reverberated across the political landscape. In a thank-you note a few days later, the chief executive officer of the Durban Chamber wrote to me: "Judging by the standing ovation you received and the media coverage of your message regarding the political situation, what you had to say was received with appreciation and enthusiasm." Congressman Donald Payne told the House Africa Subcommittee on his return that Buthelezi had been subjected to "one of the most persuasive and tough [instances of] diplomatic language I have ever heard uttered by a U.S. diplomat. . . . I am convinced that this strong, open and public diplomacy will go down in history as one of the factors bringing about [the] positive decision by Chief Buthelezi to now agree to participation in the coming elections."[25] Several people told me that, in the next two weeks, Mandela mentioned the speech to them as a significant event. Several years later, I asked one of Buthelezi's chief advisers why this particular speech had had such significance. He answered:

> The IFP had always been very close to the business community in KwaZulu/Natal and especially the sugar barons and so on. Everybody assumed [Buthelezi] was representing their interests and their views. . . . What you were saying at that point represented the business peoples' point of view. . . . Many people would assume he [also] had U.S. support or he had British support. . . . You undercut his position and exposed him. . . . He took it personally that the ambassador was undermining [his] own position.[26]

It would be a mistake, however, to credit this speech with having a definitive impact on the situation. It only contributed to the atmosphere pressuring for an agreement. There was another process under way that would provide the denouement of this protracted and dangerous situation in which the country found

itself, tottering on the brink of civil war. As Buthelezi told the congressional delegation in that end of March meeting, "Our future in South Africa is now hinged
on the outcome of international mediation."

INTERNATIONAL MEDIATION

For a long time Buthelezi had argued that there should be international mediation of the constitutional disagreements, and for most of that time the ANC and
the government had strongly rejected the idea. But in early 1994 the idea took
on a new life. In February Buthelezi proposed to Japanese ambassador Sezaki that
Japan, Italy (because of its role in Mozambique), Denmark (because its ambassador was dean of the diplomatic corps), and Switzerland (because Buthelezi
wanted to secure a venue in Geneva) undertake mediation between, on the one
hand, the Freedom Alliance and, on the other, the ANC and the government.
Japan insisted that the United States, United Kingdom, and Germany be
included and Buthelezi agreed.

I was skeptical of this proposal. As I wrote to Washington, I thought it could
very well be a trap, a way of involving the international community in Inkatha's opposition to the constitution and leaving us with some of the blame for the continuing impasse. At a minimum, I said, it could be just one more attempt by Inkatha
to delay the elections.[27] My concern was sharpened by the fact that the proposal
was originally broached to Japan by one of Buthelezi's most hard-line advisers,
Mario Oriani-Ambrosini. Ambrosini came to see me about it on February 16. He
had no answers to whether there was any indication that the parties would be
ready to compromise in this process or on other aspects of the terms of reference.
My worries were not diminished by his asking me in the same meeting
to take note of separatist movements under way in the Cape, such as the Cape
Republic Movement. Sure enough, I had a fax from this obscure group on my
desk that afternoon.

Of greater concern was the absence of agreement on the exact purpose of
the mediation. Sezaki had been given the impression that the mediators were
wanted to arrange further trilateral talks, not to mediate actively. But in my phone
conversation with Buthelezi on February 15, he indicated the purpose was to find
"common ground" between the parties. Inkatha's position on the issues was also described differently to various interlocutors. Buthelezi told me he had brought his
demands down to five. He told Sezaki that three would do. To others, he said four.

In my meetings with government officials on the idea, I found them deeply
skeptical. The government's chief negotiator, Roelf Meyer, could not see any purpose in international mediation. There was plenty of opportunity to meet and
negotiate; help was not needed for that. Meyer had become convinced by then

that Inkatha had made up its mind not to participate in the elections and that the other parties should proceed without them. Mediation was thus just a means for stalling the elections. The ANC was more ambivalent. Mbeki wondered if the proposal might be a face-saving way for the moderates in the IFP to bring the party around. He wanted to explore that possibility. Somewhat more opportunistically, Joe Slovo told the Japanese ambassador that this might be a way to split Inkatha off from its partners in the Freedom Alliance.[28]

In discussing the proposal with my diplomatic colleagues, I found they shared my caution but were clearly tempted, indeed flattered, by the proposal. I agreed that we should not walk away from something if it could in fact be critical to resolving the crisis. I suggested, however, that any mediation be linked to three conditions: (a) the request would come from all three major parties, Inkatha, the ANC, and the government; (b) there would be an understanding that the mediation would not involve any change in the election date; and (c) there would be some indications that the parties were willing to consider compromises in their respective positions. Most of my colleagues agreed to these, but at least one wanted to shy away from the election date issue, the issue that I felt was key. I also remained uneasy about any precipitous action on the part of the international community to become formally involved in a process that depended so greatly on internal consensus. In late February London contacted Washington to explore the idea of Anglo-American teams undertaking "shuttle diplomacy." I moved quickly to scuttle this idea. At that very time, sensitive negotiations were under way between the parties themselves that we should not cut across.

The proposal took on a new dimension in March after Mandela, in his meeting with Buthelezi on March 1, agreed to examine this proposal. Shortly afterward, I received a call from the ANC asking if Henry Kissinger would be available for the task. Evidently, Inkatha had been thinking of a group of international lawyers steeped in federalism. The ANC preferred prominent statesmen. They had in mind Kissinger and Lord Carrington. Yusuf Saloojee told me that the government was not yet involved in the mediation request but would soon have to be. Carrington was traveling in South Africa at the time and laid down some of the same conditions my colleagues and I had in mind, viz., the request had to come from all three parties, the terms of reference had to be clear and "sensible," and the names of all the mediators had to be known in advance.

I told Washington that the mediation idea was fraught with risks but that the new twist offered some opportunity:

> Each side approaches it with different agendas. The ANC sees a process that will bring Inkatha into the election, a quick, distinguished mediation that in essence blesses the transition arrangements with perhaps a few more constitutional concessions. The IFP sees it as the basis for reopening

the negotiations and delaying the elections. Any mediation effort that resulted in delaying the elections could end up putting the blame on the mediators.

Nevertheless, I wrote:

> Not wanting to be unhelpful if asked, there may be an advantage if the mediators . . . were chosen as individuals, not representatives or even nominees of government. That way the USG [U.S. government] can remain independent, supportive of the process as it contributes to a settlement, available to pick up the pieces should it fail to do so.[29]

The pressure for mediation mounted in the coming weeks, as tensions between the ANC and Inkatha rose to a fever pitch. The ANC scheduled a march in Natal that threatened to be violent, and major efforts had to be undertaken by the various parties to bring it under control. Inkatha, as noted above, scheduled a march in Johannesburg that would turn bloody. On March 31, de Klerk, with the agreement of the TEC, imposed a state of emergency in KwaZulu/Natal to stem the tide of violence. In this atmosphere, negotiators for the two parties struggled to pin down the terms of reference for the mediation. On March 24, Jacob Zuma, leader of the ANC in KwaZulu/Natal (and today deputy president of South Africa), and Inkatha's Frank Mdlalose met with me as part of a round of meetings with diplomatic missions to discuss the terms of reference they had agreed to between them. Zuma and Mdlalose had consistently been the moderates in their respective parties in KwaZulu/Natal and were desperately looking for a way out of the crisis. One could not doubt their sincerity or be anything but sympathetic with their efforts. However, it was not clear that the terms of reference they had developed met with approval from their superiors. The next day Roelf Meyer, after meeting with Zuma and Mdlalose, called me to reiterate that the government remained skeptical of mediation.

Sure enough, agreement soon broke down over the terms of reference. By the end of March each party was proposing its own terms. I told Thabo Mbeki that having two sets of terms would deter the mediators. Kissinger weighed in, writing on April 1 that he was waiting for the parties to close the gap. Nevertheless, a week later Kissinger felt he could not refuse to make the effort, hoping still that terms would be agreed on by the time of his arrival. On April 11, I learned that another tentative agreement between the parties had been jettisoned by Cyril Ramaphosa and I warned Kissinger that the terms remained in contention. But by this time, Lord Carrington was en route, so Kissinger felt he had no choice but to embark on this journey as well.

It is important to discuss the issue that was dividing the parties in the terms of reference, for this issue would prove crucial in the end. The sticking point was the date of the election. It was fairly clear to almost everyone that Inkatha hoped that the mediation process would lead to a delay in the election date. For that reason, Ramaphosa, who had become hardened by years of negotiating with Inkatha, insisted that the terms of reference explicitly reaffirm the date of the election or at least explicitly exclude the election date as relevant to the mediation. Meyer, similarly disillusioned with Inkatha, took the same position. Naturally, Inkatha would not agree to that formulation.

My position was that the election date had to be maintained and that the mediators would err if they embroiled themselves in that issue. My reasons were described above with regard to my speech in Durban. The government's authority was ebbing each day. Meanwhile, ANC supporters could not be expected to take any delay without protest. Agreement on a firm date for the elections had been critical to defusing the tensions after the assassination of Chris Hani. It was positively dangerous to reopen that date, especially since Inkatha could use that opening to prolong negotiations for months or longer. Moreover, the increasing confrontation between the ANC and Inkatha in the final weeks before the election only reinforced my view that there could be no peace in South Africa until there was a new political dispensation. Only a government that had legitimacy could deal with the underlying and long-term problems behind the violence with the strength and capacity required. On March 29, Washington concurred with my position. Washington also concurred that the U.S. and UK governments should facilitate the mediation as much as possible, given the distinguished persons leading it from our two countries, but that the governments should not be official parties to it.

The importance of the election date was reinforced at that time in meetings of Ambassador Albright, and later the Lewis congressional delegation, with officials of both the government and the ANC. De Klerk told Albright on March 28 that he was adamant that elections go forward on the date planned. He was prepared, as he later demonstrated, to declare a state of emergency in KwaZulu/Natal to ensure elections going ahead there as elsewhere. As for mediation, he found the terms of reference "clear as mud." I told de Klerk in that meeting that the United States had no intention of becoming involved in anything that would lead to postponement of the elections. The next day, de Klerk told the congressional delegation that elections must take place "come hell or high water" and that he was prepared to do whatever was humanly possible to ensure that the elections were free and fair. De Klerk also noted, rather candidly, that the problem of violence could be handled much better by the postelection Government of National Unity, because it would not have the same "legitimacy problem" that his government faced. Thabo Mbeki told the delegation on March 30 that, while the ANC was amenable to international mediation, the election date was "nonnegotiable." Mbeki believed that Buthelezi, for his part, was aiming at all costs to delay the election.[30]

On April 8 one more effort to find agreement among the parties themselves, this one engineered by de Klerk, failed. A meeting between de Klerk, Mandela, Buthelezi, and the Zulu king, to agree on protection of the Zulu monarchy, one of Inkatha's sticking points, ended in disarray when the king, after retiring to study Mandela's offer on the matter, sent back word of his refusal. Mandela and Buthelezi issued conflicting statements and the situation again seemed destined for conflict. In the meeting, Mandela had once again made clear that, whatever happened in the negotiations, there could be no question of postponing the election.[31]

This was the backdrop to the arrival of the international mediation team on April 12. The team now consisted of Kissinger and Carrington, plus four leading constitutional lawyers—from the United States, India, Italy, and Germany. The team's arrival was a media extravaganza, staged at the Carlton Hotel in downtown Johannesburg. The team was seated on the stage as they were introduced by prominent business representatives and other dignitaries. An unexpected event that would later take on major significance occurred just as the introductions were being made. A large African man walked onto the stage, introduced himself as Washington Okumu from Kenya, threw his arms around a startled Henry Kissinger, exclaiming "My professor!" and took his place among the mediators. No one quite knew who he was or who had selected him. For the moment he was ignored.

Kissinger had a clear idea of how the mediation should operate. It was his intention that he and Carrington alone would meet with the principals—de Klerk, Mandela, and Buthelezi—and help them find common political ground for an agreement, and that everyone would then go off to a quiet retreat, where the experts would address the detailed constitutional questions. Kissinger had already asked the American constitutional expert on the team—the distinguished Judge Leon H. Higginbotham—to work on compromises on the constitutional issues. Higginbotham believed the issues were of a long-term nature but was prepared to hammer out compromises that would allow the transition process to go forward. Kissinger and Carrington plunged into their meetings the first night of their arrival, starting with de Klerk. Immediately they found themselves faced with the problem of a lack of agreed on terms of reference.[32]

De Klerk handed them a new set of terms drafted by the ANC, which explicitly stated that the date of the elections was not a subject for mediation. De Klerk said he could accept this, for like the ANC he would not accept any postponement of the elections. But he doubted Buthelezi would accept so explicit a commitment. After providing a brilliant briefing on the constitutional issues, in which he refuted most of Buthelezi's complaints and provided advice on how the mediators could tackle the several complex issues at stake, de Klerk suggested that perhaps elections in KwaZulu/Natal could be delayed for nine months. The next day, the two chief mediators met with Buthelezi. British ambassador Reeve and I had attended Kissinger and Carrington's meeting with de Klerk, but I suggested we drop out of the Buthelezi meeting in order to give the mediators a "fresh start" with the Inkatha leader. Buthelezi told the two mediators that he could agree to finesse the election question, that is, not address it explicitly in the terms of reference (though he implied otherwise in his subsequent meeting with the press). Kissinger and Carrington then took this offer to Mandela.

Here the issue of the election came to a head. Mandela was flanked by Jacob Zuma, who had earnestly sought to keep the mediation alive, and Cyril Ramaphosa, who had been skeptical from the beginning. Thabo Mbeki, who sided with Zuma, was inexplicably out of town at this critical juncture. Zuma proved no match for Ramaphosa. Mandela initially seemed prepared to accept the finessing of the election issue, but Ramaphosa was adamant that the date be firmly protected in any agreement to go forward with the mediation. He also flatly rejected the idea of postponing the election in KwaZulu/Natal. Kissinger asked if the mediation could be separated from the implementation of its conclusions. The latter would be in the hands of the political parties. The mediators, Kissinger said, did not want to enter into those matters, especially any discussion of the election date. Zuma agreed with this approach, but Ramaphosa replied that the matter must be addressed holistically. The IFP would use any agreement reached in mediation to justify postponing the election. Thus "implementation" of the results, especially protection of the election date, had to be agreed on in advance.

Discomfited by the disagreement around him, Mandela asked Kissinger to give the ANC more time to work things out. Kissinger protested. The press was outside the door, waiting for an announcement that the mediation would go forward. The buses were standing by to take the mediators to a country retreat to begin working on the constitutional issues. Time was fleeting. A delay would look like the ANC was balking. But Mandela said he had no choice. Kissinger said that if there could be no agreement by the next day, he would have no choice but to call off the effort.

Kissinger had now come to recognize that the election issue was a poison tree that the mediators should not touch. Upon leaving the meeting with Mandela, he stated unequivocally to the press that the date would not be considered by the mediators. "The date for South Africa's liberation," he said, "is a decision for the South Africans to make."

That afternoon there was a flurry of meetings between the ANC, Inkatha, and the government, and not a small amount of confusion. Buthelezi sent a message saying that the mediators should proceed immediately to the retreat. Roelf Meyer called to say that they should not leave until hearing the results of the

three-way meetings. Meyer sided with Ramaphosa and wanted a clear commitment to the election date in the terms of reference. However, he was overruled
by the cabinet, which sided with de Klerk's readiness to have it finessed. But
Ramaphosa remained firm. The entire mediation team met in the afternoon and
decided unanimously to give the parties until lunchtime the next day to sort out
their differences, after which, if the issue was not resolved, they would go home.
That night my wife and I hosted a dinner at the Carlton for Kissinger, Carrington, the British ambassador, and one of Carrington's aides. Twice Kissinger and
Carrington left to meet with ANC officials Ramaphosa, Joe Slovo, and Mac
Maharaj to see if a compromise was possible.

But the next day Mandela told Kissinger that the ANC's position, along the
lines Ramaphosa had insisted on, was final. It was over. At a press conference that
afternoon, Kissinger said the mediators had left their homes with the perception
that agreed-on terms of reference had been negotiated and that advice they had
received from all quarters was that they should come. But the mediators could
not begin if there was no agreement on the issues they should mediate. Kissinger
apportioned no blame publicly, but privately he blamed Ramaphosa. Kissinger remained convinced that if the terms he brought to Mandela had been accepted by
the ANC, the mediation could have succeeded. Instead, he believed, Ramaphosa
and others in the ANC were out to "crush the Zulus." Kissinger claimed to have
heard this remark from one of the ANC officials, but he may have recalled it from
the meeting with de Klerk, who had referred to some within the ANC feeling
that way.[33] In any case, I later cautioned Ramaphosa and Slovo that it was imperative that the ANC avoid any such rhetoric following the collapse of the mediation and instead send out signals of reconciliation.

Kissinger's assessment about the potential for successful mediation on the
terms offered may be right, but it is doubtful. Ramaphosa and Slovo may have
been carried away in their rhetoric with their antipathy toward Buthelezi, but
their position was based on years of hard bargaining with Inkatha. There was
plenty of reason to believe that Inkatha's principal objective with the mediation
was to postpone the election, and thus increase Buthelezi's leverage in a long,
drawn-out period of subsequent negotiations. The fact that the mediation idea
was pushed by some of Buthelezi's most hard-line advisers, such as Ambrosini,
who made no secret of his desire to see the elections postponed, added to this
assessment. In any case, without agreement of all parties on the terms of reference,
Kissinger and his colleagues undoubtedly made the right decision—to depart.

All in all, the mediators felt they had done the right thing, first, simply by
coming. Otherwise, it would have looked as if the international community was
not responding to an urgent plea for help. Second, they were wise to recognize
that, if the differences in the terms of reference had not been reconciled at the

beginning, a failure later in the process, and one with worse consequences than resulted from calling off the effort, was inevitable. In my message to Washington, I said:

> The mediators were superb. Professional, totally fair and objective, diplomatic, united, and smart enough not to get caught in a political buzz saw, they maintained respect for their position throughout and gave this effort everything they had. They deserve praise for going the last mile.[34]

If it looked like it was over, it wasn't. Enter Washington Okumu, the enigmatic Kenyan who had barged onto the stage the night of April 12. It is still not clear who invited Okumu to the mediation—perhaps the OAU, perhaps Inkatha. In the end, no one cared. Okumu had known Buthelezi for some twenty years and they shared a deep and abiding Christian faith. Once the international mediation broke down, Okumu appealed to Buthelezi to reconsider his options. In a dramatic meeting at the Lanseria airport, where Buthelezi was preparing to return to Ulundi, Okumu put these options to Buthelezi in stark terms. Even the logistics of the meeting were extraordinary. Buthelezi had waited for Okumu to arrive, but when it came time for the plane to take off, he decided he could wait no longer. But shortly after takeoff the plane encountered mechanical problems and was forced to return. As Buthelezi described it, "It was as if God had prevented me from leaving, and I was there like Jonah brought back."[35]

Okumu appealed to Buthelezi's religious principles and asked that he consider the terrible costs in blood and lives of civil war. But he also was frank in laying out the political realities for Buthelezi and his party. If Inkatha stayed out of the election, Okumu argued, the result would be either political oblivion for Buthelezi and his party or a long, and almost certainly unsuccessful, guerilla campaign. Okumu stressed that armed opposition to a democratically elected South African government could expect neither sympathy nor support from the international community, including from any country in Africa. Okumu then put his alternatives to Buthelezi. Buthelezi would have to drop all attempts to interfere with the elections or have them postponed and indeed agree to participate in them. In return, the government and the ANC would have to agree to facilitate Inkatha's reentry into the elections—even though all deadlines for participating had passed —and accept amendments to the constitution to guarantee the role and status of the Zulu monarchy. Finally, all three parties would have to agree to resume international mediation of remaining constitutional differences after the elections.

Buthelezi accepted on condition that the guarantees for the monarchy be entrenched in the constitution prior to the elections. Okumu then set off on a two-day marathon of negotiations across the country, with de Klerk, with Mandela, with Buthelezi, and finally with all three parties together, until a deal was struck

on the morning of April 19. None of the proposals that Okumu offered were
really new, except perhaps the promise of further mediation after the election.
They were far less than the constitutional provisions on which Buthelezi had
been insisting for months.

Okumu's success was due to a variety of factors. One was that the collapse of
the international mediation had likely convinced Buthelezi that his hopes of postponing the elections were now virtually dead. This undercut the influence of
hard-line advisers such as Ambrosini and Walter Felgate, who had worked tirelessly toward this end and who had convinced Buthelezi that it was within his
reach. Okumu, who described them as wanting no agreement but instead wanting
Buthelezi "to go to war," set out to sideline them almost immediately. Learning
that Ambrosini had drafted his own, more extreme, set of proposals for the planned
meetings, a tactic Ambrosini had used before that would surely upset the process,
Okumu shut him off at the first meeting between the parties and insisted that
only Okumu's draft, agreed to by Buthelezi, be put on the table.

Another factor was that, within the ANC, the specter of civil war was no
more desirable than it was to Buthelezi. Okumu had a difficult time with Mandela, who insisted that his most hard-line advisers agree to the deal. Mandela was
particularly concerned about the requirement that the virtually defunct Parliament be called in once again to amend the transitional constitution. But once convinced that all of it could be accomplished without upsetting the election timetable, he accepted the agreement.[36] For both Mandela and Buthelezi, stepping
back from the brink of even greater violence was a relief. "South Africa may well
have been saved from disastrous consequences of unimaginable proportions," said
Buthelezi as the final agreement was reached. "Nothing is more precious than
saving lives," said Mandela.[37]

Finally was Okumu's style. His religious emphasis, his being African, his
"African style," as he described it, of not pressing against artificial deadlines, all
provided a more comfortable environment for Buthelezi to recede from his more
intransigent demands. There was none of the racial tension that crept above the
surface when Buthelezi was pressed by whites, particularly white South Africans.
As one person close to these negotiations commented,

> There was a long-term historical personal relationship [between Okumu
> and Buthelezi]. They shared values—religious values, a great commitment
> to the spiritual dimensions of the world that was between them. They also
> had a personal warmth—a long-term thing and I think in these situations
> that's absolutely vital.[38]

On April 25, one day before the election, the lame duck, all-white Parliament,
setting the stage for its own demise, was called in for one last act, to ratify the
agreed-on provisions as part of the transitional constitution. "I am just over the

moon," cried Archbishop Tutu on hearing of the agreement.[39] His reaction reflected the absolute joy that swept through the country with the announcement that the long confrontation with Inkatha had been resolved and the last obstacle to a peaceful transition had been removed. In one day, the financial rand, the monetary unit used for foreign-exchange transactions, jumped 15 percent in value.

President Clinton issued a statement warmly welcoming the agreement. "Throughout the historic process of change in South Africa, the leaders of that country have shown great courage and a capacity for compromise. Today's bold action by Chief Buthelezi, Nelson Mandela, and F. W. de Klerk is one more act of collective statesmanship that bodes well for the prospect of free and fair elections in South Africa and for the success of the Government of National Unity." At a time when the world was watching and wrestling with the strife and violence in the former Yugoslavia, the president underlined the significance that the transition in South Africa held for the rest of the world: "What happens in South Africa is of vital importance to us all. South Africa has the potential to alter the world trend toward greater ethnic division and establish a powerful model for democratic reform and national reconciliation."[40]

While much went into this final agreement, the role of the South African business community, conducted largely behind the scenes, deserves special recognition. It was the Consultative Business Movement (CBM), the alliance of concerned businesses described in an earlier chapter, that mobilized the funds and provided all of the logistics for the international mediation as well as the subsequent role of Okumu, just as it had done for the multiparty constitutional negotiations and various seminars on difficult constitutional issues over the previous four years. But its role was also substantive in these final moments. CBM early on consulted on a confidential basis with the Independent Electoral Commission to make sure there were no technical obstacles to bringing Inkatha into the elections, despite the late date. CBM's director, Colin Campbell, himself a former minister of the church, assisted Okumu in drafting the text that was used for the final negotiations (and that sidelined Ambrosini's efforts). He arranged for Anglo American Corporation to provide Okumu with a plane to race around the country over that fateful weekend. And in the critical meeting with Mandela, CBM arranged for Murray Hofmeyer, chairman of CBM, an elder statesman in the business community and much admired by Mandela, to be present at the meeting. It was testimony again to the South Africans' willingness to rise to the challenge and take their fate into their own hands. As Campbell concluded,

> The strategies we used—using the draft as text method, acting with speed, getting resources around us—were all very effective. I would go so far as to say that if those methods had not been applied [by CBM] the political will that in the end grasped the settlement would not have had

the opportunity to really assess that deal with any of the seriousness that
it deserved. It was by no means inevitable that the deal was going to survive the negotiations.[41]

South Africans were equally impressive in making the last-minute adjustments required of this agreement. By the time of the agreement, the IEC had
already printed the forty-five million ballots to be used. Inkatha's inclusion meant
printing up and fixing gummed labels, with Inkatha's symbol and Buthelezi's picture, to each of these ballots. (One can only suspect that some consideration had
been given to this possibility in advance.) De Klerk, who by a drawing to determine
position on the ballot was at the bottom, had been campaigning with the slogan
"Vote for the man at the bottom of the ballot." Now, to the anger of his party stalwarts, he agreed to allow Inkatha's sticker to be placed below his, nullifying that
slogan. The IEC had to quickly arrange establishment of polling stations throughout KwaZulu/Natal, to which it had been effectively barred until now.

Equally impressive was Inkatha's ability, with less than a week to go, to
swing into a massive campaign effort, especially in KwaZulu/Natal. Here there
was clear evidence that advance preparations and organization paid off. Indeed,
for months some Inkatha officials had been assuring me that Inkatha would in
the end participate, hinting that preparations were under way. Joe Matthews
described how it was done:

> I'll tell you what we did. The leader of our party was so determined that
> we were not going to participate, that he ordered my election committee,
> of which I was chairman, to stop its activities. And we thought, all right, we
> can stop all the public activities, but nothing stops us from printing posters,
> from being ready with election material and so on, in other words doing
> all the kind of work that would be done by a normal political party. So
> ... at this last meeting at the Union Building [Buthelezi] called me out-
> side and he said, "Can we participate in a week's time?" And I said yes.
> And of course that was a Tuesday. By Wednesday we had our posters up
> all over.[42]

Buthelezi himself launched into an intense barnstorming effort throughout
the province, going virtually day and night up to the day of the election. Throughout the country, the campaign was in full swing, now with growing optimism
that the end of apartheid, of isolation, of the long period of uncertainty was at
last at hand.

10

A New Dawn

Anyone who ever wore a "Free Mandela" T-shirt, lobbied a congressman, boycotted a name brand or hoisted a placard outside an embassy—people known here as "strugglelistas"— has been desperate to get here this week for the happy-scary ending to one of humankind's most riveting morality plays.
—PAUL TAYLOR, *Washington Post*

O N THE MORNING OF APRIL 27, the first full day of voting, a bomb went off at the Johannesburg airport. Eleven people were injured. For the next few hours that morning we waited to see whether this was the beginning of organized armed resistance to the election or the beginning of a new dawn. In all, eleven bombs had been detonated in the twenty-four hours before the polls opened, killing eight people and injuring nearly forty more. Within hours of the bomb blast on the 27th, however, the South African police swooped down and arrested thirty-one white extremists and charged them with causing the deaths and injuries over the previous several days. The election thereafter proceeded in an atmosphere free of violence and intimidation. It was a new dawn.

THE FINAL HURDLE: A FREE AND SAFE ELECTION

The weeks preceding the election had been filled with concerns. There were rumors that even if the election went smoothly, it would be followed by a complete collapse of services, utilities, and governance. Among some elements of the white population, there were preparations for disaster:

> Rumours of impending doom swept through parts of the white community.
> Pamphlets and facsimiles circulated warning of disruption to power and

water supplies and provided a "keep alive list" covering everything from drinking water to toilet paper as well as giving advice on how to douse petrol bomb fires. A list by the right-wing Conservative Party recommended that a survival kit should include "arms and ammunition, small Bible, and a panga or small axe." . . . Supermarkets, corner cafes and farm cooperatives were stripped of canned food, candles, rice, long-life milk, batteries and primus stoves. Whites in the northern suburbs of Johannesburg queued up for hours to fill gas cylinders. Gun dealers could hardly keep up with the demand. Newspapers reported airline flights to Lisbon, Tel Aviv and a number of European destinations were booked solid for months ahead.[1]

Among the blacks, there was worry as well but of a different kind: a lingering concern about the loyalty of the security forces, especially in the event of any serious armed white resistance.

The ANC was particularly anxious in these final days to allay the concerns of the white population and to secure the loyalty of the security forces. On April 8, the TEC issued a formal communication to all public servants, including members of the security forces, and directed to both those in the South African government and those in the service of the homelands, which would come under South African government control immediately following the election. The statement reminded them that the new constitution guaranteed that all persons previously employed in the government would continue in their jobs with all existing rights and levels of compensation guaranteed. The message went on: "Although the Constitution comes into operation only on 27 April 1994, the TEC has, on the basis of the provisions of the Constitution, [already taken steps that] guaranteed all public servants their jobs, salaries and pensions."[2]

On April 25, Mandela and de Klerk reached agreement in principle on a plan that could indemnify all persons convicted of political crimes committed through December 1993—whether in support of or in opposition to apartheid. The details would be worked out in the subsequent establishment of the Truth and Reconciliation Commission, but the implications were clear. Not only high-ranking security officials but, as one journalist noted, "even those rogue security agents who have helped fuel the violence in black townships in recent years" could go free.[3] Agreement had also been reached on the integration of former liberation fighters into the SADF, renamed the South African National Defense Force (SANDF), in a manner that preserved the basic structure of the SADF. Mandela also announced that the current chief of staff, General Georg Meiring, would remain in his job under the new government.

The United States also took steps to reassure the population. Richard Steyn, the editor of the *Star,* one of South Africa's major newspapers, approached me several weeks in advance of the election with a proposal. He believed that an interview of President Clinton by South African journalists on the eve of the election could provide a valuable message of assurance about the future, especially about the continued support of the international community once the transition had taken place. I contacted the White House and it was agreed. The interview, by both Steyn and a journalist from the black-owned *Sowetan,* took place in the White House on April 20. It was Clinton at his best. As Steyn would later recall, "In that frightening period when everybody was stockpiling, the President of the US came in with a very major interview, saying, look, we're behind you."[4]

Clinton began by elaborating on the significance of the South African election to the United States:

> I think it would be difficult to overstate the significance of the election to the American people, for many reasons. First of all, [there is] our own history of racial division. . . . So all Americans have been more drawn to the problems and promises of South Africa than perhaps other nations have been. Second our own civil rights movement has, for decades, had a relationship with the antiapartheid movement in South Africa. So this will be a great sense of personal joy to many, many Americans who have been involved in this whole issue personally. And finally, it is important to the United States because of the promise of harmony and prosperity in South Africa, and what that might mean not only to South Africa but to many other nations in the region.

Clinton went on to relate the election to the worldwide concern over ethnic hatreds being dramatized at that very time in the former Yugoslavia:

> I think if this election comes off it will send a message around the world that there is another way to deal with these problems, and that if it can be done in South Africa, how can you justify the old-fashioned killing and fighting and dying over a piece of land, over divisions which are not as important as what unites people in other places. I mean, it's amazing. Contrast what we see in Goradze with what we see about to happen in South Africa. It is a matter of enormous historical impact.

Clinton then turned to what was on the minds of many South Africans, especially those who were not supporters of the ANC. The question was whether Clinton shared the concerns about possible abuses by the new government:

> The leaders of the country have taken great steps to minimize the prospect of that development by agreeing to a constitution with a strong bill of rights and a constitutional court, and by agreeing to a government of national unity; and by also frankly siding with international global developments that are consistent with human rights—renouncing terrorism, renouncing the spread of weapons of mass destruction. All of these augur for a government that will be balanced and fair and will not tolerate as official policy the abuse of human rights.

Clinton then repeated the pledge we had made earlier about holding the new government to these principles:

> If that [abuses] should occur, I think the United States should have the same obligation to speak against it there as we did before in South Africa.

The other concern in South Africa was the commitment of the United States to stay involved after the transition. Clinton's reply:

> The message I would have is this: The United States is elated at the prospect of these elections. We have contributed to the effort to fight apartheid. We have tried to support the effort to have good elections and we want to celebrate with and support South Africa. But we realize that the real work will begin after the election, of continuing to live in harmony; of fighting the new problems every day; of making democracy work; of dealing with the social problems and the very severe economic problem. And we intend to be a partner from the beginning: we intend to be a full partner.[5]

Within the embassy, we took prudent precautions in case of even temporary disruptions. But I was sensitive to the message that our actions would be sending to the international community as well as to the South Africans. In a "town meeting" of all American employees and their families on March 21, after reviewing our preparations and recommendations, I urged them to convey our message accurately:

> Safety of our personnel is our first priority. But we also have to keep in mind that the United States mission is seen as a bellwether by other embassies and by South Africans. Therefore, it is absolutely essential that we convey accurately to our friends and contacts our expectations and position. We should not exaggerate.
>
> Thus it is important that we portray the situation accurately. When we ask you to store several days of food and water, it is because we think there could be—I repeat could be—temporary problems in the streets or interruptions in power supply, not because we feel the whole place is likely to come apart. It is important that you convey that accurately to your friends and neighbors if they ask. . . . Don't send false signals to the rest of the international community about what we expect to happen.[6]

It is hard to convey the joy, relief, enthusiasm, and euphoria that swept over the country when the election actually did take place, free of all that people feared. Millions of people stood in line for hours, patiently, to cast their vote. All fears of low turnout, of widespread violence, of intimidation or disorder vanished in this national outpouring of support for change. Jesse Jackson, heading the official U.S. observer mission, was struck by the signs of cooperation between white farmers and their black workers in Jubertina, where he had gone to observe voting in the rural areas. There he saw white farmers helping drive their black workers to the polls so that they could vote. The South African Defence Forces, contrary to what some might have expected, were projecting an image of stability and security rather than intimidation. The ten thousand polling places, quipped de Klerk, "are the safest places in the country," referring to deployment of more than one hundred thousand police and soldiers to secure the election.[7]

For everyone, white, black, Indian, and colored, there was a sense of liberation. "I feel a total sense of joy and relief," cried a white insurance executive as he stood in line with people of all colors. "I can finally look at people in the eye and not feel a burden of guilt."[8] A black woman answered a journalist, "What does it feel like to vote for the first time? It feels like at last the government is restoring the human dignity we haven't had in our lifetime. I know I'm free now."[9]

The election was not without controversy. Alarmed by reports of irregularities on the first day, principally from KwaZulu/Natal, where few observers were scattered through the rural areas, Mandela charged on television, "It is clear to me that there has been massive sabotage [which is] totally unacceptable."[10] Delayed delivery of ballots to the Transkei area, an ANC stronghold, prompted Mandela to insist on extending the deadline in some areas for twenty-four hours and to threaten to declare the election not "free and fair" unless the second day of voting was made a holiday as the first was. Buthelezi threatened to renounce the election if more ballots with the Inkatha stickers were not urgently provided. De Klerk's supporters believed they were losing as much as 8 percent of their vote to fraud.

Many of the problems resulted from poor statistics predicting voter whereabouts and turnout, while there were also the expected logistical problems in an election so hurriedly prepared. For example, the last-minute entrance of Inkatha into the election required organizing five hundred new polling sites and identifying and training thirteen thousand new people to staff those stations. But also, within the IEC, evidence of sabotage by employees from the Interior Department emerged, marring what were otherwise remarkable efforts by nearly everyone involved.[11] Altogether, the IEC fielded 180,000 election workers, supplemented by thousands of NGO observers from South Africa and abroad. When the above problems surfaced, SADF helicopters were employed to get ballots to the Transkei and millions of new ballots were printed and rushed to KwaZulu/Natal.

The U.S. observer mission took pains to provide reassuring information to the public throughout the days of the election. The president had sent a high-level official U.S. observer mission. Headed by Jesse Jackson, it included Assistant Secretary of State for Africa George Moose and NSC director for African affairs Colonel MacArthur DeShazer, along with several private citizens. The embassy was concerned enough about the safety of this high-profile team that we registered

Reverend Jackson in a hotel under a different name and refused to give out the itinerary of the team. At the same time, the message that the team had to give to the people was important. Someone of Jackson's fame would attract attention and be sought out for comment, which provided an opportunity, so we arranged for Jackson to stay in touch with the radio and print press by phone, reporting regularly on his and his team's experiences throughout the first two days of voting. The embassy fed him information from other observers around the country so that he could report on the situation overall, for example, the absence of resistance in the northwest, where it had been most expected. The message he thus conveyed was that while problems were occurring here and there, the overall election process was going extremely well. Jackson praised each step the IEC took to correct the situation, and he praised the conduct of the SADF. Above all, he urged people to see the election as a time for celebration.

Members of the IEC, UN and other observer teams, and South African leaders all called during the day to express their appreciation for Jackson's commentary countering the spread of any false rumors and helping build confidence. On the night of April 27, Jackson and the team gave a press conference at the Carlton Hotel in downtown Johannesburg, summing up their impressions from the first two days of voting.

Jackson noted that his team had split up to cover both rural and urban voting places, in both the south and the north of the country:

> The election is moving forward with great momentum. . . . In some instances there were glitches, but glitches to be understood in light of such an enormous task to be put together in just a matter of four months. In most areas, there were virtually no complaints. . . . In those areas where there are some technical problems, the IEC has been quick to move. . . . The basic flexibility of the IEC is to be commended and if there are outstanding disputes, there is a process for adjudication. We will be working all day tomorrow, visiting polling sites and talking with leadership, and talking with members of the Independent Electoral Commission, trying to gather as much information as we can. But that which we have seen today has been very impressive and encouraging.

Jackson conveyed as well some of the tremendous emotion of this event that he had witnessed. The first day of voting, April 26, had been set aside for the old and infirm:

> To watch seniors, some in their wheelchairs, who got up at three o'clock in the morning to sit in those chairs, with blankets across their legs in the chill of the morning, waiting for an opportunity to make a statement, in a life-long drive for the right to be recognized as a whole human being.

While there is great concern over how quick the housing will come, and health care will come, what has come already is the ending of humiliation in the resurgence of pride and human dignity.[12]

There were nearly five hundred American observers in all. There were sixty-seven in the United Nations' fifteen-hundred-person observer mission, a large delegation from the AFL-CIO, delegations from individual universities and NGOs, and some individuals who were acting alone. Through the coordination we had arranged with the Lawyers' Committee for Civil Rights, U.S. observers were spread out across the country, attached in most cases to South African observer groups and able to share in the joy of this unfolding miracle. For Americans who had long worked for this moment, it was especially moving. Ron Walters, a Howard University professor on the official observer mission, was too overcome with emotion to continue his remarks at the Jackson press conference. An African American AFL-CIO representative said, "This is one of the last places where the pure struggle for peoples' rights is taking place. There is something spiritual about being here."[13]

The problems that had been experienced in the voting process, however, did not end there. Ballot boxes were subsequently mishandled, charges of fraud were lodged, especially over irregularities in KwaZulu/Natal, rules for reconciling ballots and voting stations had to be jettisoned. The result was that for a week following the election the IEC and the parties were engaged in counting and bargaining. Justice Kriegler, who had appeared in television ads throughout the previous several months promising a fair and secure election, reflected the muddle in his gradually descending order of public commentary. On April 28, in the wake of the problems in the voting, he told the press, "I never promised you a rose garden." "This isn't the US or England," he said a few days later as the delay in announcing the results continued. When questions began to be raised about the ways in which the disputes were being settled, he responded, "This election is not about vote reconciliation, it is about national conciliation." "Let's not get squeamish about it," he remarked on May 4, as reports circulated about deals being made with the parties. And finally, as he was about to declare the election "substantially free and fair," he said ruefully, "When you live in a brothel, it is hard to remain chaste."[14]

There are many stories about how the results were finally determined. Though some ballot counters swore to me that they never received any instructions but to do their work as they saw fit, most people believed that the parties came together to work out a compromise. One theory is that Mandela agreed to drop any protests over KwaZulu/Natal, to the anger and frustration of the ANC chapter in that province, in return for getting the extra ANC votes from a second day's voting in the Transkei, which swelled the ANC's overall majority. A more widespread belief is that both the National Party and Inkatha dropped their protests against the ANC when it was determined that the ANC did not reach a two-thirds majority or sweep every provincial race. Whatever the actual process of compromise, all parties agreed in the end to drop their protests. De Klerk conceded on May 2, three days before the final results were officially announced.

The general outcome of the election was never in doubt, and the population remained calm during this period, basking in the delight of what had transpired. The only uncertainties were in the margin of victory for the ANC, whether it achieved the two-thirds needed to ratify a new constitution without the support of other parties, and the outcome in such hotly contested provinces as KwaZulu/Natal. In the end, the ANC was awarded 62.6 percent of the vote, de Klerk's National Party 20.4 percent, Inkatha 10.5 percent—each crossing the 10 percent threshold for participation in the Government of National Unity. General Viljoen's party captured only 2.7 percent and the Democratic Party polled 1.7 percent. The PAC fared worse, with 1.3 percent of the vote. The ANC lost only two of the nine provincial elections: the Western Cape to the National Party and KwaZulu/Natal to Buthelezi's Inkatha. Mandela professed to be relieved that the ANC had not won a two-thirds majority. "We have to be very careful," he said, "not to create the fear that the majority is going to be used for the purpose of coercing the minorities."[15]

Buthelezi won far more support than some of his detractors had predicted, especially in KwaZulu/Natal, where his hold on the rural vote was virtually uncontested. In the bitter conflict between the ANC and Inkatha over the previous several years, ANC stalwarts sometimes derided Buthelezi as representing "nobody," not even 5 percent of votes as Mandela once said to me. On the other side, Buthelezi's admirers would exaggerate his support, as if all Zulus, making up 20 percent of the population, were behind him. In fact, as we often pointed out in our discussions during this period, Buthelezi's strength in the rural areas of KwaZulu/Natal, mobilized through local chiefs and assiduous courting of tradition, was virtually unchallengeable, whether at the polls or through force and intimidation. As I once said to Mandela, "You cannot beat Buthelezi on his own ground." At the same time, Buthelezi's support in the cities, among urban and union-member Zulus, was much less. Thus Inkatha secured a bare majority of forty-one out of eighty-one seats in the predominantly Zulu province. And notwithstanding the intense violence that had taken place between Inkatha-held hostels and ANC activists in the townships outside Johannesburg during 1993–94, Inkatha gathered only three out of eighty-one seats in the Transvaal legislature. Here as elsewhere outside KwaZulu/Natal Inkatha showed itself with virtually no strength.[16]

All the disputes and controversies seemed to fade into the background as the events of the next several days unfolded.

On May 9, the newly elected Parliament, with all the pomp and ceremony that had been traditional in that body under the old regime, assembled and voted Nelson Mandela president of South Africa. "This is the day for which we have been waiting for more than 300 years," said Archbishop Tutu. Cyril Ramaphosa, who had led the arduous negotiations for the ANC over the previous four years, exulted as he strode into the building "we have been storming all these years. . . . Suddenly through negotiations, the doors are open, and we are walking in majestically."[17]

Perhaps nothing was more moving nor more significant in this week of extraordinary events than seeing, together on the floor of the Parliament, all the great rivals for power in South Africa—Mandela, de Klerk, Buthelezi, Viljoen, the PAC's Makwetu, the Democratic Party's Leon—not in the streets nor in the bunkers but now walking across the aisle, shaking hands, preparing to govern as members of a common Parliament, members of a united system of government. Mandela entered the building that day with de Klerk at his side. He warmly embraced Buthelezi, whom he would name minister of home affairs, and the members gave these two a standing ovation. As one journalist recorded the event, "African adversaries embraced, world leaders hailed a miracle and ordinary people danced in the streets."[18]

On May 10, before 150,000 people from all over the country and dignitaries from all over the world, Nelson Mandela was inaugurated as president on the steps of the Union Building in Pretoria. Foreign governments were asked to limit their delegations to ten persons, but, as is often the case with the United States, the official U.S. delegation exceeded the limit, numbering more than sixty, including both a White House and a congressional contingent. Somehow, the South African government found seats for all of them. Vice President Al Gore headed the American delegation, which included his wife, Tipper, Hillary Clinton, General (rtd.) Colin Powell, members of the cabinet, and many distinguished leaders of the anti-apartheid movement, including Maya Angelou, Jesse Jackson, Ron Dellums, and John Lewis.[19]

There are many stirring memories from the inauguration. It is hard to describe the emotion of seeing Nelson Mandela, so long a prisoner, so long almost more a symbol than a reality, being sworn in as president of South Africa, surrounded by all the trappings of power, saluted by the still white-led military, joined on the dais by his former adversaries. For those who campaigned for more than twenty years to "Free Mandela," for those who feared that the final liberation of this deeply divided society could come only through bloody civil war, this must have seemed a dream, beyond even their greatest expectations.

Among the many memories, two moments from that day stand out for my wife and me. When Mandela stepped up to the podium, he was followed by the chiefs of staff of all the military branches. As he took his seat in the front row, they took theirs behind him. "That moment" said Colin Powell, "marked the real transfer of power." In the midst of the ceremony, South African planes came into view. For just a moment, a ripple of fear ran through the audience. Then one black man remarked to his neighbor, "It's all right. They're ours now." And the audience cheered as the planes saluted the new president in a magnificent flyover.

Part III
Afterword

11

A New Relationship

FOR MORE THAN A YEAR, the United States had been preparing for the new relationship with South Africa that a new dawn would bring. Over and over U.S. spokespersons had been assuring South Africa that American interest would not fade away after the election, when the many problems of reconstruction and reconciliation would have to be addressed. The problem lay in the realities of the 1990s. American aid levels were declining; at the same time, demands were being placed on the United States for new programs in the former Soviet Union and the transitional countries of Eastern Europe. For those who wanted to make a dramatic statement of support for the new South Africa, these were formidable barriers. Under the circumstances, the administration put together an impressive package of assistance. But given the historic character of the change taking place in South Africa, and how much Americans in all walks of life had been involved in encouraging it, what we felt was a good faith effort would fall short in the eyes of the man whom everyone wanted to impress the most: Nelson Mandela. It was not fatal to the new relationship, but it cast a shadow on it.

There were other adjustments as well. Normalcy brings new opportunities, but also new problems. The new South Africa found itself enmeshed in trade disputes with the United States, with lingering problems of arms sales and indictments, and with new foreign policy challenges. Nevertheless, the foundations of a strong new relationship were built. Shared principles and shared world objectives would be at the heart of this relationship.

THE AID ISSUE: PEANUTS ARE AN AMERICAN SUCCESS STORY

The controversies over the U.S. aid program are a good example of the problems encountered. For more than a year prior to the 1994 election, the U.S. government had worked on what package of support we could provide the new government.

225

I was cautious in the months leading up to the election, saying in several speeches in South Africa that the aid level might not rise at all, but that emphasis would be given to mobilizing private investment and the financing of the World Bank. But this was caution on my part only. The United States, I knew, had to do something much greater. Behind the scenes, a bureaucratic struggle was under way. Brian Atwood, administrator of AID, was experiencing severe cuts by Congress in the overall assistance program. As a result, he had made the decision to close twenty-two USAID posts, many in sub-Saharan Africa. He could not see robbing the Africa program even more in order to provide substantially additional aid to South Africa, which on the surface was richer than most other African countries. Indeed, Atwood pointed out, in this age of declining aid, South Africa at $80 million was already the largest program in sub-Saharan Africa. Atwood was also concerned that South Africa's liberation could detract from development in the southern Africa region as a whole by causing the United States to concentrate too much on South Africa. Atwood thus began work on a regional initiative within which he would fit the South Africa program.[1]

For the State Department and other agencies, such as Commerce under Ron Brown, that had played such active roles in the run-up to the election, this was unthinkable. I sympathized with Atwood, having served in AID for nearly twenty years and knowing the difficulties he was facing. He was right too that the United States should not be seen as turning its back on South Africa's neighbors, who, while celebrating the victory over apartheid, for which they had all paid a price, were also concerned that South Africa could dominate the region to their own diminishment. But I also knew that the U.S. response to the end of apartheid had to be more dramatic than a relatively vague regional proposal.

When Atwood visited South Africa in January 1994 to announce the additional election assistance, we had several talks. Atwood finally agreed that there would have to be two packages, one explicitly for South Africa and another for the region. We discussed a package that would include not just direct grant assistance but housing finance guarantees and use of the Overseas Private Investment Corporation, the Export-Import Bank, and other U.S. government resources. Atwood complained, however, that the Office of Management and Budget had just rejected his request for an increase in the housing guarantee program and that Congress was criticizing it as well. I told Atwood that I would personally help draft the housing guarantee proposal to meet Congress's latest objections and would help lobby for its approval. Housing was one of the most critical and visible needs in South Africa, I argued. Americans could not have visited the segregated black squatter communities all these years and then not offer help in this sector when the opportunity arose. USAID was making excellent progress in developing proposals along this line. Atwood agreed to include a substantial housing guarantee program.

These discussions broke the logjam in planning. But because the situation in South Africa had remained so tenuous throughout 1993, the administration had not requested a major package of assistance for South Africa in the FY94 budget. Thus everything that could be put into the package had to come from some other cause or line item. As the date of the inauguration drew near, the administration scrambled for funds to fill the package. Asked about this in his interview with the *Star* and the *Sowetan*, President Clinton was candid:

> We are looking, we are scouring the government accounts for things, money that won't be spent that we can put into this. . . . Now, next year and the year after—we're going to stay after this on a multiyear basis—we may be able to do better. But I think, given the condition of our budget laws and where the money is right now and the fact that we are in the middle of a fiscal year, we're going to do quite well.[2]

On May 4, in a ceremony on the South Lawn of the White House, President Clinton unveiled the U.S. program. It was a three-year commitment of $600 million, combining grant technical assistance, the largest component, with a number of guarantees that would mobilize private funds. The USAID program would rise from $80 million to $136 million, plus housing guarantees for an additional $30 million in private financing. The balance of the $200 million-per-year program would come from OPIC, USIA, and the Trade and Development Agency. There was, as in all such packages, a good deal of "smoke and mirrors." The real increase in direct aid was in the near doubling of USAID funds, and given the stringent conditions in AID, this was a tremendous achievement. The South Africa program would become one of the largest in the world. But much of the balance was in the funds from private sources that would be mobilized by U.S. guarantees, for example, $30 million for housing and $35 million for investment.

The president announced several other non-aid parts of the package. The United States Trade Representative would grant South Africa special trade preferences under the Generalized System of Preferences, in effect giving more than four thousand South African products duty-free entry into the United States. The Commerce Department would designate South Africa as one of the "big emerging markets," thus permitting a range of new trade-promotion services. A high-level minister-counselor would be assigned as commercial officer in Johannesburg, one of only ten such positions worldwide. In addition, Ex-Im would continue to provide whatever export financing the market demanded and the Defense Department would reestablish the broken relationship with the South African military, offering $100,000 in training funds.[3]

If the United States was satisfied that it had made a tremendous effort, Nelson Mandela was not. When Vice President Gore paid his call on Mandela the day after the inauguration, the new president was abnormally stiff and seemingly preoccupied. No sooner had the two exchanged the normal pleasantries and congratulations than Mandela asked to see Gore alone. When Gore emerged, he told me that Mandela had expressed shock at the U.S. offer. He saw it as well below what other countries were offering—a subject of continuing debate between the United States and South Africa afterward. But most of all, Mandela saw it as threatening his whole concept of what the U.S.–South Africa relationship should be. Mandela told Gore he wanted to fly to Washington urgently, address a joint session of Congress, and ask for a tripling of the offered amount. Taken aback, Gore urged Mandela to discuss the matter with me before making any decision along these lines.

What prompted so strong a reaction? Several things. The United States had made South Africa's liberation a cause célèbre. Over the years, but especially in the final years of negotiation and transition, South Africa had received countless high-level American visitors, innumerable messages of encouragement, and most recently promises of continued support in the postelection years. I have no doubt that some of Mandela's visitors during this period told him, in private conversations, that South Africa freed from apartheid would become a second "Israel," the focus of a Camp David–type commitment on the African continent to match the deep American involvement in the Middle East. Camp David, it will be recalled, ushered in a U.S. aid commitment of nearly $3 billion annually to the two participants. In that light, $200 million a year, largely in technical assistance, as large as it loomed in the U.S. bureaucracy, was pitifully small in Mandela's eyes.

But second, as Mandela explained to Gore and later to President Clinton, he had had to convince his more radical colleagues in the ANC, long imbued with anti-U.S. feelings, that the relationship with the United States was going to be one of South Africa's most important in the post–Cold War world. Partly, he had argued, that would be because American support for the many tasks of reconstruction and overcoming of the apartheid legacy would be irreplaceable. Mandela also saw the relationship as part of a broader one encompassing key international values and efforts for peace and development in the region. The U.S. offer, however, was so below expectations that it would undercut these efforts. The United States would be seen as doing less than even smaller countries in Europe and Asia. Anti-U.S. feelings would be rekindled. In his meeting with Gore, Mandela talked of the many youth who had paid the price of imprisonment under apartheid, many of whom were now without education and had been rearrested for crime. These people desperately needed a lifeline of hope, for which Mandela would appeal to Congress.

Some within the administration were intrigued by the prospect of Mandela making such an appeal. I was not. I doubted that any increase in aid to South Africa would be additional but would only cut further aid elsewhere in Africa. I also was not sure this was the best way for the new relationship to begin, with an appeal for more aid. Gore had warned Mandela that this could worsen, not improve, relations. Most of all, the U.S. aid program, if increased, would likely continue to be largely in the form of technical assistance. This was not what Mandela was looking for. U.S. aid no longer funded large capital projects such as infrastructure and housing. For this type of funding, South Africa would have to look to the World Bank or to private investment. The days of such investment from U.S. aid were over.

I met with Mandela on June 17 to follow up. I tried to put our program in context and to suggest that what additionally the United States could do most usefully was to help attract private investment to South Africa. Mandela was conciliatory and responsive. His reaction to the U.S. aid announcement, he said, was in response to criticism of it from the more radical wing of the ANC. He said that President Clinton had in fact followed up on everything he had ever asked of him, beginning with raising South Africa's needs with the G-7 in 1993. It was a point Mandela would make many times in the future. He said that U.S. leadership was very important to him and that the relationship was thus important. He was sensitive to Gore's caution about the effect of another aid request. His main concern, however, was to mobilize financing for the ANC's Reconstruction and Development Program (RDP), the cornerstone of its new economic policy, to help overcome the ravages of apartheid. I said that the United States would be interested in hosting or organizing with the South African government a conference aimed at mobilizing private investment for such purposes. Mandela responded positively, and a few days later he set up an interministerial meeting to work on it. Mandela also said he would like to preside at our first aid agreement signing, and, true to his word, he did so when in September we signed an agreement with the Ministry of Justice to help overhaul the court system, which was then still staffed and structured from the apartheid era.

But this was not the end of the controversy. First of all, despite months of meetings and planning, the proposed conference never came off. The United States had in fact sponsored a major conference on South Africa in Atlanta just after the inauguration. The administration had put considerable pressure on Deputy President Thabo Mbeki to attend, along with other key South African officials. The conference, titled "Investing in People: US–South Africa Conference on Democracy and Economic Development," was a huge public relations success and brought together people to discuss all aspects of the new South Africa.[4] It would have been hard to manage a second one so soon afterward, even if it had been more sharply focused. Second, the South African government was determined to set its own economic agenda. It had arranged, with support from the UN Development Program, for a major conference of its own on the RDP in October, to which all donors were invited. The government poured much of its efforts into this conference, producing voluminous documentation and project proposals. The European Union had meanwhile scheduled a conference with the Southern Africa Development Community to look at regional development. Perhaps most important, Alec Erwin, the deputy minister of finance and later minister of trade and industry, to which the planning for the U.S. conference was assigned, was never keen on the conference. While always polite and expressing support for the idea, Erwin kept putting off a decision and finally indicated that the United States should consider folding the conference into a broader one involving other countries as well.

In the end, the idea was simply overtaken by events. There were many other activities on the part of the United States to promote private investment, including a proposed visit by all the major U.S. pension funds, active work of the new minister-counselor from the Department of Commerce, and numerous meetings with individual American investors. But the special conference on private investment never materialized.

Meanwhile, despite the good feelings in our June meeting, the issue of U.S. aid levels continued to fester in Mandela's mind. In October, Mandela arrived in the United States for a state visit. It would be a triumphal one and would seal the personal relationship between Mandela and Clinton, who would go out of his way to attend numerous events for Mandela in Washington and New York and deliver some magnificent speeches. But it started out rocky. In the arrival ceremony on the lawn of the White House, Mandela, speaking without notes, first praised former president George Bush, then African Americans who had contributed so much to the anti-apartheid movement, then the American people, before getting to any reference to his host. Mandela also bluntly asked for a "blank check" from America. President Clinton, and for that matter the crowd, was a little uneasy at this less than gracious opening. That evening at the state dinner, Mrs. Clinton, puzzled, asked me, "Did someone tell him that a bipartisan approach would get him more money?"

Fortunately, Mandela got word that his remarks had upset people. From that point on, he not only was upbeat in his public statements, but lavished praise on Clinton. But what was on his mind at the start became clear on the second day, when Vice President Gore hosted a meeting preparatory to the meeting with President Clinton. Mandela told Gore and the assembled group of cabinet secretaries and officials that the U.S. aid level was "miserable" compared to that of the Japanese and others. Mandela compared it as well to the aid the United States

provided to the Middle East. The left wing in South Africa was making an issue
of it, he said. Mandela intended to raise this with Clinton the next day. I told
South Africa's foreign minister that I did not think "miserable" was the right word
for our program, but Mandela's staff, including the ambassador to the United
States, Harry Schwartz, were on the same sheet of music with their president.

The next day, Mandela, though more politely, raised the issue with President
Clinton. Secretary of State Christopher was blunt. In the Middle East, he said,
"we have strategic interests." Gore painstakingly took apart the comparison with
other donor pledges to South Africa, pointing out that most of the others' offers
were export credits, at not insubstantial interest rates, compared to our largely grant
program and guarantees that would raise private, not government, loans. We too
were offering export credits, through the Export-Import Bank, but we did not include these in our aid figures. Mandela backed off a bit and simply asked Clinton
to do the best he could. Clinton commented that Mandela's visit would surely
help with Congress in obtaining funds for South Africa.

Yet it was still not over. Back in South Africa in November, Mandela,
responding to a question from the press, commented that the American aid program to South Africa was "peanuts." The remark set off a flurry of press and official commentary.[5] I found it coming up in conversations with officials in the capital and the provinces, with American and South African businessmen. Some
jumped on the bandwagon, with the criticism spreading to the level of American
investment compared to that of other countries—even though the United States
was indeed ahead of nearly every other nation in this regard. It was particularly
painful to hear this from black businesses when we had structured so much of our
program and private investment promotion to assist this group.[6] However, some
commentators worried that Mandela was unnecessarily ruffling the feathers of
the United States.[7] One correspondent noted that Mandela's remarks came just a
week after Republicans, with pledges to cut government spending, had gained
control of Congress. "If he thinks it's peanuts, he doesn't have to eat them," one
Republican was reported to have commented.[8] Many South Africans, seeing this
added to other issues discussed below, began to wonder whether the U.S.–South
African relationship was going downhill.

I was concerned about the reactions and felt that a formal response was necessary. Indeed the press anticipated it.[9] But first I wanted to go back over the facts
and comparisons with Mandela. We had a brief conversation on the phone a few
days after his remarks to the press. Mandela defended his statement, reiterating
the need to bring around the radicals in their attitude toward the United States.
He chided me, asking that the Americans not ask him never to criticize the
United States. He made comparisons again to other U.S. aid programs, including
the one to Egypt. As for other donors whose programs, I reminded him, were

actually smaller than ours, Mandela said they were doing "more than on the surface." This appeared to be a reference to contributions to the ANC, a reprise of Mandela's discussion with Clinton in 1993. We went around on these points for several minutes and I disagreed especially with his belief that his remarks might actually help us with Congress. It was a strained conversation, and we ended by agreeing to discuss the issue further.

I went to see Minister Jay Naidoo, who was responsible for the RDP. He assured me that our grant program was indeed substantially greater than others and well integrated with the RDP. He was fulsome in his praise of cooperation with USAID. However, he said there was disappointment within the government that the United States had not responded to South Africa as we had to Russia and Ukraine, adding to the comparisons! He also intimated that there was disappointment that Mandela had not found something akin to these expectations during the state visit. I checked with the Japanese ambassador to see if my understanding of his program was correct. It was, he said. But he knew some governments, though not Japan, were making contributions to the ANC, some for prestige purposes, others for jockeying within the Nonaligned Movement (NAM). Most of Mandela's foreign trips, to Indonesia, Malaysia, Saudi Arabia, and elsewhere, were believed to be for fund-raising.

As concerned as I was over both the growing amount of disinformation about our program and its deeper impact on the relationship, I did not want to pick a public fight with so great and fundamentally friendly a figure as Mandela. Indeed, in a meeting on another matter the following January, Mandela went out of his way to emphasize the importance he gave to the relationship with the United States and that the "peanuts" remark had been taken out of context. His full statement on the matter had made the point that the relationship with the United States had to be seen in terms not just of aid but of "the support they have given us on a wide range of issues." He reiterated the same point in a phone call to me the next day.

That same week, I sent Mandela a letter on which I had been working for a long time. I wanted to clarify the facts about our aid as well as alert him to my plans to go public and the reasons for my doing so:

> I appreciated the opportunity to discuss with you over the phone your comments on the United States aid program. While I understand the background and context of your remarks, as you explained them to me, they have nevertheless unleashed a spate of attacks on the United States by officials of the Government, Provincial MECs [Ministers] and others, many of whom have no knowledge of the magnitude or details of our program. One Minister, not involved with our aid program, gave an interview to an American newspaper saying that the South African Government would soon propose a total restructuring of our aid program. . . . Other

officials have accused us of racism, insensitivity, etc., then been amazed when we told them the facts about our program.

This "open season" on the United States has the potential of harming our relations, which is of course exactly the opposite of what you intended. I will be undertaking a series of speeches and interviews with the media in the coming weeks to correct the vast amount of misinformation about our program.

I went on to provide Mandela with a detailed rebuttal of the various charges and false comparisons that were being made. I would not criticize other donor programs in public. After all, I wrote, President Clinton had appealed to G-7 members to double their aid, and we were not in competition with them. Nevertheless, in this letter I pointed out that, excluding commercial credits that the South African government itself had said it did not want counted as "aid," the U.S. program was three times that of the United Kingdom, more than three times larger than that of France, and equal to Japan's. Furthermore, while our program was the same in size as that of Japan, Japan's was 15 percent grant, ours 65 percent; the balance of Japan's package was in tied loans, a type the South African government had chosen to utilize virtually none of. By contrast, nearly $200 million of our aid was already committed. I also reported my meeting with Minister Naidoo and his assurances that our program fit well into the priorities of the RDP and that he was accessing the exact technical assistance he needed. As for our programs in Russia and Ukraine, I reported to Mandela that on a per capita basis, our aid to South Africa was twice that to Russia and three times that to Ukraine. I closed by expressing my hope that Mandela would help me in "turning away unfair criticisms that are being leveled not only at our program but at the fundamental nature of our relationship."[10]

For the public response, I chose the annual general meeting of the American Chamber of Commerce in February 1995. I wanted to set the record straight, but I also wanted to take the sting out of the issue. So I titled my speech, a copy of which I sent to Mandela in advance, "US–South Africa Economic Relations (Or Peanuts Are an American Success Story)." I opened it with a long account of the work of George Washington Carver, the African American scientist who, seeing the devastation to southern farmers in the United States from the collapse of the cotton market, closeted himself in his laboratory with only peanuts to sustain him. There he developed, from this one crop, meal, instant and dry coffee, vinegar, cheese, milk, molasses, bleach, stain remover, wood filler, metal polish, ink and paper, and, perhaps his most famous invention, peanut butter. Carver's work revolutionized the southern agricultural economy. By 1938, peanuts had become a $200 million crop and were, besides, restoring the soil that had been leached by decades of cotton farming. I concluded:

> I tell this story because I am sure that it was the ubiquitousness, the diversity, the high value and the contribution to economic growth of this particular product that President Mandela had in mind when he likened our program to peanuts.

I then went into a defense of our program. I was candid that controversy over the aid program arose from exaggerated expectations, due in part to the very importance we in the United States had given to the transition in South Africa. I then went into detail, as I had with Mandela, on how our program in South Africa compared to those in Russia and Ukraine, two countries of great strategic importance to the United States. Even some of the figures cited in the press for Israel confused our grant aid with a $10 billion housing guarantee loan that Israel was obligated to repay.

I described the areas in which we were working that were important to South Africa, for example, housing, where we had already mobilized in one year the guaranteed loans anticipated over three years; education, where we were helping upgrade the formerly black and colored colleges; training at all levels of government; and health. Answering another popular criticism of U.S. aid, that it went largely to American contractors and experts, I pointed out that 60 percent of our aid went directly to South African experts, entities, NGOs, and universities. More than half of these were black South Africans or black-led organizations. Finally, addressing the criticism of U.S. investment so far, I pointed out that more than three hundred American companies were now operating in South Africa, well above the number during the period of sanctions.[11]

The speech was widely reported and seemed, with the touch of humor, to cut through much of the tension that had arisen, and the controversy died down.[12] But the disappointment remained in the minds of many South Africans, including Mandela. Thus from time to time, along with other criticisms of the program, the peanuts accusation lingered, an object lesson in the dangers of building expectations that cannot possibly be fulfilled.

Mandela would lash out at the aid program again in 1997, in relation to another issue. On this occasion, in a speech to the ANC, he sharply criticized some South African NGOs that in his words were corroding the ANC movement. In unusually sharp terms, he called such NGOs "instruments of foreign governments and institutions that fund them to promote the interests of these external forces." Though it was in a separate section of the speech that he lashed out at the USAID program for not being sufficiently responsive to South Africa's needs, the criticism seemed linked to the earlier criticisms of the NGOs. This accusation, which some attributed to Mbeki, was a reflection of the growing sensitivity of the ANC government by then to internal criticism and posed a challenge to programs like that of USAID, which sought not only to lend support to the new government but to maintain support to the representatives of civil society, some of whom were indeed independent critics of government. USAID moved quickly to close this breach, but in the process was accused by some of these critics of bending too far in the other direction.[13] As some observers noted, looking back on USAID's long history of support to NGOs, "Thus, in the end, USAID–South Africa's strength ended up being its Achilles Heel."[14]

But aid was only one such issue.

Foreign Policy

Soon after the TEC had been formed and had established a foreign affairs committee, I had discussed with its members the areas of foreign policy that would be sensitive between our two countries under the expected ANC government. The principal issues revolved around the so-called pariah states, later designated "rogue states" and subsequently "states of concern" to the United States. These were Iraq, Libya, Iran, Cuba, and North Korea as well as controversial ones such as Sudan. Mandela had already made clear that he would not turn his back on Libya and Cuba, which had aided the ANC in the days when it was outside the pale for most Western countries. I urged the incoming officials, however, to establish close consultation with us in order to avoid any unforeseen repercussions. There were provisions in U.S. law, for example, that would cut off aid to any country providing arms to some of these states or aiding others.

Such issues were bound to be controversial, however, especially for a new government looking to establish its independence and break with its past. Moreover, the new government was itself struggling with legacies from its predecessor.

One example of the latter was the issue of assisting the government of Sudan. In early 1994, we learned that South Africa had agreed to help Sudan repair some of its planes and helicopters. I demarched the Department of Foreign Affairs (DFA) on this matter in January, arguing that such assistance only contributed to the civil war in that country. DFA replied that, while South Africa would not assist with the repair of military planes, such as MIGs, it was assisting on C-130s and helicopters. I questioned whether one could make the distinction over the latter as purely for civilian use. Shortly after Mandela's government was inaugurated, I raised the issue with the new deputy minister of foreign affairs, Aziz Pahad, who promised to look into it. He later told me that the assistance would not continue past the existing contract. But nearly a year later, Minister of Defense Modise told me that Sudan, with the connivance of South African arms agents Armscor and Denel, had "tricked" the government into letting in two more helicopters for repair. Modise balked when he learned of this, for South Africa had determined that Sudan fell into the category of countries to which South Africa would sell no arms.

Much more in the public eye were the questions of South African relations with Cuba and possible South African cooperation with Iran. At the United Nations, in the fall of 1994, South Africa voted against the U.S.-sponsored resolution criticizing Cuba's human rights record. In July 1995, South Africa announced plans to send an ambassador to Cuba. This announcement elicited a strong reaction from Congresswoman Ileana Ros-Lehtinen, a Cuban American who had fled Cuba and who had just taken over as chair of the House Subcommittee on Africa. She and three other members of Congress wrote to South Africa's ambassador in Washington protesting the decision and urging even more strongly that Mandela not invite Castro to South Africa for a state visit.[15]

At almost the same time, controversy arose over Iran. Ironically, the pressure for developing cooperation with Iran came more from holdover elements of the previous government. Pik Botha, the longtime foreign minister of the previous regime, was named energy minister in the Mandela government. He soon embarked on an ambitious schedule of travel while searching out new agreements as South Africa emerged from the long period of sanctions on oil imports. One possible venture was utilizing South African storage capacity for Middle Eastern oil, which would thus be closer to its ultimate markets in the West. Iran was a prime candidate for such an enterprise because it was already one of South Africa's main suppliers. The United States was not happy with this prospect but became even more alarmed over Botha's comments about possible nuclear cooperation with Iran. The controversy arose just as Secretary of Energy Hazel O'Leary was visiting South Africa to develop cooperative projects in the energy field.[16]

On August 22, 1995, I buttonholed Botha as he was going into a meeting with O'Leary. I pressed him about his plans for nuclear cooperation. Botha responded with a long, strong defense of South Africa's sovereign rights to engage in foreign policy for its own interests and to make such decisions on its own. But having delivered himself of these principles as only Botha could, he then said, "But in fact, we will not engage in any military-related nuclear cooperation with Iran, perhaps not even peaceful areas." The next day, I met with Foreign Minister Alfred Nzo, who reiterated this latter position. Indeed, DFA had been miffed by Botha's freelancing in foreign affairs—he apparently was not able to leave his old responsibilities behind him—and had drafted a strong letter to him on the Iran matter.[17]

At Nzo's initiative, he and I went directly before the press following our meeting, and Nzo made clear that South Africa would adhere strictly to its obligations under the International Atomic Energy Agency and as a member of the Nuclear Suppliers Group. As such, he said, South Africa "would never at any stage be involved in any activity with any country that is likely to produce a result in which that country produces nuclear weapons or weapons of mass destruction."

He put to bed speculation that there was a serious rift in U.S.–South African relations. On the contrary, Nzo said, even where disagreements may exist, there was a regular process of consultation between us.[18]

I appreciated Nzo's doing this, for indeed the press had written extensively about the Iran and Cuban matters, touching off a debate about South Africa's foreign policy and its relations with the United States. Press opinion was mixed. In March, the *Sunday Times* of Johannesburg had written an editorial titled "SA Should Not Meet Goliath Head On." It was an appeal for South Africa to be pragmatic in its relations with the United States. But the editorial was hardly complimentary about the United States. "To co-exist with the United States is like sharing a lifeboat with an elephant," it quoted a European banker as saying. "It takes infinite caution simply to survive." It concluded:

> If this tiny nation is tempted into confrontation with the United States, neither its influence nor its moral intentions will last very long. The American can deploy every kind of weapon, from bombs, to trade boycotts to bribes, to destructive propaganda, in overwhelming degree, and they are utterly ruthless in doing so.[19]

Another editorial, titled "US Could Destroy a Good Friendship," was at least more polite:

> The debt of gratitude we owe the US does not, however, give it undue leverage on our foreign policy. The US should know as well as anyone that any country's foreign policy seeks to further its own self-interest. . . . Thus, US pressure now being applied against South African plans to store oil for Iran and to open an Embassy in Havana, borders uncomfortably on interference.[20]

A longtime career official in DFA, smarting over our demarches on both Sudan and Iran, remarked bluntly to me, "Some in DFA resent that 'the big guy' [the United States] wants South Africa to go in a certain direction yet provides no proof of why it should do so."

There were of course many foreign policy issues on which the United States and the Mandela government cooperated closely from the beginning. These included Angola, Mozambique, Nigeria, and central Africa. But even when South Africa and the United States were cooperating in foreign affairs, there was the potential for misunderstanding and friction. One example was Haiti. Ironically, when Vice President Gore met with Mandela after the inauguration, he cautioned Mandela about the demands that would come to him from around the world and said that he should ration his and his country's involvement. Yet only four months later, the Clinton administration, eager to round up as much international involvement as possible in its intervention in Haiti, asked South Africa to provide some police trainers as part of the peacekeeping effort there. I had opposed this idea, for the very reasons Gore had put to Mandela in May, and especially as this was a situation totally outside South Africa's sphere of interest. Moreover, it seemed strange to ask South Africa for police trainers given the history of the South African police. Nevertheless, I and others in the administration who shared my view were overruled. President Clinton himself called Mandela on this request in early September, suggesting as many as forty to fifty personnel.

Unfortunately, when Mandela turned to his staff for advice the call went to the Defense Ministry. That touched off rumors that the United States had asked South Africa for troops. The Defense Ministry leaked the story and told the press, "No way." The next day, the *Cape Times* headlined, "SA No to US." A signing ceremony for an aid project was postponed for unrelated reasons, but the *Times* linked it to the "troop request." Shortly after, I met with de Klerk to clarify the request. He called back to ask if sending two to four police trainers, "this scaled-down proposal," would be satisfactory. I said (without checking with Washington) it would. However, de Klerk reported that Mbeki would like the request to come from Aristide rather than from just the United States. I said this was not practical and de Klerk agreed. Then, when we thought it was all agreed, de Klerk called me back a few days later to say that because of all the press on the issue, the cabinet had decided to defer a decision. Eventually this small contingent went to Haiti, but the controversy was instructive.

A much more significant area of cooperation was the negotiations for extension of the Nonproliferation Treaty (NPT), which again revealed the sensitivities involved in this new relationship. In many ways, this was the most important test of the new relationship. President Clinton had made indefinite extension of the NPT one of his highest-priority foreign-policy objectives in 1995. When Thabo Mbeki visited the United States in March 1995, President Clinton met with him and made this the main topic of conversation. Clinton emphasized the tremendous importance the United States accorded to this matter. Subsequently, President Clinton, Vice President Gore, and former chief of the Joint Chiefs Colin Powell all wrote to the South Africans urging support. The issue was complicated. The treaty provided that twenty-five years after its entry into force, a conference would be convened to decide whether it should continue in force indefinitely. The decision was to be taken by a majority of the parties to the NPT. Thus, at the 1995 NPT Review Conference, a decision would be taken that would affect the future of the treaty that was the cornerstone of the international regime to prevent the spread of nuclear weapons.

However, an opinion held by many of the nonaligned countries was that indefinite extension would deprive nonnuclear weapon members of any leverage on the nuclear powers. There was considerable unhappiness that, while the non-nuclear weapon members had adhered to their pledge not to develop such weapons—and indeed several countries, such as Brazil, Argentina, and of course South Africa, had forgone that option when they had the means—the members with nuclear weapons (China, France, Russia, the United Kingdom, and the United States) had not done very much on their treaty requirement to work toward total nuclear disarmament. There were thus deep feelings about what were seen as inequalities in the treaty, and indefinite extension threatened to harden them. South Africa was caught in the middle. As a country that had destroyed its nuclear weapons, and with a new president deeply committed to nonproliferation, South Africa had good reasons to support the strongest possible outcome for the NPT. Because of the highly developed state of its nuclear industry, moreover, South Africa was a member of the Nuclear Suppliers Group, an association of industrialized countries that controlled the export of nuclear materials and technology. But as a newly liberated country, one that was taking its place of leadership within the Nonaligned Movement and indeed would become its chair in 1998, South Africa had cause to sympathize with the treaty's critics. South Africa's peculiar position between two worlds made it all the more important in the debate that would take place.

Within the South African government, opinion was divided. There were strong sentiments for opposing indefinite extension. Thabo Mbeki made the final decision, in favor of indefinite extension. But South Africa contacted the United States to say that there must be some changes in the rules of review and that there must be a statement of principles that would guide further implementation. The United States replied that it would be open to suggestions along these lines. South Africa developed the guidelines, including a strengthened review process. The United States concurred. To show support for these principles, the United States moved in the Security Council to provide further guarantees to nonnuclear states of protection against nuclear attack. Clinton also accelerated work on the Comprehensive Test Ban Treaty. In June, thanks to South Africa's lobbying and diplomacy (supported within the NAM by tiny Benin), the vote for indefinite extension was unanimous.

What seemed to many of us in this matter a model of diplomatic cooperation, based on extensive discussion and exchange of considerable technical and legal documentation, was however seen quite differently by political figures and the press.[21] Almost immediately, as the issue surfaced in the public, there were charges of the United States pressuring South Africa, indeed threatening it, and of South Africa buckling to pressure rather than standing on principle. After South Africa indicated the conditions it was seeking in return for supporting indefinite extension, the press reported it as a "row" with the United States. Even those voices arguing for going along with the U.S. position did not do so on the basis of principle. A professor at the University of Witswatersrand was quoted as saying that there was no point in jeopardizing relations with the superpower for the sake of "a great and idealistic moral stand. I think South Africa will have to back down if the US is totally immovable. The US will use all kinds of pressure to get its way."[22]

The United States was accused, in fact, of using all kinds of pressure. Numerous references were made to the demarche I made to the foreign minister on March 10. There were hints that the United States had threatened to cut off cooperation on the peaceful uses of nuclear energy, that we had conditioned our support for South Africa's membership in the Nuclear Suppliers Group on support for indefinite extension of the NPT, that even withdrawal of aid was threatened.[23] Equally disturbing was the assumption that if South Africa came to the position of supporting indefinite extension, it had somehow lost its independence and moral standing, that it could not have reached this decision on its own and in support of its own principles.[24]

I looked for a South African government response to these charges, but the government seemed cowed by the criticism and unwilling to make a public defense of its evolving position. Particularly disturbed by the charge that somehow the NPT was an "apartheid" treaty that South Africa should oppose in principle, I decided to write my own reply for publication. I began by clarifying the actual legal implications of anything but indefinite extension, pointing out that "not one of the reports nor any of the experts quoted" in the numerous articles on the subject had focused on the technical problem that was driving the debate over how to extend the NPT. If the treaty were to lapse, I wrote, "the prospect is chilling." I continued:

> There may be many things wrong with the present treaty, and much that should be fixed. But surely, the problems of inequality, lack of security for non-nuclear states, and pressures for further disarmament would not be ameliorated by having the number of nuclear states go from five to ten or twenty and for international norms and mechanisms to disappear.
>
> I am horrified to see the NPT described as an "apartheid treaty," as if the spread of nuclear weapons was some desirable good to be enjoyed by everyone. It is in fact the poorer (or more responsible) nations, who cannot or will not spend the billions of dollars to acquire nuclear weapons, that are most threatened by neighbors who would.

I then dismissed the idea that the United States had pressured South Africa into its position. And oddly, it fell to me to defend the South African government's decision-making process:

I know it sounds good, especially for those who prefer drama over reality, to say that diplomacy is carried out by "threats," "pressure," etc. But it is not the way it is done. Contrary to reports that South Africa "buckled" under US pressure, or made its decision on this matter because of threats of non co-operation in nuclear matters, or that South Africa had failed to use its moral ground effectively, the South African response has been careful, responsible and, above all, principled. From the first discussion of this matter, the South African Government made clear that it would make up its mind only after carefully investigating the issue, and after discussing it with its OAU and NAM partners, with the Parliament, and in the Cabinet.

South Africa assembled an analysis of their concerns with the treaty and their demands. South Africa conveyed back to us that unless these concerns were addressed the majority that we and others sought for indefinite extension could not be obtained. We listened carefully to South Africa and to others raising these issues. . . . President Clinton moved to strengthen the UN Security Council guarantees to non-nuclear states and to press forward with the Comprehensive Test Ban Treaty. Minister Nzo's speech to the NPT conference was this, not a "capitulation" to the US or other nuclear states, but the product of a careful and principled investigation of the issue.

There was some uneasiness in the U.S. delegation to the NPT conference over publication of my article (I had not cleared it with Washington), because of concern that it might compromise South Africa in the final days of the ongoing negotiations. But in fact the reaction within South Africa was positive. Although I had sent the article to the *Weekly Mail and Guardian,* whose previous coverage of the issue I found particularly galling, it was picked up by at least half a dozen newspapers.[25] I was also pleased that South African government officials, rather than being embarrassed, quietly thanked me for saying what they had been unable to.

The cooperation on this issue opened the door to cooperation on a matter of particular importance to South Africa. Shortly after the decision on the NPT, South Africa made clear that the Africa Nuclear Weapons Free Zone (ANWFZ) Treaty was of special importance to it, especially in the wake of the NPT debate. This was a very popular cause among African states, and South Africa was eager to be supportive after breaking with the early OAU consensus on the NPT. The final negotiations were in fact taking place in South Africa later that year. The United States, as the major nuclear power, had to adhere to this treaty if it was to have any meaning. The United States had some initial questions about the treaty, but, sensitive to South African concerns, the United States worked through the issues and adhered to the treaty without reservations in April 1996. The combined cooperation on the NPT and the ANWFZ Treaty was, as I concluded in my article about the NPT negotiations, "diplomacy at its best."

Foreign policy thus offered areas of cooperation and differences. Because the new South Africa shared so many of the values and objectives important to the United States—respect for human rights, nonproliferation, peaceful resolution of conflicts, multiracial democracy—the opportunities for collaboration were great. It was important to keep this fact in the forefront, for the United States would have to accept that on some issues there would be differences. On some of these, no amount of persuasion would change South Africa's view. This would be particularly the case with Mandela's attitude toward Libya and Cuba. The issue touched a nerve and would continue to arise. In February 1996, in response to American criticism over his possibly inviting one or both of those countries' leaders to South Africa, Mandela stated that he would not be dictated to on these relationships, "not at all, by anybody. . . . These are our friends, who were with us when we were all alone. . . . The enemies of the West are not my enemies."[26] In 1997, when Mandela, against strong American urging, traveled to Libya to help mediate the turning over of suspected Libyan terrorists for trial, he was blunter: "Those who say I should not be here are without morals." He characterized the American attitude on this issue as "arrogant and racist."[27]

During President Clinton's warm and even celebratory visit to South Africa in March 1998, Mandela at their joint press conference took the occasion to respond bluntly to yet another State Department criticism of South Africa's approaches to Libya:

> One of the first heads of state I invited to this country was Fidel Castro. I have received in this country ex-President Rafsanjani of Iran. I have also invited brother Qaddafi to this country. And I do that because our moral authority dictates that we should not abandon those who helped us in the darkest hour in the history of this country. . . . And those South Africans who have berated me for being loyal to our friends, literally, they can go throw themselves into a pool.[28]

Mandela went on to suggest that the example of South Africa's transition showed that the United States should sit down with its enemies as the ANC had sat down with its apartheid foes. It was important for the United States to remember that, these loyalties notwithstanding, South Africa took steps, as described with regard to Iran and as will be detailed in other cases below, to keep such "friends" from obtaining technology relevant to weapons of mass destruction, and that South Africa would not sell them arms.

Indeed, in the warmth of President Clinton's visit to South Africa, both men wisely went on from this issue to work on those that bound them together.

Two years later, Clinton would extend his second visit to Africa in order to respond to Mandela's appeal that Clinton join him in seeking to bring peace to Burundi, a chancy hope but one to which Clinton willingly lent his presence. In September 2001, Mandela's successor, President Thabo Mbeki, would condemn the terrorist attacks on the United States as "repugnant and indiscriminate acts of murder." Every political party in South Africa's Parliament supported a resolution making a similar statement.[29]

Armscor: The Legacy Issue

Perhaps no issue was more troubling and more challenging to the relationship in the first two years of the Mandela regime than the U.S. Justice Department's case against South African arms companies Armscor, Kentron, and Fuchs and seven individuals. This was an old issue, indictments having been issued in 1991. The case grew out of discovery that the South African arms industry had arranged for South Africa not only to evade the sanctions against importing U.S. arms and military technology but also to sell U.S. technology to Iraq on the eve of the Gulf War. American-captured Iraqi weapons showed that South African firms had supplied U.S.-made proximity fuses and other technical equipment to Iraq. The case was extraordinarily complex, involving not only legal charges against individuals and the companies, but also a demand for follow-up oversight of South Africa's arms industry to ensure compliance with U.S. requirements before sanctions related to the case could be lifted. The Justice Department was also seeking South Africans to testify against an American in a related case. While the Justice Department had the responsibility for the criminal case, the State Department had the responsibility for civil enforcement proceedings and oversight requirements. There were also both criminal and civil fines to be negotiated. Adding to this already complex case, Armscor was a South African government-owned corporation; Denel, which had been spun off from Armscor as its manufacturing arm, was affected by the sanctions because it had incorporated Kentron; Fuchs was private, owned by one of South Africa's most prominent conglomerates, Barlow Rand. This made coordination of positions among the parties enormously difficult.[30]

Under the de Klerk government, there already had been strong pleas for a "political" settlement of the case. South African officials told us that some of South Africa's most prominent industrialists could be caught up in the case, having been on the boards of these companies or otherwise involved. It was argued that they had acted at the government's request and for what they believed were patriotic objectives. De Klerk urged that the case be dropped or settled with minimum punishment, in the spirit of the changes going on in South Africa. At one point, de Klerk's minister of defense, Kobie Coetsee, sought a meeting with Attorney General Janet Reno and hinted darkly that he would expose "secrets" about U.S. operations in South Africa if a deal could not be struck. Reno turned down the meeting.

I had little sympathy or liking for Armscor. In an early call on me to discuss the case, Armscor CEO Tielman de Waal said frankly that his company had indeed violated U.S. laws and as long as he thought it necessary would continue to do so. Some months later, when I was being pressed by Pik Botha to have this case settled as "old business," I repeated this comment. Botha was embarrassed and complained to de Waal. The next time I saw de Waal, he said, "I will be careful in what I say to you." Good advice.[31]

The U.S. government position was that a "political" settlement was out of the question. The State Department could not force the Justice Department to drop the criminal charges, nor would it even want to recommend doing so. We strongly urged Armscor and its erstwhile partners to settle the case through direct negotiations with the Justice Department. This was the position we had taken consistently over several years with the de Klerk government. With the inauguration of the Mandela regime, we thought this issue might disappear from the political agenda. How wrong we were!

For whatever reasons, and I suspect they were complex, the Mandela government took up the issue with even greater zeal than its predecessor had shown. This was partly because Armscor executives early on sold the new leadership on the importance of South Africa's arms industry as a source of jobs and foreign exchange. They implied that the fines and restrictions that could come out of the case could cripple that potential. Further, they spread the story that the U.S. motive was not so much justice as squelching South African competition in the lucrative international arms market. This came to be a major issue in 1994 in connection with a large British tender for military helicopters, as described below. I suspect also that influential people involved in this case reached the upper levels of the new government about the implications for them if the case was pursued too vigorously. Finally, rallying unanticipated allies around the industry that had once contributed so much to the brutal suppression of the majority population, the issue came to be seen as touching on South African sovereignty and thus as one that should be stoutly defended by the ANC regime.

The issue rose early to the highest levels. South Africa had developed a prototype attack helicopter, the Rooivalk. Not even the SADF had adopted it, but Denel's Atlas Aviation subsidiary, which had developed the Rooivalk, continued to hope it could be sold abroad. In 1994, in a gesture that was more political than substantive, the United Kingdom said it would entertain a bid from South Africa for its forthcoming tender for helicopters, reportedly worth $3 billion. The hitch was that, to be compatible with NATO requirements, the Rooivalk would have to incorporate special gun sights available only from the United States. The American corporation Loral, among others, offered to provide the technology if the sanctions could be waived for this purpose. Mandela himself took up this challenge on his state visit in October. In his meeting with Vice President Gore and President Clinton, Mandela said he had many problems with the South African arms industry and its practices—an illegal shipment to Rwanda had just been uncovered —but in the case of the helicopters South Africa's economic interests were paramount. He pressed Clinton to obtain a waiver. Clinton said only that he would look into it.

Over the next several days, officials in the State Department, the NSC, and the Justice Department scrambled to see what should or could be done. Both in Justice and within State, especially in the secretary's office, there was considerable hesitation about having the president interject himself into this case. Some of us suggested a range of options, for example, a waiver of sanctions for this one sale accompanied by South African agreement on oversight, but in the end the president received only two extreme options—grant the waiver or leave the case alone. The president chose the latter. For several weeks after the visit, the embassy was pressed for an answer from the president. In the end, we had to say that a waiver would be granted only in the context of an overall settlement of the case— the Justice Department position.

Although the United Kingdom gave Armscor extra time, without the waiver the Rooivalk bid was dead. That led to charges that the real U.S. motive in denying the waiver was to keep the way clear for the American Apache helicopter to win the British tender. In an article in the Johannesburg *Sunday Times,* a DFA source was quoted as saying, "They are deliberately trying to sabotage the deal." The story went on that this "cynical elimination of the bid has deepened the rift between the South African arms industry and the US."[32] We knew too that Chief of Staff Georg Meiring felt strongly that the United States had ulterior motives. When asked by a visiting Pentagon official if he was interested in visiting the United States, Meiring replied sarcastically that because South Africa had been involved in illegally importing American technology in the past, he might risk arrest. He visited the U.S. European Command headquarters instead. The subject came up with nearly every American visitor to the Defense Ministry. Armscor's offices were in the same building, and on one occasion a senior Pentagon official was taken off guard by an Armscor executive being invited in by ministry officials to discuss the case.

The case grew even nastier shortly afterward. South Africa changed lawyers just as a settlement seemed in sight. The new lawyer withdrew some of the previous offers of his predecessor and the Justice Department responded by pulling off the table nearly every compromise it had offered. Thabo Mbeki called in my deputy on two occasions in December, when I was away, to question the Justice Department's tactics and communications. This was the one instance when I had a serious disagreement with South Africa's new ambassador to the United States, Franklin Sonn. In an emotional call, I pleaded with him not to have South Africa change strategies and reopen the entire negotiation. But South Africa was embarked on a more aggressive strategy, questioning a number of the aspects of the case and taking an increasingly hard line on the questions of sovereignty, for example, asking whether the United States even had the right to fine an entity owned by another government or whether oversight should be carried out by an American or someone neutral.

On a visit to Washington in February 1995, Thabo Mbeki said that bilateral relations with the United States could not be normalized until this issue was settled. "You can't say that everything else is normal except for this little corner."[33]

Despite the growing confrontation over the issue, one of the significant factors that would help to bring about a settlement of this matter was the consultation that was going on separately on South Africa's development of a new arms export control regime. Under the previous regime, Armscor had extraordinary powers. It not only manufactured and sold, but approved and licensed, South Africa's arms exports. In other words, there was little if any political control over these sales. The Mandela government had determined to maintain an arms industry but wanted to establish greater accountability. The new government had been embarrassed by the discovery of a shipment marked for Yemen that was actually destined for Rwanda, a fellow African country wracked by civil war.

The United States was also anxious to see South Africa establish such a system to help in control of arms shipments worldwide. Beginning with a visit by Assistant Secretary of State for Political-Military Affairs Thomas McNamara in late 1994, the United States shared with South Africa details of our own system and the legislation behind it. In 1995, McNamara's deputy, Frances Cook, made two trips; the first was to exchange views with the South Africans on a broad range of political-military issues, while in the second she brought a number of experts and extensive materials on arms exports, specifically. These discussions brought together the Foreign Affairs, Intelligence, and Defense ministries in South Africa, some of whom had been blocked out of a role in arms controls in the past. In September, South Africa announced establishment of an interministerial committee that would oversee arms exports. It was to be headed by Kader Asmal, minister of forests and water, who was selected for his political will, managerial abilities, and distance from the security services. The criteria for approving arms deals would resonate with our own, that is, the human rights situation in the receiving country, no re-export, and political control over the decisions. Among those countries placed in "Category 3," to whom arms exports were prohibited, were Iraq, Sudan, Libya, and Syria.

Even as this process progressed, the Armscor dispute dragged on. In June 1995, a settlement seemed close but once again foundered.[34] Ambassador Sonn, who had brokered this last effort, was discouraged at the power and influence of the forces opposed to settlement, who held sway over the government's final position. The issue became a perennial subject between Deputy President Mbeki and Vice President Gore in meetings of the Binational Commission that was established following Mandela's election. It was through the BNC that the two sides were eventually brought together. In July 1996, after a marathon negotiation session in Washington ordered by the two cochairs, a settlement was agreed on.[35] Fines were assessed in a manner acceptable to the South African government and follow-up mechanisms were put in place. This brought to a close one of the most contentious issues in the relationship.

TRADE: "IT'S TOUGH BEING PALS WITH UNCLE SAM"

One of the benefits of a normal relationship is the growth in trade, which had been stymied between the United States and South Africa during the era of sanctions and disinvestment.[36] But trade has rules and is subject to considerable friction. This is part and parcel of a normal situation and the friction has to be contained within the context of the broader relationship. This is certainly true in the relationship between the United States and Europe, in which trade disputes often become extremely contentious but never threaten the alliance. For South Africa, however, the newness of the rules and problems, coming so soon after the euphoric celebration of its transition, often came as a rude shock.

One of the first disputes arose over trademarks. South Africa had on its books a law that stipulated that registered trademarks that were not utilized for five years expired unless there were exceptional circumstances. During the period of sanctions, American companies such as McDonald's, Victoria's Secrets, and Toys R Us chose to boycott South Africa. In that period, enterprising South Africans registered the names of some of these companies, and some even opened small businesses with those titles. When sanctions ended, these firms sought to have their original trademarks respected. The initial reaction of the government was not friendly. Trevor Manuel, Mandela's first minister of trade and industry, told me in one of our first meetings on the subject that American firms had an inordinate head start in tying up names and copyrights and had thus stymied entrepreneurs from developing countries. Over time, the new South African government recognized that its laws had to be brought up to the standards and practices of international agreements under the WTO and the World Intellectual Property Organization.

Franchisers such as McDonald's, moreover, offered substantial opportunities for the development of South African entrepreneurs.

But much water flowed under the bridge, court cases were filed, and many difficult exchanges took place before the issue was settled. At one stage, the United States placed South Africa on its Section 301 "watch list" of countries in violation of such standards, with the threat of sanctions. Not until 1997 were South African laws sufficiently adjusted that the country was removed from that list.[37]

An even more serious dispute arose over South African stainless steel exports to the United States. Increases in stainless steel capacity constituted one of the few large investments made by South African investors in the period of the political negotiations. But South Africa was one of several countries targeted by both the United States and the European Union for antidumping actions. The severity of the findings stunned both South Africa and its American importers.[38] In December 1998, the Commerce Department in this case imposed antidumping margins ranging from 3 to 68 percent against six countries, including South Africa, and an additional countervailing duty of up to 15 percent.[39] An irritated Alec Erwin, minister of trade and industry, told me that year that South Africa would postpone trying to negotiate a free-trade agreement with the United States, because "you are too litigious."[40] Steel continues to be a source of contention. In August 2001, the U.S. International Trade Commission decided to impose further antidumping duties on exports of hot-rolled steel from South Africa and other countries. Not surprisingly, Erwin, chairman for South Africa of the UN Conference on Trade and Development, made U.S. antidumping laws an issue at the WTO talks in Doha, Qatar.[41]

Of course, trade negotiations are complex with any partner. South Africa's negotiation of a free-trade agreement with the European Union took several years and was delayed in the final stages for months by disputes over the labeling of South African wine and the entry of South African fruits into the European market. The European Union has still to ratify the agreement. As noted, the European Union, like the United States, took action against South African steel imports. But the strain of trade issues undoubtedly took some of the bloom off the rose of the postapartheid aura of good feeling between the United States and South Africa. Normalcy has its price.

Yet the fundamentals of improving trade remained attractive. This was demonstrated in the results from the Africa Growth and Opportunity Act (AGOA), passed by Congress in 2000. This act, a cornerstone of Clinton administration policy in Africa, provides significant duty-free access and larger quotas for African goods entering the U.S. market. What made AGOA controversial was that it attached these provisions to conditions outlining the economic and political reforms that would be necessary for African countries to qualify. Almost every African country endorsed the act as it made its way—tortuously over nearly two years—through Congress. But South Africa did not. South Africa bristled at the conditions, which it saw as neocolonialist. It also believed the act heralded a movement away from aid, which South Africa felt was critical to the poorer countries on the continent. This was indeed the second point of contention during President Clinton's visit to South Africa in 1998. At that same press conference at which Mandela stated his views on relations with Libya, among others, he pronounced AGOA "unacceptable." Under pressure from other African countries and the United States, South Africa later recanted its position. South Africa's ambassador in Washington, Franklin Sonn, sent a letter of endorsement to all members of the Senate in April and, when the bill passed in June, Thabo Mbeki called it "a very good signal . . . an important step."[42]

But what surprised the South Africans was how good AGOA proved to be, not only for Africa in general but for South Africa. African trade with the United States jumped sharply after passage, reaching over $4 billion. Alec Erwin, an erstwhile critic, predicted that South African exports to the United States would rise 30 percent in the first year after passage, compared to a 15 percent rise in previous years. He was particularly pleased with the opportunities for South Africa to provide African-origin raw material to other African countries that could not meet the U.S. requirement for such material. Erwin believed that joint South African–Lesotho cooperation resulting from AGOA would produce ten thousand new jobs in Lesotho—that small, impoverished, landlocked country within South Africa's borders. The U.S. Trade Representative Office predicts that AGOA will create sixty-six thousand new jobs in South Africa, as well as promote hundreds of millions of dollars in new foreign direct investment.[43]

Not only did the fundamentals remain good, but so also did our respective senses of humor. On my final day in South Africa as ambassador, in December 1995, I met Trevor Manuel—my longtime companion and counterpart in the trademarks dispute—in the airport. "I have a confession," he said. "Upcountry, about 100 km from Pretoria, I passed a little ramshackle roadside restaurant. The sign on the entrance said 'Pizza Hut.' I never told you." "That's all right," I said. "I've driven by the same restaurant and I never mentioned it to you, or to Washington."

BIOLOGICAL AND CHEMICAL WEAPONS: REDUX

The resolution of the chemical and biological weapons problem carried over well into the Mandela administration. Despite our efforts to reach Mandela on this issue even before the election, it would be nearly a year later before we and our British colleagues could sit down with him and chart a course for the future. We were not only concerned about pinning down cooperative arrangements with the new government, but also concerned over reports of trips to Libya by the infamous Wouter Basson and at least one other scientist who had been involved with the program.[44] Mandela was briefed on this issue on several occasions by his own experts but postponed meeting with us. During his state visit to the United States in October 1994, President Clinton urged Mandela to address it expeditiously. Mandela responded that he would, but that there were "problems" within his administration. Mbeki had earlier indicated to me that there was resistance within the security services about our demands in this matter. Mbeki was also weighing the implications of investigating the allegations of past uses, that is, whether such investigation would threaten the very stability of the Government of National Unity. Mbeki was discomfited as I went through the ramifications of what we were asking of the new government.

Throughout 1994 these same issues were debated extensively within the U.S. government and with the British. The U.S. position, as it evolved, was that the question of usage had to be investigated by the South African government. We lacked the information to make a definitive determination of the accuracy of these allegations, but in briefings to Congress and in our own policy deliberations we had to acknowledge such allegations and take them seriously. If convincing evidence did emerge, moreover, it would challenge the South African government's continued insistence that the program had been "defensive." The South Africans, we felt, not only had an obligation to investigate the allegations, but had to realize that they could easily become public, forcing a government response. As noted earlier, the United States had taken the position, and it continued to do so, that if the issue became public we would make clear that we had raised these allegations with the South African government, both de Klerk's and Mandela's, and had urged that they be pursued. As long as these issues remained unresolved, the United States and Britain opposed South Africa's entry into the Australia Group, an important nonproliferation body.[45]

The British were not initially inclined to put such weight on the usage question. They believed we should be more "forward looking." They were especially concerned that our insistence on this sensitive issue not upset the cooperation we were receiving on nonproliferation matters nor destabilize the Government of National Unity. It took until the end of 1994 to resolve the balance of these issues in our joint position. In the meantime, we continued to press for a meeting with Mandela, which finally took place on January 13, 1995.

The meeting with Mandela went extremely well. He broadened the participation from the earlier meetings we had had with de Klerk to include the minister of foreign affairs, Alfred Nzo, and the deputy minister of defense, Ronnie Kasrils. After the British ambassador and I had made our presentation, Mandela said our concerns were very reasonable. He emphasized that the Government of National Unity would never condone what the ANC had previously opposed, that is, programs of weapons of mass destruction. Moreover, with obvious reference to our concerns over Libya, Mandela assured us that there were no relations with any country that would justify sharing this technology. Following a somewhat defensive presentation by Surgeon General Daniel Knobel, Mandela reiterated his belief that the U.S. and British concerns were reasonable and he pledged full cooperation. Gently chiding Knobel, and with a bit of advice for us, Mandela said, "The Afrikaner can be very stubborn but, if handled correctly, can be the best of friends." He phoned me the next day to say he appreciated the "frank way" we had addressed the matter and that he would press his people to cooperate in every way.

We had anticipated, correctly, that under pressure from within his security forces Mandela would not agree to destroy the data or turn it over to an international body. Thus we offered as a fallback that the safeguards initiated by de Klerk be reaffirmed and that further consultations take place on those safeguards. Mandela agreed. Mandela left, turning the meeting over to Nzo and Kasrils. We quickly agreed on ways to consult in detail on the CBM. The thorniest issue was how to control the travel of scientists such as Basson and others to places such as Libya. Kasrils and other officials confessed alarm over the extent of such travel. Although there were difficulties involved—for example, Basson was then already under investigation for smuggling drugs and other offenses—the South Africans agreed to proceed to rehire him into the government as a way to stop his foreign travels and keep him under wraps. As he was a cardiac surgeon, he was hired back into the military in that capacity, a decision that would later cause Mandela some embarrassment, but that was the only recourse that appeared practical at the time.[46]

Our problems were not over, however. As discussed in the previous chapter, on February 26 the London *Sunday Times* published a front-page story on South Africa's biological and chemical weapons program. Quoting British and American intelligence sources, the story reported Western alarm over the program, in particular, the danger of the technical information being "sold" to the Libyans. It implied Mandela was having difficulty with his military in bringing the program under control and reported the allegations of uses against individuals and ANC fighters in Namibia and Angola under the previous regime.[47] There was little in the story to convey the degree of cooperation we had been receiving from de Klerk or Mandela. The story set off a chain reaction in the press in South Africa. Knobel and others in the military were taken aback and saw the article as a breach of faith on the part of the United States and the United Kingdom. Knobel and other SANDF officials angrily denied the charges of uses having been made of such weapons, denials that would of course later prove unfounded. Knobel also accused the Western countries of jealousy: "They are jealous of what we achieved and now want to find out who supplied us with the information. But we are not going to tell them."[48]

In the days that followed, Knobel suggested the story had been leaked on purpose to put pressure on Mbeki, who was scheduled to arrive in Washington the very next day. Knobel informed me that the meetings with our next team of experts, which had been agreed on at the meeting with Mandela, would now have to be postponed. South Africans, he claimed, were leery of sharing information with us if it was not to be treated confidentially. Another source within the government told me only Mbeki and Kasrils could now approve the meetings' going ahead. I phoned both of them in early March and a sympathetic Kasrils, and subsequently Mbeki, gave us the go-ahead. It still took some effort to smooth things over with Knobel in order to give the team the access and cooperation needed. The United States delegation told Knobel that the U.S. government had no interest in such public stories, especially when it denigrated the degree of cooperation we had received. The delegation assured him there was no deliberateness on the part of the U.S. government; indeed, we had begun an investigation into the leak.

Once the air was cleared, the meetings went well and reestablished the level of cooperation we desired. The United States and the United Kingdom shared copies of our own CBMs as well as of legislation designed to secure data. There was a lengthy discussion of the details of South Africa's past programs. The United States decided to sidestep further the question of the CBM. The information the South African government now put forward was "internally consistent," but it was still in the context of a defensive program. Our position was that any proof of uses would undermine the South African government's insistence that the program be described as "defensive," and we had no desire to have them make such a statement to the BWC, even if we did not have the basis ourselves to challenge it. We continued to urge that these allegations be investigated. With much greater understanding of the past programs, it was possible for the United States and the United Kingdom to focus thereafter on steps to avoid proliferation. These included a range of discussions and exchange of ideas and material.

It is ironic what developed afterward. Basson was brought before the Truth and Reconciliation Commission (TRC). In the course of its investigation, the commission discovered that Basson had kept copies of at least some of the data in boxes in his house as well as on the computer disc over which we had had so much negotiation. The government took control of these boxes and was indeed nervous over access, even by the TRC. The TRC investigated some of the allegations of uses of chemical and biological agents, but was hampered in its inquiry by the South African government, which worried about both leaks of sensitive data and harm to its own case against Basson. As a witness, Basson of course was as enigmatic and contradictory as ever. The government subsequently brought charges against Basson on drugs and embezzlement infractions, but the court threw out charges of murder in Namibia, Angola, and elsewhere outside South Africa's jurisdiction. These horrible instances, including the use of a muscle relaxant to commit large-scale murder of Namibian liberation soldiers, whose bodies were subsequently thrown from an aircraft into the sea, thus remain beyond reach of any justice system, though the truth of them is now generally accepted. The court case that remained went on for more than a year, filling the airways and the press with the lurid activities of a program, and of a man, who was totally out of control of any rational or humane direction.[49]

These allegations of use, to poison and incapacitate opponents of apartheid, belied the South African government's continued claim that its program was defensive. Knobel would argue later, in his testimony before the TRC and at Basson's trial, that such uses were unauthorized and without his knowledge. Straining credibility, he argued that, as they were unauthorized, the program was thereby officially defensive. But the command-and-control structure within the apartheid regime for such matters was not totally unofficial, as Goldstone's investigations into "third force" activities clearly demonstrated. Knobel is to some an enigma—how could he not know what was happening in his own program?—to others an outright liar. I came to know him well. Whatever he knew or chose not to know, Knobel's self-image is of a doctor, a man of healing. He took pride that in the days of apartheid, when the South African military was ostracized from other international contacts, he could attend international meetings of surgeons general. Understanding the importance of that image was key to obtaining the cooperation and access we needed in the days of early investigation of this program. Today, Knobel is a tragic figure. Distanced from his former military colleagues because of the extensive court testimony he gave against Basson, but shunned too by those horrified by what went on under his ostensible direction, he clings alone to his self-image and struggles to maintain his pride.

This issue, which so preoccupied the embassy and much of Washington for two years, strained U.S. relations with some of South Africa's security forces but only strengthened trust between the United States and Mandela. The United States recognized from the beginning that investigation into the past uses of these devices, like much else in South Africa's apartheid past, would be bruising and potentially destabilizing. It was important for South Africa to find its way to addressing it, as it has done along with so much else that was painful in that period. While there was legitimate concern with the use issue in Washington from the point of view of the integrity of the BWC and the precedent that such use represented, the primary objective in this case had to be to encourage South Africa to investigate it and deal with it. Over time, worries about the effect on stability have given way to a search for the truth, though much remains to be discovered. Our other concern was to ensure South Africa's commitment to nonproliferation of this capacity. In a statement to the press in 1998, during the TRC's inquiry into the program, the South African government reiterated the principles and practices that had been at the heart of this long endeavor:

> [The] Government wishes to clarify that this programme has been termi-nated and the material for offensive purposes in government storage has been destroyed. This was done in co-operation with countries which pos-sess expertise in matters relating to these programmes, and in full compli-ance with relevant international treaties.
>
> The South African Government ... does not have any interest in de-veloping weapons of mass destruction, least of all offensive chemical and biological weapons. The government is also committed to ensuring that the knowledge and expertise gathered in this area should, under no circum-stances, become available to any other country, individual or companies.
>
> We wish to assure the nation and the international community that the information on the country's CBW defensive capacity is, as allowed by the international treaties, safely kept under lock and key. The transfer of the keys from the previous government and its agencies has taken place.
>
> This government is outraged by the on-going revelations [of use], and is as interested in answers to these questions as the people of our country and the rest of humanity are.[50]

BUILDING A SOLID FOUNDATION FOR THE FUTURE: THE BINATIONAL COMMISSION

When Vice President Gore attended the inauguration of Nelson Mandela, he recognized the wider importance of this transition. He saw the transitions under way in Russia and South Africa as two of the most crucial in terms of world sta-bility. As he later articulated,

> There are two transitions under way in the world the success of which will be of especially great significance. That in Russia is vitally important to Eurasia and the entire world. . . . Similarly just as the world used to face a threat from communism and the Cold War, the world faced and still faces a threat from ethnic violence and hatred. . . . Every day that the new South Africa continues moving forward and building its future is a day when the rest of the world has more hope.[51]

Gore proposed that the United States establish a high-level binational commission to deepen the relationship between the two countries and ensure a level of coop-eration that would enhance the prospects for South Africa's success. Similar commissions had been inaugurated with Russia and Egypt. The BNC was launched the following year, under the joint chairmanship of Gore and Thabo Mbeki. Initially comprising subcommittees, at cabinet level, on agriculture, science, trade and investment, education, the environment, and energy, it later added committees on justice and defense. The BNC was one of the most important instruments of the new relationship between South Africa and the United States. It kept the relationship from drifting downward, from losing the potential that seemed so great on that sunny day in May 1994, when the impossible happened—South Africa inaugurated Nelson Mandela as its president and the white establishment took its seat behind him.

A plethora of programs have flowed from the BNC. These include programs in solar energy, housing, training of scientists, biomedical research, trade and investment, and law enforcement.[52] But what makes this vehicle most important is that it has provided a basis for resolving issues at high levels, for developing cooperation on major issues, and for developing relationships that will outlast the aid program. It is a statement, as Presidents Clinton and Mandela said at the BNC's inauguration, "by our two peoples that each nation regards its relationship with the other as being sufficiently important to warrant a very heavy investment of time, thought, and energy" on both sides.[53]

It was during Thabo Mbeki's participation in the BNC meeting in Washington in 1995 that President Clinton impressed on him the importance the United States gave to the indefinite extension of the Non-Proliferation Treaty, leading to Mbeki's critical decisions in favor of South Africa's role in making that happen. It was at the 1996 meetings of the BNC that the basis for resolving the bitter Armscor case was found, with the direct involvement of the cochairs in bringing the matter to conclusion. Much of the work in resolving the trademarks dispute and other trade issues came about through the Trade and Investment Committee and the private-sector Business Development Committee under the BNC.

Even though a defense committee was not established until 1997, the early meetings of the BNC provided a vehicle for discussing the whole range of political-military matters of concern to the two countries, including arms sales, AIDS, and relationships with states of concern to the United States. As Gore said in 1996, "Deputy President Mbeki and I have an ongoing dialogue on what we call 'off line' issues. And they encompass virtually every issue in the relationship."[54] As sensitivities on such issues were gradually overcome, the BNC established a Defense Committee in 1997 and a Justice and Anti-Crime Cooperation Committee in 1999. U.S. assistance in law enforcement, to address South Africa's serious crime problems and U.S. concerns over drug smuggling, has been one of the fastest-growing areas of U.S.–South African cooperation. Today the FBI, DEA, Secret Service, and INS all have offices in Pretoria.[55]

One potential of the BNC, however, has not been fully realized. By engaging the several departments of the U.S. government directly in this commission, it was hoped that programs of *mutual* interest would develop, such that the U.S. costs would become part of the departments' own budgets and not be aid-dependent. Otherwise, they would last only as long as the aid program, which is always problematical. If the relationship is to be truly deep, like that between the United States and its European partners, aid should not be the determining factor. Some of the BNC programs are part of the respective departmental budgets, but most of them look to USAID for funding. The USAID program has declined from that first postapartheid level of $136 million to $50 million, already putting pressure on these programs. If these programs cannot be sustained by individual departments, then the next best solution is for USAID to endow some of these programs before the aid program closes. As indicated in the next chapter, failure to provide sustainability to such programs is a mistake the United States has made elsewhere.

At the outset of the George W. Bush administration, the future of the BNC was in doubt. However, the administration decided to revamp it, not eliminate it. It will become the U.S.–South Africa Cooperation Forum, which will not regularly meet at the vice presidential level, or even necessarily at the cabinet level. This may be a natural evolution for such an organization. The BNC at its outset signaled the desire for a special relationship, and much of that is in place. The Bush administration has signaled moreover that South Africa along with Nigeria and Kenya are the "natural partners" of the United States in Africa.[56] The key determinant of whether this evolution is truly successful, however, will be in the follow-up in all the original BNC's program areas and the sustainability of its initiatives.

LINGERING QUESTIONS

In the years since Mandela's election, much has transpired that demonstrates the strength of South Africa's transition to democracy. Mandela made one of his greatest contributions to Africa and his country by insisting on only one term. His successor, Thabo Mbeki, elected in 1999, cerebral, managerial, private, is of another kind, as are the challenges. Some question Mbeki's commitment to transparency, his seemingly extreme sensitivity to criticism, and his tendency to concentrate power not only at the top but within the presidency, with few around him who can speak openly and forcefully about matters gone wrong.[57] There is concern over what have been vituperative attacks on the press. There has been what the opposition calls a "reracialization of politics" in South Africa, in contrast to Mandela's emphasis on racial reconciliation. Some of these concerns are valid; some are at least exaggerated—certainly the opposition has done as much to press Mbeki's "buttons" on race as he has done to raise the issue.[58]

Mbeki has also been roundly criticized for not being more forceful with neighboring Zimbabwe's president, Robert Mugabe, when the latter began inciting land grabs by black "veterans" against white farmers and oppressing political opponents. However, Mbeki has little personal influence with Mugabe and rightly is concerned that if South Africa put too much pressure on Zimbabwe, for example, through the water and power supply it provides to the country, it could provoke an enormous refugee crisis spilling into South Africa. Nevertheless, Mbeki has had to reassure the business community that his hesitation was not a sign of sympathy with such redistributive steps and that he still adheres to economic policies that recognize the importance of the private sector.[59]

Despite all these concerns, the institutions of democracy remain strongly intact, with the Constitutional Court ruling as many times against the government as with it, with the press free, and with civil society still vibrant. Moreover, no one can gainsay what have been major achievements of the postapartheid period. While reducing short-term foreign debt by 80 percent, reducing inflation from an average of 15 percent to little more than 6 percent, and reaching in 2001 perhaps the first budget surplus in decades, the government has at the same time made major inroads into the social and economic deprivations of the people. More than nine million people have been given access to clean water, and 1.5 million more have electricity. The government has built nearly one million houses for those who lacked shelter and provides a basic lunch for every child in primary school. As other countries struggle with the concept of a "social safety net," South Africa has introduced basic pensions for the elderly poor to supplement an existing pension system for all levels of retired government employees, including teachers and nurses, black and white. If the remaining tasks are monumental— three million still lack electricity and eight million lack access to clean water—the progress to date is still exceptional.[60]

Where the economy has not progressed nearly as hoped is in growth and employment. In spite of what adherents of the "Washington consensus" would have to consider stellar policies of fiscal and monetary discipline, and of trade liberalization and at least a good deal of encouragement of the private sector, growth has struggled at no better than 3 percent in most years since 1994 and has been as low as 1 percent in two of those years. Unemployment in the formal sector has thus grown, not receded, as some five hundred thousand jobs have been lost in the formal sector. Foreign direct investment (FDI) has also not been at the levels anticipated, with South Africa attracting per head one-third to one-tenth of the investment attracted by other emerging economies.[61] Not all of this is due to

South African policies; a large part has to do with the limited market South Africa still offers and problems of competitiveness as an export platform.[62]

Nevertheless, problems of skills and productivity, deep structural problems in the education system, plus labor laws that in many experts' views inhibit the growth of small and medium industry make overcoming economic problems a long-term process. South Africa ranks near the bottom of forty-seven countries surveyed for their competitiveness in human capital.[63] Meanwhile, the lagging economy has sharpened disagreements within the ANC alliance, with the labor movement becoming increasingly aggressive in challenging the government's conservative economic policies and fighting the government's plans for further privatization, the area that has attracted much of the FDI so far. On the eve of the UN Conference on Racism in Durban, in September 2001, COSATU staged a two-day general strike over these issues, to the anger and embarrassment of the government.[64]

But where South Africa has lost prestige the most, in the United States and elsewhere, is in the struggle against HIV/AIDS, and responsibility for this lies at the door of President Mbeki. The explosion of the epidemic in South Africa has nearly overwhelmed anyone dealing with the issue. Perhaps one of every four adults, as many as 4.2 million people, is now infected and South Africa has the largest infection rate in the world. The impact on the economy is growing. Anglo American, one of the largest mining companies in the country, finds that 21 percent of its staff is infected. Many firms are hiring several people to fill each job, with long-term training becoming a questionable investment. The most optimistic estimate is that HIV/AIDS will reduce South Africa's growth by 0.4 percent annually in the coming years; others feel it will be much more costly. The social costs are even more numbing, with predictions that the number of AIDS orphans will rise from one hundred and forty thousand to as many as two million by 2010, that a skewing of the future population will occur because of a shortage of both productive women and workers, and that life expectancy will drop from sixty to forty by 2008. Already, several hundred thousand people a year are dying from the disease.[65]

The government was not prepared for this and stumbled badly in its first few years. But Mbeki compounded the problem when, in 1999, he questioned the scientific basis for AIDS, that is, the link with HIV; argued further that proven antiretroviral drugs were dangerous and even a plot against Africa; and thereby created a mountain of confusion that to this day hobbles the government.[66] Just about everyone I know who knows of my involvement in South Africa has asked me to explain Mbeki's pronouncements on this issue, so I will try to do so here.

What Mbeki meant, in my view, was the following: It would be wrong of the West to treat the AIDS epidemic in Africa the way it is treated in the West, that is, by treating the people living with HIV with life-extending drugs and carrying out a prevention program. Such an approach in South Africa would ignore the role that poverty, malnutrition, social dislocations from migrant labor in the mines, and the lack of a basic health infrastructure play. Malnutrition associated with poverty aggravates the virulence of the HIV strain and enhances the prevalence of opportunistic infections from AIDS, such as tuberculosis and malaria.[67] Migrant labor creates special problems in prevention that can be overcome only with long-term economic and social reconstruction. As a South African researcher notes, "If you wanted to spread a sexually transmitted disease, you would take thousands of young men away from their families, isolate them in single-sex hostels, and give them easy access to alcohol and commercial sex. And that is basically the system of migrant labor we have."[68]

Furthermore, the lack of health infrastructure makes it difficult to administer anything like a sophisticated drug therapy program, even a program to treat opportunistic infections. Finally, the costs of following the Western model of treatment would—in the estimate of the government—be ten times the entire current health budget of the government, which is already a substantial percentage of total expenditures. In more combative terms, Mbeki might be said to be saying that the West wants to rush in and treat the symptoms of the problem, leave South Africa with a dependency on expensive drug therapy, and depart leaving all the underlying problems of poverty and malnutrition intact. Even with drug companies now offering their products at extremely low prices, Mbeki asks if this will be true as long as they will be needed on the continent.

Had Mbeki made these points in this way, as indeed Ambassador Sheila Sisulu and her staff in Washington do quite articulately, the world might well have listened, as it should. Indeed, many of these ideas calling for a more comprehensive approach to the problem in developing countries found their way into the communiqué and plan of action at the UN General Assembly's Special Session on HIV/AIDS in June 2001. South Africa is also spending considerable amounts on HIV/AIDS, making its program probably the largest, in dollar terms, in Africa. The Ministry of Health has requested $300 million for the years 2002–2004 for this purpose.[69] But Mbeki has stubbornly clung to his questioning of the relationship of HIV to AIDS, in addressing the world AIDS conference in Durban in July 2000 and again in his address to the National Press Club in Washington in June 2001. In these and other statements, he has thereby convinced many that he does not appreciate the magnitude of this crisis. Not surprisingly, this has become a contentious issue within the country, with AIDS activist groups suing the government and even quasi-governmental bodies disputing Mbeki's statistics and arguments, for example, his latest assertion, an incorrect one, that violence is a greater cause of death among young South Africans than is AIDS.[70] In July 2001, I conducted, at the South African government's request, an advocacy workshop for the South African National AIDS Advisory Council, a joint government–civil society body. All the participants put the best face on the government's efforts, but underneath one could feel the confusion, the lack of clarity in the policy, and the lack of top-level oversight and priority, all factors that undermined the government's effectiveness.

The AIDS crisis will continue to dog South Africa's reputation, even as it drags down its potential. But it would be wrong to leave the discussion of South Africa and of President Mbeik on this point. Mbeki has also staked his reputation and much of his international effort on being a bridge between the developed and developing world in addressing the issues of globalization. As with the NPT, South Africa sees itself as a hybrid country, a developing country in many aspects, but also one with a highly developed infrastructure and economic base. Thus Mbeki has sought to position South Africa not as a country fighting globalization and linkages with the world economy, but as one that embraces them but speaks for the inequities that leave so many poor countries behind. He has enunciated these themes in many speeches, within the G-20, as head of the Nonaligned Movement, and most recently in championing a New Economic Partnership for African Development, which would couple basic commitments to democratic government, human rights, and sound economic policies on the part of the African countries with major debt relief, much greater market access, aid, and technological transfer from the industrialized countries. Mbeki has challenged some traditional positions within the developing world on this score and has been forthright in criticizing Africa's record on human rights and governance.

Neither in the Clinton administration nor so far in the Bush administration has the potential for partnership on these issues been taken up. It is a pity, for the industrialized countries, undertaking a new round of trade talks and wanting to extend the progress of global economic integration, will need voices of reason and candor on these issues, a bridge from the developed to the developing world that will articulate ways to make the global economy a more equitable and far-reaching good.

WHERE WE HAVE COME

When Nelson Mandela made his state visit to the United States in October 1994, he drew crowds, not only in the halls and dinner venues but also on the streets. Washington cab drivers, normally immune to the many dignitaries who come through the city, stopped to wave. People crowded onto the sidewalks whenever he appeared. In New York, in Washington, wherever he went, the admiration and awe extended to him were overwhelming. The initial coolness he exhibited on the White House lawn gave way to a tremendous feeling of partnership with

America. When President Clinton paid his visit to South Africa in 1998, that energy was renewed.

But relationships between countries cannot rest on personalities alone. That between the United States and South Africa rests on something much more. It rests on a history of shared experiences, of our peoples joining together in a fight for freedom and racial equality. It rests on a recognition that South Africa—with its unique place between the developing and the developed world, with democracy more firmly institutionalized than in most other transition countries, as a force for human rights, and as a partner in developing the global economy—is a critical partner for the United States in every aspect of our foreign policy—just as the United States is critical to every aspiration of South Africa.

In the period of South Africa's historic transformation, the United States played its role. We were facilitators and we played this role about as well as it could be played. Out of that shared experience, a new respect and basis for cooperation was established. Institutions were put into place to deepen that relationship further. Much has been built upon those foundations in subsequent years, by outstanding American and South African ambassadors and by other officials, business leaders, and devoted individuals.[71] The full product of this partnership may yet to be harvested. Above all, it is the task of both countries not to squander that promise, not to lose the potential that was created.

12
Lessons Learned— and Relearned

Then at last, if never before, Adams acquired education. What he had sought so long, he found; but he was none the wiser.
—HENRY ADAMS, *The Education of Henry Adams*

IT HAS BECOME A CLICHÉ that the South African transition, not without bloodshed but without the devastation of civil war, was a "miracle." Even analytical academics have deemed it such:

> Neither history nor analysis would have predicted a negotiated outcome to the internal conflict in South Africa. In history there is no precedent anywhere for successful negotiations allowing a poor majority to take over from or even to share power with a rich minority when majority and minority identify and are identified ascriptively. That only happens by revolution or by postcolonial replacement. From an analytic standpoint, all the reasons . . . for the difficulty of negotiating an internal conflict exist so strongly in South Africa as to make negotiation there appear impossible. For negotiation to succeed in South Africa an apparent sociopolitical miracle would be required.[1]

The problem with painting South Africa so often as a "miracle" is that it leads to seeing it as an aberration, a special case with limited relevance to other conflicts. South Africa did have special characteristics as it approached the final stages of the transition. It had juridical and constitutional institutions that, while applied mostly to the whites, offered space for some of those opposed to the apartheid system and precedent for the wider application of such institutions afterward. There were extraordinary leaders and a host of outside events that played into the final process. South Africans are in many ways special people. But one must recall that in the previous decade, almost no one saw these factors as definitive. On the contrary, South Africa was seen as a country en route to disaster. Moreover, some of those characteristics that made South Africa "special" were the product of decisions made decades earlier and were reinforced by influences both indigenous and external.

In particular, there are lessons in the South African experience that lend themselves to the role of external actors in conflict situations. These lessons deserve our attention.

BUILDING CAPACITY FOR PEACE

Surely, one of the lessons from South Africa is that building capacity, enhancing dialogue, developing ideas, and promoting confidence are of extraordinary value in enabling a society to overcome the pressures of conflict. In South Africa's case, those processes took place over decades. They continued during periods when prospects for reform in the country looked bleak, during periods when isolation and revolution were deemed by many the only means for achieving fundamental change. The work of the American foundations, described in an earlier chapter, bringing South African jurists and lawyers together with the best minds in the United States, bringing together representatives of disparate political outlooks so that stereotypes and misunderstandings could be dissolved, providing scholarship programs that developed an impressive cadre of skilled persons who were able to address the many aspects of the transition and assume positions of leadership in the new era—these were some of the building blocks of the South Africa "miracle." USAID's scholarship program may have seemed small in the 1980s when it began. But by the mid-1990s, thirteen hundred South African black recipients who otherwise would not have had the opportunity had graduated from universities and were beginning to take their places in government, business, and the NGO world.

The lesson is continuity and patience. Facilitating communication, breaking down stereotypes, and promoting dialogue are recognized as part of the conflict resolution process; what some authors have described as "pre-mediation." But conflict resolution studies also talk much about "ripeness" of a conflict for resolution, when the parties through stalemate or some external shock come to the conclusion that continuing the conflict is more costly than resolving it. What South Africa teaches us is that there is a fruitful process well before the conflict is "ripe" and that building dialogue and a capacity for negotiation may take more than workshops and quiet meetings, valuable as those are when the time comes. In South Africa, some of the programs described above went on for more than twenty years before they bore full fruit. Some people opposed them, arguing that

consorting with the representatives of apartheid society only softened the isolation that the system deserved. The U.S.–South Africa Leadership Development
Program (USSALEP) suffered such criticism. But like so many other programs
that brought people out of their immediate surroundings and opened them to new
ideas, USSALEP contributed to the atmosphere that made possible, many years
later, the outcome in South Africa.

In other countries, the challenge may be greater and the outcome less certain.
Countries that have prohibited discussion, crushed economic opportunity, and
persecuted opposition members offer little scope for those encouraged from outside. Many from those countries, educated and exposed to new ideas, may therefore choose exile or be forced into it, possibly lost to the development of their
countries. Marina Ottoway cautions, moreover, that in countries not yet democratic, the contribution to democracy of such donor-assisted skills and organizations may be dependent on more radical and at times violent movements that
have the muscle to force change—movements normally outside the donor's pur-
view.[2] Certainly, without a strong liberation movement in South Africa, the contribution of those professional and educated cadres described above would have
been much less. But it is also true that liberation movements that come to power
without these skills to draw on may prove ineffective in governing and are likely
to drift toward being autocratic.

What works much less well is the stop and start of American involvement.
In the first excitement of Nigeria's independence in the 1960s, the United States
through its aid and exchange programs developed cooperative programs with
nearly every major Nigerian university. Then in the 1970s, when Nigeria's oil
wealth flourished, the programs were closed. Nigeria was too "rich" for aid. When
I came to Nigeria as ambassador in the mid-1980s, I found a whole generation of
Nigerian academics with little or no contact with America, isolated and angry over
the nondemocratic governments under which the country had suffered, and faced
with a devastating deterioration of the universities. Their isolation and anger led
them into strategies that did little to change the political situation and only contributed more to the deterioration of the university structure. A true prodemocracy movement only developed in Nigeria in the late 1990s, partly under the spur
of Nelson Mandela.[3]

In those intervening years, from the 1970s to the late 1990s, nothing like a
Binational Commission had been created between the United States and Nigeria
to provide continuity and encouragement. It took AID and Congress decades to
find a way, with the experience in Eastern Europe, for our aid programs to operate in other than the poorest countries, to operate in those "middle-income"
countries that are by definition of special influence and importance. In the new
century, with Nigeria once again poor and in the wake of a return to democracy,

the United States seeks to rebuild those ties again. Nigeria is once again a recipient of one the United States' largest aid programs. Pity that a generation has been lost.

However, this process should not be the work of government alone. Some of the most dynamic and meaningful programs in South Africa were operated by private foundations and organizations. These have had more freedom and flexibility. Unfortunately, there has been a turning away from international programs by the major foundations in recent years. After many years of early investment in African universities, the Rockefeller Foundation went on to other priorities. Only now is it returning to an area where it once made a major contribution. Some other foundations are also now returning to the work they did so well in past decades. Pity that they, too, lost nearly a generation of sustained effort.

KEEPING THE PROCESS IN THE HANDS OF THE PARTIES

There is no question that outside mediation is often necessary and effective in resolving conflict. But there is a temptation to believe that it is indispensable, even the preferred route. Mediators are led to believe that they must provide the solution, the deadlock-breaking proposal, the guiding hand to the combatants. Quite a few books have been written in recent years on conflict resolution. Many of them are prescriptions for mediators. There is no question they provide valuable lessons.[4] But there is less written on a more subtle process, that of facilitation of a peace process, a policy predicated on keeping the process in the hands of the contending parties.[5]

The temptation to mediate is understandable. Conflicts can be horrible and threaten wider international peace. The parties may be unable to come together without some outside help. And outsiders, such as the United States, the United Nations, and the European Union, are pressed by the media and the public to intervene. There is a sort of hubris in being a mediator as well. But for all the successes of mediation—and there are many, for example, between Iran and Iraq in 1988, in El Salvador in 1991, in Mozambique in 1992, in Cambodia in 1993, and between Ethiopia and Eritrea in 2000—there are also costly failures. There is the danger, in Herman Cohen's words, of "signature obsession," the pressure to get a deal when the fundamentals are not there to support it.

Analysts may disagree whether the failure of the successive peace agreements in Angola during the 1990s was the fault of insufficient external engagement or simply the lack of commitment of at least one of the contending parties to the process, but surely the agreements, to which so much international effort was invested, lacked strong, sustaining internal support.[6] In the developments leading up to the NATO bombing in Kosovo, in 2000, mediators at Rambouillet sought in effect to ram an agreement down the throats of the two sides, particularly the Serbs, that they could not accept. Ironically, the settlement drafted by the G-8 and passed through the UN Security Council at the end of the bombing campaign gave the defeated Serbia more than offered at Rambouillet.[7] The Lome agreement in 2000 to settle the civil war in Sierra Leone was another example, an agreement that broke down almost immediately with brutal consequences and that the mediators themselves later sought to repudiate. President Clinton's dramatic end-of-term effort to mediate a settlement of the Israeli-Palestinian conflict is perhaps another example.

By contrast, the process of facilitation is designed precisely to avoid becoming the mediator, to keep the responsibility with the parties, making the solutions theirs. Facilitation, compared to mediation, may take patience. It may require standing relatively aloof, especially avoiding that temptation to mediate, when the parties refuse to come together. But it is not a recipe for passivity, for a policy of inaction. Rather, as shown in the South Africa case, it can involve the most intense diplomatic efforts, the most dynamic programming of resources, and the mobilization of a broad array of supportive elements to bring pressure on the participants. External actors can surround the process with expertise, constantly put pressure on the parties to remain or return to the table, and implement sanctions where necessary. Public and private diplomacy can play a part. Heavy investment in indigenous capacity, at both the grassroots and the senior levels, can make a substantial difference.

Above all, facilitation can contribute to a solution that is firmer and lasting. One of the most important factors in South Africa's transition was that it was the South Africans' negotiations, their agreements, their transition. As noted earlier in this book, offers of mediation were rejected. Thus the compromises that were accepted were ones borne by and defended by the South Africans. It is hard to imagine a Government of National Unity fostered by outside mediators functioning as well and with as much legitimacy as the government did in South Africa. Accepting a Government of National Unity, a formal power-sharing agreement, was one of the most difficult compromises the ANC had to make. But once it came to that conclusion, the ANC took on the task of justifying it to its constituents and making it an integral part of its own transition strategy. On the other side, it was de Klerk who gave up his quest for a "white veto" in the new government and accepted a consensus voting basis instead, and who gave up his alliance with Buthelezi to negotiate primarily with the ANC. It is hard to imagine the solidity of the security forces behind the settlement or the strength of governmental pressure on Buthelezi had these accommodations been imposed from outside.

PERSONALITIES BORN AND MADE

One might argue that South Africa was unique, or at least most fortunate, in the extraordinary quality of its leadership at this time in its history. If ever there was evidence that personalities affect history, South Africa is it. Without question, Mandela's breadth of vision, his humanity, his genuine commitment to nonracial democracy, and his charisma had a major impact on the very possibility of negotiations' being accepted by his own followers as well as by the ruling party, and on the direction and outcome of those negotiations. F. W. de Klerk is also a man of vision, perhaps the only leader in history to negotiate a transition from president to the third-ranking position in a new government. He is also a man of exceptional leadership ability, to be able to bring along the full force of the security establishment and the bulk of his constituency in giving up so much of their power. Moreover, both men were surrounded by extraordinary people, with talent and vision and with commitment to the process. Our faith in the ability of these leaders to achieve a favorable outcome strengthened our own commitment to facilitation rather than mediation.

Yet leaders are not just born: they are often shaped. As has been pointed out in earlier chapters, many of those in South Africa who were charged with the tremendously important negotiation of the details of constitutional issues, integration of institutions, and creating a full democracy had had years of exposure to the best minds in the world, opportunities to study, to reflect, and to prepare for these momentous times. Those experiences also gave us entrée to their deliberations, common grounds on which to appeal, shared values with which to work together.

There will of course be conflict situations in which leaders are much less honorable, much more venal, sometimes incredibly cruel. Reaching them and convincing them of the need to negotiate, to compromise, will take different tactics, different forms of leverage. But even then, the more one brings them to the table, making them participants in the decisions, the stronger will be the outcome. And in the meantime, as noted above, investing in building new leaders, with new values and capabilities, should be a priority.

South Africa has exported its experience to other conflict situations. It has experienced some of these limitations in leadership in the process. When Nelson Mandela reported to the UN Security Council in January 2000 on his role in seeking to bring peace to Burundi, he was careful to describe his role as one of facilitation and adamant that only the Burundians could produce a settlement. He chastised them for failing to assume their full responsibility: "It is time for Burundians to get down to business! No one can reach an agreement on their behalf. The responsibility rests squarely with their leaders now to find the necessary arrangements by which Burundians can live together."

Echoing the experience of the ANC in bringing along its constituents through the tortuous process of negotiation and compromise, Mandela urged the Burundian parties to do the same:

> Common sense tells that if an agreement signed in Arusha [Tanzania, where the negotiations were taking place] were not acceptable to public opinion in Burundi, it could not be successfully implemented. The responsibility for ensuring that link lies solely with the leadership of the parties conducting the negotiations. This means the leaders need to do groundwork at the grassroots level in order to persuade their constituencies that the price of agreement, and lasting peace, will be concession and compromise on certain major issues.[8]

Mandela may fail in his efforts. He surely has had to play a more active facilitating role than any outside entity did in South Africa. But the lesson he carried from South Africa was nevertheless clear and relevant and remains true in Burundi today. South Africans have similarly carried lessons from their experience to Northern Ireland. In retreat sessions and regular exchanges, South Africans have emphasized to the parties in Northern Ireland the importance of direct negotiations among the stakeholders, of building trust between them, and of the principles of transparency and compromise.[9]

FACILITATION IS NOT CHEAP: THE NEED FOR PEOPLE AND RESOURCES

In the 1990s, the U.S. embassy in South Africa had a corps of talented political officers led by the sophisticated John Campbell; three consulates, including one in the volatile province of KwaZulu/Natal; USAID and USIA missions of dedicated officers both American and South African; and representatives from the Defense Department, the Agricultural Department, and the Commerce Department. Two of our political officers were Afrikaans speakers, able to stay in touch with the range of conservative political forces as well as the developments within the "colored" community. One of our political officers, first Pamela Bridgewater and later Robin Hinson-Jones, spent virtually all day, every day at ANC headquarters, coming to know and be trusted by the leaders and the other party officials there. We had a full-time labor attaché who threw himself into the most difficult and sometimes dangerous work of labor politics in KwaZulu/Natal and elsewhere. The consulate in Durban, in KwaZulu/Natal, had only two or three professional officers, but they were our outreach to the events there, to the officials of Inkatha and their rivals, and our regular liaison with Chief Buthelezi.[10] Without the eyes and ears of these dedicated people, without their outreach and contacts, their day-to-day monitoring of events, their energy and innovation, and their recommendations, the embassy and the U.S. government would have been flying blind. Surely none of the judgments that I made as ambassador would have had the same value.

Yet in the 1990s, the United States allowed its diplomatic capacity to atrophy. By the end of the decade, the nonmilitary international affairs budget was 20 percent less in current dollars than it was on average during the late 1970s and 1980s.[11] Human resource policies and budgets, labeled "dysfunctional" by outside experts, had left the Department of State with a deficit of seven hundred foreign service officers, or 15 percent of requirements. Communications and information management systems were outdated, with 92 percent of posts equipped with obsolete classified networks.[12] Other resources were similarly allowed to decline. Foreign aid declined to $10.4 billion, or 0.6 percent of federal budget outlays, compared to $18.5 billion, or 3.06 percent of federal spending, in 1962—this despite the massive increase in resources that had to be devoted to the former Soviet Union and Eastern Europe in the past decade.[13] Colin Powell, in one of his first acts as secretary of state, requested of Congress a 13 percent increase in the department's budget for 2002, an important step in reversing this long period of decline.

How this decline has affected the capacity of the United States to play a facilitative role can be demonstrated in two key African situations. In Congo, the United States has no presence in the eastern part of the country and thus is out of touch with the rebellious movements that, with foreign encouragement and involvement, are destabilizing that country. Our embassy in Kinshasa, while extremely well led through much of the war by Ambassador William Swing, has been closely bound to the information provided by and dealings with the weak central government. In Nigeria, my very able colleague Howard Jeter took up his duties as ambassador in 2001 without a senior political counselor, which meant no one to supervise a political section made up of almost all young, inexperienced officers. He is without a consulate in the north—the one there was closed several years ago—though this is where the traditional power of Nigeria resides. Nor is there a consulate or any embassy presence in the delta, not only the source of Nigeria's oil wealth and most American investment but now one of the most volatile regions. He has no Hausa speakers on his staff, though this is the language of the Muslim half of the population. Yet, in this country of more than one hundred million people and more than one hundred different language and ethnic groups, Ambassador Jeter is expected to facilitate Nigeria's path to stable democracy; to help it avoid breaking apart under regional, religious, and ethnic conflicts; and for these purposes to oversee an aid program of more than $100 million. I can only wish him well.

The lack of depth can be seen elsewhere. In the late 1990s, the United States responded to the several conflicts raging in Africa with the appointment of numerous special envoys. There were high-profile ones, such as Jesse Jackson, presumably an envoy for all of Africa but especially involved in a flawed effort in Sierra Leone; the serious and dedicated former congressman Howard Wolpe, for Burundi and the Great Lakes region; experienced career officers such as Richard Bogosian for the Great Lakes region and Howard Jeter for Liberia and Sierra Leone; and Tony Lake, who worked quietly and ultimately successfully with Ethiopia and Eritrea. They worked tirelessly throughout this period, traveled endlessly to the region, talked with other envoys, and lent their every talent to bringing about peace. But in almost every case they were without the depth of staff support, consistent high-level backing, and availability of flexible resources needed to make a significant impact. In some people's eyes, they were substitutes for policy rather than indicative of a serious U.S. commitment. Not surprisingly, one of Colin Powell's first acts as secretary of state was to abolish half the special envoy positions.[14] Hopefully, rather than representing a lessening of commitment to these peace processes, this will lead to a more organized and sufficiently resourced program of conflict resolution. Former senator John Danforth, when appointed by President Bush as a special envoy to Sudan in September 2001, made a point of saying he expected his work to be fully integrated and supported by the department.[15]

Encouraging in this regard, Powell moved quickly as secretary to obtain congressional support to address the shortage of personnel as well as other resource shortfalls in the department. The department will increase hiring by 43 percent in fiscal year 2002 and add similar numbers for each of the next two years. Several new and diverse hiring programs are being established to recruit a wide variety of specialized as well as general skills.[16] The terrible terrorist attack on the United States of September 11, 2001, will most likely result in further strengthening of a broad array of foreign affairs skills. This will begin to reverse a long and costly decline.

THE SOUND OF TWO HANDS CLAPPING

When I was in Washington for consultations in early 1993, Deputy Secretary of State Clifford Wharton told me over lunch one day that he and his wife had long differed over the question of sanctions against South Africa. He had been in favor of them, believing that they were necessary both to bring pressure on the government and to demonstrate solidarity with the liberation movement. His wife, a businesswoman, opposed them. She argued that the impact of sanctions fell mostly on the black population, that those who were most in need would pay the largest price. Instead, not only did business development in South Africa provide jobs, but the pressures of economic modernization were helping break down the structure of apartheid. "If it makes you feel any better," I replied, "you were both right."

What we can learn from South Africa is that processes of engagement and restraint, reward and punishment, do not have to be seen always in competition with each other. Indeed, they are perhaps best worked in tandem.

South Africa's experience in this regard is not just of historical value. South Africa resurfaced as a reference point during 2000 in two policy debates. One instance involved the question of whether to provide permanent normal trade relations with China. Opponents of such relations argued that the business community's defense of its role in bringing about change in China was "as hollow as the same claims made by that community in South Africa" in the 1980s.[17] The second was the debate over the role of the World Trade Organization (WTO). Leaders of the demonstrations against the WTO meeting in Seattle that year argued that if the WTO had been in existence in the 1980s, sanctions against South Africa would have been ruled illegal.[18] The questions raised in both cases are whether sanctions or engagement is most effective in bringing about change in a repressive society and whether, if sanctions are a proper instrument, their role should for this purpose outweigh trade standards alone.

South Africa offers some valuable lessons in this area. Sanctions "worked" in South Africa, but they did in part for reasons related to the South African situation. One was that the leaders of the liberation movement, and many of their rank and file—who would indeed suffer from them—were willing to pay the price of sanctions. As Archbishop Tutu said, "We were not just looking to make our shackles comfortable."[19] There is no doubt, moreover, that sanctions became so significant for the liberation movement in the 1980s that not to support them was to separate ourselves from that movement in a dangerous way. Sanctions also had an effect on the ruling elite. The economic impact was significant but may have been mixed. One assessment was that overall attempts to evade restrictions cost South Africa between $15 billion and $27 billion.[20] At the same time, some white-led South African firms profited from sanctions, buying at bargain prices foreign firms that were disinvesting, concentrating economic power domestically and through sanctions busting.[21] But the principal effect was probably psychological, adding to the sense of insecurity, isolation, and loss of confidence among the white population generally. As has been pointed out in this book, removing sanctions and South Africa's isolation was a major objective of de Klerk in his reform policy and a major selling point for those reforms with his white constituency.

Sanctions would not necessarily work that way in other situations. If there is no organized popular movement to articulate the trade-offs and calculate the allowable pain, the impact on the populace can be the opposite of that in South Africa. A case in point may well be Iraq, where the regime has used the sanctions to turn popular anger against the perpetrators of the sanctions, not the internal oppressors. Targeted sanctions are now considered better in such cases. But even with sanctions targeted on the leaders, where the oppressors are immune to international opinion or independent of real pressure, sanctions are of limited value. Nigeria in the 1990s under General Sani Abacha was one such case. Abacha could not have cared less about international opinion and, lacking a full international oil embargo, was able to amass great wealth through oil exports, among other means, largely unbothered by the various travel and other restrictions that were imposed on him and his government. South Africa was different. For all their faults, white South Africans saw themselves as part of the Western world and felt deeply about their isolation.

But the other lesson from South Africa is that economic development did help undermine the foundations of apartheid. South African corporations realized by the 1980s if not earlier that keeping workers far from their places of employment and other restrictions of apartheid were simply inconsistent with the demands of a modern industrialized economy. They had begun buying up apartment buildings in Johannesburg under their own names and housing black workers there, in violation of the law. Apartheid was coming apart, as leaders such as de Klerk came to realize, even before the government moved to abolish it. If not absolutely courageous about it, business leaders were not actively opposed to change, and many actively facilitated it. Concomitant with a modernizing economy, the growth of black unions, whose recognition came as a result of internal business, as much as political, pressures, provided extraordinarily important vehicles for black political as well as economic development. As described in chapter 2, black trade unions became a major organizing force in alliance with the United Democratic Front in the 1980s and in all the political mass actions over the next decade. There, the leader of one of the strongest of those unions, the United Mineworkers, honed his negotiating skills, which he later employed brilliantly as the chief ANC negotiator of the political transition.

American firms did not start out as social or political reformers in South Africa. A survey of managers of American firms in the early 1970s found most of them immune or opposed to such objectives.[22] But under pressure, and with adoption of the Sullivan Code, American firms set an example of social investment that outshone, and continues to outshine even today, their South African counterparts' performance.[23] They may not have been as significant in bringing about change as their supporters claimed during the disinvestment debates, and their continued presence rankled for many years among the veterans of the liberation movement, but they did provide important examples of corporate responsibility and at least softened the impact of sanctions for their workers. Surely they did less harm than their critics charged.

Finally, there is no question that the much-maligned policy of "constructive engagement" did provide a source of encouragement to reformers within the

Afrikaner establishment and an avenue of American influence, in particular on resolution of the regional issues. That it was abused by the South African government and failed in its public diplomacy does not take away from that.

The lesson is that following dual, or parallel, or, if one prefers, seemingly inconsistent policies in the face of such a situation is not at all a bad thing. It adds up to a valuable array of tools by which to influence a situation. The difficulty is to be able to manage such a dual policy effectively, for example, to allow those forces of modernization to undermine strictly authoritarian systems, while not becoming simply an apologist for small but insignificant changes, for what Richard Moose described as "change" that is not "progress." It takes balance and judgment. It takes case-by-case decisions on where to draw the line, where to apply the brakes on cooperation, how to develop incentives, and what to hold back. It is hard enough in any case, but it is almost impossible to do it well if there is no consensus on such a dual policy. The tragedy of U.S. policy toward South Africa in the 1980s was that differences, deep and emotional, over U.S. policy made applying such careful balance nearly impossible. Instead, we seemed to be jolting between two policies, one driven by public pressures and eventually Congress, the other driven by the administration. China may offer us a better opportunity, though the balance has always to be recalibrated.

BUT SINGING WITH ONE VOICE

When Ed Perkins went out as ambassador to South Africa in 1986, he had an agreement that he would not use the term "constructive engagement." He even sidestepped it in his confirmation hearings. Friends of his urged him to not even take the assignment, arguing that as an African American he was being exploited. Representing one's country when it is so divided at home is never easy. Perkins had his hands full not only in South Africa but also at home.

One of the great strengths of U.S. policy in the 1990s was that these differences had faded away and there was a unanimous focus on assisting the transition process. By the end of 1992 the accusations, for example, that the process was not yet legitimate or that de Klerk's intentions were anything but honorable, had dropped away. This allowed the United States to deploy all its resources, governmental and nongovernmental, toward a single objective.

But our success was due to more than that. Washington during this period gave those of us in the field rather extraordinary leeway and support. There was virtually no second-guessing. This was true of both the State Department and the National Security Council. We in the field thus set the tone of our relationships with counterparts and developed the strategy and employment of our public diplomacy—I confess I never cleared a single speech that I gave with Washington, though I always sent them copies after the fact. We developed the strategy for use of our aid resources and acted aggressively in carrying out the policy, without fear of contradiction or repudiation. It was not entirely by chance.

My view of the role of an embassy is to provide both the best analysis and the best recommendations. If an embassy simply reports to Washington and awaits a response, then the complex bureaucratic process in Washington will make the analysis and set the policy response. The embassy may not like the result. In South Africa, we worked at remaining in control of policy and its implementation. With a first-rate staff, our belief that we were in touch with the relevant parties, and of course our understanding of the overall policy set in Washington, we believed we were in the best position constantly to place events in context, to propose next steps and reactions to events, and, within limits, to take policy initiatives. It was gratifying that Washington agreed. The only issue over which there was a significant difference between Washington and the field, though it was more between agencies in Washington, was nonproliferation. In that case, competing scientific analyses, as well as policy differences, had to be ironed out. By coming back on consultation to Washington and working those issues through personally, I was able to bring about agreement that was absolutely essential if we were to be effective in this area.

The backing we got from Washington was more than gratifying. Washington, especially the Office of Southern African Affairs under Ambassador April Glaspie and Assistant Secretary George Moose, mobilized the necessary interagency approvals, argued our case with other agencies, and secured us people and resources. They also challenged us when they thought we were wrong. That too was valuable. But the tone of their advice, even when questioning or critical, was always one of support.

Equally critical is making use of all U.S. government resources in the field. Management of U.S. government representation overseas is becoming one of the most challenging demands on ambassadors today. When I was ambassador in South Africa, there were seven U.S. government agencies represented within the embassy community. Today in South Africa there are twenty-five. Theoretically, the ambassador is in charge of all such representation, but that is in theory. Agencies such as the FBI and the DEA tend to operate independently, sharing little with the ambassador and sometimes working at cross-purposes with other policy objectives.[24]

The positive side of this is that the potential from such a resource base is enormous. The first rule, however, is for the ambassador and his or her staff to respect the fact that each agency represented has its own mandate, sometimes legislated, and gets guidance and rewards from its headquarters in Washington. Once that respect, and the support from the ambassador that goes with it, is accorded, it should be possible to inspire those representatives to share in the overall U.S. objectives and to promote cooperation across agency lines toward them. As former undersecretary of state David Newsom has written,

> It has long been myth, reinforced by letters issued by each President, that U.S. Ambassadors are in charge of their Embassies. The fact is that good Ambassadors achieve that control not through letters, but by overcoming obstacles, establishing confidence among their staff, and leading.[25]

In South Africa, we achieved that synergy. For example, the agricultural attaché's job was to sell American wheat and rice and other American agricultural products, and to report to the U.S. Department of Agriculture on the local agricultural scene. I supported him in that, even though commerce with South Africa was not yet one of our priorities. But also, caught up in the importance of our overall objectives for the transition, he became in the course of his travels around the country an important source of information on the views of the farming community, both black and white, about the political process under way. He put me in touch with farm leaders of both races and provided access we would otherwise not have had. The defense attaché's job was to provide liaison with the South African Defense Force. But Colonel Kim Henningsen, with extensive experience with the Zimbabwean transition before coming to South Africa, was also critical to us in opening up contact with the ANC's armed wing and advising it on its integration into a new national defense establishment. I have described elsewhere how closely USAID and the U.S. Information Service worked to develop flexible and responsive programs in support of the transition. Chaired by the political counselor, there was a democracy committee that met regularly to see how the combination of all our resources and capabilities could be deployed for this purpose in the most effective way.

NEVER FORGET YOUR FRIENDS

The United States emerged as the principal external actor in this period. But others were extremely important and it was essential to maintain as much unity and cooperation among all the external players as possible. Britain and Germany were the most important, but Japan became increasingly so and the European Union as a whole loomed large as resources became important in the run-up to the election. With Britain and Germany, sharing assessments and ideas was critical. It was especially important to align our policies with regard to Buthelezi. Both Britain and Germany had histories of support to Buthelezi and strong domestic constituencies on his side. It was important that we stay together. As noted, the three ambassadors met regularly for this purpose and were candid among ourselves about who could do what and under what circumstances.

Winning the confidence of our partners, through sharing of information and assessments, also helped avoid end runs or competing initiatives. It didn't hurt that my deputy chief of mission, Priscilla Clapp, spoke fluent Japanese and Russian and kept in good contact with the Russian and Japanese ambassadors. Japan rebuffed Buthelezi's proposal for an international mediation that would have excluded the United States, an initiative that would have complicated the process. The European Union, at the urging of Denmark's ambassador, took initiatives in stepping up support for the electoral process, to which we responded immediately and positively and to which we lent strong support and eventually leadership. As a result, there was remarkable coordination of the thousands of international election observers and other support to the election. In the delicate matter of biological and chemical weapons, the coordination between the British ambassador and me, and between our staffs, could not have been closer.

JUDGMENT

In commenting on the craft of mediation, Chester Crocker has written that some things are a matter of "feel and instinct."[26] So, too, one might add, in making key judgments on when and where to take sides, when and where to stay strictly neutral, and many other key steps in the process of facilitation. Judgment is not chance.

During the period of the transition, we made many critical judgments in the embassy, some that were not without risk. We trusted the principal parties, the government and the ANC, to be able to manage the process. We put considerable confidence in, and a major effort into securing, Constand Viljoen's decision ultimately to join the electoral process rather than lead his supporters into war. We did so based largely on our assessment of him, but also of the people around him. At the same time, we pretty much wrote off the Conservative Party, not only as largely hopeless but also in the end as potentially irrelevant. We made the decision to take an increasingly confrontational attitude toward Buthelezi while at the same time keeping open every opportunity to reach him. Unlike some in Washington and within the ANC, we never underestimated his power base and relevance to a successful outcome. We also did not, as some South Africans tried to persuade us and others to do, overestimate it as bearing on the country as a whole. Perhaps most risky of all, we made the judgment that the process would hold, that a coup or intervention of some kind by the security establishment was a real threat but less than likely. As a result, we stuck to our position in opposition to outside peacekeepers, or for that matter to pleas for further delays in the election timetable.

These judgments were not made by the seat of our pants. They were made based on the extensive outreach to the whole country, to the many factions, to the academics, to the power brokers, to the farmers, and to the security forces. They were made based on the quality of people in our country team and the quality of their analyses. They were based too on "feel," our feel for the people, for the country, for the nature of the process under way. They may have been risky judgments in some cases; sometimes in looking back on them I realize even more how risky some of them were. But they were not chance.

PUBLIC DIPLOMACY

In quite a few countries, the American ambassador has extraordinary access to the press. Many of his or her speeches are reported, sometimes printed in full. It is an asset to be used carefully and for a clear purpose. An ambassador should give "The Speech" only once. That speech, almost obligatory of a new ambassador, is on "American policy toward Country X." It covers the basics. After that, public diplomacy should be husbanded and used to get specific messages across at specific times.

The venue and distribution of a speech deserves careful attention. I eschewed speeches and avoided major venues when I had nothing new I wanted to say. The speech on constitution making, which I felt was very important, did not make much of a splash at the time, but, put in the hands of editors and those influencing opinion, with whom we had established a relationship and a reputation for speeches worth reading, it later got wide publicity and had considerable impact. A policy analyst at the South African Center for Policy Studies told me that the five key points of the influence of the United States in the entire transition process were the "sweeteners" for the release of Mandela, the position taken on federalism, the warnings on violence, the holding of parties to their preelection commitments, and my speech on constitution making!

I wrote almost all my own speeches, in part because Foreign Service officers are not trained to write speeches. As I would tell them, "A speech is not a memo. It has a different style, a different rhythm, a different objective." But most of all I did it because writing speeches allowed me to gather together my thoughts on developments and to use the speech to advance policy, first in my own mind and then publicly, to the next step. I also wanted to think carefully about how to modulate the message. It is possible to put ideas across that are in effect critical of the host government's position without cutting off one's access or doing it in a way that angers more than persuades. Although we did not shy away from stating to de Klerk and his key staff our belief that the equivalent of a "white veto" was neither a realistic nor an appropriate objective for the government's strategy, we made the same point in public without directly attacking the government per se. The message was clear enough for all to see, but argued in terms of general principle and aimed at the white population more than at the government.

It is also possible to use public diplomacy to capture attention, as I did with the South African business community in early 1993. And if one believes in transparency, the message need not be new to key parties. As described earlier in this book, I went out of my way to share my thoughts and the draft of the speech on foreign aid with President Mandela before publicly answering his criticisms of the program.

Sometimes confrontation in public is unavoidable if the stakes are high enough. I regretted the depth of anger created between myself and Buthelezi but do not for a moment regret stating our position as I did when I did. It proved important to mobilize public support from his own constituency in order to help avoid the bloodbath that loomed so large. It was also necessary to make clear where the United States stood, given the history of support Buthelezi had enjoyed within American political circles. Given the nature of the man, and given our own interests, we were able to resume a productive relationship following the election, when he assumed the position of minister of home affairs. There was a respect between us that did not get lost. As I was preparing to leave in late 1995, Pamela Bridgewater, our consul general in Durban, gave me a farewell lunch, which Buthelezi graciously attended. In his toast, he said, "You will excuse me for saying it this way, Pamela. The ambassador and I spoke to each other as men do."

EXORCISING OUR OWN DEMONS

In confronting apartheid in South Africa, America had to confront its own racial problem, what Gunnar Myrdal called "an American dilemma." It was easy for Americans to look on apartheid as a most extreme and repellent form of racial discrimination, to feel almost smug in that regard. But the very resonance of the civil rights and anti-apartheid movements reminded us that both nations faced the problem of racial divisions and how to resolve them. In addressing the issue in South Africa, we could not but look at ourselves in how we did so. We were revealed in all our strengths and our weaknesses. The Defense Department struggled initially with this issue but ultimately proved up to the challenge. AID in Washington proved less capable, at great cost to some of its finest practitioners.

My predecessor, Bill Swing, and I both battled for some time with the U.S. Marine Corps on the question of racial representation. We believed that the United States should practice what we preached in South Africa, that our presence should reflect America, not just its racial makeup but the values of racial partnership and pluralism. Yet the U.S. Marine Corps had been steadfast in refusing to station an African American within the embassy's two marine guard detachments. The marine hierarchy argued that with the instances of racial discrimination such a marine might encounter, for example, in a bar or restaurant, there would likely be fights between the marines and the owners of such places. Morale would suffer.

I knew the rigors with which candidates were selected for the embassy marine security guard detachments, that they were among the most impressive, loyal, patriotic, and disciplined group of young persons one could ever find. I doubted that they could not manage the situation. Most of all, an all-white Marine detachment seemed to me an especially blaring anomaly as we approached the South African Defence Force with offers of help about racial integration. So energetically did I pursue this matter that one of my staff, returning from a visit to Washington, told me the Marine Corps complained I was "abusing" it. But to its credit, the corps relented. Not only did it begin assigning African Americans, but the first was as the "gunny" sergeant in charge of the detachment in Cape Town. Others soon followed. Needless to say, the individuals and the detachments as a whole performed flawlessly.

The experience with AID was quite different. As documented in earlier chapters, the USAID program in South Africa was distinguished by its singularly political purpose, to help overcome apartheid and to prepare for democratic rule. One of the problems the program encountered, as had those of the foundations before it, was that many of the better-organized and better-structured anti-apartheid organizations in South Africa to which assistance could be directed were white led. It was a reflection of the advantages that whites had both in education and resources and thus in their ability to manage the complexities of foreign grants.[27] These organizations—such as the Institute for Democratic Alternatives in South Africa, the Legal Resources Center, Black Sash, and many others— were vital and courageous and deserving of support. But even before I arrived in South Africa I had begun hearing of complaints from black South Africans that the USAID program was not really responding to the very purposes of the CAAA, that is, to assist those most disadvantaged by apartheid and to build their capacity for contributing to the future leadership of a democratic South Africa. Their complaints were borne out by the facts: in 1990 black-led organizations, in a population nearly 80 percent black, received approximately 27 percent of USAID obligations to South African entities.[28]

Leslie "Cap" Dean, director of USAID, and his deputy, Bill Ford, both of whom arrived in South Africa in 1992, set out to rectify this situation. Through greater outreach, employment of accounting firms to help small black-led organizations set up their books and handle USAID funds, and greater flexibility and risk taking, they were able by 1994 to raise the percentage of black-led organizations receiving assistance to 51.[29] Many of the leaders of these organizations would take the skills they had developed into the postelection government, some would take them to the private sector, and others remained leaders of civil society. It was a major achievement. Dean and Ford also sought to make USAID a model of equal opportunity. Doors opened for African Americans, other minorities, and women, many of whom had long been active in the anti-apartheid movement, to help play a role in the new South Africa.

These achievements should have been celebrated in the USAID mission and in AID headquarters. But they raised, perhaps in sadly revealing fashion, racial antagonism within the American community. Some within USAID, unhappy with the changes, misrepresented the policy to white-led South African organizations, suggesting that no funds would henceforth come their way. I personally answered the anxious inquiries of many such organizations and, once the policy was correctly explained, not a single one disagreed. They soon discovered, moreover, that the policy was corrective, and neither arbitrary nor irrational. Like many other white-led groups, for example, Black Sash, an organization of white women of privilege who set out with great courage to challenge the apartheid system—who indeed became a symbol to the world of white resistance to the apartheid system —continued to receive assistance.

However, a disaffected USAID employee complained to AID in Washington and members of Congress and later filed a formal grievance, alleging that USAID was following a policy of "reverse discrimination," with regard to both South Africans and African Americans. It was charge that should have been promptly investigated and dismissed. But instead AID began a series of inquiries, investigations, and further investigations that lasted nearly a year and a half, the organization seemingly unable to face the issue squarely. An investigation by the inspector general produced a set of "exhibits"—mainly interviews and documents—five inches thick. The impact on USAID morale was devastating, as the staff responded over and over to these inquiries, had e-mails and other correspondence exposed and publicized, and were distracted from their duties. I appealed to Brian Atwood, administrator of AID, to recognize that this was perhaps AID's most effective program anywhere and to say so publicly, as I did in a statement on March 24. But Atwood issued only a lukewarm statement.[30] Politics and the fear of congressional criticism were driving the response from Washington. So traumatized was AID by these charges that, when a later evaluation refuted nearly every one of them, AID held back publication of the report for six months, until complaints from within AID forced it to be brought out.[31]

The controversy received considerable attention in South Africa as well as in the American press. Critics of the United States took pleasure in it, this seeming American "hypocrisy," and grossly misrepresented the facts.[32] Other South Africans found it curious, even amazing, that there could be any controversy over an emphasis on assisting the disadvantaged community in apartheid South Africa.

"Who should you be assisting?" I was asked by some incredulous black South Africans. Others were saddened by what they felt was a pillorying of a sensitive and meaningful program, one that had reached out with more than just funding. One black leader wrote: "The human context must not be allowed to slip from view and leave only the rational. We speak of a humanscape long before we think of a landscape. And that is something the current USAID Pretoria management have become acutely accustomed to."

The evaluation report mentioned above found that, in meeting the true goals of the CAAA, USAID had done extremely well and, given the historical need and population balance, could hardly have been considered to have had a bias against white-led groups. The latter were still funded at two-and-one-half times their representation in the population. As for the charges regarding African Americans, the report found that "the data do not support the contention of a few vocal critics. Of the $176 million that has been channeled through US intermediaries, only $35 million, or 20 percent have gone to [minority firms] and only a half dozen of [these] are African-American."[33]

Of even greater significance, the report found that more than 70 percent of South African NGOs surveyed felt that USAID had made a considerable contribution to black political and social empowerment, to education, and to the advancement of human rights. More than two-thirds said that the USAID program had strengthened relations between South Africa and the United States. The evaluators concluded, "This finding is especially important given the fact that USAID started out in South Africa . . . with a negative image of its ideology and actions."[34]

But AID could not celebrate these achievements or reward its risk takers. Dean was sidelined on his return to Washington and, seeing the handwriting on the wall, soon retired. The Africa Development Foundation, a separate U.S. government agency dedicated to supporting nongovernmental social development programs, had the good sense to save Bill Ford from a similar fate and made him the foundation's president. He led that organization with distinction for the next five years.

There are two ironies—two lessons—in this story. Toward the end of the decade, as AID found itself ill-equipped to respond to postconflict situations and provide support for emerging democracies, it established the Office of Transitional Initiatives (OTI), which had greater flexibility and quicker response capability than normal AID programming to address such situations. In early 2001, I listened to an OTI representative describe its programs in Nigeria, where it was reaching out to support Nigerian NGOs and other prodemocracy groups. As I listened to the plans for technical assistance and other means to enable these organizations to manage U.S. funds, I said, "This sounds like the methods USAID used in South Africa." "Yes," she replied, "that's our model."

But the most telling experience for me came on the night of the elections in South Africa in April 1994. One of the USAID grants that had generated the most controversy had been to the Martin Luther King Jr. Center to train young voter educators in both election procedures and the principles of nonviolence. Critics charged that USAID had given the center undue assistance in developing its proposal, despite the fact that this was the very first overseas program the center had undertaken. As described in an earlier chapter, the program was a great success. Coretta Scott King came to South Africa as an election observer. On the night of the final day of voting, I hosted a small dinner in her honor at the Carlton Hotel in downtown Johannesburg. As we were dining, we learned that Nelson Mandela and the ANC were having a victory celebration on a floor below. I asked her if she would like to attend, and of course she said yes. As we entered the hall, people were dancing, singing, crying, and embracing, as the reality of this victory, this final step of liberation, was coming true. Immediately upon our entering, Mandela recognized Mrs. King and drew her onto the stage. There, arms around each other, dancing to South African rhythms, they cried out the phrase that had defined the civil rights struggle in the United States as it had the struggle against apartheid, "Free at last! Free at last!"

As I stood and watched them, I thought to myself, how foolish, how insensitive, how deaf to history the United States would have been had it not found a way to include the Martin Luther King Jr. Center in this moment of triumph.

Living the American dream is the best policy for the United States to follow, at home and abroad. It is a lesson we can take away from South Africa.

Appendix

U.S. Secretary of Commerce Ron Brown,
Speech at the University of the
Western Cape, South Africa,
on November 30, 1993, at 10:15 A.M.

THANK YOU VERY MUCH; it is indeed an honor to be at this wonderful and historic university and to be introduced by your distinguished rector. I am privileged to share this moment with you at this decisive phase in the history of South Africa and in the history of our world. You have struggled long and hard against apartheid and you have demonstrated to the world that justice and right will ultimately prevail. As a wise woman once said, the future belongs to those who believe in the beauty of their dreams. We are here today because thousands of men and women who believed in the beauty of their dreams gave us the leadership that we needed and we are here to carry on their long, hard fight to see that those dreams in fact come true. Your generation has inherited those dreams, dreams which were by far the most fragile and valuable possession of millions of people denied the more substantial acquisitions of justice and of democracy. Your generation will be defined and remembered by the action you take to preserve and to enhance your precious legacy.

As I look at the students of this university my heart is full and my mind, as it has done so often since I arrived here in your beautiful nation, weaves its way through the complex pattern of our histories. In 1966 another American came to speak in Cape Town. His name was Robert Kennedy and we remember him for his dreams of a more just world. He came to South Africa to learn and to meet South African youth, whom he defined in this way: not just those young in years but those of every age who are young in the spirit of imagination and courage and an appetite for the adventure of life. He came to speak to young people, much like those who attend this university, and to encourage their fight for social justice. And he said of our two nations, we are like you, a people of diverse origins and we too have a problem, though less difficult than yours. A problem of learning to live together regardless of origins, in mutual respect, enhancing together the rights and well-being of our people.

I come here to South Africa to exchange views with you on what we together can do to meet the challenges of our time. This is the spirit in which I, too, come today. I come as the United States secretary of commerce but I also come as an African-American, who came of age during the great struggle for civil rights in the United States. I come as a supporter of the changes taking place in your nation. I have come to share what I have learned and to learn from you, so that together we can continue to meet the challenges of our time.

It is said that the great problem of the twentieth century has not just been the color line, but all the lines that separate us, one from another, be they lines of class or gender or race or belief. Each line, every artificial barrier that we erect, weakens us. They deprive us of our dignity. They falsely exonerate us from the responsibilities of brotherhood; these lines are in fact iron bars which imprison and which isolate us. So the great challenge of the twentieth century has been to break down these lines and to build in their place a circle of fellowship and common humanity. Before we consider today the daunting challenges and limitless opportunities that now lie before the South African people, we should pause hard for a moment and recall the world as it was only a generation ago. In 1966 as Bobby Kennedy journeyed through South Africa, Martin Luther King Jr. was fighting for his dream of civil rights in America. As cities across the United States erupted into long hot summers and demonstrators marching from Selma to Montgomery, Alabama, were beaten and jailed, the Reverend King remained steadfast, saying, and I quote, "I refuse to accept the idea that the 'isness' of man's preservation makes him morally incapable of reaching up for the 'oughtness' that forever confronts him."

In 1966 Nelson Mandela had already been in prison for four years. No amount of injustice, no amount of cruelty or persecution could weaken his spirit or his faith. For thirty years no jail cell could contain his dream of the world without racism, of a South Africa without apartheid. In 1966 Stephen Bantu Biko joined the National Union of South African Students and formally began his struggle for liberation. He called upon his people to rise and attain the envisaged self. In 1966 Helen Suzman was the sole member in Parliament to oppose apartheid; hers was a voice that said no to injustice when all others said yes and a voice that will echo throughout the chamber when a multiracial parliament is seated next year. We have witnessed extraordinary, tremendous, and beneficial changes in both of our nations, and in fact in the world, since 1966. Changes, though, purchased at great cost. The courage and sacrifice of Dr. King or Steve Biko have been matched by thousands whose names we do not even know, and by some Americans as well, Americans like Amy Biehl who believed in the dream and the promise of South Africa. Thousands of mothers and sisters and brothers and husbands who gave their hearts and hands, and too often their lives, to the cause of freedom and justice and democracy.

Many of you have fought these hard and bitter battles, you have met the fierce resistance that inevitably greets and treats those who threaten the status quo. You have sacrificed and you have won, you have changed the face of South Africa. You all give testament to the great power of the individual, you show how even in the face of overwhelming obstacles each man and woman, clad in the armor of a just cause, can really make a difference. When Robert Kennedy spoke in Cape Town he said, each time a man stands up for an ideal or acts to improve the lot of others, or strikes out against injustice, he sends forth a tiny ripple of hope, and crossing each other from a million different centers of energy and daring, those ripples build on a current which can sweep down the mightiest walls of oppression and resistance. Yours is the power that is generated when people of all races, of both sexes, of diverse origins come together. This power has changed South Africa and has given new meaning to Robert Kennedy's immortal words.

Since the 2nd February, 1990, when President de Klerk prepared the way for constitutional change, South Africa has climbed an arduous road to democracy and created change that would have been inconceivable just five years ago. Six months from now all of the people of South Africa, regardless of gender, race, color, or belief, will be joined in the historic uplifting act of electing a government. This is an awesome fact and I know that to many April 27th may seem like the end of the long, hard struggle. But I have learned through experience that elections in and of themselves do not create change, they only create the opportunity for change. And I ask you, the people of South Africa, to make sure that April 27th is not an end but is a beginning, make sure that it is the first day in a dynamic new South Africa. Make it the birthday of your new dreams and fill your dreams with the lessons you have learned, for even the most troubled path contains inalienable truths. Remember the power of each individual voice and remember the beauty and energy that erupts when different voices join in harmony. Dream about what you can accomplish when one voice becomes a thousand, when a thousand voices become 36 million, when 36 million voices become one. Because a nation is not anything if it consists of each of us, but it becomes great when it consists of all of us.

Fill your dreams with the wisdom of Bishop Tutu, who says that freedom is indivisible, no-one is truly free until all are free everywhere. Injustice and racism anywhere pose a threat to freedom and justice everywhere. Do not build new lives that separate you from each other or from other nations. In the division of apartheid your country focused inward. In the unity of the new South Africa you must look out to the rest of the world. Take the outstretched hands of the United States and of other countries. This is not just a time of great change for South Africa; it is a time of change for all of us. Our world has become global, inter-connected and interdependent. Great change brings great opportunity and difficult challenges. Young people have a pivotal responsibility in rebuilding the new South Africa. You are the new pioneers; you carry the flame; you hold the dream. To you falls the task of weaving these magnificent dreams into tangible progress that touches every man and woman in this nation. And as we accept that each person contributes in his or her own singular way, we must know ourselves to be unique as well. We must never let others define us, or limit us, or dictate to us what we must believe.

In my life I have worked as a social worker and as a businessman and as a political leader. I have worked as a corporate lawyer and now work as the secretary of commerce of the United States and I have always tried to reject those who would categorize me by my profession. I have learned firsthand that there is no easy division between those who fight for democracy and those who strive to create prosperity. The truth is that these goals are intertwined. Resolution of the political crisis is only part of the picture. Hard-won political freedoms must be matched by growing economic opportunities. And in the most critical business of nation building we know that that is the task of business itself. You generate an environment that welcomes private investment, creates jobs and spurs economic growth. You do a great service to your country. South Africa has enormous economic potential. The transition to democracy, the lifting of sanctions and South Africa's integration into the world community all portend well to the future economic growth and business confidence that is much needed. Already there are promising signs. After four years of recession South Africa's economy grew for the first time in 1993. South Africa still has the largest economy in Africa. Your physical location near trade routes and in the highest growth area in Africa makes this country an important base for international commerce and a natural spring-board for business opportunities in the region and on the entire continent. Few countries rival South Africa's mineral wealth and its potential. Your challenge is to turn this generation's energy and this generation's creativity to developing these vast resources, building factories and building businesses, creating products and services and reaching for markets beyond your own community to the rest of Africa and indeed throughout the world. South Africa, I believe, can be the anchor for economic, political and social development on the entire continent. And you must labor to bring every South African into the economic system, as consumers, as managers, as skilled laborers and as entrepreneurs. Because a critical post-apartheid dividend, the creation of a growing just and inclusive economic system, must come from the unleashing of the energy, drive and intellect of every single South African.

I cannot possibly stress enough the importance of education in meeting the challenges you face. For knowledge is truly powerful, not just for the skills and the facts that it offers us, but for the process of discovery which it entails, for the vision which it brings us. Today I stand before you representing the president and the people of the United States because I, too, believe in my dream and because my ancestors believed in theirs. They came from Africa. Some two hundred years ago they were led in chains onto slave ships bound for the Caribbean and for the American South. For generations they labored in the fields, dehumanized, disrespected, reduced to the status of a machine, but they survived. And then when declared free they labored again under the chains of racism and the chains of poverty, but again they survived. They began the fight, the movement, the struggle that we carry on today and their son now stands here in this chamber as secretary of commerce of the United States of America. A man whose ancestors were brought to America by the international slave trade now helps shape the international trade policy of the United States.

So when we think of our nation and how far we have to go, let us remember how far we have come. If we have learned anything in the past few years, it is that nothing is forever, that everything is possible, that people can rise above difficult circumstances and recreate themselves, recreate their people and recreate their nation. The more time I spend in your country, the more I believe that South Africa can be a beacon for the world, that you will prove that a nonracial democracy can exist in peace and in prosperity. I call on you, the youth of South Africa, those of every age who are young in the spirit of imagination and courage and have an appetite for the adventure of life to march together into the dawn of a new day for South Africa. Have the courage to dream, have the strength to believe in your dreams and have the dedication to make your dreams a glorious new reality for all the people of South Africa.

Nothing is impossible; together you can make your nation into a beacon for the world. You have in fact earned the right to truly spread your wings and soar, making a difference as individuals and as a nation reborn. The new South Africa will not be built in a day. Sometimes the pace of change will be agonizingly slow. Press on my friends, keep the faith, together you can make our dream a reality for all of the people of South Africa.

Thank you very much.

Notes

1. Who Owns This Negotiation?

1. In my first meeting with Nelson Mandela, in September 1992, his opening remark was about how much he admired and appreciated President George Bush: "He always calls me when there is something important. Even when he is going to do something with which I might disagree, he calls me first to tell me."

2. Apartheid

1. Allister Sparks, *The Mind of South Africa* (New York: Ballantine Books, 1991), 28.

2. Ibid., 29–30.

3. Ibid., 43.

4. Thomas Pakenham, *The Boer War* (New York: Avon Books, 1979), 8.

5. The account of these wars is dramatically told in Noel Mostert, *Frontiers* (London: Jonathan Cape, 1992).

6. Ibid., 121.

7. Pakenham, *Boer War,* 612–613. For an account of black casualties during the war, see pp. 608–609.

8. Naboth Mokgatle, *The Autobiography of an Unknown South African* (Berkeley: University of California Press, 1971), 262–263.

9. Study Commission on U.S. Policy toward Southern Africa, *South Africa: Time Running Out, Report of the Study Commission on U.S. Policy toward Southern Africa* (Berkeley: University of California Press, 1986), 41.

10. Study Commission, *Time Running Out,* 69.

11. Antjie Krog, *Country of My Skull* (Johannesburg: Random House, 1998), 70–71.

12. Kader Asmal, Louise Asmal, and Ronald Suresh Roberts, *Reconciliation through Truth* (Cape Town: David Philip, 1996), 99–100.

13. Desmond Tutu, *No Future without Forgiveness* (Johannesburg: Rider, 1999), 94.

14. See, for example, his January 2, 1903, petition to Joseph Chamberlain, colonial secretary, in Fatima Meer, ed., *The South African Gandhi*, 2d ed. (Durban: Madiba and the Institute for Black Research, University of Natal, 1996), 272–273. He was equally polite if firm in his correspondence with Smuts. See pp. 425–517.

15. Tom Lodge and Bill Nasson, *All Here and Now: Black Politics in South Africa in the 1980s* (New York: Ford Foundation and the Foreign Policy Association, 1991), 5–7.

16. Sparks, *Mind of South Africa*, 289.

17. Lodge and Nasson, *All Here and Now*, 200. For a discussion of the reasoning behind the government's decision, see Robert Price, *The Apartheid State in Crisis* (New York: Oxford University Press, 1991), 122–125.

18. Ibid., 48.

19. Lodge and Nasson, *All Here and Now*, 260.

20. Price, *Apartheid State*, 59.

21. For example, in 1985 the Soweto Parents Crisis Committee sought unsuccessfully to negotiate reforms that would lead the students to return to school. The effort evolved instead into a campaign to overhaul the education system altogether. Price, *Apartheid State*, 211–212.

22. F. W. de Klerk, *The Last Trek, a New Beginning* (New York: St. Martin's, 1999), 99.

23. For an account of these talks, see Allister Sparks, *Tomorrow Is Another Country* (Johannesburg: Struik Book Distributors, 1994), 21–36.

24. Confidential discussion, January 28, 1994.

25. David Steward, former director-general of de Klerk's presidential office, interview by author, November 18, 1999, Pretoria. De Klerk also endorsed the repression in principle, if claiming at the same time to have been largely shut out of the deliberations of the State Security Council and its apparent endorsement of extreme actions. De Klerk, *Last Trek*, 114, 117. Ironically, important black leaders of resistance saw their efforts in a similar way, not to expect the "immediate transfer of power," but to shift the "balance of forces in our favor." See the speech of Zwelakhe Sisulu, quoted in Lodge and Nasson, *All Here and Now*, 84.

26. De Klerk, *Last Trek*, 103.

3. Passion, Passivity, and Pragmatism

1. Reverend James Scott, a white missionary of the Free Church of Scotland, in 1904, quoted in Elliott P. Skinner, *African Americans and U.S. Policy toward Africa, 1850–1924* (Washington, D.C.: Howard University Press, 1992), 199.

2. Jean Strouse, *Morgan: American Financier* (New York: HarperPerennial, 2000), 441–442.

3. Skinner, *African Americans and U.S. Policy*, 394.

4. Study Commission on U.S. Policy toward South Africa, *South Africa: Time Running Out. Report of the Study Commission on U.S. Policy toward South Africa* (Berkeley: University of California Press, 1986), 133–135. About 80 percent of the direct investment was accounted for by four firms: Mobil, Ford, General Motors, and Caltex Oil.

5. Boutros Boutros-Ghali, *The United Nations and Apartheid* (New York: United Nations Reproduction Section, 1996), 10–15, 166–169.

6. "Charles Runyon III—Posthumous Award," award citation by the United Nations Association of the National Capital Area, at the Human Rights Day award luncheon, December 10, 1999, Washington, D.C.

7. Elliott Skinner, *Beyond Constructive Engagement* (New York: Praeger, 1986), xi–xii, 237–239. Pauline Baker suggests that Nixon's policies toward South Africa were influenced by his "southern strategy" of courting southern conservatives in the United States, the counterpoint to Carter being influenced by civil rights leaders. Pauline H. Baker, *The United States and South Africa: The Reagan Years* (New York: Ford Foundation and the Foreign Policy Association, 1989), xi–xii.

8. William Schaufele, assistant secretary of state for African affairs, statement before the American Academy of Political and Social Science, April 16, 1977, Document 1 in Office of the Historian, U.S. Department of State, *The United States and South Africa: U.S. Public Statements and Related Documents, 1977–1985*, Research Project no. 1467 (Washington, D.C.: Department of State, September 1985), 1–2.

9. Walter Mondale, statement at a news conference, Vienna, May 20, 1977, *U.S. Public Statements*, 10–11.

10. Richard Moose, "South Africa: Four Years Later" (speech before the African Studies Symposium at Pennsylvania State University, October 13, 1980), *U.S. Public Statements*, 19–20; Donald McHenry, U.S. Permanent Representative to the United Nations, statement before the U.N. Security Council, June 13, 1980, *U.S. Public Statements*, 34.

11. Quoted in Robert Kinloch Massie, *Loosing the Bonds: The United States and South Africa in the Apartheid Years* (New York: Nan A. Talese, Doubleday, 1997), 193–194.

12. Ibid., 201–203.

13. Ibid., 307.

14. Randall Robinson, *Defending the Spirit* (New York: Plume, 1999), 109–110.

15. "Department of State Daily Briefing, January 5, 1993," Document 99, *U.S. Public Statements*, 162.

16. Robert Price, *The Apartheid State in Crisis* (New York: Oxford University Press, 1991), 176–177.

17. Robinson, *Defending the Spirit*, 157.

18. Chester A. Crocker, *High Noon in Southern Africa: Making Peace in a Rough Neighborhood* (New York: W. W. Norton, 1992), 259–267, 277.

19. Robinson, *Defending the Spirit,* 147.

20. Joseph Lelyveld, *Move Your Shadow* (New York: Times Books, 1985), 233.

21. Skinner, *Beyond Constructive Engagement,* 132.

22. Crocker, *High Noon in Southern Africa,* 253.

23. Ibid., 263.

24. George Shultz, *Turmoil and Triumph* (New York: Charles Scribner's Sons, 1993), 1121–1122; Crocker, *High Noon in Southern Africa,* 322.

25. Massie, *Loosing the Bonds,* 616.

26. Aurora Associates International, Inc., and Creative Associates International, Inc., *Program Evaluation: USAID/SOUTH AFRICA* (Pretoria: United States Agency for International Development, April 21, 1995), 18, 318.

27. Pauline Baker, "The United States and South Africa: Persuasion and Coercion," in *Honey and Vinegar: Incentives, Sanctions and Foreign Policy,* ed. Richard Haass (Washington, D.C.: Brookings Institution Press, 2000), 110.

28. Report of the Study Commission, *Time Running Out.* The commission would also sponsor a number of important and influential books by American and South African scholars over the next several years, covering such topics as white and black politics in South Africa, U.S. policy, and civil liberties.

29. David Devlin-Foltz, interview by author, New York City, April 26, 2001. Devlin-Foltz developed several of these programs for the Carnegie Corporation, the Rockefeller Foundation, and other foundations.

30. Franklin Thomas, interview by author, New York City, May 25, 2000; Richard Goldstone, interview by author, Washington, D.C., February 7, 2000.

31. Penuel Maduna, interview by author, Cape Town, November 11, 1999.

32. Arthur Chaskelson, interview by author, Johannesburg, November 12, 1999.

33. Conversation with Paul Fray, Washington, D.C., May 3, 2001. Fray was editor of the *Saturday Star* of Johannesburg and a 2000–01 Nieman fellow. Not all Nieman fellows were "transformed" by their experience in the United States. Several continued to write strongly progovernment, even propagandist, material on their return and through the turbulent 1980s. Allister Sparks, Nieman fellow in 1962–63, interview by author, Washington, D.C., June 1, 2000.

34. United States–South Africa Leadership Development Programme, *1998 Annual Report, Fortieth Anniversary Commemorative Edition* (Washington, D.C.: USSALEP, 1998), 18–20.

35. Colin Eglin, member of the Democratic Party, interview by author, Cape Town, November 10, 1999.

36. United States–South Africa Leadership Development Programme, *1998 Annual Report,* 10–11. Among the organizations partnered with USSALEP were the African-American Institute, the Boston University School of Communication, the National Institute of Trial Advocacy, the National Science Foundation, Partners for

International Education and Training, the Phillips Academy at Andover, and the School of Advanced International Studies at Johns Hopkins University.

37. Brenda Bryant et al., "Training for Disadvantaged South Africans: Review and Design" (presented to the United States Agency for International Development by Creative Associates International, Inc., Washington, D.C., July 2, 1989), executive summary, 1; vol. 1, 76, 82. See also Institute of International Education, *South Africa Education Program* (New York: Institute of International Education, 1994).

38. Sheila Avrin McLean and Rona Kluger, *U.S. Foundation Giving to Enhance Educational Opportunities for Black South Africans,* Information Exchange Working Paper no. 1 (New York: Institute of International Education, May 1987), 5, 11.

39. Anthony Sampson, *Mandela* (New York: Alfred A. Knopf, 1999), 317.

40. For a description of the USAID program in this period, see Aurora Associates and Creative Associates, *Program Evaluation, 20–22.*

41. John Stremlau, Rockefeller Foundation, interoffice correspondence, March 28, 1984.

42. Thomas, interview.

43. Carl Beck, interview by author, Washington, D.C., August 17, 2000.

44. Baker, *Reagan Years,* 51.

45. Beck, interview.

4. THE WIND SHIFTS

1. State Department, Report on South Africa Conference, July 29, 1992.

2. Pauline Baker, *The United States and South Africa: The Reagan Years* (New York: Ford Foundation and the Foreign Policy Association, 1989).

3. Ibid., 50; Chester Crocker, *High Noon in Southern Africa: Making Peace in a Rough Neighborhood* (New York: W. W. Norton), 143–144.

4. F. W. de Klerk, *The Last Trek, a New Beginning* (New York: St. Martin's, 1999), 79–89, 156.

5. Allister Sparks, *The Mind of South Africa* (New York: Ballantine Books, 1990), 398.

6. De Klerk, *Last Trek,* 162–163.

7. Herman Cohen, interview by author, Washington, D.C., December 26, 2000.

8. Thabo Mbeki, remarks at the Carnegie Endowment's South African breakfast meeting, Washington, D.C., October 2, 1989.

9. Cohen, interview. For more on the positive ANC reaction to the Bush administration, see Anthony Sampson, *Mandela: The Authorized Biography* (New York: Alfred A. Knopf, 1999), 382.

10. Carl Beck, interview by author, Washington, D.C., August 17, 2000.

11. Cohen, interview.

12. Howard Wolpe, remarks at the Carnegie Endowment's South African breakfast meeting, Washington, D.C., January 17, 1990

13. William Gray, remarks at the Carnegie Endowment's South African breakfast meeting, Washington, D.C., March 20, 1990.

14. Robert Kinloch Massie, *Loosing the Bonds: The United States and South Africa in the Apartheid Years* (New York: Nan A. Talese, Doubleday, 1997), 669.

15. Massie, *Loosing the Bonds,* 671.

16. De Klerk, *Last Trek,* 189.

17. F. W. de Klerk, interview by author, Cape Town, November 11, 1999.

18. Neil Van Heerden, interview by author, Johannesburg, January 12, 2000.

19. De Klerk, *Last Trek,* 183.

20. Roelf Meyer, interview by author, Johannesburg, November 15, 1999.

21. De Klerk, interview; *Last Trek,* 140–141.

22. De Klerk, *Last Trek,* 188.

23. Ibid., 190.

24. David Steward, interview by author, Pretoria, November 18, 1999.

25. De Klerk, interview.

26. Essop Pahad, interview by author, Pretoria, November 15, 1999.

27. Ibid.

28. Barbara Masakela, interview by author, Johannesburg, November 19, 1999.

29. Nelson Mandela, meeting with President Clinton, October 5, 1994.

30. For his account of British diplomacy in this period, see Robin Renwick, *Unconventional Diplomacy in Southern Africa* (New York: St. Martin's Press, 1997), 109–158.

31. Meyer, interview.

5. FROM MEDIATION TO FACILITATION

1. For a description of the function of each working group, see F. W. de Klerk, *The Last Trek, a New Beginning* (New York: St. Martin's, 1999), 235.

2. Ibid., 88, 229–232.

3. Patti Waldmeir, *Anatomy of a Miracle* (London: Penguin, 1997), 198–204; Allister Sparks, *Tomorrow Is Another Country* (Johannesburg: Struik Book Distributors, 1994), 133–137.

4. Sparks, *Tomorrow Is Another Country,* 136.

5. Waldmeir, *Anatomy of a Miracle,* 202–204; Sparks, *Tomorrow Is Another Country,* 136–140.

6. Sparks, *Tomorrow Is Another Country,* 140.

7. Boutros Boutros-Ghali, *The United Nations and Apartheid* (New York: United Nations, 1996), 93–98.

8. Chester Crocker, *High Noon in Southern Africa: Making Peace in a Rough Neighborhood* (New York: W. W. Norton, 1992), 90.

9. Boutros-Ghali, *United Nations and Apartheid,* 118–120.

10. Herman Cohen, interview by author, Washington, D.C., December 26, 2000.

11. George Bush to F. W. de Klerk, June 25, 1992.

12. F. W. de Klerk to George Bush, June 27, 1992.

13. F. W. de Klerk, interview by author, Cape Town, November 11, 1999.

14. Patrick "Terror" Lekota, remarks at the Carnegie Endowment's South African breakfast meeting, Washington, D.C., February 13, 1990.

15. Kader Asmal, interview by author, Cape Town, November 10, 1999.

16. Ibid.

17. Ibid.

18. De Klerk, interview.

19. U.S. Senate Committee on Foreign Relations, *South Africa: Hearing before the Committee on Foreign Relations,* 102d Congress, 2d session, 23 September 1992; testimony by Herman Cohen, assistant secretary of state for African affairs.

20. Richard Goldstone, interview by author, Washington, D.C., February 7, 2000.

21. *Sunday Times* (Johannesburg), July 17, 1992.

22. Ibid.

23. A controversy that arose from this meeting was a humorous reminder of how evidence of foreign support was one of the chips in the game under way. As noted, I had been given carte blanche by the Foreign Ministry to engage in various meetings prior to presenting credentials, and I had informed the ministry that this included a meeting with Mandela. But some clever people in the ANC saw an opportunity and told the press that I was coming to present my "credentials" to Mandela, before doing so with President de Klerk, in recognition of the ANC as the government in waiting. The South African government reacted furiously. I, of course, denied it, and Mandela, when I informed him of the sensitivity of this matter, graciously corrected the public version.

24. U.S. Senate Committee on Foreign Relations, *South Africa: Hearing,* 3.

25. Essop Pahad, interview by author, Pretoria, November 15, 1999.

26. U.S. embassy, Pretoria, analysis, January 1993.

27. Oral report to the author on visit to the European Community "Troika" (the Troika is made up of the past, current, and next chairman of the European Union) by the British ambassador to South Africa, September 1992.

28. Brian Pottinger, "Time Running Out for SA Says Ambassador," *Sunday Times* (Johannesburg), November 15, 1992.

29. Nelson Mandela, conversation with author, December 9, 1992.

30. F. W. de Klerk, conversation with author, December 11, 1992.

6. LENDING WEIGHT TO THE PROCESS

1. Chester Crocker, *High Noon in Southern Africa: Making Peace in a Rough Neighborhood* (New York: W. W. Norton, 1992), 263.

2. Herman Cohen, conversation with author, March 3, 1999.

3. F. W. de Klerk, interview by author, Cape Town, November 11, 1999.

4. Helen Grange, "Keeping Course in Stormy Waters," *Star* (Johannesburg), January 20, 1993.

5. Desmond Tutu, interview by author, Atlanta, March 27, 2000.

6. Barbara Masakela, interview by author, Johannesburg, November 19, 1999.

7. Joe Slovo, *The Unfinished Autobiography* (Randburg: Ravan Press, 1995), 194.

8. Joe Slovo, interview, *Jewish Affairs* 50, no. 1 (1995): 11.

9. For insight into this most complex scene of South Africa's worst political violence, which continues to this day, see Rian Malan, *My Traitor's Heart* (New York: Vintage Books, 1990).

10. Donna Shalala, speech at the funeral of ANC president Oliver Tambo, Nasrec Stadium, Johannesburg, May 2, 1993.

11. USIA funds could not be used for military training. Thus we structured the visit as an educational trip, without any military training and minimal Department of Defense involvement. The emphasis was on exposure to academic and other expertise on racial integration efforts in the U.S. military and police forces. Once sanctions were removed, the Department of Defense provided high-level advice to the newly integrating South African forces based on U.S. experience in this area.

12. For a detailed account of the dissension within National Party ranks and the defections, see Raymond Louw, "As National Party Support Drains Away, the Right Wing Struggles to Take Advantage and the ANC Takes Fright," *Southern Africa Report* 11, no. 23 (June 11, 1993).

13. Roelf Meyer, interview by author, Johannesburg, November 15, 1999.

14. David Steward, interview by author, Pretoria, November 18, 1999. Steward argues that de Klerk was never wed to formulas of weighted voting within the cabinet or other devices to give the white polity something close to veto power within the new government. He claims that these were ideas pushed by the right wing within the cabinet, and that de Klerk dutifully pursued them but readily conceded to the principle of consensus in November 1993. However, if this was the case, it was not apparent during the negotiations or in the public statements of the government.

15. Princeton N. Lyman, speech to the 702 Breakfast Club, Johannesburg, April 27, 1993.

16. F. W. de Klerk, interview by author, Cape Town, November 11, 1999; Steward, interview; Denel (Pty) Ltd. News Release, June 30, 1993.

17. "Statement by Acting State President Mr. R. F. (Pik) Botha Regarding the Termination of the Further Development of a Space Launch Vehicle by Denel, Pretoria, June 30, 1993"; as released by the government.

18. De Klerk also told the foundation representatives that he did not want to suffer the ignominy of being heckled in the United States by those who might object to his receiving the medal. Mandela told the foundation that he would "walk with de Klerk so that if there are hecklers, both of us will be the target." Hecklers protesting the award to de Klerk were present in Philadelphia but were not prominent. Franklin Thomas, interview by author, New York, May 25, 2000.

19. "U.S. Envoy Surprised at F. W.-Mandela Reports," *Citizen* (Johannesburg), July 8, 1993.

20. F. W. De Klerk, *The Last Trek, a New Beginning* (New York: St. Martin's, 1998), 280.

21. Steward, interview.

22. De Klerk, interview.

23. Richard Sten, interview by author, Johannesburg, November 17, 1999.

24. Aubre Hamersma, interview by author, Johannesburg, November 17, 1999.

25. Don Robertson, "U.S. to Fund Millions for Penicillin Plant in S.A.," *Sunday Times* (Johannesburg), March 21, 1993; "R1,35-m U.S. Grant for S.A. Penicillin Development," *Citizen*, March 23, 1993.

26. Kader Asmal, interview by author, Cape Town, November 10, 1999.

27. Committee of Investigation into Intergovermental Fiscal Relations in South Africa, "Working Paper Regarding Future System of Fiscal Relations between Different Levels of Government," July 1992.

28. The agreement on regional boundaries proved unexpectedly easy when a natural division presented itself—the one that existed for South Africa's football teams, each of which had strong regional support and seemed to reflect the existing regional loyalties.

29. Consultative Business Movement, *Multi-Tier Fiscal Relations: Financing Regions in South Africa—Report for Discussion with Political Parties, Internet Groups, and the Public at Large* (Johannesburg: Consultative Business Movement, September 1993).

30. Anthony Sampson, *Mandela* (New York: Alfred A. Knopf, 1999), 428–429.

31. However, Mboweni told us he found the American antitrust laws and procedures too litigious and leaned instead toward those of the United Kingdom.

32. *South Africa's International Economic Relations in the 1990s: Conference Report* (Washington, D.C.: Aspen Institute, April 27–30, 1993), 26.

33. Sebastian Mallaby, *After Apartheid: The Future of South Africa* (New York: Times Books, 1992), 53–65.

34. Essop Pahad, interview by author, Pretoria, November 15, 1999.

35. One visiting journalist, commenting on these conflicting interests, reversed the nostrum then current in South Africa, that is, that white fears and black expectations for change were surely to come into conflict after the election. She said wryly that she worried about white expectations and black fears: whites expect there will be no changes and blacks fear they are right!

36. Helen Grange, "Keeping Course in Stormy Waters," *Star*, January 20, 1993.

37. "Business, Media, and Rival Groups React Coolly to Mandela's Proposal to Lift Sanctions," U.S. embassy, Pretoria, to U.S. State Department, Washington, D.C., declassified cable 00779, January 1993.

38. Princeton N. Lyman, "The Role of Business in the New South Africa" (speech to the Pretoria News/Burgerspark Business Club, November 18, 1992).

39. Princeton N. Lyman, "American Investment and the Role of the Business Community" (speech to the SEEF–Cape Times Executive Breakfast Club, March 9, 1993).

40. Gavin du Venage, "Input Needed from Business in Economic Debate, Says Lyman," *Business Day*, May 26, 1993; David Braun, "With Talks Comes Investment," *Weekend Mercury* (Durban), February 27, 1993; Audrey D'Angelo, "SA Cannot Afford to Wait before Investing," *Cape Times*, March 10, 1993; "A Battle Already Won," *Sunday Times*, March 14, 1993; "Risk of Success," *Star*, April 29, 1993; "SA Business Must Start Taking Risks," *Sowetan*, May 11, 1993; Shirley Woodgate, "Business Urged to Take Risks for SA," *Business Day*, April 28, 1993; Kelvin Brown, "Washington Considers Tapping Pension Funds for Investment in SA," *Business Day*, April 28, 1993; Curt von Keyserlingk, "Groot beleggings km vir SA—ambassadeur" (Great investments come to South Africa—ambassador), *Beeld*, April 28, 1993; "SA Promised 'Generous Non-Partisan' Aid," *Cape Times*, April 29, 1993.

41. Consultative Business Forum, *Managing Change: A Guide to the Role of Business in Transition* (Johannesburg: Consultative Business Forum, 1993).

42. Ken Owen, editorial, *Sunday Times*, July 31, 1993.

43. Princeton N. Lyman, speech at the Johannesburg Press Club, October 28, 1993.

44. William Pretorius, editorial, *Beeld*, October 30, 1993.

45. William Pretorius, editorial, *Die Burger* (Cape Town), October 30, 1993.

46. Shaun Johnson, "Our Constitution-Makers Are Not Unique in Their Stupidity," *Star*, December 4, 1993.

47. Ibid.

48. Rocky Williams, "Coming to Grips with Covert Operations: Who Does What and Where?" briefing paper for international observers, December 3, 1992.

49. Richard Goldstone, *For Humanity: Reflections of a War Crimes Investigator* (New Haven: Yale University Press, 2000), 40–58.

50. Dutch Violence Observation Mission, *Violence in the Vaal,* report by a Dutch Violence Observation Mission to the Vaal Triangle in South Africa, March 4–25, 1993.

51. Rian Milan, *My Traitor's Heart* (New York: Vintage, 1990); A. de V. V. Minnaar, *Mafia Warlords or Political Entrepreneurs? Warlordism in Natal* (Pretoria: Centre for Conflict Analysis, Human Science Research Council, December 1991).

52. U.S. embassy, analysis based on South African Police daily unrest report and data from the Human Rights Commission.

53. Dutch Violence Observation Mission, *Violence in the Vaal,* 18.

54. Princeton N. Lyman, keynote address, American Chamber of Commerce and National Peace Accord Gala Dinner, Johannesburg, October 9, 1992.

55. For an excellent account of how the community-based peace committees functioned, see Susan Collin Marks, *Watching the Wind: Conflict Resolution during South Africa's Transition to Democracy* (Washington, D.C.: United States Institute of Peace Press, 2000).

56. In addition to supporting the local peace committees, King refused to be drawn into challenges to the authority of the Goldstone Commission. She firmly rejected the proposal of Transkei ruler Bantu Holomisa that the UN mission, rather than the Goldstone Commission, take charge of investigations into charges of violence emanating from that homeland.

57. For assessment of the strengths and weaknesses of the peace committees, see Mark Shaw, *Crying Peace Where There Is None? The Functioning and Future of Local Peace Committees of the National Peace Accord,* Research Report no. 31 (Johannesburg: Centre for Policy Studies, August 1993), and United Nations, *Report of the Secretary-General on the Question of South Africa,* A/48/845. S/1994/16, January 10, 1994, 10–14.

58. United Nations, *Report of the Secretary-General,* 12.

59. Princeton N. Lyman, "U.S. Economic Assistance to South Africa" (speech to the Institute for Multi-Party Democracy, Durban, July 22, 1993).

60. "All Leaders Must Stop Crying Fire," *Sunday Times,* July 25, 1993; David Breier, "Loose Talk of Civil War, Say Experts," *Star,* July 25, 1993; "US Favors a Federal System in SA," *Citizen,* July 23, 1993; Tim Cohen, "US Aid Focuses on SA," *Natal Mercury,* July 23, 1993; Vasantha Angamuthu, "US Aid Booster," *Durban Daily News,* July 23, 1993.

61. Editorial, *Durban Daily News,* January 5, 1994.

62. For an analysis of the history and problems associated with this force, see *The National Peacekeeping Force, Violence on the East Rand and Public Perceptions of the NPKF in KATORUS* (Johannesburg: Human Resources Research Council and the Institute of Defense Policy, June 1994).

63. Consultative Business Movement, *Information Update,* no. 13 (September 17, 1993), 12–13.

64. During the visit of de Klerk and Mandela to Washington in July, anti-apartheid activists had persuaded the National Security Council to include in the official statement about the visit that the United States would postpone assistance to the TEC and the electoral process until sanctions had been lifted. I convinced the NSC to drop this reference in the statement, arguing that we needed to begin assisting these processes as soon as possible.

65. In September 1993, the TEC, with full ANC and other parties' support, endorsed a special drought emergency loan from the IMF. This loan had less-stringent conditionality than would a standby. But it is significant that in the negotiations of this loan, the TEC agreed in principle with a number of economic policies endorsed by the IMF that would guide South Africa in the future, already an indication of the directions the ANC-led government would take.

66. Report of the American embassy, January 24, 1993.

67. ANC Policy Guidelines for a Democratic South Africa, As Adopted at the National Conference, May 28–31, 1992, 26.

68. R. W. Johnson, "When That Great Day Comes," *London Review of Books,* July 22, 1993, 9.

69. Office of the President, "Remarks Prepared for Delivery by Vice President Al Gore at the US–South African Binational Commission Joint Press Conference," July 23, 1996, http://usinfo.state.gov/regional/bnc/usafrica/2pcgore.htm; Office of the Vice President, U.S.–South Africa Binational Commission, Trade and Investment Committee, "Vice President Gore Signs Bilateral Tax Treaty to Facilitate U.S.–South Africa Trade," February 17, 1997, http://usinfo.state.gov/regional/bnc/ usafrica/ trade17.htm.

70. Indicative of the resistance to doing so among longtime anti-apartheid activists were the comments of state legislators from Massachusetts and New Jersey at an embassy briefing in August 1994, three months after Mandela had been inaugurated as president. They wanted to wait still further, until there was more progress on dismantling the legacies of apartheid, including the level of black unemployment. The fact that holding back investment would only make that harder was lost on them.

71. "Code of Conduct Not Only for U.S. Firms, Says Brown," *Weekly Mail* (Johannesburg), December 3, 1993.

72. A survey of American firms in 1998 found 34 percent of firms that responded were still spending in excess of R500,000 on such programs annually, while another 34 percent were spending between R100,000 and R500,000. Khulisa Management Services and Deloitte and Touche, "Report of the Corporate Social Investment Programmes of the Members of the American Chamber of Commerce" (1998).

73. Princeton N. Lyman, "Investing with Social Responsibility in South Africa," in *Attracting Capital to Africa* (Washington, D.C.: Corporate Council on Africa, 1999).

74. Jacob Gayle, USAID, memorandum to Ambassador Princeton N. Lyman, July 25, 1994; UNAIDS, *Report on the Global HIV/AIDS Epidemic,* Geneva, June 2000, 9.

75. Jon Jeter, "Death Watch: S. Africa's Advances Jeopardized by AIDS," *Washington Post,* July 6, 2000.

76. Tony Klouda, "It's Called Fiddling while Rome Burns," *AIDS Analysis Africa: Southern Africa Edition* 5, no. 2 (August-September 1994): 7.

77. "S.A. Will Stay on Right Path: U.S. Commerce Sec," *Citizen*, December 1, 1993.

78. Thabo Leshilous, "US Visitors Are Upbeat," *Argus* (Cape Town), December 4–5, 1993.

79. U.S. secretary of commerce Ron Brown, departure statement, December 2, 1993.

80. Sean Feely, "Brown-SA," *SAPA* news release, November 28, 1993.

7. THE BUTHELEZI DILEMMA

1. Messages to Chief Buthelezi, Nelson Mandela, and F. W. de Klerk delivered through the U.S. embassy in Pretoria, September 9–10, 1992.

2. Essop Pahad, interview by author, Pretoria, November 15, 1999.

3. Princeton N. Lyman, "U.S. Economic Assistance to South Africa" (speech at the Institute for Multi-Party Democracy, Durban, July 22, 1993).

4. When we responded negatively to the idea, he replied, "Too bad. It would be a friendly country."

5. Princeton N. Lyman to Mangosuthu Buthelezi, July 29, 1993.

6. Ibid.

7. Ibid.

8. Mangosuthu Buthelezi to Princeton N. Lyman, August 2, 1993.

9. House Committee on International Relations, Africa Subcommittee, *South Africa: Hearing before the Africa Subcommittee,* 103d Congress, 2d session, September 30, 1993, testimony by George Moose, assistant secretary of state for African affairs.

10. The statement by the European Community was more nuanced. Without reference to what the community might do if such agreements were not honored, it called on all the parties in South Africa "to ensure that all agreements reached in the multi-party negotiations are adhered to." "Declaration on Recent Events in South Africa," European Political Co-Operation Press Release of September 25, 1993.

11. Nelson Mandela, speech at the dedication of Chris Hani Hall, Johannesburg, November 4, 1993.

12. Though Ciskei and Bophuthatswana were ruled by black leaders, they were represented at negotiations by white advisers, at least one of whom had worked for more than one "homeland."

13. Franklin Thomas, interview by author, New York, May 25, 2000.

14. "Memorandum for Presentation to the Honorable Harry Johnston, Chairman, U.S. House of Representatives Africa Subcommittee by Chief Mangosuthu Buthelezi, January 7, 1994."

15. "Memorandum for Discussion with Archbishop Desmond Tutu by Chief Mangosuthu Buthelezi, December 15, 1993."

16. Ibid.

8. LOOKING LEFT AND RIGHT

1. Tom Lodge and Bill Nasson, *All, Here, and Now: Black Politics in South Africa in the 1980s* (New York: Ford Foundation and Foreign Policy Foundation, 1991), 142–150.

2. Anthony Sampson, *Mandela* (New York: Alfred A. Knopf, 1999), 530.

3. Allister Sparks, *Tomorrow Is Another Country* (Johannesburg: Struik Book Distributors, 1994), 192.

4. George Moose, speech at the Carnegie Endowment's South African breakfast meeting, Washington, D.C., June 15, 1993.

5. Moseneke, who in the 1980s was known as a "radical," was at this time one of South Africa's few black "advocates," equivalent to English barristers. He would go on to become vice chairman of the Independent Election Commission, the duties of which he carried out with great distinction. Following the election, he became chairman of the board of Telkom, South Africa's telecommunications parastatal, where he engineered its partial privatization.

6. Patricia de Lille, interview by author, Cape Town, November 11, 1999.

7. Nelson Mandela, quoted in Ismail Lagardien, "Focus on Mandela," *Sowetan*, December 18, 1992.

8. As pointed out below, the Transkei did not fall into the category of a "neighbor," since only South Africa recognized it as independent. A raid on the Transkei, however, would have placed the ANC in a terrible dilemma and perhaps made the situation with the Transkei all the more difficult.

9. Desmond Tutu, *No Future without Forgiveness* (London: Rider, 1999), 24.

10. It is hard to describe adequately the extraordinary response of the Biehl family to Amy's death. Absent of recrimination or a desire for revenge, they instead have dedicated themselves to making of Amy's memory a memorial of good works in South Africa, to carry on her own work. The Amy Biehl Foundation is today engaged in reducing the sources of rage and anger among South African youth, providing training, counseling, and economic opportunities. Most extraordinary, the project operates among other places in Guguletu itself, and the Biehls have even reached out to the families of those who killed their daughter. I consider it a privilege to know them and an honor to have been asked to serve as a member of the foundation's Technical Advisory Board.

11. "Mob Slays U.S. Student: 2 Arrested," *Pretoria News,* August 26, 1993; "Hundreds Throng to Service for Amy," *Star* (Johannesburg), August 30, 1993.

12. U.S. embassy press release, August 26, 1993.

13. Princeton N. Lyman to Gora Ebrahim, September 1, 1993.

14. F. W. de Klerk, *The Last Trek, a New Beginning* (New York: St. Martin's, 1999), 286.

15. Another PAC mistake was campaigning heavily on the land issue. Land reform was surely justified in a country where the majority had been forced off the best lands for more than three generations. But in that time, black South Africans had become overwhelmingly urban, or peri-urban, in the townships that surrounded most cities and towns. Even in the countryside, few made their living wholly by agriculture. The issues for most in the 1990s, therefore, were jobs, housing, and political freedom.

16. De Lille, interview.

17. Ibid.

18. Kriel would sit back when I asked a searching question and say, "Very interesting question," and then go into a carefully modulated reply. At the end of our meetings, with his enigmatic smile, Kriel would say, "I enjoy our conversations." In 1994 Kriel would be elected premier of the Western Cape province, the only province in which the National Party won a majority.

19. De Klerk, *Last Trek,* 264.

20. Ibid.

21. "South Africa: Will the Right Resort to Violence?" telegram from the U.S. embassy, Pretoria, to Washington, January 13, 1994, Pretoria 595.

22. Sparks, *Tomorrow Is Another Country,* 172–178.

23. De Klerk, *Last Trek,* 265.

24. Private communication with the author, February 16, 1994.

25. Private communication with the author, July 1993.

26. Pierre Steyn, interview by author, Pretoria, November 17, 1999.

27. Ibid.

28. Ibid.

29. Sparks, *Tomorrow Is Another Country,* 202; Steyn, interview.

30. Alex Boraine, deputy chairman of the Truth and Reconciliation Commission, speech at the United States Institute of Peace, March 8, 2000. Mandela told me in our meeting on February 22, 1994, that he would be meeting with the SADF leadership on February 23, which may well have been the meeting to which Boraine referred.

31. De Klerk, *Last Trek,* 349–350.

32. See, for example, Jakkie Cilliers and Paul-Bolko Mertz, "Military and Democracy: Concept and Role of Armed Forces and Political Control of Defence in a Democratic South Africa," *South African Defence Review,* Working Paper Series, no. 8

(Johannesburg: Institute of Defence Policy, 1993); Pierre Steyn, "Challenges and Prospects for the SA Defence Industry: Equipping the Armed Forces of the Future," *South Africa Defence Review*, Working Paper Series, no. 11 (Johannesburg: Institute of Defence Policy, 1993).

33. Steyn was surprised and impressed by the cooperation between the State Department and the Department of Defense. "Normally, you don't find Defense Department and State Departments working together, but you did that, and it was so clearly in sync, it had to be successful." Steyn, interview.

34. "South Africa: Will the Right Resort to Violence?" telegram from the U.S. embassy. We assumed the military intelligence assessment would reach de Klerk. However, when we discussed the issue years later, de Klerk told me it had not and chided me for not bringing it to his attention. F. W. de Klerk, interview by author, Cape Town, November 11, 1999.

35. The SADF was still feeling resentment at its isolation under sanctions and it showed this by refusing to schedule a formal call for Freeman on the chief of staff. But General Meiring himself chose to attend the American defense attaché's reception for Freeman, where the two had the chance for a long talk. Meiring told Freeman that, if necessary, he would utilize the Citizen Force or commandos from regions other than their home areas to control any uprising from the right. Other briefings, the exchanges at the IDP event, and a luncheon that I hosted also brought Freeman's delegation into contact with senior SADF officers. Overall, Freeman's visit did much to break down the negative attitudes toward the United States within the SADF.

36. Princeton N. Lyman, "Flying through the Storm" (speech at Johannesburg, March 23, 1994).

37. Sparks, *Tomorrow Is Another Country*, 204.

38. Patti Waldmeier, *Anatomy of a Miracle* (London: Penguin, 1997), 239.

39. For example, Mangope's minister of defense, Rowan Cronje, had served in the government of Ciskei as well as other homelands within South Africa.

40. In the always amazing vista of South African politics, miracles happen even for the conservatives. In the 1999 election, Mangope was elected to Parliament as a member of his newly formed United Christian Democratic Party, which won a total of three seats. "Jurassic Parliament," *Weekly Mail & Guardian* (Johannesburg), June 11, 1999.

41. Sparks, *Tomorrow Is Another Country*, 206–219.

42. Constand Viljoen, interview by author, Pretoria, November 8, 1999.

43. Sparks, *Tomorrow Is Another Country*, 199–200.

44. The generals included, besides Viljoen, Tienie Groenewald, former chief of military intelligence; Kobus Visser, a retired police general; and Douw Steyn, a veteran of the Angola war who commanded a group of military-trained white farmers called the Boerekrisis Aksie (Boer-Crisis Action). Sparks, *Tomorrow Is Another Country*, 202.

45. So fractured was the right wing that the AVF, which was created for Viljoen to lead, brought together no less than eighteen individual parties or organizations.

46. Meeting between Constand Viljoen and Secretary of Commerce Ron Brown, Johannesburg Airport, December 1, 1993.

47. So opportune was its appearance on the scene in the spring of 1993 that rumors arose that the new front had been secretly created by the government in order to put pressure on the ANC, as well as to bring more pragmatism to the right wing, a rumor for which, however, there is no evidence. See Raymond Louw, "Editor," *Southern Africa Report* 11, no. 25 (June 25, 1993): 1, in which the National Party is described as using the generals, with their more moderate stance, to marginalize the Conservative Party.

48. Viljoen, interview.

49. Ibid.

50. De Klerk, interview.

51. A smaller Afrikaner group, headed by an academic, Carl Bishof, advocated establishing the *Volkstaat* in a relatively remote section of the Northern Cape province. Its adherents appealed for a return to Afrikaners' settler roots. But the Afrikaner population had long since become more urbanized than that.

52. Viljoen, interview.

53. Sparks, *Tomorrow Is Another Country*, 204–205, 232; meeting between Thabo Mbeki, Assistant Secretary of State George Moose, and the author, Johannesburg, December 14, 1993.

54. Not all the members of the CP went along with Hartzenberg's policies. The Mulder brothers—Pieter and Connie—who were CP members of Parliament and scions of one of South Africa's premier conservative families, moved to Viljoen's side. They added considerably to the AVF's political skills and intellectual depth as Viljoen wrestled with the choices in front of him.

55. Sparks, *Tomorrow Is Another Country*, 209–210. However, Viljoen claims he undertook the operation in secret from the SADF. Viljoen, interview.

56. Ibid.

57. Viljoen, interview.

58. Ibid.

59. Ibid.

60. Ibid.

61. U.S. embassy, Pretoria, retrospective analysis, sent to the U.S. State Department, Washington, D.C., July 25, 1995.

62. Viljoen, interview.

63. Meeting with Senators Jim Jeffords and Clairborne Pell, Pretoria, April 12, 1995.

64. Viljoen, interview.

9. DENOUEMENT

1. Martin Meredith, *South Africa's New Era: The 1994 Election* (London: Mandarin, 1994), 181.

2. See, for example, Lawrence Schlemmer, "Results of the Opinion Polls and Implications for the Future," and Mark Shaw, "The Impact of Violence on Prospects for a Free and Fair Election," in *The Election and After: Implications for the PWV Region: Proceedings of a Preelection Briefing Held in Johannesburg, April 18–19, 1994* (Johannesburg: Centre for Policy Studies, 1994), 1–2, 18–19.

3. Paul Taylor, "South African Election Declared Free, Fair," *Washington Post,* May 7, 1994, A15.

4. Bill Dalbec and Craig Chaney, "Voter Education Research" (SABC Election Research Unit, 1994). This is a twelve-page summary of survey results provided to USAID by the authors.

5. Joe Matthews, interview by author, November 10, 1999, Cape Town.

6. Chandre Gould and Peter I. Folb, "The South African Chemical and Biological Warfare Program: An Overview," *Nonproliferation Review* (fall-winter 2000): 10–23; Truth and Reconciliation Commission, *Truth and Reconciliation Commission Final Report,* vol. 2, chapter 6, "Special Investigation into Project Coast: South Africa's Chemical and Biological Warfare Program" (October 29, 1998), available on-line at http://www.polity.org.za/govdocs/commissions/1998/trc2chap6c.htm; Stephen Burgess and Helen Purkitt, *The Rollback of South Africa's Biological Warfare Program,* INSS Occasional Paper no. 37, Counterproliferation Series (Colo.: United States Air Force Institute for National Security Studies, United States Air Force Academy, February 2001); Tom Mangold and Jeff Goldberg, *Plague Wars* (New York: St. Martin's, 1999), 224–282. Mangold and Goldberg's book is not always accurate, especially in its accounts of the dates and tone of meetings, the nature of U.S.-British cooperation, and South African reactions. Some corrections are provided above.

7. Truth and Reconciliation Commission, "Special Investigation," 518.

8. James Adams, "South Africa: Libya Said Seeking Secret Biological Weapons," *Sunday Times* (London), February 26, 1995. We had been alerted to the story several days before it was published. State Department press guidance on this question said, "We have been discussing these allegations with the South African Government since first learning of them." "Alleged Use of Biological Weapons by South Africa: Press Guidance," Department of State document, February 24, 1995.

9. Specifically, de Klerk had ordered that all lethal agents be destroyed; work on nonlethal crowd control and incapacitating agents could continue. Gould and Folb, "South African Chemical and Biological Warfare," 19. These meetings in 1994 were not the first time de Klerk had heard some of these allegations. General Pierre Steyn's report on "third force" activities in December 1992 included allegations of an SADF chemical weapons attack on Mozambican soldiers. F. W. de Klerk, *The Last Trek, a New Beginning* (New York: St. Martin's, 1999), 263.

10. De Klerk reiterated to me his appreciation for how this issue was handled during this period, both in our allowing him to brief Mandela rather than our doing so first and in our focusing on the nonproliferation aspects in the first instance, leaving the allegations of use to be addressed by South Africa in both the Truth and Reconciliation Commission and the courts. F. W. de Klerk, interview by author, Cape Town, November 15, 1999.

11. On the very morning of May 4, a member of the NSC called me to question whether going to Mbeki would be breaking faith with de Klerk. We were walking a fine line, I told him, by not mentioning even the nature of the proliferation threat, but keeping faith with the new leadership. In any case, I told my interlocutor, Mbeki was being informed as we spoke.

12. For many whites, this display of mass black action, indeed having direct exposure to the reality of the black majority of the population, was a new experience. One resident of Johannesburg remarked, "They were very organized but I wouldn't like it very much if they came to the city every day." *Argus,* January 18, 1994.

13. Mangosuthu Buthelezi, "Memorandum for Presentation to the Hon. Harry Johnston, Chairman, House Foreign Affairs Africa Sub-Committee," Ulundi, January 7, 1994.

14. Telegram from the embassy to the State Department, Pretoria 2551, February 18, 1994.

15. Mangosuthu Buthelezi, "Statement Made at a Meeting with Mr. Nelson Mandela, President of the African National Congress," Durban, March 1, 1994, faxed to the U.S. consulate, March 1, 1994.

16. Patti Waldmeir, *Anatomy of a Miracle* (New York: Penguin Books, 1997), 245.

17. Mangosuthu Buthelezi, "Vote of Thanks by Mangosuthu Buthelezi to the Honourable Andre Fourie, M.P., Minister of Regional and Land Affairs, for Officially Opening the 1994 Session of the KwaZulu Legislative Assembly," Ulundi, March 17, 1994, faxed to the U.S. consulate, March 17, 1994.

18. Mangosuthu Buthelezi to John Major, March 21, 1994.

19. Mangosuthu Buthelezi to William J. Clinton, March 15, 1994.

20. .See note 17 above.

21. Waldmeir, *Anatomy of a Miracle,* 248.

22. Pat Schroeder, *24 Years of House Work and the Place Is Still a Mess* (Kansas City, Mo.: Andrews McMeel, 1998), 90–91.

23. Princeton N. Lyman, "The Choices ahead of Us" (speech to the Durban Chamber of Commerce dinner, March 30, 1994).

24. Jim Fisher-Thompson, "US Legislators Visit South Africa," *USIA Wireless File,* March 29, 1994, 1.

25. House Committee on International Relations, Africa Subcommittee, "U.S. Policy toward South Africa on the Eve of the Election," April 20, 1994, testimony by Donald Payne.

26. Joe Matthews, interview by author, Cape Town, November 10, 1999.

27. "Inkatha Calls for International Mediation of Constitutional Impasse," telegram from the embassy to the State Department, Pretoria 2381, February 16, 1994.

28. Ibid.

29. "ANC Asks about Availability of Henry Kissinger for Mediation," telegram from the embassy to the State Department, Pretoria 3636, March 10, 1994.

30. "South Africa: CODEL Lewis Meeting with President de Klerk," telegram from the embassy to the State Department, Pretoria 4664, March 30, 1994.

31. De Klerk, *Last Trek,* 324.

32. The subsequent description of the mediation effort is based on my direct participation and the report sent to Washington, "International Mediation Unsuccessful," telegram from the embassy to the State Department, Pretoria 5299, April 14, 1994.

33. Henry Kissinger, conversations with the author, April 14, 1994, and October 16, 1996.

34. "International Mediation," telegram.

35. Mangosuthu Buthelezi, "Statement by the President of the Inkatha Freedom Party," press release of the Inkatha Freedom Party, Pretoria, April 19, 1994.

36. "South Africa: Kenyan Mediator Tells Ambassador of His Role in Bringing Buthelezi into the Elections," telegram from the embassy to the State Department, Pretoria 6012, April 27, 1994. See also Bill Keller, "Zulu Leaders Agree to Call Off Boycott," *New York Times,* April 20, 1994.

37. Paul Taylor and William Claiborne, "Buthelezi Ends Boycott of South African Vote," *Washington Post,* April 20, 1994.

38. Ron Kraybill, "Bringing in Buthelezi," *Track Two* (Johannesburg), May–September 1994, 30.

39. Taylor and Clairborne, "Buthelezi Ends Boycott."

40. "Clinton Hails Agreement in South Africa," text of the White House statement of April 19, 1994 (United States Information Service, Pretoria, April 20, 1994).

41. Kraybill, "Bringing in Buthelezi."

42. Matthews, interview.

10. A New Dawn

1. Martin Meredith, *South Africa's New Era: The 1994 Election* (London: Mandarin, 1994), 182. The food and other basic supplies would later go to good use. In the wake of the Rwanda genocide and an appeal for assistance to the refugees, South Africans emptied their overstocked larders to contribute generously.

2. "Statement by the Transitional Executive Council Regarding Public Servants," Pretoria, April 8, 1994.

3. Paul Taylor, "Historic Election Begins in South Africa," *Washington Post,* April 27, 1994.

4. Richard Steyn, interview by author, Johannesburg, November 17, 1999.

5. Bill Clinton, transcript of April 20 interview, USIA Wireless File, April 22, 1994, 15–20.

6. Princeton N. Lyman, remarks at the "Town Meeting," March 21, 1994.

7. Paul Taylor, "South African Vote Hits Snags on Second Day," *Washington Post,* April 28, 1994.

8. Ibid.

9. Michelle Singletary, "Hours in Line Ease Years of Oppression," *Washington Post,* April 28, 1994.

10. Anthony Sampson, *Mandela: The Authorized Biography* (New York: Alfred A. Knopf, 1999), 483. Patti Waldmeir counted hundreds of ballot boxes from KwaZulu/Natal with broken seals, filled with grass instead of ballots or with ballots neatly stacked by illegal hands. "The election was a mess," she concluded. Patti Waldmeir, *Anatomy of a Miracle* (London: Penguin, 1997), 259–260.

11. Meredith, *South Africa's New Era,* 186–188; Kenneth B. Noble, "Voting Difficulties Arise in Natal Province," *New York Times,* April 28, 1994; Lynne Duke, "In South Africa's Zulu Heartland, Voting Snafus Bring Charges of Foul," *Washington Post,* April 28, 1994. In his meeting with Jesse Jackson on April 28, 1994, Mandela charged that the shortage of ballots in the Transkei was the result of "massive sabotage." Members of the IEC later confided to me that evidence of sabotage could be laid at the feet of Interior officials who had been given much of the responsibility for logistics.

12. Jesse Jackson, USIA informal transcription of the press conference given by Jackson and the official delegation to South Africa, Carlton Hotel, Johannesburg, April 27, 1994.

13. Paul Taylor, "The Election Onlookers: Ogling As History Happens," *Washington Post,* April 26, 1994, E2.

14. Meredith, *South Africa's New Era,* 187, and personal notes from press briefings.

15. Nelson Mandela, statement to the *Guardian,* April 29, 1994, quoted in Sampson, *Mandela,* 484.

16. Sampson, *Mandela,* 185.

17. Paul Taylor, "Mandela Elected President of South Africa," *Washington Post,* May 10, 1994, 1.

18. Neil McMahon, "South African Parliament Formally Elects Mandela," *Washington Times,* May 10, 1994, 1.

19. One very prominent activist who was not present was Randall Robinson. Robinson had had a falling-out with Mandela over the latter's failure to attend a major fund-raiser for TransAfrica during his visit to Washington in 1993. But Robinson had another reason to stay away: he was in the midst of a hunger strike to protest U.S. policy toward Haiti and Haitian refugees. Robinson called me on the day of the ceremony to ask that I make sure the man he had sent to represent him and TransAfrica had a ticket and means of transportation to the event, which I did.

11. A NEW RELATIONSHIP

1. U.S. Agency for International Development, *The Initiative for Southern Africa: Realizing the Potential of Peace through Partnership for Economic Progress* (Washington, D.C., U.S. Agency for International Development, November 26, 1993); Brian Atwood, "Remarks of the Honorable J. Brian Atwood [at the] Southern Africa Development Community Conference (SADC)," Gabarone, Botswana, January 27, 1994 (Washington, D.C., U.S. Information Agency).

2. Bill Clinton, transcript of April 20 interview, 1994, USIA Wireless File, April 22, 1994, 15–20.

3. White House, Office of the Press Secretary, "Fact Sheet: Trade, Aid and Investment Package for South Africa," May 5, 1994. See also White House, Office of the Press Secretary, "Remarks by the President and the Vice President at South African Event, the South Lawn," May 5, 1994. For an analysis of the Commerce Department's Big Emerging Markets program, which included South Africa along with nine other countries, see John Stremlau, "Clinton's Dollar Diplomacy," *Foreign Policy* 97 (winter 1994–95): 18–35.

4. John Sedlins, "USIA Focuses US–South Africa Policy with Atlanta Conference," *USIA World* 13, no. 4 (1994): 2–4. For the texts of statements at the conference by Vice President Gore, Commerce Secretary Ron Brown, and then treasury undersecretary Lawrence Summers, and for a summary of agreements reached, see the "Africa English File," prepared by the U.S. Information Service, Pretoria, June 6, 1994, 1–8.

5. "US Aid to SA Scanty—Mandela," *Sowetan*, November 18, 1994; Brian Stuart, "US Offered Us Only 'Peanuts'—Mandela," *Citizen* (Johannesburg), November 18, 1994, 8; "Mandela Calls US Aid Package 'Peanuts,'" *Business Day*, November 18, 1994, 1; Esther Waugh and Kaizer Nyatsumba, "US Aid to South Africa 'Peanuts,'" *Star* (Johannesburg), November 18, 1994; Paul Taylor, "Mandela Complains That US Aid to South Africa Is 'Peanuts,'" *Washington Post*, November 19, 1994, A20.

6. The attack on American investors was launched at a breakfast meeting between a visiting American investor and a group of leading black businessmen. The account was given to me by a South African lawyer who had attended the event.

7. "Lyman lees dalk Leviete voor" (Lyman might tell their fortune), *Beeld* (Johannesburg), February 8, 1995; Philip Tufano, "Peanuts Remark Could Affect US Aid Package," *Business Day*, February 23, 1995; Peter Fabricius, "Peanut Remark on US Aid Was Poor Timing," *Pretoria News*, November 20, 1994. See also Paul Taylor,

"Mandela Complains That US Aid to South Africa Is 'Peanuts,'" *Washington Post*, November 19, 1994, A20.

8. Fabricius, "Peanut Remark."

9. "Lyman lees dalk Leviete voor"; "Bruising Money Talks," *Sunday Times* (Johannesburg), February 12, 1995.

10. Princeton N. Lyman to Nelson Mandela, January 10, 1995.

11. Princeton N. Lyman, "US–South African Economic Relations (Or Peanuts Are an American Success Story)" (speech to the annual general meeting of the American Chamber of Commerce, February 23, 1995).

12. Ross Herbert, "US Aid to SA Not Peanuts, Says Envoy," *Star*, February 24, 1995, 4; "US Has Largest Aid Package to SA: Lyman," *Citizen*, February 24, 1995, 13; Mark Ashurst, "Peanuts Aid Package Reflects US Success Story," *Business Day*, February 24, 1995.

13. R. W. Johnson, "Destroying South Africa's Democracy: USAID, the Ford Foundation, and Civil Society," *National Interest* 53 (fall 1998): 24–28.

14. Chris Landsberg and David Monyae, "Fifteen Years of USAID's Foreign Political Aid to South Africa," in *The Reality behind the Rhetoric: The United States, South Africa, and Africa*, ed. Greg Mills and John Stremlau (Johannesburg: South Africa Institute of International Affairs and the Center for Strategic and International Studies, 2000), 93.

15. Chris Steyn, Terry Van der Walt, and John MacLennan, "Tensions on the Rise as US Objects to SA Oil Storage Deal with Iran," *Sunday Independent* (Johannesburg), July 30, 1995, 2.

16. O'Leary sought to play down the issue on the eve of her visit and in fact was not eager to address it. "Bid to Defuse Squabble over SA, Iran Link-Up," *Argus* (Cape Town), August 16, 1995.

17. Edyth Bulbring, "US Fears SA-Iran Nuclear Linkage," *Sunday Times* (Johannesburg), August 20, 1995. One deputy minister told me that in the aftermath of Botha's visit to Iran, Iranian officials showed up in Defense Minister Modise's office, expecting to be able to buy arms.

18. "No SA Nuke Secrets to Iran, Says Nzo," *Citizen*, August 23, 1995.

19. "SA Should Not Meet Goliath Head On," *Sunday Times* (Johannesburg), March 26, 1995, 24.

20. "Uncle Sam," *Business Day*, August 22, 1995, 14.

21. Rusty Evans, DFA director general, believed the negotiations on the NPT provided a model for good cooperation on foreign affairs. The key lessons one could take away from this experience were the importance of communications at the highest levels of the two governments and of accompanying exchanges of background papers and positions. That allowed for an elaboration of the South African government's position with full knowledge of American concerns and analysis. "DFA Director

Discusses US-SA Relations," telegram from the American embassy, Pretoria, to Washington, Pretoria 6875, June 2, 1995.

22. Peter de Ionno, "SA in Nuke Row with US," *Sunday Times* (Johannesburg), March 26, 1995, 7.

23. See, for example, Peter Fabricius, "Nuclear Issues Could Cause Rift," *Pretoria News,* March 28, 1995, and Peter Fabricius, "All Eyes on Nzo at UN," *Pretoria News,* April 19, 1995, 9.

24. Peter Vale, a political scientist at the University of Cape Town, made a particularly sharp attack on the decision in the *Weekly Mail and Guardian* (Johannesburg) of April 21–27, 1994. See also David Dig, "Foreign Policy in Foreign Hands," *Weekly Guardian and Mail,* April 28 to May 4, 1994, 8.

25. For example, in addition to the *Weekly Mail and Guardian,* April 28 to May 4, 1995, 8, it appeared in whole or in part in the *Star,* April 28, 1995, the *Citizen,* April 25, 1995, and the *Pretoria News,* April 28, 1995, 5.

26. Report from the American embassy, Pretoria, February 1, 1996.

27. "Despite U.N. Ban, Mandela Meets Qaddafi in Libya," *New York Times,* October 23, 1997, 3; Joseph Fitchett, "Mandela Begins Visit to Gadhafi as US Protests, Calling Washington's Policy Arrogant," *International Herald Tribune,* October 23, 1997, 1; "Mandela Given a Hero's Welcome in Tripoli," Deutsche Presse Agentur, October 22, 1997. Despite American criticism, Mandela's subsequent comments in London on the need to end the decade-long impasse over this issue gave voice to the erosion of international support for the sanctions against Libya and helped spur the U.S. and UK offer to have the trial in the Hague rather than either the United States or Scotland. This offer eventually resolved the issue. See Princeton N. Lyman, "Saving the UN Security Council: A Challenge for the United States," in *Max Planck Yearbook of United Nations Law,* ed. J. A. Frowein and R. Wolfram (Netherlands: Kluwer Law International, 2000), 132–133.

28. White House, Office of the Press Secretary, "Press Conference by President Clinton and President Mandela," Cape Town, March 27, 1998.

29. Donald Pressley, "All Parties Condemn US Attacks," *Business Day,* September 13, 2001, 1.

30. The details of the case, as well as the U.S. position, are well covered in three articles by Simon Barber: "Time to Exorcise the Living Dead of the Arms Industry," *Business Day,* November 8, 1994; "Arms Case Sours Relations with US," *Sunday Times* (Johannesburg), December 25, 1994; "US Prosecutors Are Still Clawing at Throat of Sanctions-Buster Armscor," *Business Day,* June 23, 1995.

31. The exchange was reported later in the press. Barber, "Arms Case," 4.

32. "US Accused of Sabotage as Rooivalk Deal Flops," *Sunday Times* (Johannesburg), December 12, 1994, 1. See also "US Blocks Rooivalk Sale," *Diamond Fields Advertiser,* March 9, 1995, 4, quoting at length an article in the London-based *Africa Confidential.*

33. Peter Fabricius, "US, SA Ties: Armscor Indictment Cannot Be Separated Says Mbeki," *Star,* February 28, 1995.

34. Peter de Ionno, "Fines Drama Jeopardizes US Trade Deal," *Sunday Times* (Johannesburg), June 18, 1995; Kevin O'Grady, "Armscor to Pay Sanctions Busting Fines," *Business Day,* June 14, 1995, 1; "R47-m Fines Could Settle US Arms Case," *Citizen,* June 14, 1995.

35. Thomas Lippman, "Arms Dispute Near End: South Africa and US Agree on Terms," *International Herald Tribune,* July 27, 1996.

36. "It's Tough Being Pals with Uncle Sam" was the headline of an article by Cyril Madlala in *Sunday Times* (Johannesburg), December 10, 1995, 4.

37. U.S.–South Africa Binational Commission, *Third Meeting, February 14–17, 1997,* http://usinfo.state.gov/regional/bnc/usafrica/3rdmtg.htm, 3.

38. Neil Buckley, "European Producers to Lodge Dumping Complaint," *Financial Times* (London), November 11, 1998, 6. See also Sue Kendall, "Industrial Countries Pledge to Keep Steel Markets Open," Agence France Presse, November 6, 1998, for a discussion of the wider steel problem.

39. T. Grant John, "Flat-Rolled Stainless Paradox: Good Demand, Consumption Struggle for Profit," *American Metal Market Specialty Steel Supplement,* December 15, 1998, 10a. For a description of political dimensions of the issue in the United States, see David E. Sanger, "Clinton Pressed for Curbs on Steel Imports," *New York Times,* November 6, 1998, C2.

40. Alec Erwin, at a meeting in Pretoria, September 5, 1998.

41. U.S.–South Africa Business Council, *Business Report* (Washington, D.C.: U.S.–South Africa Business Council, August 2001).

42. Africa News Service, "United States and Africa: South Africa States Support for US/Africa Trade Bill, May 8, 1998"; U.S.–South Africa Business Council, *Business Review* (Washington, D.C.: U.S.–South Africa Business Council, June 2000), 7.

43. Alec Erwin, speech to the U.S.–South Africa Business Council, June 27, 2001; Rosa Whitaker, deputy U.S. trade representative for Africa, speech to the Organization of African Unity, June 22, 2001, quoted in Manchester Trade, *Africa Business Update* (newsletter, Washington, D.C.), October 11, 2001.

44. In his testimony before the Truth and Reconciliation Commission, Basson claimed to have traveled to Libya on several occasions between 1992 and 1995, ostensibly to work on transport, energy, and a hospital program. Chandre Gould and Peter I. Folb, "The South African Chemical and Biological Warfare Program: An Overview," *Nonproliferation Review* (fall-winter 2000): 20; Stephen Burgess and Helen Purkitt, *The Rollback of South Africa's Chemical and Biological Warfare Program* (Maxwell Air Force Base, Ala.: U.S. Air Force Counterproliferation Center, Air University, April 2001), 57–64. See also Peter Fabricius, "Bio-Warfare Scientist Is in Libya," *Weekend Star,* March 4, 1995.

45. With all that has since become public about the South Africa program, it is indicative of how closely held and sensitive the subject was at the time that neither the U.S. nor the UK government could inform their Australia Group partners of the reasons for opposing South Africa's membership.

46. Tom Mangold and Kevin Goldberg, *Plague Wars* (New York: St. Martin's, 1999), 275. There was considerable irony in this appointment. At our meeting, Kasrils joked that if Basson were so hired, he would hope not to seek medical help for any heart problems at a military hospital, imagining himself looking up to see Basson standing over him. As it happened, some years later, General Knobel, en route to a military ceremony, felt pangs in his heart. Driving to the nearest military hospital, he was admitted to the care of who else: Wouter Basson. Knobel said Basson was very professional and expert. Daniel Knobel, at a meeting in Pretoria, November 17, 1999.

47. James Adams, "Gadaffi Lures South Africa's Top Germ Warfare Scientists," *Sunday Times* (London), February 26, 1995, 1.

48. "Chemical Arms Claim Denied," *Citizen,* February 28, 1995, 1. See also Mark Ashurst, "Chemical Weapons for Defense," *Business Day,* February 28, 1995; Helen Grange, "Chemical Capability Defensive," *Star,* February 28, 1996; and Sarel van der Walt, "Mandela weet van chemiese navorsing in SA," *Beeld,* February 28, 1995.

49. Gould and Folb, "South African Chemical and Biological Warfare," 18–19.

50. Government Communications (GCIS), "Statement of TRC Hearings on the CBW Programme," June 15, 1998.

51. "Gore, Mbeki Hold Joint Press Conference," December 5, 1995, and "Gore: South Africa Has a Chance to Be 'Beacon of Hope,'" December 6, 1995, U.S.–South Africa Binational Commission, http://usinfo.state.gov/regional/bnc/usafrica/1stmt-gwf.htm#agpact.

52. Details of these programs can be found in the annual reports of the BNC at www.usinfo.state.gov/regional/bnc/usafrica.

53. "U.S., South Africa Sign Agreement Renewing Commercial Ties," July 23, 1996, U.S.–South Africa Binational Commission, http://usinfo.state.gov/regional/bnc/usafrica/sfmetc.htm.

54. Ibid.

55. Mark Shaw, "A Special Agent? US Assistance to Fight Crime in South Africa," Mills and Stremlau, ed. *Reality behind the Rhetoric,* 125–137.

56. Walter Kansteiner, assistant secretary of state for African affairs, as quoted in e-mails to members from the U.S.–South Africa Business Council, June 14, 2001.

57. Princeton N. Lyman, "The Mbeki Administration," *Perspectives on Africa* 3, no. 2 (fall 1999): 12–18. See also Howard Barrell, "Mbeki: One Year On," *Daily Mail and Guardian,* June 2, 2000, in which the author concludes, "He may need to get himself advisers unafraid to argue forcefully against his instincts and viewpoints, and able to think outside the accepted parameters."

58. Provoked by the opposition's criticism of his "African approach" to HIV/AIDS, Mbeki gave an extraordinary speech on the occasion of the Second Oliver Tambo lecture in Johannesburg in August 2000. Quoting liberally from Franz Fanon, W. E. B. DuBois, and Malcolm X, Mbeki warned the "petite black bourgeoisie" of South Africa against a class rather than a "liberation" identity and to avoid "accommodation with the dominant bourgeoisie," whom it opposed during apartheid. For more on these themes, see Tom Lodge, "Party Politics: African National Congress," and Xolisa Vapi, "A Transformed Media Is Key to Deepening SA's Democracy," papers presented at the State Department conference, "South Africa: Future of Democratization," Washington, D.C., April 5, 2001.

59. South African Press Association, "Mbeki Delights Business with 'Rubicon' Speech" (Cape Town, October 20, 2000); "South Africa: Africa's Great Black Hope," *Economist*, February 24, 2001, 12–13.

60. Ibid., 4.

61. Ibid., 11–12. Ann Bernstein, *Policy-Making in a New Democracy: South Africa's Challenges for the Twenty-first Century*, CDE Research Policy in the Making, no. 10 (Johannesburg: Centre for Development and Enterprise, 1999), 53 and passim; Ben Turok, "South Africa's Response to Globalisation" (paper presented at the North-South Roundtable, State of the World Forum, New York, September 5–9, 2000).

62. Market size and growth were the principal reasons for investor caution re South Africa, according to a survey conducted by the Global Business Council. Global Business Council, *Communiqué*, no. 1 (2000): 4.

63. Bernstein, "Policy-Making in a New Democracy," 57.

64. David Welsh, "Tensions in the Alliance," *Insight* (a newsletter from Omega Investment Research, Ltd.) 14, no. 396 (August 7, 2001).

65. UNAIDS, "Report on the Global HIV/AIDS Epidemic" (Geneva: UNAIDS, June 2000), 9; "Great Black Hope," *Economist*, 8–9; Erica Barks-Ruggles et al., *The Economic Impact of HIV/AIDS in Southern Africa*, Conference Report, no. 9 (Washington, D.C.: Brookings Institution, September 2001): 3.

66. Mark Schooes, "South Africa Acts Up," *Village Voice*, special reprint of an eight-part Pulitzer Prize–winning series, "AIDS: The Agony of Africa," November 9, 1999, 24.

67. Mbeki's actual comments on HIV and AIDS include the following: "I am saying that you cannot attribute immune deficiency solely and exclusively to a virus. A whole variety of things can cause the immune system to collapse, . . . endemic poverty, malnutrition, contaminated water, and repeated infections of malaria or sexually transmitted diseases." "Mbeki Dissents on AIDS: Says HIV May Not Be the Only Cause," Associated Press dateline, Pretoria, September 1, 2000.

68. Schooes, "South Africa Acts Up," 24.

69. U.S.–South Africa Business Council, *Business Report* (Washington, D.C.: U.S.–South Africa Business Council, September 2001), 5.

70. Becoming increasingly defensive about his stance on AIDS, Mbeki told a BCC interviewer on August 6, 2001, that the largest single cause of death in South Africa is violence and accidents, not AIDS. However, South Africa's Medical Research Council issued a report showing that AIDS had become the leading cause of death in the country, accounting for 40 percent of deaths among those between the ages of fifteen and forty-nine, and 20 percent of deaths overall. The report projected that AIDS would account for the deaths of between five million and seven million South Africans by the year 2010 if more resources were not devoted to the disease. Jon Jeter, "Challenging South Africa's AIDS Policy," *Washington Post,* October 19, 2001, A25.

71. A good example is the United States–Southern Africa Center for Leadership and Public Values, a joint program of Duke University and the University of Cape Town, established in 2001 by my successor in South Africa, James Joseph, and funded by private donations. Another example comes from Linda and Peter Biehl, the parents of Amy Biehl, whose tragic death was described in chapter 8. Through the Amy Biehl Foundation they have honored Amy's memory by dedicating themselves to helping overcome the roots of violence and despair in the very township areas where Amy died and have drawn support from all across America.

12. LESSONS LEARNED—AND RELEARNED

1. I. William Zartman, ed., *Elusive Peace* (Washington, D.C.: Brookings Institution, 1995), 147.

2. Marina Ottoway and Thomas Carothers, eds., *Funding Virtue: Civil Society Aid and Democracy Promotion* (Washington, D.C.: Carnegie Endowment for International Peace, 2000), 90.

3. During the dictatorial rule of Sani Abacha in the late 1990s, prodemocracy Nigerians traveled to South Africa to solicit Mandela's support for international sanctions against Nigeria. Mandela pointedly told them that, yes, sanctions could be useful —they had been in South Africa—but without an indigenous democracy movement, they would not do much. South Africa had had one, he told them, in the ANC; Nigerians did not.

4. Some recent examples are Chester Crocker, Fen Osler Hampson, and Pamela Aall, eds., *Herding Cats: Multiparty Mediation in a Complex World* (Washington, D.C.: United States Institute of Peace Press, 1999); I. William Zartman, *Ripe for Resolution: Conflict and Intervention in Africa* (New York: Oxford University Press, 1989); Zartman, *Elusive Peace;* Fen Osler Hampson, *Nurturing Peace: Why Peace Settlements Succeed or Fail* (Washington, D.C.: United States Institute of Peace Press, 1996); Cameron Hume, *Ending Mozambique's War: The Role of Mediation and Good Offices* (Washington, D.C.: United States Institute of Peace Press, 1994).

5. One very valuable example of such analysis is provided by Jan Egeland, "The Oslo Accord," in *Herding Cats,* ed. Crocker et al., 529–546. Egeland's subsequent efforts to facilitate peace in Colombia are described in Larry Rohter, "U.N. Envoy Tries to Aid Peace Effort in Unique Colombia War," *New York Times,* July 10, 2000, A8.

6. Cf. Fen Osler Hampson, *Nurturing Peace,* 122, which blames the failure of the Bicesse agreement of 1993 in part on the lack of commitment and staying power of the third parties, and Paul Hare, "Angola: The Lusaka Peace Process," in *Herding Cats,* ed. Crocker et al., 661, which says, regarding the Lusaka agreement of 1995, "In the end, Savimbi chose the option of war over peace. That is the reason why the Lusaka peace process failed."

7. Edward McWhinney, *The United Nations and a New World Order for a New Millennium* (Netherlands: Kluwer Law International, 2000), 68.

8. Permanent Mission of South Africa to the United Nations, "Briefing to the United Nations Security Council, New York, by H. E. Mr. Nelson Mandela, Former President of the Republic of South Africa, on the Burundi Peace Process" (report issued in New York, January 19, 2000), 3–4.

9. Padraig O'Malley, *Northern Ireland and South Africa: "Hope and History at a Crossroads"* (Boston: John W. McCormack Institute of Public Affairs, University of Massachusetts, March 2000).

10. The skill of these diplomats was demonstrated by Pamela Bridgewater, now ambassador to Benin. In her work with the ANC, she became admired and closely trusted by Nelson Mandela. When she was promoted to consul general in Durban, some questioned whether that association would harm her ability to establish a relationship with Buthelezi. On the contrary, she gained the same level of trust there. When Mandela and Buthelezi met in Durban in March 1995, they joked over their "rivalry" for Bridgewater—one of the few light moments of that meeting.

11. Richard N. Gardner, "The One Percent Solution: Shirking the Cost of World Leadership," *Foreign Affairs* (July-August 2000): 3.

12. *State Department Reform: Report of an Independent Task Force Cosponsored by the Council on Foreign Relations and the Center for Strategic and International Studies* (Council on Foreign Relations and the Center for Strategic and International Studies, Washington, D.C., 2001), 1.

13. Gardner, "One Percent," 8.

14. Al Kamen, "Not So 'Special' After All," *Washington Post,* March 5, 2001, A17.

15. John Danforth, remarks in a White House ceremony announcing his appointment, September 6, 2001.

16. Colin Powell, "We Are All Recruiters," *State Magazine,* September 1, 2001, 2; Neal Walsh, "Now Hiring: Diplomatic Readiness Task Force Begins Work," *State Magazine,* 15–17.

17. *Washington Post,* March 27, 2000.

18. Paula G. Kawken, "Skeleton Woman in Seattle," *Sun* (Chapel Hill, N.C.), April 2000, 38–46.

19. Desmond Tutu, interview by author, Atlanta, March 27, 2000.

20. Pauline H. Baker, "The United States and South Africa: Persuasion and Coercion," in *Honey and Vinegar: Incentive, Sanctions and Foreign Policy*, ed. Richard Haass (Washington, D.C.: Brookings Institution, 2000), 95.

21. Aubre Hamersma, Standard Bank, interview by author, Johannesburg, November 17, 1999.

22. Robert Kinloch Massie, *Loosing the Bonds* (New York: Nan A. Talese, Doubleday, 1997), 266–270.

23. Princeton N. Lyman, "Investing with Social Responsibility in South Africa," *Attracting Capital to Africa, 1999* (Washington, D.C.: Corporate Council on Africa, 1999), 245–247.

24. See, for example, David A. Vise, "New Global Role Puts FBI in Unsavory Company," *Washington Post*, October 29, 2000, A1, A30.

25. David D. Newsom, "Why State Doesn't Need *These* Reforms," *Foreign Service Journal* 78, no. 3 (May 2000): 28. One of the nicest compliments I ever received was as ambassador to Nigeria when the State Department's inspector reported to me, after interviewing the country team members, "Each one told me, 'The ambassador takes a special interest in my program.'"

26. Crocker, *High Noon in Southern Africa: Making Peace in a Rough Neighborhood* (New York: W. W. Norton, 1992), 481.

27. In 1987, one of the objectives of foundations was to "strengthen the small but growing number of black community–based . . . organizations rather than helping the comparatively well funded, white liberal–led groups." The same problem had been identified in 1978 but remained. Sheila Avrin McLean and Rona Kluger, "U.S. Foundations Giving to Enhance Educational Opportunities for Black South Africans," Information Exchange Working Paper no. 1 (Institute of International Education, New York, May 1987; from the Rockefeller Foundation archives), 4; internal memorandum on Carnegie Corporation programs, unnumbered.

28. Aurora Associates International, Inc., and Creative Associates International, Inc., *Program Evaluation: USAID/South Africa* (Washington, D.C.: U.S. Agency for International Development, April 21, 1995), 62.

29. Ibid.

30. Atwood said the program had been "vital" to the empowerment of millions of South Africans and received high praise from South Africans of all colors. However, he then devoted four paragraphs to the charges against it, promising that they would be taken "very seriously." J. Brian Atwood, "Statement of J. Brian Atwood, Administrator, U.S. Agency for International Development, on Office of Inspector General Review of USAID South Africa Mission" (Washington, D.C.: U.S. Agency for International Development, March 25, 1995).

31. AID official, confidential interview by author, December 10, 2000.

32. David Morris, "Aid Abuse Probe," *Argus* (Cape Town), March 24, 1995, 1; Peter Fabricius, "US Aid Programme Accused of Reverse Discrimination," *Star* (Johannesburg), December 12, 1994, 14; "US to Probe Aid Bias toward Blacks," *Citizen* (Johannesburg), March 28, 1995; "US Aid Inquiry," *Cape Times*, March 28, 1995; "US to Investigate Claims of Impropriety in SA Aid," *Natal Mercury*, March 28, 1995; "Aid Agency Investigates Allegations of Favouritism," *Business Day*, March 28, 1995. A particularly critical and slanted presentation was in Simon Barber, "Racial Criteria Applied in US Aid Programmes," *Business Day*, November 28, 1994, 14. Barber concludes, "The rebels' cause was, and is just. Help to vindicate them by rubbing US Vice President Al Gore's nose in the doings of Dean, Ford and Lyman when Gore shows up next week, accompanied by his self-congratulatory cast of hundreds." In the American press, see Paul Taylor, "Aid to S. Africa Assailed as Tilted toward Blacks," *Washington Post*, March 27, 1995, A1.

33. Aurora Associates and Creative Associates, *Program Evaluation*, 62.

34. Ibid., 55–56.

Index

Bush (George H. W.) administration
on apartheid and transition, 3–4,
43, 48–50
certification of conditions stated
in CAAA, 78
letters after Boipatong violence,
61–62, 129
letters on proposed mass
actions, 65–66
resistance to pressure for further
sanctions, 78
praised by Mandela, 230
sanctions, 115
Bush (George W.) administration
BNC during, 256
partnership possibilities with
South Africa, 260
Business Development Committee,
255
Buthelezi, Chief Mangosuthu, 20,
46–47, 59–60, 67, 68, 72, 80,
82, 93, 100, 174, 276, 277
accommodation of demands,
131–132, 193–198, 201–202
as administrator of KwaZulu, 128
alliance with right-wing parties, 195
on communism, 194
constitutional demands made by,
137–138, 186
international mediation,
202–211
constitutional referendum proposed
by, 128–129
correspondence with Clinton, 197,
199
denunciation of Record of Understanding, 128, 132–133
desire for constitution drafted
before elections, 133
desire to postpone election, 196
election issues, 217
election results, 220
ethnic violence and, 129

feeling of betrayal by de Klerk
government, 196–197
formation of Freedom Alliance, 141
formation of IFP, 127
inclusion of in election process,
194–212
letter from Bush, 129
Mandela and, 108, 195–196
meeting with Brown, 144–145
meetings with Lyman, 128–129,
132–133, 139–140
movement to political right, 130
negotiations with South African
government and U.S., 87, 144
reaction to Lyman's Durban
speech, 198, 199, 200–201
reaction to South African Constitutional Bill, 145
rejection of ANC's military arm as
part of security force, 140–141
security concerns, 133
stance on federalism in new
regime, 94, 131, 194
talks with Okumu, 209–210
U.S. liaison with, 269
U.S. support for, 129, 130
See also Inkatha Freedom Party
(IFP)
"Buthelezi dilemma," 129–130, 279
BWC. See Biological Weapons
Convention (BWC)

CAAA. See Comprehensive Anti-
Apartheid Act (CAAA)
Cabelly, Robert, 68
Campbell, Colin, 211–212
Campbell, John, 269
Cape Times, 238
Carnegie Endowment for Inter-
national Peace, 39
Carnegie Foundation, 37
Carrington, Lord, 203, 204, 206,
207, 208

About the Author

Princeton N. Lyman has over three decades of diplomatic experience in both the U.S. Department of State and the U.S. Agency for International Development (USAID). He was U.S. ambassador to South Africa from 1992 through 1995, and has served as assistant secretary of state for international organization affairs, as ambassador to Nigeria, and as director of the U.S. Aid Mission to Ethiopia at USAID. He was a senior fellow at the United States Institute of Peace in 1999–2000, and had previously been a visiting fellow with the Overseas Development Council. Lyman is currently the executive director of the Global Interdependence Initiative, Aspen Institute. He is the coauthor of *Korean Development: The Interplay of Politics and Economics* and has written numerous articles, including "South Africa's Promise," "Ethics in Diplomacy," and "Saving the UN Security Council: A Challenge for the United States." His honors include the President's Distinguished Service Award, the Department of State Distinguished Honor Award, and the Secretary of State's Career Achievement Award. Lyman holds a Ph.D. in political science from Harvard University.

United States Institute of Peace

The United States Institute of Peace is an independent, nonpartisan federal institution created by Congress to promote research, education, and training on the peaceful management and resolution of international conflicts. Established in 1984, the Institute meets its congressional mandate through an array of programs, including research grants, fellowships, professional training, education programs from high school through graduate school, conferences and workshops, library services, and publications. The Institute's Board of Directors is appointed by the President of the United States and confirmed by the Senate.

Chairman of the Board: Chester A. Crocker
Vice Chairman: Seymour Martin Lipset
President: Richard H. Solomon
Executive Vice President: Harriet Hentges
Vice President: Charles E. Nelson

Jennings Randolph Program for International Peace

This book is a fine example of the work produced by senior fellows in the Jennings Randolph fellowship program of the United States Institute of Peace. As part of the statute establishing the Institute, Congress envisioned a program that would appoint "scholars and leaders of peace from the United States and abroad to pursue scholarly inquiry and other appropriate forms of communication on international peace and conflict resolution." The program was named after Senator Jennings Randolph of West Virginia, whose efforts over four decades helped to establish the Institute.

Since 1987, the Jennings Randolph Program has played a key role in the Institute's effort to build a national center of research, dialogue, and education on critical problems of conflict and peace. More than a hundred senior fellows from some thirty nations have carried out projects on the sources and nature of violent international conflict and the ways such conflict can be peacefully managed or resolved. Fellows come from a wide variety of academic and other professional backgrounds. They conduct research at the Institute and participate in the Institute's outreach activities to policymakers, the academic community, and the American public.

Each year approximately fifteen senior fellows are in residence at the Institute. Fellowship recipients are selected by the Institute's board of directors in a competitive process. For further information on the program, or to receive an application form, please contact the program staff at (202) 457-1700.

Joseph Klaits
Director

PARTNER TO HISTORY

This book is set in Adobe Caslon. The Creative Shop designed the book's cover; Mike Chase designed the interior. Helene Y. Redmond made up the pages. David Compton copyedited the text, which was proofread by Karen Stough. The index was prepared by Sonsie Conroy. The book's editor was Nigel Quinney.